**Research Methods in Li** ~~...~~ **..ɔtudies**
Series Editors: Ronald . ~~...~~ ᴄ ʟynn Westbrook

*Library Anxiety: Theory, Research, and Applications* by Anthony J. Onwuegbuzie, Qun G. Jiao, and Sharon L. Bostick

# Library Anxiety

## *Theory, Research, and Applications*

Anthony J. Onwuegbuzie
Qun G. Jiao
Sharon L. Bostick

*Research Methods in Library and
Information Studies, No. 1*

The Scarecrow Press, Inc.
Lanham, Maryland, and Oxford
2004

# SCARECROW PRESS, INC.

Published in the United States of America
by Scarecrow Press, Inc.
A wholly owned subsidiary of
The Rowman & Littlefield Publishing Group, Inc.
4501 Forbes Boulevard, Suite 200, Lanham, Maryland 20706
www.scarecrowpress.com

PO Box 317
Oxford
OX2 9RU, UK

British Library Cataloguing in Publication Information Available

**Library of Congress Cataloging-in-Publication Data**

Onwuegbuzie, Anthony J., 1962–
  Library anxiety : theory, research, and applications / Anthony J. Onwuegbuzie, Qun G. Jiao, Sharon L. Bostick.
    p.   cm.— (Research methods in library and information studies ; no. 1)
  Includes bibliographical references and indexes.
  ISBN 0-8108-4955-0 (pbk. : alk. paper)
  1. Library anxiety.  2. Library users—Psychology.  3. Library research—Psychological aspects.  I. Jiao, Qun G.  II. Bostick, Sharon L., 1953–.
III. Title.  IV. Series.
Z711 .O59 2004
025.5—dc22                                                          2003017677

# Contents

# Foreword

It was almost twenty years ago in a small, crowded classroom at the University of Tennessee at Chattanooga that the term *library anxiety* was born. I had been collecting data on the reactions of freshman students to the library instruction sessions I presented. As I listened to Sheila Tobias describe her work with math anxiety, the symptoms began to sound very familiar. These were the same feelings students were using to describe their attitudes about using the university library for research. A talk with Ms. Tobias confirmed the similarity of separate findings, and shortly thereafter the concept of *library anxiety* was introduced into the vocabulary of the field.

Several years later, Sharon L. Bostick contacted me with her dissertation proposal that focused on converting the early research on library anxiety into a quantitative scale. It was a pleasure to be involved with her rigorous development of the Library Anxiety Scale (LAS) and to follow in the literature the research interest generated by this new instrument. With the development of an easily applicable measurement tool, library anxiety began to take its place as a viable research topic, both nationally and abroad.

Although my personal research moved in another direction, I continued to be interested in the study of library anxiety by reviewing manuscripts on this topic submitted to various library publications. In this way, I became familiar with the library anxiety research being conducted by Qun G. Jiao and Anthony J. Onwuegbuzie. Both have contributed greatly to defining, clarifying, and extending the concepts underlying library anxiety. It therefore seems appropriate that this book, the next logical step in

the development of library anxiety as a legitimate field of study, should
come from these three researchers.

This book, the first to be published on the topic of library anxiety, provides a new, and much needed, milestone in library-related research.
After the publication of my initial articles on library anxiety, I was invited
to present workshops all over the United States and Canada. One of the
most fascinating aspects of my travels was talking with reference librarians about the topic. "We've known about this for years," I was constantly
being told, "but no one had given it a name." Providing a name seemed
to legitimize the topic for study. Librarians were delighted to be talking
openly together about something they knew existed but had never discussed. More researchers became intrigued by various aspects of library
anxiety and began to study and write about it. This gave reference librarians and those using their services new and better data to draw on as they
wrestled with the stress of using our increasingly complex libraries. I am
certain that the practicing librarians from whom I learned so much, and
the researchers who are currently studying library anxiety, will welcome
this new advancement along the path to better serving our library users.

Constance A. Mellon, Ph.D.
Professor and Director of Library Science Graduate Studies
East Carolina University, Greenville, North Carolina

# Preface

Although the characteristics of library anxiety have been observed for years, detailed analysis and scientific understanding of the phenomenon is of relatively recent origin. The last two decades have brought remarkable advances in our knowledge of library anxiety and its debilitating effects on users' ability to perform library information–seeking tasks. Some research findings are in the process of being assimilated into the main body of library and information science literature. Our increased understanding of library anxiety, especially in academic library settings, is also being translated into innovative approaches to the intervention and prevention of the undesirable effects of library anxiety. The urgent need for help with diverse library anxious users in the information age has resulted in a surge of interest in this emergent field of study among librarians, educators, researchers, administrators, and graduate students in this country and many foreign countries. This popularity is causing some confusion about library anxiety research and creating the need for a reliable review of the current status of the research, as new methodological variations and techniques and claims of effectiveness are beginning to enter the research literature. Yet, a book of this nature has not previously been available because library anxiety research seems to cover a restricted domain of study in a relatively well-defined situational context within the general library and information science problems. We have written this book in an attempt to present an overview of the current state of library anxiety research. We hope that the presentation of accumulated research evidence will help resolve some of the confusions and myths about library anxiety research.

It is apparent that a large proportion of the information on library anxiety has accumulated over the past 10 to 15 years. Although much has been learned, a great deal remains to be explored. Some areas are still in need of more definitive research. For instance, there have been few controlled studies to substantiate the effectiveness of intervention and mediation procedures, despite tentative claims. This is not unique in the field of library and information science, which is undergoing a transition and theory-building phase. The reported correlations between library anxiety and other related variables and some claims of successful intervention procedures are not yet supported by substantial, irrefutable evidence. Only time will tell which of these developments are fads and which represent true progress in the intervention of library anxiety effects. It will probably be decades until definitive data can be collected, analyzed, and applied. In the meantime, however, despite its nascent state of development, many of us have been impressed by what we have already learned during such a short period of time, concluding that this field of research deserves serious exploration. By reviewing the current status of research and pointing out promising research areas, we hope that potential researchers will form some perspectives on this field and have some kind of direction to follow in their pursuit of library anxiety study. Interested readers of this book will learn what can be expected to appear in the literature in the coming years.

This book is written for educators, researchers, librarians, and advanced students in library and information science who seek to understand better the nature of library anxiety and its measurement and intervention procedures. It is also for administrators, counselors, psychologists, teachers, and professors in public schools, colleges, and universities who have to deal with a variety of anxieties and related psychoeducational problems in their daily lives. The book is designed to be used as a general reference book in the field of library anxiety study, a textbook for library and information science students, a guidebook for practitioners in library and educational settings, and a source of information about specific aspects and problems of library anxiety research for those who wish to expand our knowledge of the subject through further investigation. In addition, this book can serve as a miniresearch methodology textbook for people in the field of library and information science.

We have already received many intellectual and emotional rewards for our work in this area. We have enjoyed being pioneers in this emergent field of research. Through this book, we hope that more people will join us and share with us the pleasure and excitement of conceptualizing the nature of library anxiety and developing effective and generalizable intervention procedures for helping our users to achieve their lifelong goals. Specifically, we hope that we can succeed in inspiring graduate students and librarians, as well as library science researchers, in this endeavor.

This book is organized into the following four parts: Background, Theory, Research, and Application. Specifically, Part 1 contains chapter 1, which provides background information about the development of the Library Anxiety Scale (LAS), the most widely used measure of library anxiety. Also presented in this chapter is a comprehensive delineation of the psychometric properties of the LAS. Part 2 includes chapters 2 and 3. Chapter 2 provides a comprehensive description of the nature and etiology of library anxiety, including the antecedents and symptoms. Chapter 3 outlines five theoretical models of library anxiety. Four of these models have not been presented previously. Part 3 contains chapters 4, 5, and 6. Chapter 4 discusses data collection and research design issues pertaining to quantitative, qualitative, and mixed methodological research. Chapter 5 provides a framework for conducting quantitative, qualitative, and mixed methodological data analyses. Chapter 6 discusses data interpretational issues in quantitative, qualitative, and mixed methodological research, particularly those relating to threats to validity and legitimation. Part 4 contains chapters 7 and 8. Chapter 7 presents and summarizes the existing library anxiety prevention and intervention procedures and strategies. Chapter 8 provides a detailed discussion of the potential areas for future research on library anxiety and also discusses the issues and challenges involved in this line of research.

*Chapter One*

# Development and Validation of the Library Anxiety Scale

## OVERVIEW

The concept of library anxiety was formally introduced by Constance A. Mellon in 1986. However, it took nearly six years before a scale was developed that could be used to undertake empirical studies in this area. This Library Anxiety Scale (LAS; Bostick, 1992) has been used in virtually every quantitative study of library anxiety. The purpose of this chapter is to describe the LAS. First, the development of the scale is reviewed. An outline of the original research design, population, and sample is provided, and an explanation of the types of items is presented. This is followed by a delineation of the psychometric properties of the instrument (i.e., score reliability and validity) yielded by the norm group. Finally, score reliability and validity information reported by other researchers are summarized. This includes a summary of the findings from the first study to use confirmatory factor analysis techniques to test the multidimensional structure of library anxiety.

## THE DEVELOPMENT OF THE LIBRARY ANXIETY SCALE

### Synopsis

The development of the Library Anxiety Scale (LAS) involved the following 14 steps: (a) developing a list of key components relating to library anxiety, (b) sending the list to experts for validation, (c) examining responses or commonalities and contradictions, (d) restructuring the outline, (e) resending the outline to experts, (f) linking items with a list of key components, (g) sending items to a panel of experts, (h) developing a pilot instrument, (i) assessing the scale for readability and clarity, (j) editing items based on assessment, (k) conducting a pilot study, (l) performing an exploratory factor analysis, (m) editing instrument and retaining viable statements, and (n) assessing test-retest score reliability. These steps are displayed in figure 1.1. The scale development process is described in more detail in following sections.

## Population of Library Users

The population targeted for the development of the LAS was composed of students at colleges and universities who had an opportunity or a need to use an academic library as part of their educational programs. This population was not limited to any specific level of student but included all levels from first year through postgraduate. The rationale for including all levels of students is that it assumes that library anxiety is not limited to first-time users but is consistent across the continuum of learning in a university setting (Onwuegbuzie, 1997a). Because the library is a dynamic institution continuously updating and changing systems, adding new technologies, and becoming more diverse, it is further assumed that even students who have been enrolled without interruption can experience anxiety when confronted with these changes. The population was not limited to any geographic location because it was presupposed that the anxiety felt by students affects all areas, regardless of geographic setting.

## Sample of Library Users

Several samples of students from all levels were used to develop the LAS. These students were drawn from formal classes, with the entire class completing the instrument in each case. Students were also approached individually to complete the instrument in order to maximize the representation of all students, from those enrolled in classes to those working on directed studies, including doctoral dissertations.

In selecting the students for the development and validation phases, the

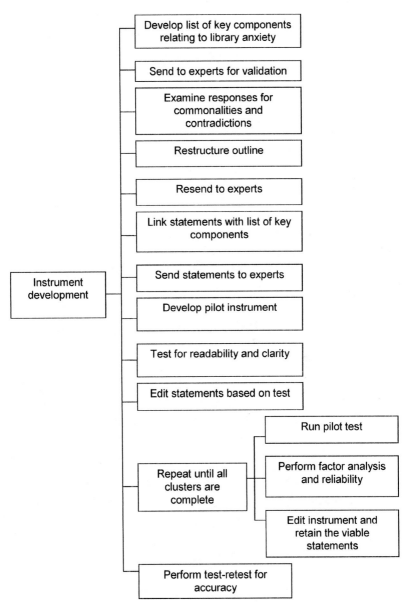

**Figure 1.1 Procedures used in the development of the scale.**

goal was to obtain samples that were large enough to provide adequate representations of the population. In so doing, it was hoped that sampling error would be kept to a minimum. As the development of the instrument progressed through the piloting process, different students were selected to complete the instruments. No student was asked to complete this instrument more than once, regardless of the stage of development.

## Sample of Expert Evaluators

A group of 11 experts from the field of library and information science was selected to evaluate the LAS at its various stages of development. The criteria for selection of the experts included their professional reputation, number of publications and speeches made, and professional affiliation, particularly between public and private institutions. All the experts were affiliated with colleges and universities. Further, all the selected professionals agreed to participate in the study, although the same ones were not necessarily involved in all aspects of the instrument's development. Four experts represented private institutions; seven were affiliated with public institutions. All were professional librarians. The panel included reference librarians, library administrators, and library school faculty members.

## STAGES OF THE LIBRARY ANXIETY SCALE DEVELOPMENT PROCESS

### Table of Key Components

The first step involved development of a listing of key components relating to library anxiety. This list was arranged in tabular form. The table of key components relating to library anxiety was developed based on an extensive review of the literature; discussions with university faculty, students, and librarians; and the instrument developer's professional experience. This table, in outline form, was the preliminary step in creating a master list of key components. The table consisted of the following five sections: (a) staff, (b) resources, (c) technology, (d) reference, and (e) policies and procedures. Each component was included on a separate page so that the experts could edit or respond directly on the form. The table, along with a cover letter, was sent to the experts for their opinions and recommendations.

The feedback provided by the experts was analyzed by looking for emergent themes and commonalities. These were put into a large matrix and then transferred back into the outline. The experts' responses were italicized on the outline to differentiate them from items on the original table, creating a master list of key components. Not all responses were put onto the master list. Some were not usable because some experts felt they could not respond to the subject presented or did so in a way that, after careful evaluation, was considered not to be relevant to the development of the scale. Some responses were too institution specific and, thus, could not be generalized to other educational institutions. As such, these responses could not be used in the scale development. A sixth component, encompassing the psychological factors directly relating to Mellon's theory, was added at this time. The master list became the guide for creating the first set of statements.

## Statements

The next step involved the creation of statements (e.g., "It's easy to find my way around the library"), some of which would lead to the Library Anxiety Scale (e.g., "I get confused trying to find my way around the library"). These statements were written to correspond to the components on the master list. The goal here was to produce 300 statements to send to the experts for their opinions. The large number of initial statements ensured that an adequate number would be retained after analysis and deletions of unfavorable statements. These statements were designed to be used on a Likert-type scale, utilizing the following guidelines: clarity, relevance, and avoidance of the past tense and of ambiguous language. Each statement was to be short and contain only one idea.

The instrument developer enlisted the aid of other librarians, university faculty, and students to create the statements. A total of 268 statements were thus created, divided into categories that were based on the six components. The statements at this time were numbered consecutively and sent to the experts for comments, additions, and deletions. New statements suggested by the experts were added to the original 268 because the categories were for convenience only. The statements were sent for comments to the experts with a cover letter asking for their return.

The statements were edited to reflect the experts' comments. One expert noted that only three of the statements in the psychological/theoretical category were positive. Three more were changed to positive wording, but the theory was stated in negative form and the statements reflected this fact. The final number of statements was 294. The distribution of the statement revisions is presented in table 1.1. The number of statements representing each of the six components is presented in table 1.2.


## Pilot Study 1

The statements were arranged randomly for the first pilot instrument. A numbering key comparing the original numbers with the new numbers was developed to track the statements. While a booklet format for the statements was initially desirable, the size and bulk of the 294 statements made this option too cumbersome. Instead, they were photocopied on both sides of each page.

Students selected for this phase were asked to respond to the statements on machine-readable forms. The forms would then be scanned at the University of Toledo, which used NCS equipment. Unfortunately, the forms for this equipment only allowed for 240 items. This problem was solved by coding the data forms as page 1 and page 2. Also, they were coded for identification purposes, beginning with 001. Thus, each form had a four-digit number coded onto it, reading as 0011, 0012, 0021, 0022, and so forth.

The instrument was distributed as a packet, including an instruction sheet, the pilot version of the LAS, and the machine-readable forms. Brief

**Table 1.1    Distribution of statement revisions: Pilot 1.**

| Statement Category | Number |
| --- | --- |
| Original statements sent to experts | 268 |
| Statements omitted | 1 |
| Statements added | 16 |
| Statements edited for grammar | 6 |
| Statements unchanged but noted as areas of concern | 3 |
| Final total | 294 |

Table 1.2 **Distribution of components: Pilot 1.**

| Component | Number of Statements |
|---|---|
| 1. Staff | 56 |
| 2. Resources | 67 |
| 3. Technology | 61 |
| 4. Reference | 36 |
| 5. Policies and procedures | 44 |
| 6. Theoretical and psychological | 31 |

instructions also were placed on the top of each page. A cover sheet of instructions for the administrators (i.e., course instructors) of the instrument was included. The packets were distributed to a variety of classes at the University of Toledo, Wayne State University, Macomb County Community College, and Madonna College. The class levels ranged from first-year students to graduate students.

The initial round of instrument administration revealed several problems. First, the initial pilot instrument, which was 13 pages in length and which took about 45 minutes to complete, was found by many students to be problematic. These students felt that responding to this amount of items was boring, irksome, and redundant. Second, they found the back-to-back format unwieldy. Third, the instructions explaining the Likert-format scale listed the options as 5 = Strongly Agree, 4 = Agree, 3 = Undecided, 2 = Disagree, and 1 = Strongly Disagree. In direct contradiction, the machine-readable forms were numbered in reverse direction, that is, from 1 to 5. This was very confusing to most students. As a result, the instrument was recopied with the instructions matching the form. Also, the back-to-back format was eliminated. The third problem concerned the machine-readable forms. Specifically, the size of the instrument and the limitations of the form prevented sequentially numbered sheets. This turned out to be confusing, causing many students to lose their place while responding. To minimize this problem, the correct numbers, in groups of 10, were lightly penciled on the second sheet. These numbers were erased before the sheets were scanned.

The total number of students completing the first pilot instrument was 281. These completed forms were scanned at the University of Toledo, and the data were placed in the instrument developer's computer account there. Four of the 281 completed forms contained errors. These flaws stemmed from the fact that two selections were made for one item. The errors were given a code of "9" to eliminate blank spaces in the data set. The statistical analysis of the data consisted of an exploratory factor analysis to eliminate items that did not cluster with other items in a meaningful way. An exploratory factor analysis is a statistical procedure that can be utilized on a set of items (i.e., statements) to determine which items in the set form meaningful subsets or factors that are statistically independent from each other. These factors thus are assumed to represent the underlying phenomena that are responsible for the observed correlations among the items. In this case, the overall goal of factor analysis is to reduce the dimensionality of the set of items and to summarize patterns of correlations among the observed items (Tabachnick & Fidell, 1996). (A more complete discussion of factor analyses can be found in chapter 5.)

Unfortunately, the initial factor analysis conducted by Bostick (1992) failed to reach convergence when all variables were entered simultaneously, despite using mainframe computers at the University of Toledo, the University of Michigan, and Wayne State University. In each case, the amount of memory was insufficient to compute the analysis. That is, the factor analysis of the 294 items needed more iterations to converge than the computers would permit.

In order to compensate for this convergence problem, the factors were divided into their original six components as determined by the instrument developer and verified by the experts. Independent factor analysis was performed on each topic area. Only variables with factor loadings greater than .30 were retained for the analysis, as recommended by Lambert and Durand (1975). Eighty-eight items were retained using this criterion. These 88 items were used to undertake a subsequent factor analysis in an attempt to determine whether the selected items would cluster on the predetermined factors or form their own categories.

The factor analysis initially provided 24 factors using the eigenvalue-greater-than-one rule, also known as K1 (Kaiser, 1958), which was implemented to ascertain an appropriate number of factors to retain. The instrument developer decided to force the analysis into six factors to determine if they would match the original six components. Using a varimax procedure (Kieffer, 1999), the analysis reached convergence in 21 iterations. The factors were examined to determine the strength of the relationships. While the categories that developed appeared to be conceptually meaningful, several items factored on more than one category. Further, all six key components were not represented. It was decided to retain all 88 items for the second round of pilot administration.

A reliability analysis also was performed in this initial pilot administration. The classical-theory reliability estimate, as measured by Cronbach's alpha, was .80 for these 88 items. The 95% confidence interval for this reliability estimate was .77 to .83. Using Nunnally and Bernstein's (1994) criteria of .70, this internal consistency reliability estimate was deemed very acceptable.

The instrument developer then decided to force a four-factor solution on these 88 items. Again, using the varimax procedure, the analysis reached convergence in 11 iterations. When examined to determine the strength of the relationships, the 88 items fitted neatly into the four factors, which were labeled as follows: (a) Staff Assistance in Using the Library, (b) Comfort in Using the Library, (c) Constraints to Using the Library, and (d) Knowledge of the Library and Library Independence. Factor 1 contained 33 items and explained 19.4% of the total variation; Factor 2 contained 21 items, accounting for 5.4% of the total variation; Factor 3 contained 18 items, providing for 3.3% of the explained variation; and Factor 4 contained 16 items, explaining 3.0% of the variation. Thus, these four factors, in combination, explained 31.1% of the total variance, exhibiting room for improvement. Information regarding the number of items, eigenvalue, and proportion of variance explained is presented in table 1.3.

## Pilot Study 2

The second pilot study of the instrument involved a revised scale containing the 88 remaining items. These statements were renumbered from 1 to

Table 1.3   Description of four factors derived from factor analysis: Pilot 1.

| Factor Description | Number of Variables | Eigenvalue | Percent of Explained Variation |
|---|---|---|---|
| 1.  Staff barriers | 33 | 17.29 | 19.4 |
| 2.  Facilitators | 21 | 4.80 | 5.4 |
| 3.  Environmental barriers | 18 | 2.96 | 3.3 |
| 4.  Affective barriers | 16 | 2.67 | 3.0 |

88, and another number key was created. The packet remained essentially the same except for the instructions at the top of each page, which were reduced to just the answer scale. Due to the type of machine-readable forms available, the responses were indicated using an A to E scale, with A = Strongly Disagree, B = Disagree, C = Undecided, D = Agree, and E = Strongly Agree. The instrument was administered to students from first-year to graduate level at the University of Toledo, Wayne State University, and Macomb County Community College.

A total of 415 students took the second pilot administration. After these forms were returned and scanned, the responses were factor analyzed to eliminate variables that did not contribute adequately to any factors. Twenty-two factors met the eigenvalue-greater-than-one rule. As with the first pilot stage, a second factor analysis was performed, specifying that the data be forced into six factors. Here, any item that failed to have a factor loading of at least .50 was eliminated (Hair, Anderson, Tatham, & Black, 1995). Of the original 88 variables, 43 remained in the study. Score reliability, using Cronbach's alpha, indicated a coefficient of .83 for the 43 items (95% confidence interval [CI] = .81, .85).

Additional factor analyses were performed using these data, but limiting the factor analysis to the 43 items remaining in the study. The variables were forced into four factors, which accounted for a total of 45.5% of the variation in library anxiety. Using a varimax procedure, the analysis reached convergence in six iterations. When examined to determine the strength of the relationships, the 43 items remained in four categories. The categories became more specific and were named: (a) Barriers with Staff, (b) Facilitating Influences, (c) Environmental and System Barriers, and (d) Affective Barriers. Factor 1 contained 12 items and explained 26.7% of the total variation; Factor 2 contained 12 items, accounting for 7.6% of the total variation; Factor 3 contained 10 items, providing for 5.7% of the explained variation; and Factor 4 contained 9 items, explaining 5.2% of the variation. Each factor explained at least 5% of the total variance, as recommended by researchers (Hair et al., 1995). These four factors combined explained 45.2% of the total variance. Information regarding the number of items, eigenvalue, and proportion of variance explained is presented in table 1.4.

Table 1.4   Description of four factors derived from factor analysis: Pilot 2.

| Factor Description | Number of Variables | Eigenvalue | Percent of Explained Variation |
|---|---|---|---|
| 1. Staff barriers | 12 | 11.48 | 26.7 |
| 2. Facilitators | 12 | 3.28 | 7.6 |
| 3. Environmental barriers | 10 | 2.45 | 5.7 |
| 4. Affective barriers | 9 | 2.24 | 5.2 |

## Pilot Study 3

The third pilot study of the instrument involved the use of the 43-item revised scale. The goal of this pilot study was to determine the psychometric properties of this shortened scale. Of particular interest were the internal consistency, test-retest reliability, structural validity, and construct-related validity of scores yielded by this latest measure of library anxiety. Also, scale invariance was examined.

The 43-item LAS was administered to three classes: a community college class, an undergraduate class at a private college, and a graduate class at an urban university. A total of 69 students completed both the test and retest of this instrument. A special section was used on the response forms to elicit certain demographic factors. Specifically, students were asked to indicate their birth date, gender, and class level. The class level was broken down as follows: (a) freshman, (b) sophomore, (c) junior, (d) senior, (e) Master's level, (f) specialist level, (g) Doctoral level, and (h) none of the above.

The response forms were coded as was the case for the previous pilot administration, with a unique identifier beginning with "001." Because it was essential to identify the same respondent for the test and the retest, the forms were put into a packet and numbered "0011" for the first test and "0012" for the retest. The second form was placed in a manila envelope, and the first form was paper clipped to the front. The entire packet, with the instrument booklet, was distributed to the students. These students were instructed to remove the first form, sign their names on the manila envelope, and return the envelope to the instructor. They then responded to the first form and, once completed, returned it to the instructor.

For the retest, which occurred three weeks later, the envelopes and test booklet were distributed to the same students by name. They were instructed to remove the second form from the envelope and to complete it. These forms were then returned to the instructor; the students kept or discarded the envelopes.

When the test-retest process was completed, the forms were collated and the demographic section was checked for consistency. A problem was discovered with the class level relating to community college and under-graduate students. Using the codes, there was no way to determine which freshman and sophomore students were attending community colleges. Fortunately, the instrument developer was able to ascertain the students' class levels because the packets were initially reviewed by each class to which they were administered. Thus, the codes could be changed for com-munity college students to differentiate them from freshman and sopho-more university students.

## Score reliability

Reliability is the extent to which scores that are generated from an instru-ment demonstrate consistency (Kerlinger, 1999; Onwuegbuzie & Daniel, 2002b, in press). Cronbach's coefficient alpha provides information about the degree to which the items in a scale measure similar characteristics (Kerlinger, 1999). In order to test for internal consistency, Cronbach's alpha was computed on the 43 items. The resultant alpha coefficient of .80 provided evidence of adequate internal consistency. The 95% confidence interval for the reliability estimate was .73 to .86. Further, the three-week test-retest reliability estimates, as measured by Pearson's product-moment reliability coefficient, for the factors were as follows: Barriers with Staff ($r = .60, p < .05$); Affective Barriers ($r = .75, p < .05$); Comfort with the Library ($r = .35, p < .05$); Knowledge of the Library ($r = .19, p < .05$); and Mechanical Barriers ($r = .58, p < .05$). The test-retest score reliability estimate for the total scale was ($r = .70, p < .05$). With the exception of the Knowledge of the Library factor, all the test-retest coefficients represented moderate to large effect sizes (Cohen, 1988).

## Construct-related validity

Validity is the extent to which an instrument yields scores that measure what the instrument is supposed to measure (Campbell & Stanley, 1990; Gay & Airasian, 2000, 2003; Kerlinger, 1999). Furthermore, construct-related validity is the extent to which an instrument can be interpreted as a meaningful measure of some characteristic or quality (Campbell & Stanley, 1990; Gay & Airasian, 2000, 2003; Kerlinger, 1999). Establishing structural validity is an important step in providing evidence of construct-related validity (Campbell & Stanley, 1990; Gay & Airasian, 2000, 2003; Kerlinger, 1999).

In an attempt to assess the structural validity of the LAS scores, an additional exploratory factor analysis was performed using the data from the first phase of the test-retest. Specifically, an exploratory factor analysis was used to assess the structural validity of the instrument. Moreover, a maximum likelihood (ML) factor analysis was employed to determine the number of factors underlying the scale. This technique, which is more valid for identifying the number and nature of the latent factors that are responsible for covariation in a data set than is principal components factor analysis (Bickel & Doksum, 1977; Hatcher, 1994), is perhaps the most commonly used method of common factor analysis (Lawley & Maxwell, 1971). Using a varimax rotation and a criteria of .3 or greater for deeming a factor loading practically significant (Lambert & Durand, 1975), the ML factor analysis revealed five interpretable factors with eigenvalues greater than 1.0. These three factors combined explained 51.8% of the total variance. Interestingly, this proportion of total variance explained is consistent with that typically explained in factor solutions (Henson, Capraro, & Capraro, 2001; Henson & Roberts, in press). Table 1.5 provides the number of items, eigenvalues, and proportion of variables explained by each of the five factors.

The factor loadings of the 43 items (not presented) ranged from .32 (i.e., "The library won't let me check out as many items as I need" [Affective Barriers factor]) to .80 (i.e., "Librarians don't have time to help me" [Barriers with Staff factor] and "I don't know what resources are available in the library" [Affective Barriers factor]). Only 2 items (both in the Affective Barriers factor) had loadings between .30 and .39, a fur-

**Table 1.5  Description of five factors derived from factor analysis: Pilot 3.**

| Factor Description | Number of Variables | Eigenvalue | Percent of Explained Variation |
|---|---|---|---|
| 1. Barriers with staff | 15 | 10.93 | 25.4 |
| 2. Affective barriers | 12 | 3.44 | 8.0 |
| 3. Comfort with the library | 8 | 3.19 | 7.4 |
| 4. Knowledge of the library | 5 | 2.61 | 6.1 |
| 5. Mechanical barriers | 3 | 2.09 | 4.9 |
| Total | 43 | | 51.8 |

ther 9 items had loadings between .40 and .49, 8 items had loadings between .50 and .59, 11 items had loadings between .60 and .69, 11 items had loadings between .70 and .79, and 2 items had loadings of .80.

## Invariance of the Library Anxiety Scale

As noted earlier, students who completed the test and retest were asked to answer three questions regarding themselves. These questions comprised their level in college, age, and gender. These questions were used to assess the invariance of the LAS. That is, the three subsidiary questions were posed to determine if the LAS would differentiate among types and groups of students: (a) Does the instrument discriminate among levels of college students? (b) Does the instrument discriminate among college students by age? and (c) Does the instrument discriminate among college students by gender?

The first question was answered by summing the responses for each of the factors developed through the factor analysis to form a total anxiety score for each student. These total anxiety scores, as well as the five subscale scores, were used as the dependent variables, with the level of the responding student serving as the independent variable. (For this and for all subsequent comparisons undertaken by the instrument developer, the lowest LAS scores represent the highest levels of library anxiety.) The levels compared were community college students, undergraduate students at a private university, and graduate students at a public, urban university. A one-way analysis of variance (ANOVA) was used to test for differences. The results of the ANOVA are presented in table 1.6.

As can be seen from table 1.6, the results of the ANOVA conducted for each of the five factors and the overall score yielded one statistically

Table 1.6  Library anxiety scale scores as a function of level of college student.

| Factor | Community College M | Community College SD | Undergraduate M | Undergraduate SD | Graduate M | Graduate SD | DF[1] | F-Ratio |
|---|---|---|---|---|---|---|---|---|
| Barriers with staff | 38.09 | 6.09 | 38.71 | 6.83 | 34.56 | 4.84 | 2/66 | 2.49 |
| Affective barriers | 32.00 | 6.72 | 31.29 | 7.08 | 27.75 | 4.67 | 2/66 | 2.22 |
| Comfort with library | 23.41 | 1.87 | 23.26 | 2.57 | 23.31 | 2.89 | 2/66 | 0.02 |
| Knowledge of the library | 17.45 | 2.20 | 17.58 | 2.80 | 19.13 | 2.39 | 2/66 | 2.46 |
| Mechanical barriers | 7.45 | 2.04 | 7.77 | 1.86 | 9.38 | 2.33 | 2/66 | 4.63[2] |
| Total | 118.41 | 12.34 | 118.61 | 15.80 | 114.13 | 10.35 | 2/66 | 0.64 |

1. DF = Degrees of Freedom
2. p < .05

significant result. Specifically, a statistically significant difference emerged among the three college groups with respect to the Mechanical Barriers factor ($F$ [2, 66] = 4.63, $p < .05$). A post-hoc test (i.e., Tukey's Honest Significance Difference) revealed that graduate students ($M = 9.38$, $SD = 2.33$) reported statistically significantly higher levels of library anxiety than did community college students ($M = 7.45$, $SD = 2.04$) and undergraduate students ($M = 7.77$, $SD = 1.86$). The effect sizes associated with these pairwise differences were 0.89 (graduate vs. community college) and 0.79 (graduate vs. undergraduate), both of which represent large effect sizes (Cohen, 1988). On the other hand, neither the four remaining scales nor the total scale discriminated the three college levels. These findings suggested that the LAS is relatively invariant with respect to level of college student.

A one-way ANOVA also was used to assess library anxiety as a function of age. The ages were divided into categories of 10-year increments. These categories became the levels of the independent variable, whereas each of the five factors and the composite score on the LAS was treated as the dependent variables. The results of the ANOVA are presented in table 1.7.

As can be seen from table 1.7, the results of the ANOVA conducted for each of the five factors and the overall score produced statistically significant differences on the total instrument score, and for Barriers with Staff, Comfort with the Library, and Knowledge of the Library. Post-hoc tests on these main effects (i.e., Tukey's Honest Significance Difference)

**Table 1.7   Library anxiety scale scores as a function of age.**

| Factor | 30 and Under | | 31 to 40 | | 41 to 50 | | Over 50 | | F |
|---|---|---|---|---|---|---|---|---|---|
| | M | SD | M | SD | M | SD | M | SD | |
| Barriers with staff | 38.23 | 6.12 | 40.07 | 6.83 | 35.85 | 6.30 | 31.50 | 3.87 | 2.82* |
| Affective barriers | 31.90 | 6.38 | 30.20 | 4.78 | 30.45 | 7.96 | 24.75 | 4.86 | 1.48 |
| Comfort with the library | 23.47 | 1.93 | 24.27 | 1.58 | 22.95 | 2.61 | 20.50 | 5.07 | 3.02* |
| Knowledge of the library | 17.63 | 2.09 | 18.33 | 2.41 | 18.60 | 2.01 | 14.75 | 6.18 | 2.95* |
| Mechanical barriers | 7.60 | 2.28 | 8.87 | 1.06 | 8.25 | 2.22 | 7.25 | 3.20 | 1.45 |
| Total | 118.83 | 12.73 | 121.73 | 9.25 | 116.10 | 14.06 | 98.75 | 19.24 | 3.56 |

*$p < .05$

revealed that for Barriers with Staff, none of the pairwise differences between the age groups were statistically significant, even though the omnibus $F$-test was statistically significant. On the other hand, for Comfort with the Library, students in the over-50 age groups reported statistically significantly higher levels of library anxiety than did the group that was between 31 and 40. The effect size associated with this difference was 1.47, which, using Cohen's (1988) criteria, is extremely large. Similarly, for the Knowledge of the Library, the over-50 group reported statistically significant higher levels of anxiety than did those between 40 and 50. The associated effect size of 1.31 also was extremely large (Cohen, 1988).

In fact, when the means of the four age groups were examined, it was found that the oldest group, namely, those students more than 50 years old, had the lowest scores on all of the subscales, indicating higher levels of library anxiety. Thus, the subscales did not appear to differentiate students whose ages were under 50 years but did yield differences between those more than 50 years of age and one or more of the other age groups.

In order to discover whether the gender of the students played any role in the pattern of library anxiety scores that emerged, the same sample, comprising 56 females and 13 males, was examined. To answer this research question, a series of independent samples $t$-tests was employed. The results of the ANOVA are presented in table 1.8. This $t$-test yielded no statistically significant differences between males and females on any of the factors or the composite score of the LAS. However, caution should be exercised in interpreting these results because of the relatively small number of men in the sample. That is, it is possible that the lack of statisti-

Table 1.8 Means and standard deviations for library anxiety scale scores as a function of gender.

| Factor | Female | | Male | | |
|---|---|---|---|---|---|
| | M | SD | M | SD | t |
| Barriers with staff | 37.67 | 6.36 | 37.08 | 6.40 | 0.30 |
| Affective barriers | 31.25 | 6.50 | 28.31 | 6.75 | 1.46 |
| Comfort with the library | 23.20 | 2.28 | 23.85 | 3.00 | − 0.87 |
| Knowledge of the library | 17.66 | 2.52 | 18.92 | 2.72 | − 1.60 |
| Mechanical barriers | 7.91 | 2.22 | 8.62 | 1.71 | − 1.07 |
| Total | 117.68 | 13.72 | 116.77 | 13.48 | 0.22 |

$* p < .05$

cal power stemming from the small number of males in the sample led to the nonstatistically significant findings. In any case, this finding provides some evidence that the scale does not distinguish males and females in determining levels of library anxiety.

As a set, the above three findings suggested that the LAS is relatively invariant with respect to gender and level of college student. On the other hand, the LAS, to some extent, appears to vary as a function of age. However, it is not clear the extent to which these results are generalizable. Indeed, the findings pertaining to gender (i.e., Jacobson, 1991; Jiao & Onwuegbuzie, 1997; Jiao, Onwuegbuzie & Lichtenstein, 1996; Mizrachi, 2000; Shoham & Mizrachi, 2001), age (i.e., Bostick & Onwuegbuzie, 2002a; Jiao & Onwuegbuzie, 1997; Jiao et al., 1996; Mizrachi, 2000; Shoham & Mizrachi, 2001) and year of study (i.e., Jiao et al., 1996; Mech & Brooks, 1995; Mizrachi, 2000; Onwuegbuzie & Jiao, 1997b; Shoham & Mizrachi, 2001) have been somewhat contradicted in more recent studies, as outlined in chapter 2. As such, caution should be exercised in interpreting the instrument developer's conclusions regarding the invariance of the LAS.

## Final Version of the Library Anxiety Scale

The final version of the LAS was finally created in 1992 (Bostick, 1992) after several phases of instrument development. This scale is provided in Appendix A, with the scoring protocol for the LAS presented in Appendix B. Clearly, the LAS underwent rigorous development. As has been documented above, the developer of the instrument provided evidence that the LAS yields scores that appear to have good psychometric properties. In particular, this 43-item scale yielded adequate score reliability estimates. Specifically, the internal consistency for the total scale score was .80 (95% CI = .73, .86), and the test-retest reliability index for the full scale was .74, both coefficients providing adequate evidence of score reliability.

With respect to score validity, evidence of content-related validity was provided logically via the use of a master list of key components, as well as via several rounds of opinions provided by a panel of experts. Additionally, evidence of construct-related validity was furnished empirically via an exploratory factor analysis, which yielded five factors. This analysis indicated that library anxiety is a multidimensional construct, with Barriers with Staff explaining the largest variances in library anxiety scores (i.e., 25.4%).

Thus, the careful development of the LAS paved the way for empirical studies to be undertaken in the area of library anxiety. As such, librarians and other information professionals were, for the first time, able to measure levels of anxiety experienced by students in academic library settings, using a self-report scale that took less than 15 minutes to complete and which had been found to yield reliable and valid scores.

## SUBSEQUENT VALIDATION STUDIES ON THE LIBRARY ANXIETY SCALE

### Construct-Related Validity

Recently, Jerabek, Meyer, and Kordinak (2001) attempted to conduct what they called "a confirmatory maximum likelihood factor analysis" of the LAS (p. 285). Using an exploratory factor analysis with a varimax rotation, these researchers also found that the LAS scores produced five meaningful factors. According to these investigators, Factor 1, which explained 13.02% of the variance, referred to students' perceptions of "the people working in the library and their lack of helpfulness." Factor 2, accounting for 8.74% of the variance, comprised items "concerned primarily with comfort." Factor 3, explaining 8.32% of the total variation in scores, involved items related to "confidence using the library." Factor 4, which accounted for 7.79% of the variance, "dealt primarily with non-computer technology in the library." Finally, Factor 5, explaining 3.36% of the variance, contained "items dealing with directions and instructions." These five factors combined explained 41.22% of the total variance, approximately 10% less than Bostick's (1992) finding. Although using an exploratory factor analysis to undertake a confirmatory factor analysis has received much criticism in the literature (Henson & Roberts, in press; Henson et al., 2001; Kieffer, 1999; Onwuegbuzie & Daniel, 2003; also see chapter 5), the fact that the same number of factors were extracted as in Bostick's (1992) study provides incremental validity to Bostick's (1992) originally reported multidimensional structure of the LAS.

Evidence of construct-related validity of the LAS also has been provided via qualitative techniques. Specifically, Onwuegbuzie (1997a) analyzed reflexive journals, anxiety questionnaires, and research proposals of graduate students from nonstatistical disciplines who were enrolled in an introductory research methodology course. Using a thematic analysis, Onwuegbuzie (1997a) replicated Bostick's (1992) five factors. Interestingly, a sixth factor emerged, namely, what Onwuegbuzie (1997a) termed resource anxiety (see chapter 2).

Most recently, Onwuegbuzie and Jiao (2002e) conducted a more conventional confirmatory factor analysis on the LAS using a data set containing 489 college students. Specifically, the confirmatory factor analysis tested the adequacy of Bostick's (1992) five-factor model. This analysis provided support for the multidimensional structure of the LAS. Indeed, an examination of the goodness-of-fit indices (e.g., Tucker-Lewis index, comparative fit index, relative fit index, normed fit index, goodness-of-fit index, adjusted goodness-of-fit index) suggested that Bostick's (1992) five-factor model provided an adequate fit to the data. Indeed, with the exception of two items, all standardized regression coefficients in the model were larger than .50. Both items with the smallest factor loadings (i.e., standardized regression coefficients) belonged to the Barriers with Staff subscale. These items were: "I can always ask a librarian if I don't know how to work a piece of equipment in the library" (Item 21, standardized regression coefficient = .45) and "The library is a comfortable place to study" (Item 22, standardized regression coefficient = .27). However, these loadings were still large enough to justify their inclusion in the five-factor model.

Jiao and Onwuegbuzie (2002b) compared the efficacy of each of the five subscales of the Library Anxiety Scale in predicting overall library anxiety, as measured by the total LAS scores. Across several data sets, they found that the Barriers with Staff scale consistently was the best predictor of overall LAS scores, explaining, by itself, as much as 86% of the total variance in LAS scores (using Onwuegbuzie & Jiao's [in press] data). This result is consistent with that of Bostick (1992) and Jerabek et al. (2001), who found from their exploratory factor analyses that Barriers with Staff explained the highest proportion of variance in library anxiety scores.

## Criterion-Related Validity

Criterion-related validity indicates the extent to which scores generated by an instrument either predict future performance (i.e., predictive validity) or estimate current performance on another scale that is hypothesized to measure a similar construct (i.e., concurrent validity) (Campbell & Stanley, 1990; Gay & Airasian, 2000, 2003; Kerlinger, 1999). Evidence of criterion-related validity is provided by significantly relating performance on one instrument to performance on another criterion either in the present or in the future (Gay & Airasian, 2000, 2003).

### Concurrent validity

In recent years, evidence of concurrent validity of LAS scores has been documented by several researchers. Specifically, library anxiety has been found to be related statistically significantly to several types of academic-related anxiety, including research anxiety, statistics anxiety, writing anxiety, computer anxiety, and attitudes toward the educational use of the Internet (Collins & Veal, in press; Jerabek et al., 2001; Mizrachi, 2000; Onwuegbuzie & Jiao, 2002c; Shoham & Mizrachi, 2001). Interestingly, the effect sizes associated with these relationships typically have been moderate to large.

Divergent validity involves correlating scores from the target measure with scores from a construct that measures the opposite of the construct. More specifically, divergent validity exists if no correlation is found between the two sets of scores. Further, discriminant validity has been established if it can be demonstrated that the scores on the target scale are not correlated with scores on another instrument designed to measure a construct that should theoretically not be related to the target construct (Johnson & Christensen, 2000). Evidence of both divergent and discriminant validity have been provided by Mech and Brooks (1995, 1997), Jerabek et al. (2001), and Jiao and Onwuegbuzie (1999a), who each reported no statistically significant relationship between library anxiety and measures of trait anxiety among various student populations (e.g., undergraduate students, graduate students). As noted in chapter 2, this set of results suggests the relative independence of the library anxiety construct from trait anxiety among college students.

*Predictive validity*

Evidence that LAS scores have predictive validity has been provided by Onwuegbuzie (1997a). This researcher found that library anxiety predicted students' ability to write a research proposal. In particular, Onwuegbuzie (1997a) found that affective barriers ($r = -.35, p < .001$) and knowledge of the library ($r = -.27, p < .001$) were moderately negatively related to the quality of research proposals completed by graduate students. Even more noteworthy, using structural equation modeling techniques, Onwuegbuzie and Jiao (in press) observed that library anxiety not only predicted the quality of research proposals among graduate students, it also mediated the relationship between levels of performance of this task and several cognitive and affective variables (i.e., age, academic achievement, learning style, academic procrastination, and self-perception) (see chapter 3).

## Reliability

Reliability, or rather *unreliability*, can adversely affect the internal validity of findings (i.e., instrumentation; Campbell, 1957; Campbell & Stanley, 1963; Gay & Airasian, 2000, 2003; Johnson & Christensen, 2000) through an inflation of Type I error or a reduction in statistical power. Low reliability indices not only adversely affect null hypothesis significance testing but also negatively impact effect-size measures. This is because low reliability coefficients stem from scores that do not behave in a consistent manner (Gay & Airasian, 2000, 2003; Johnson & Christensen, 2000; Onwuegbuzie & Daniel, 2002b, in press), and it is these scores that are used to calculate both test statistics in null hypothesis significance testing and effect-size measures. As such, researchers should never assume that because Bostick (1992), or any other researcher, reported a large reliability coefficient in the past, this guarantees a high reliability estimate in their own studies. That is, reliability is not a function of the instrument but of scores (Onwuegbuzie & Daniel, 2002b, in press; Thompson & Vacha-Haase, 2000; Vacha-Haase, 1998; Wilkinson & the Task Force on Statistical Inference, 1999). Consequently, researchers using the LAS, as well as all other scales, always should report reliability estimates pertaining to their own data. In fact, alongside reliability coefficients, confidence intervals around these estimates should be provided (Onwuegbuzie & Daniel, 2002b, in press; Thompson & Vacha-Haase, 2000; Vacha-Haase, 1998; Wilkinson & the Task Force on Statistical Inference, 1999).

Jiao and Onwuegbuzie (2002c) examined the score reliability reported on the Library Anxiety Scale in the extant literature. Although score reliability has not always been reported when the LAS has been used, they noted several distinct patterns among the score reliability coefficients that have been documented. First and foremost, with the exception of Bostick's (1992) reliability estimate of .80, all other studies ($n = 9$) in which score reliability has been reported for the total scale yielded coefficients in the .90s. In fact, Onwuegbuzie and Jiao (1998b), Jiao and Onwuegbuzie (2001a) and, most recently, Collins and Veal (in press), Onwuegbuzie and Jiao (2002e), and Bostick and Onwuegbuzie (2002a) each reported reliability estimates of .95 for the full scale. Bearing in mind that .70 is considered acceptable for score reliability estimates pertaining to affective measures (Nunnally & Bernstein, 1994), these values are extremely noteworthy. Thus, not only does the LAS produce scores that yield extremely reliable estimates, but these estimates are remarkably consistent across samples with different, cultures, nationalities, ages, years of study, gender composition, educational majors, and so forth.

Second, the five LAS subscale scores also have yielded reliability coefficients across studies that have been very consistent. For example, across 12 studies in which subscale score reliabilities have been reported, Jiao and Onwuegbuzie (2002c) found that in all but one study (i.e., Onwuegbuzie & Jiao, 1998c; Cronbach's alpha = .79) the Barriers with Staff scale yielded the highest reliability estimate. Indeed, as has been the case for the full scale scores, the reliability estimate in these studies always has been in the .90s, with Bostick and Onwuegbuzie (2002a) and Onwuegbuzie and Jiao (2000) both reporting reliability indices of .95. In contrast, across these 12 studies, the Knowledge of the Library and Mechanical Barriers subscales yielded scores with the lowest reliability estimates. This perhaps should not be surprising because Knowledge of the Library and Mechanical Barriers subscales contain the smallest number of items, comprising five and three items, respectively. Indeed, holding all other components equal, smaller items generate lower score reliability estimates (Crocker & Algina, 1986). The Knowledge of the Library subscale has generated score reliability coefficients that have ranged from .60 to .84, whereas the Mechanical Barriers subscale has produced reliability estimates that have ranged from .60 to .88.

As demonstrated by Onwuegbuzie and Daniel (2002b, in press), statistical power can be affected greatly by the level of reliability inherent in the scores. Thus, the fact that the LAS to date has consistently yielded extremely reliable scores provides incremental validity to findings from studies in which this instrument has been utilized. Further, the level of reliability coefficients is particularly encouraging and should serve as a motivation for future research using this instrument.

## SUMMARY AND CONCLUSIONS

The present chapter has provided a comprehensive objective critique of the psychometric properties of the Library Anxiety Scale (Bostick, 1992). In particular, the composite scores have been found to yield extremely large reliability coefficients, indicating that this scale generates minimal measurement error (Crocker & Algina, 1986; Onwuegbuzie & Daniel, 2002b). For example, a score reliability estimate of .95, has been found repeatedly for the LAS, indicates that 95% of the observed score variance is attributable to true score variance and that only 5% of the observed score variance is attributable to error score variance (Crocker & Algina, 1986). Clearly, the LAS thus far has yielded full-scale scores with exceptional reliability coefficients. Further, the score reliability estimates yielded by the five subscales also have been very encouraging. In particular, the Barriers with Staff, Affective Barriers, and Comfort with the Library subscales have yielded large reliability indices, with Barriers with Staff being especially noteworthy. However, although the Knowledge of the Library and Mechanical Barriers subscales have tended to yield adequate reliability coefficients, the fact that these estimates have, at times fallen below Nunnally and Bernstein's (1994) criteria of .70, suggests that they may benefit from a few more parallel items being written to increase these estimates across studies (Crocker & Algina, 1986).

As important as it is for instruments to generate reliable scores, this is superseded by the provision of scores that are a valid measure of the underlying construct. In other words, although score reliability is essential, score validity is the most critical property for an instrument to possess. If a score is not valid, then it cannot be reliable (Gay & Airasian, 2003; Onwuegbuzie, 2000b). Thus, it is even more encouraging that multiple evidences of content-, criterion-, and construct-related validity have been provided by Bostick (1992) and, subsequently, by other researchers. This evidence helps explain the high reliability estimates that have been documented in the extant literature.

In conclusion, based on the evidence provided thus far, the Library Anxiety Scale possesses extremely sound psychometric properties. Clearly, the rigor used in developing this scale is responsible for the encouraging reliability and validity data reported. These data provide incremental validity to the published and unpublished findings that have stemmed from the use of this instrument. Nevertheless, researchers should continue to assess the psychometric properties of the LAS. It is only by continuing to scrutinize the LAS that we can ensure that it continues to advance the field of library science.

## Chapter Two

# Nature and Etiology of Library Anxiety

## OVERVIEW

In broad terms, library anxiety is described as "an uncomfortable feeling or emotional disposition, experienced in a library setting, which has cognitive, affective, physiological, and behavioral ramifications" (Jiao et al., 1996, p. 152). An initial step in designing effective intervention strategies for the reduction of library anxiety is to elucidate the very nature and etiology of that anxiety, as well as the antecedents and symptoms. Therefore, the present chapter is an attempt to further our understanding of the phenomenon of library anxiety by discussing the nature and etiology of it. First, the construct of general anxiety is discussed. This is followed by a description of the nature of library anxiety, including an identification of the population group who is most at risk for experiencing it, as well as the prevalence rates. Third, some of the major symptoms of library anxiety are delineated. Next, a discussion of the components of library anxiety is provided. The chapter ends with a summary of the antecedents of library anxiety that have been identified in the extant literature thus far. Throughout this chapter, the phenomenon of library anxiety is described within a theoretical framework by combining the literature on general anxiety, general test anxiety, and other forms of academic-related anxiety.

## THE CONSTRUCT OF GENERAL ANXIETY

General anxiety as a reaction to an event or situation has probably been in existence since the beginning of time. However, the study of anxiety as a psychological construct is, for the most part, a phenomenon that has only emerged this century. In fact, the number of studies on anxiety, both experimental and correlational, increased steadily in the 1950s and 1960s. Spielberger (1972) estimated that approximately 5,000 anxiety-related publications appeared in the research literature between 1950 and 1970. The interest in studying anxiety seems to have continued to the present day (Edelmann, 1992; Onwuegbuzie & Daley, 1999a). Indeed, using the keyword "anxiety," a recent review of the ERIC (Educational Resource Information Center) database revealed 8,949 documents and articles indexed with that term. Even more compelling is the fact that using the keyword "anxiety" in the PsycINFO database retrieved more than 9,995 records on this topic since 2000.

General anxiety has been described as an "emotional state with the subjectively experienced quality of fear or a closely related emotion" and "feelings of uncertainty and helplessness" (Endler & Edwards, 1982, p. 39). Some authors believe that anxiety is a basic human characteristic (Spielberger, 1966, 1972). In any case, general anxiety is both subjective and experiential, and, as a result, has led to an array of definitions. Although there is a lack of consensus regarding the definition and characterization of anxiety, there is basic agreement on three types of indicators of anxiety: behavioral, physiological, and phenomenological (Phillips, Martin, & Meyers, 1972).

## Components of Anxiety

Many researchers agree that general anxiety comprises two distinct but interrelated components, namely, state anxiety and trait anxiety (Cattell, 1966). Gaudry and Spielberger (1971) and Zuckerman (1972, 1976) defined trait anxiety as the relative stable proneness within each person to react with anxiety to situations that are perceived as being stressful. State anxiety is defined as the temporary emotional state of an individual. Moreover, state anxiety is a construct that varies in intensity and fluctuates over time.

Cattell and Scheier (1961) also defined anxiety within a two-component framework. These theorists categorized anxiety as being either overt or covert. Whereas overt anxiety represents a conscious state that is related to specific events in a person's life, covert anxiety refers to an unconscious stable measure of anxiety.

## The Nature of General Anxiety

The consequences of anxiety are complex and interactional in nature and vary from one situation to another. Although these consequences are usually negative and debilitating, there are occasions when they can be facilitating. The latter is often the result of dealing with anxiety in a positive manner. In this instance, anxiety can act as a motivator (Phillips et al., 1972).

Anxiety has been shown to interfere with cognitive functioning (e.g., Waid, Kanoy, Blick, & Walker, 1978; Ward & Salter, 1974). This interference seems to occur in a variety of educational settings and with a variety of instructional methods. General anxiety has been shown to be negatively related to measures of intellectual and academic performance (Hill & Sarason, 1966; Spielberger, 1966), self-concept (Lipsett, 1958; Mitchell, 1959; Rosenberg, 1962), and peer relations (Phillips, 1971).

Research (e.g., Hollandsworth, Glezski, Kirkland, Jones, & Van Norman, 1979) indicates that students with low levels of anxiety were physiologically aroused during examinations but viewed their arousal as helpful. Highly anxious students, on the other hand, considered their state of anxiety to be debilitative. Fein (1963) postulated a curvilinear relationship between general anxiety and achievement.

Several studies (e.g., Brett & Kernaleguen, 1975; Butterfield, 1964; Feather, 1967; Joe, 1971; Ray & Katahn, 1968; Watson, 1967) have reported that college students who are assessed as having an external locus-of-control are more anxious than are those assessed as having an internal locus-of-control. However, Gold (1968) and Procicuk and Breen (1973) did not find a significant relationship between locus of control and test anxiety.

With regard to the relationship between gender and general anxiety, research findings have been mixed. Whereas some authors have found that females score higher on measures of general anxiety than do their male counterparts (Biaggio & Nielsen, 1976; Gall, 1969; Sarason, 1963; Sarason, Davidson, Lighthall, & Waite, 1958), others have reported no gender differences (Dunn, 1965; Feld & Lewis, 1967).

## Symptoms of General Anxiety

Cattell (1966), Duffy (1962), and May (1950) derived lists of physiological reactions associated with high levels of anxiety. These include increase in heart rate, respiration rate, and blood pressure; increase in overall muscle tension; contraction of the smooth muscles of the internal genital organs; decrease in skin temperature; decrease in skin resistance; increase in metabolic rate; dilation of pupils; standing on end of body hair; suspension of digestive activity; drying of mouth; and sweating of palms. Anxiety also has been shown to induce some psychosomatic symptoms such as asthma, migraine, and hypertension (Edelmann, 1992; Wolpe, 1973).

McReynolds (1976) documented behavioral signs of anxiety that include biting one's nails, restlessness, crying, stuttering, and voice tremors. Fear, frustration, and learned-helplessness are often symptoms of anxiety (Mandler, 1972). Disturbingly, high levels of anxiety can manifest itself in excessive smoking, alcoholism, and eating disorders (Hall, 1972; Koenig & Masters, 1965), as well as sexual dysfunctions (Razani, 1972).

Affective symptoms of anxiety include apprehension and emotional instability (Krug, Scheier, & Cattell, 1976). According to Spielberger (1972), severe anxiety is associated with unrealistic and disproportionate perceptions of ego threat, which often have debilitating consequences. Individuals develop methods of trying to control or to reduce their levels of anxiety. These methods include the defense mechanisms described by Sigmund Freud, such as repression, denial, and projection (Spielberger, 1972).

## Antecedents of General Anxiety

Epstein (1972) conceptualized three basic antecedents of anxiety: (a) primary overstimulation, (b) cognitive incongruity, and (c) response unavailability. Primary overstimulation involves frantic feelings of being overwhelmed with a stimulation that exceeds the level of tolerance. Cognitive incongruity pertains to situations in which there is a discrepancy between an individual's expectation and reality, coupled with a failure to cope with this predicament. Anxiety states that are associated with cognitive incongruity include confusion, despondency, and disorientation. Response unavailability represents an anxiety state that occurs when a waiting period is required before a response can be made.

As mentioned above, trait anxiety can be defined as a relatively stable and permanent personality characteristic. That is, trait anxiety is neither time- nor situation-specific. On the other hand, state anxiety can be conceptualized as a temporary condition that fluctuates over time. Simply put, state anxiety is time- and situation-specific. Gaudry and Spielberger (1971) reported that students with high levels of trait anxiety exhibit state anxiety elevations more frequently than do those with low levels of trait anxiety because they tend to interpret a wider range of situations as being threatening.

Research has consistently shown that state anxiety adversely affects learning and achievement (Joesting & Whitehead, 1977; Waid et al., 1978; Ward & Salter, 1974). Because anxiety induced in educational settings tends to be time- and situation-specific, many types of academic-related anxiety have been identified, including *computer anxiety* (Gressard & Loyd, 1987; Jennings & Onwuegbuzie, 2001; Loyd & Gressard, 1984), *research anxiety* (Onwuegbuzie, 1997a, 1997b, 1997c, 1997d), *statistics anxiety* (Onwuegbuzie, 1997a, in press-a; Onwuegbuzie, DaRos, & Ryan, 1997; Onwuegbuzie, Slate, Paterson, Watson, & Schwartz, 2000; Roberts & Bilderback, 1980; Schacht & Stewart, 1990; Zeidner, 1991), *mathematics anxiety* (Byrd, 1982; Fennema & Sherman, 1976; Harris & Harris, 1987; Richardson & Suinn, 1972; Rounds & Hendel, 1980; Tobias, 1980; Wigfield & Meece, 1988), *writing anxiety* (Daly & Miller, 1975a, 1975b, 1975c; Daly & Shamo, 1976, 1978; Daly & Wilson, 1983; Onwuegbuzie, 1997a, 1998a, 1999a; Onwuegbuzie & Collins, 2001), *foreign language anxiety* (Bailey, Onwuegbuzie, & Daley, 1998, 2000a, 2000b, 2000c, in press; Horwitz, Horwitz, & Cope, 1986; MacIntyre & Gardner, 1991a, 1991b, 1991c; Onwuegbuzie, Bailey, & Daley, 1999a, 1999b, 2000, 2001, 2002; Young, 1991), and *general test anxiety* (Everson, Millsap, & Rodriguez, 1991; Hill, 1984). However, as noted by Jiao and Onwuegbuzie (2002a), library anxiety appears to be among the most prevalent forms of academic-related anxiety, presumably because most students are compelled to use the library at some point in their programs of study. It is to this form of academic-related anxiety that we now turn.

## THE CONSTRUCT OF LIBRARY ANXIETY

For many decades, some students have reported feeling more comfortable while utilizing libraries than do their counterparts. Moreover, librarians and library educators have noticed these differences in comfort levels among their patrons. However, until recently, the finding that a student can experience a high level of apprehension about using academic libraries stemmed from informal and/or casual observations. That is, only in the last 18 years have formal, systematic studies been conducted on the nature, etiology, characteristics, or consequences of this phenomenon (Jiao & Onwuegbuzie, 1999a). The phenomenon is formally known as *library anxiety*. Indeed, at the time of writing this book, only 26 research articles, identified via database searches (e.g., ERIC, PsycINFO), have been published in the area of library anxiety.

In her seminal two-year qualitative study involving 6,000 students, Mellon (1986) noted that between 75% and 85% of undergraduate students described their initial library research experiences in terms of anxiety. Library-anxious students tend to experience interfering responses during one or more stages of the information-search process (Kuhlthau, 1983, 1985, 1987, 1988a, 1988b, 1989, 1991, 1993, 1994; Kuhlthau, Turock, George, & Belvin, 1990). As such, anxious library users tend to focus less of their time, energy, and attention on the task itself, thereby impeding the attainment of their goals (Mech & Brooks, 1995; Mellon, 1988).

Library anxiety is time- and situation-specific inasmuch as the symptoms only appear when students are in or are contemplating a visit to the library (Jiao & Onwuegbuzie, 1997). That is, library anxiety is more a state-based anxiety than a trait-based anxiety. In support of this contention, Mech and Brooks (1995, 1997) found no statistically significant differences between students' levels of library anxiety and trait anxiety. Based on this finding, Mech and Brooks (1995) concluded that, for undergraduate students, library anxiety is "a separate condition from the trait of general anxiety" (p. 175). Somewhat consistent with this finding, Jerabek, Meyer, and Kordinak (2001) found no relationship between library anxiety and general anxiety, as measured by the IPAT Anxiety Scale (Krug et al., 1976) among male undergraduates. However, it should be noted that these researchers found a moderate statistically significant association between these two variables among their female counterparts.

At the graduate level, Jiao and Onwuegbuzie (1999a) noted that library anxiety was not statistically significantly related to trait anxiety, as measured by the State-Trait Anxiety Inventory (STAI; Spielberger, Gorsuch, & Lushene, 1968). These researchers concluded that library-anxious graduate students typically are those who are not anxious in other areas of their lives. Indeed, the findings of Mech and Brooks (1995) and Jiao and Onwuegbuzie (1999a) suggest the relative independence of the library anxiety construct from trait anxiety for both undergraduate and graduate students. Moreover, these findings provide credence to the assertion that library anxiety represents a situation-specific disposition.

According to Mellon (1986), feelings of anxiety stem from one or more of the following four sources: (a) the relative size of the library; (b) a lack of knowledge about the location of materials, equipment, and resources; (c) a lack of knowledge about how to initiate library research; and (d) a lack of knowledge about how to proceed with a library search. In Mellon's (1986) inquiry, the following is a compelling example of a student who was overwhelmed by the library:

> Using the library is a scary prospect, especially when I think about in-depth research. I know that research cannot be done without frequent visits to the library and I know that nothing in here will hurt me but it seems so vast and overpowering. (p. 162)

Mellon (1986) also provided evidence of how a lack of knowledge of how to initiate and to proceed with a library search can elevate levels of library anxiety:

> Oh! Now I have to begin my research paper and what am I to do? Although I have been using the University's library for a little more than one semester, I'm still frightened each time I push those wide glass doors open. (p. 162)

The following account documented in Mellon's (1986) study illustrates how library anxiety can be increased by a lack of knowledge of the location of materials:

> When I first entered the library, I was terrified. I didn't know where any-
> thing was located or even who to ask to get some help. It was like being in
> a foreign country and unable to speak the language. (p. 162)

Further, students with high levels of library anxiety typically believe that
other students are adept at using the library, whereas they alone are inept;
their incompetence is a source of embarrassment and consequently should
be concealed; and asking librarians questions reveals their ignorance
(Mellon, 1988, 1989).

## Symptoms of Library Anxiety

A student who experiences library anxiety usually undergoes either emotional or physical discomfort when faced with any library or library-
related task, whether it is a routine responsibility such as returning a
library book or a more complex task such as conducting an extensive
library search (Kuhlthau, 1988a, 1991; Mellon, 1986, 1988, 1989;
Onwuegbuzie, 1997a). Library anxiety may arise from a lack of self-con-
fidence in conducting research, lack of prior exposure to academic libraries, and the inability to see the relevance of libraries in one's field of
interest or career path.

Mild anxiety can actually be useful inasmuch as it can facilitate motivation to utilize the library. This is referred to in the literature as facilitative
anxiety (Alpert & Haber, 1960). However, more severe anxiety from
which panic, learned helplessness, or mental disarray ensue is extremely
detrimental to the student. Furthermore, high levels of library anxiety can
threaten graduate students' ability to finish their degree programs by preventing them from conducting library searches and thus completing their
theses/dissertations (Onwuegbuzie & Jiao, 1998a, 1998b). Some of these
students will go to great lengths to avoid using the library (Onwuegbuzie,
1997a).

As is the case for general anxiety and several academic-related forms
of anxiety, library anxiety is characterized by a myriad of symptoms. In
particular, Onwuegbuzie (1997a) found evidence of symptoms that
included increase in heart rate, respiration rate, and blood pressure.
Onwuegbuzie (1997a) also documented affective symptoms such as
apprehension, frustration, and learned helplessnesss. High levels of

library anxiety also are characterized by tension, fear, uneasiness, negative self-defeating thoughts, feeling of uncertainty, and mental disorganization, all of which have the propensity to debilitate information literacy (Kuhlthau, 1988a, 1991). Thus, library-anxious students typically use the library the least (Onwuegbuzie & Jiao, 1997a). Interestingly, contrasting the lowest third with the highest third of the library anxiety distribution, Jiao and Onwuegbuzie (2002b) found that high-anxious students are approximately two-and-a-half times (odds ratio = 2.42; 95% confidence interval = 1.56, 3.77) less likely to visit the library than are low-anxious students.

Levels of library anxiety are conceptualized as lying on a continuum (Jiao & Onwuegbuzie, 1999a). However, as noted by Jiao and Onwuegbuzie (1999a), in order to describe the nature and etiology of library anxiety, it is useful to characterize prototypical high- and low-anxious students. For high-anxious students, using the library often is an extremely negative experience (Fliotsos, 1992). As is the case for test anxiety (Liebert & Morris, 1967), students with high levels of library anxiety exhibit both worry and emotionality (Onwuegbuzie, 1997a). Once in the library, library-anxious students often display many symptoms. For example, when searching for books or periodicals, a high-anxious student may misread or overlook signs and maps, misinterpret directions and cues, refrain from asking for help, or give up their search relatively quickly (Keefer, 1993; Kuhlthau, 1988a, 1991). Compared to their less-anxious counterparts, high-anxious students often lack confidence in their ability to effectively utilize the library in general and to conduct library searches in particular. These perceptions, whether accurate or inaccurate, typically culminate in shame, concealment, and subsequent avoidance behaviors. These behaviors, in turn, prevent high-anxious students from developing appropriate library skills (Mellon, 1986). Apparently, the reluctance of high-anxious students to share their feelings of anxiety can culminate in instructors overestimating their students' library skills (Jacobson, 1991).

Low-anxious students represent the other end of the continuum. In sharp contrast to their high-anxious peers, these individuals typically feel comfortable in the library and may spend long periods of time merely browsing (Onwuegbuzie 1997a). In fact, as noted by Jiao and Onwuegbuzie (1999a), it is not unusual for low-anxious students to use the library as a sanctuary from the distractions of their homes. Moreover, low-anxious students tend to use better coping strategies when faced with obstacles in the library and tend to use the most effective problem-solving techniques (Onwuegbuzie, 1997a).

Jiao et al. (1996) contrasted low- and high-anxious students with respect to their reasons for using the library. These researchers found that when library-anxious students visit the library, they tend to do so either to use the online/computer index, to return a book, to conduct a library search for a thesis/dissertation, to obtain a book or article for an assignment, or to study for a class project. In a more recent study, Onwuegbuzie and Jiao (2002a) found that using the online/computer index, conducting a library search for a thesis/dissertation, obtaining a book or article for an assignment, studying for a class project, and searching for information about potential employers were more likely the reasons cited by high-anxious students for utilizing the library. On the other hand, meeting friends was more likely to be the reason cited by low-anxious library users.

Many myths surrounding academic libraries exacerbate anxiety. These types of false belief systems help to create, to maintain, and to elevate levels of library anxiety. For example, it is often believed by students, particularly by international students in the United States or by international students using libraries in their home countries, that college libraries are primarily places to study, rather than places to conduct library searches and the like (Koehler & Swanson, 1988; Pearce, 1981). Such a misperception can lead students to deem the librarian as " 'the keeper of knowledge' who gives access to this treasure only to a select few, and therefore s/he should not be lightly disturbed, invoked, or interrupted" (Onwuegbuzie & Jiao, 1997b, p. 259).

As noted by Onwuegbuzie and Jiao (1997b) and Jiao and Onwuegbuzie (2001b), international students often come to the United States armed with erroneous beliefs and myths about the function of U.S. libraries. These beliefs unduly influence their expectations of library services (Mood, 1982). Students who believe that libraries play a minimal role in their academic success are likely to be overwhelmed and intimidated by the scope of information available and the resources by which they can obtain this information (Onwuegbuzie & Jiao, 1997b). Thus, using a college library can be a negative experience, at least initially, for many international students (Wayman, 1984).

Library searches are perceived by many to involve one path, in which success is guaranteed only if the correct path is taken, regardless of how much effort is expended in conducting the library search. This incongruity between effort and "success" promotes anxiety. Moreover, as stated by Kuhlthau (1991), "uncertainty, a natural and necessary aspect of the early stages of the ISP [Information Search Process], causes discomfort and anxiety which in turn affects articulation of a problem and judgments of relevancy" (p. 364).

Because librarians often tend to be women, library education is seen by some as belonging to the female domain. Thus, it is perhaps not surprising that males have been found to have higher levels of library anxiety than do females (Jiao et al., 1996). Indeed, Jiao et al. (1996) concluded that this finding provides incremental validity to Jacobson's (1991) contention of the existence of a female-based "library culture."

Another myth held by some students is that academic libraries are needed only by more advanced undergraduate students (e.g., seniors) and graduate students because they receive more complex educational assignments and requirements (e.g., extended term papers, theses/dissertations) than do other types of students. Consistent with this observation, Jiao et al. (1996) found that library anxiety declines linearly as a function of year of study, with freshmen and sophomores reporting the highest levels of library anxiety, followed by seniors, juniors, and, lastly, by graduate students. Further, freshmen and sophomores reported statistically significantly higher levels of library anxiety than did graduate students.

A final myth centers around the perception that some students do not have the propensity to be adept in libraries. In fact, as noted earlier, these students often believe that their peers are proficient at utilizing the library, whereas they alone are incompetent (Collins, Mellon, & Young, 1987; Mellon, 1986, 1988, 1989). In accordance with this observation, level of self-perception has been found to be an important predictor of library anxiety (Jiao & Onwuegbuzie, 1999b).

## Components of Library Anxiety

Library anxiety has been found to be a multidimensional construct. Specifically, using exploratory factor analysis techniques, Bostick (1992) identified five dimensions of library anxiety, namely, *barriers with staff, affective barriers, comfort with the library, knowledge of the library,* and *mechanical barriers.*

*Barriers with staff* refer to students' perceptions that librarians and other library staff are intimidating, unapproachable, and inaccessible. Further, librarians are perceived as being too busy to provide assistance in using the library and as having more important duties to perform than helping library users. Students with this perception tend to report high levels of library anxiety (Mellon, 1986).

*Affective barriers* stem from students' feelings of ineptness about using the library. These feelings of inadequacy are elevated by the assumption that they alone possess incompetent library skills (Mellon, 1986).

*Comfort with the library* pertains to how safe, secure, welcoming, and nonthreatening students perceive the library to be. Students who are not comfortable in the library tend to have higher levels of library anxiety (Jiao et al., 1996).

*Knowledge of the library* refers to how familiar with the library students feel they are. A lack of familiarity tends to culminate in frustration and anxiety and, subsequently, to further avoidance behaviors (Mellon, 1988, 1989).

Finally, *mechanical barriers* relate to feelings that arise from students' reliance on mechanical library equipment, including computers, computer printers, photocopy machines, and change machines. Students who have difficulty operating one or more pieces of the library equipment tend to experience high anxiety levels. (Complete details as to how these factors were extracted were discussed in chapter 1.) Interestingly, Jiao and Onwuegbuzie (2001b) found that mechanical barriers induced statistically significantly the highest levels of library anxiety among college students enrolled in an urban university. This was followed by affective barriers, barriers with staff, comfort with the library, and knowledge of the library, respectively. Similarly, Onwuegbuzie (1997e) reported that mechanical barriers generated statistically significantly higher levels of library anxiety than did the other four components.

Onwuegbuzie (1997a) studied the role of library anxiety as well as other types of academic-related anxiety when graduate students are attempting to write research proposals. Using qualitative research techniques, Onwuegbuzie (1997a) noted that library anxiety comprised the following six components: *interpersonal anxiety, perceived library com-*

*petence, perceived comfort with the library, location anxiety, mechanical anxiety,* and *resource anxiety.*

According to Onwuegbuzie, *interpersonal anxiety,* which is similar to Bostick's (1992) *barrier with staff* dimension, relates to an increase in anxiety levels when a student contemplates or is in the process of seeking help from a librarian or other library staff. The following account provides an example of a student who is high on this dimension:

> Although I found a few articles using ERIC, I thought I could get more from MEDLINE. But I could not figure out how to use the MEDLINE system and I did not want to disturb the librarian by asking them [*sic*] how to use what is probably a simple software, so I left the library frustrated. (p. 15)

*Perceived library competence,* like Bostick's (1992) *affective barriers* dimension, refers to an increase in levels of anxiety culminating in a student having a negative perception of her or his ability to utilize the library competently. The following statement is representative of this component: "I feel so overwhelmed in the library because I never know what I am doing or where to begin" (Onwuegbuzie, 1997a, p. 16).

*Perceived comfort with the library,* which is identical to that of Bostick (1992), pertains to the anxiety that arises from a student's perception of how safe and welcoming the library is. One student in Onwuegbuzie's (1997a) investigation declared: "I'll probably have to go to the other library. I hate going to that library. There is always construction and it's not in the best neighborhood" (p. 16).

*Location anxiety,* which is equivalent to Bostick's (1992) *knowledge of the library* dimension, pertains to the student's level of perceived familiarity with the library. The following statement exemplifies this form of library anxiety: "I get so frustrated and anxious because I never know where everything is in the library" (Onwuegbuzie, 1997a, p. 16).

*Mechanical anxiety,* like Bostick's (1992) mechanical barriers, refers to the elevations in anxiety levels when students are contemplating using, attempting to use, or actually using mechanical library equipment, including CD-ROMs, computers, computer printers, photocopy machines, and microfiche. For instance, a student in Onwuegbuzie's (1997a) inquiry revealed:

I went to the library at 10:30 A.M. I searched through the computer for two hours. Finally, I asked the librarian for assistance. She checked with some guy on call. It turns out that the Internet was down. My results? Today was a waste of time and not very productive in reference to my paper. (p. 17)

A library that has an inadequate number of computers is problematic for students and thus can be a source of anxiety. As one high-anxious library user noted: "I have been at the library from 10:30 A.M. until 4:00 P.M. typing my proposal. I had to wait about 20 minutes for a computer. There has been a real traffic jam in the computer lab here lately" (p. 17).

Using the library CD-ROMs also can induce resource anxiety. For instance, Onwuegbuzie (1997a) illustrated how anxiety can ensue when the key words students select to use for their computer library search turn out to be ineffective:

I went to the library to do a search for cholesterol in the elderly. This topic was hard to find any articles. I decided I wasn't using the correct key words so I asked a librarian to help me. We ended up having to use the word hyper-cholesterolemia instead of high cholesterol to find articles. ERIC sure is picky! (p. 17)

Finally, *resource anxiety* refers to the anxiety that stems from a student selecting an article or a book from a library computer search that was not available at the library. Here, not having the needed resource can lead to frustration, which, in turn, can elevate anxiety levels, as illustrated by the following statement:

Even though I found many articles about alcohol, I am so frustrated and disappointed about the insufficient sources in our library because so many articles which I need are not available in our library. (p. 18)

Interestingly, Onwuegbuzie (1997a) found resource anxiety to be one of the most prevalent dimensions of library anxiety. The library parking lot often is another source of resource anxiety:

I went to the library, and I became terribly frustrated when I could not park on the lot in front of the library. You must have a pass card to park on the lot during the week. As I drove around the campus to find a parking space,

I suddenly did not want to go to the library. The only parking space I could find was nearly two blocks away from the library. I went home. (p. 19)

Most recently, Mizrachi (2000) and Shoham and Mizrachi (2001) developed a Hebrew version of Bostick's (1992) Library Anxiety Scale, which they called the Hebrew Library Anxiety Scale (H-LAS). Using exploratory factor analysis techniques, these researchers identified the following seven factors: *Staff, Knowledge, Language, Physical Comfort, Library Computer Comfort, Library Policies/Hours,* and *Resources.*

The *Staff* factor pertains to students' attitudes toward librarians and library staff and their perceived accessibility. The *Knowledge* factor refers to how students rate their own library expertise. The *Language* factor reveals the extent to which using English-language searches and materials produce discomfort. The *Physical Comfort* factor assesses how much the physical facility adversely influences students' satisfaction and comfort with the library. The *Library Computer Comfort* factor measures the perceived trustworthiness of library computer facilities and the quality of directions for using them. The *Library Policies/Hours* factor concerns students' attitudes toward library rules, regulations, and operating hours. Finally, the *Resources* factor involves the perceived availability of the desired material in the library collection. Unfortunately, the authors of the H-LAS did not report how much of the total variance that these seven factors explained. Moreover, caution should be exercised in interpreting the following factors because they yielded low score reliability estimates: Physical Comfort (Cronbach's $r = .60$), Computer Comfort ($r = .51$), Library Policies ($r = .45$), and Resources ($r = .52$). All of these score reliability coefficients were lower than .70, which is the level considered adequate for affective measures (Nunnally & Bernstein, 1994; Onwuegbuzie & Daniel, 2002a, in press).

## Antecedents of Library Anxiety

As is the case for mathematics anxiety (Byrd, 1982) and statistics anxiety (Onwuegbuzie et al., 1997), the antecedents of library anxiety can be dispositional, situational, or environmental. Dispositional antecedents pertain to factors that an individual brings to the setting. Situational antecedents refer to factors that are in the immediate environment that

surround the stimulus. Finally, environmental antecedents relate to demographic factors that place an individual at risk for library anxiety or to
events that occurred in the past.

The major difference between a dispositional and an environmental
antecedent is that the former is internal to the person, whereas the latter is
external (Byrd, 1982). All three classes of antecedents (i.e., dispositional,
situational, and environmental) interact to determine the overall level of
library anxiety. Figure 2.1 displays the variables that have been found to
predict library anxiety as a function of antecedent type. Each of these predictors is discussed below.

## Dispositional antecedents

Dispositional antecedents include self-esteem and self-concept. As mentioned earlier, students' levels of library anxiety are exacerbated by their
beliefs that (a) they lack adequate library skills; (b) their peers are accomplished library users, whereas they alone are incompetent; and (c) their
incompetence is shameful (Mellon, 1986, 1988, 1989). Similarly, students' feelings of ineptness about utilizing the library, as identified by
Bostick (1992), represent a situational determinant of library anxiety.
More recently, Jiao and Onwuegbuzie (1999b) found that graduate students with the lowest levels of perceived academic self-competence, intellectual ability, creativity, and social competence tend to have the highest
levels of library anxiety associated with affective barriers and comfort
with the library. This result is consistent with relationships found between
self-perception and test anxiety (Hunsley, 1987), foreign language anxiety
(Onwuegbuzie et al., 1999a), mathematics anxiety (e.g., Gourgey, 1984),
and statistics anxiety (Onwuegbuzie, 2000a).

Jiao and Onwuegbuzie (1999b) concluded that the fact that library anxiety is related to perceived scholastic competence and perceived intellectual ability provides incremental evidence that library anxiety is an
academic-related phenomenon. Further, because high levels of library
anxiety were associated with low levels of perceived social acceptance,
these researchers contended that library anxiety also is a socially based
phenomenon. Based on their findings, as well as that of Mellon (1986)
regarding library-anxious students' feelings of relative ineptness, Jiao and

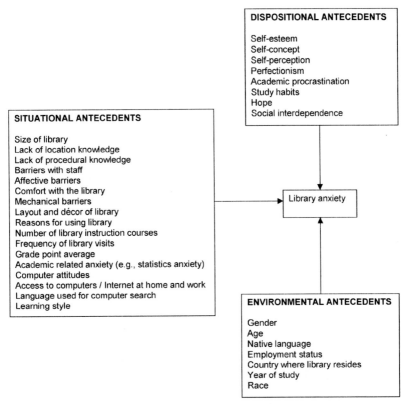

**Figure 2.1** Conceptualization of antecedents of library anxiety.

Onwuegbuzie (1999b) concluded that fear of negative social evaluation is an important (dispositional) antecedent of library anxiety. According to these authors, it is likely that students with low perceived social acceptance also tend to hold unrealistically high standards for themselves with respect to performing library tasks. Apparently, this desire to keep their perceived ineptness secret leads to avoidance behaviors, in which library-anxious students are reluctant to seek help from librarians for fear of having their perceived ignorance exposed (Mellon, 1988, 1989). Additionally, the relationship between library anxiety and perceived social acceptance indicates that learned helplessness prevails among many library users, stemming from a discrepancy between a person's behavior while undertaking library tasks and the perceived unrealistic standards prescribed by others. As noted by Jiao and Onwuegbuzie (1999b), such incongruities likely increase the propensity for search avoidance behaviors.

Perfectionism also represents a dispositional antecedent of library anxiety. Specifically, Jiao and Onwuegbuzie (1998) reported that graduate students who maintain a perceived need to attain standards and expectations prescribed by significant others (e.g., friends, family, professors, and classmates), known in the literature as socially prescribed perfectionism (Hewitt & Flett, 1991a, 1991b), tend to have higher levels of library anxiety associated with affective barriers, comfort with the library, and mechanical barriers than do their nonperfectionistic counterparts. This finding is consistent with Onwuegbuzie and Daley (1999b), who found that graduate students who hold unrealistic standards for significant others (i.e., other-oriented perfectionists) and those who maintain a perceived need to attain standards and expectations prescribed by significant others (i.e., socially prescribed perfectionists) tend to have higher levels of statistics anxiety associated with interpretation anxiety, test and class anxiety, computational self-concept, and fear of asking for help. Jiao and Onwuegbuzie (1998) noted that this finding

> suggests that perfectionistic students may perceive that not only should they be entirely familiar with the library but they should have expertise with all library equipment. Consequently, it is likely that once they begin to utilize the library and/or once the complexity of their library searches increases, these students realize that they are not as competent in library usage as they expected or desired and, as such, experience elevations in library anxiety . . . [leading] to search avoidance behaviors. (pp. 368–369)

Academic procrastination is another dispositional antecedent that has been linked to library anxiety. In particular, Onwuegbuzie and Jiao (2000) documented that overall academic procrastination was statistically significantly positively related to the following dimensions of library anxiety: affective barriers, comfort with the library, and mechanical barriers. Further, academic procrastination resulting from both fear of failure and task aversiveness was related significantly to barriers with staff, affective barriers, comfort with the library, and knowledge of the library. These results also are in accordance with the extant literature that has reported a relationship between procrastination and generalized and specific kinds of anxiety such as test anxiety, statistics anxiety, and social anxiety (Ferrari, 1991; Milgram, 1991; Solomon & Rothblum, 1984).

Study habits represent a set of behaviors that can be classified as dispositional antecedents of library anxiety. Interestingly, Jiao and Onwuegbuzie (2001a) found that students with the highest levels of library anxiety were more likely than those with the lowest levels of anxiety (a) not to seek help from their instructor when they had difficulty with their work, (b) not to tape record lectures instead of taking notes, (c) to rely on rote memorization, (d) not to complete assigned readings before their instructor discussed them in class, (e) to consume plenty of coffee and other caffeine-based drinks in order to stay awake, (f) not to utilize advance organizers before reading a chapter of a textbook, (g) not to recopy their lecture notes as soon as possible after class, and (h) not to break large amounts of information onto small clusters that can be studied separately. These behaviors were classified by the researchers as pertaining either to note taking, study techniques, or reading. The investigators concluded the following:

> Because many students utilize the library to study it is possible that, once in the library, students with the highest levels of anxiety tend to select inappropriate behaviors. For example, in an effort to minimize time spent in the library due to feelings of apprehension, high-anxious students might initiate short cuts while studying, including attempting to memorize the exact words in a textbook and not making outlines of book chapters prior to reading them. Additionally, it is possible that library anxiety leads to avoidance behaviors such as not utilizing the library to complete assigned readings before the instructor discusses them in class and not recopying lecture notes as soon as possible after class. (p. 78)

Hope also appears to be a dispositional antecedent of library anxiety. Specifically, Onwuegbuzie and Jiao (1998c) found that students who have the poorest sense of successful determination in relation to their goals and who have the least positive appraisals of their ability to generate ways to overcome goal-related obstacles and to reach their goals tend to have the highest levels of library anxiety associated with comfort with the library and knowledge of the library. Also, students with the poorest sense of successful goal-related determination tend to have the highest levels of library anxiety associated with barriers with staff, affective barriers, comfort with the library, knowledge of the library, and mechanical barriers.

Finally, social interdependence can be considered to be a dispositional antecedent of library anxiety. Using a canonical correlation analysis, Jiao and Onwuegbuzie (2002a), in their award-winning article, found that cooperative attitudes were related significantly to barriers with staff, comfort with the library, and knowledge of the library. Specifically, students who had the greatest cooperative orientation tended to have the lowest levels of library anxiety stemming from barriers with staff, comfort with the library, and knowledge of the library. Individualistic attitudes, affective barriers, and mechanical barriers served as suppressor variables.

## Situational antecedents

Situational antecedents relate to the nature of libraries. Many situational antecedents to library anxiety have been identified. In particular, the four sources that induce library anxiety reported by Mellon (1986) (i.e., size of the library; lack of knowledge about the location of materials, equipment, and resources; lack of knowledge about how to initiate library research; lack of knowledge about how to proceed with library searches) represent situational antecedents. Knowledge of the library and how to conduct library searches are other situational factors that contribute to library anxiety (Bostick, 1992; Kuhlthau, 1988a, 1989, 1991; Onwuegbuzie, 1997a).

The following variables also appear to play a role in elevating levels of library anxiety: how readily available and approachable librarians make themselves (i.e., barriers with staff); how much comfort the library induces; the extent to which librarians acknowledge students' feelings of apprehension as legitimate and then attempt to lessen feelings of inadequacy, confusion, and failure by providing positive experiences to counteract the anxiety; and the extent to which library equipment function efficiently and that students are comfortable using it (i.e., mechanical barriers) (Bostick, 1992; Collins et al., 1987; Mellon, 1986, 1988, 1989; Swope & Katzer, 1972; Zahner, 1993).

Similarly, library anxiety can be influenced by the layout and decor of the library, as well as by whether the library has appropriate signs and floor plans, uncluttered aisles, and appropriate access for physically challenged users. That is, design aspects of the library represent situational antecedents of library anxiety. Also, the myths surrounding academic libraries held by many students discussed above (e.g., librarian as "the keeper of knowledge"; libraries representing the female domain) serve as situational antecedents of library anxiety.

Students' reasons for using the library can be regarded as situational antecedents of library anxiety. In particular, Jiao and Onwuegbuzie (1997) found that students who use computer indexes and online facilities tend to have the highest levels of library anxiety with respect to all five of Bostick's (1992) dimensions of library anxiety (i.e., barriers with staff, affective barriers, comfort with the library, knowledge of the library, and mechanical barriers). Further, students who use the library to study for a class project tend to report relatively lower levels of anxiety stemming from barriers with staff, affective barriers, and knowledge of the library, whereas students who utilize the library to search and obtain information for a thesis or dissertation tend to report the most problems associated with barriers with staff, comfort with the library, and mechanical barriers. Also, those who use the library to read current newspapers tend to report the most problems stemming from barriers with staff. As noted by Jiao and Onwuegbuzie (1997), this latter finding

suggests that either (1) these students have had negative experiences with staff while they are reading newspapers—perhaps, there is a perception that librarians do not appreciate them reading newspapers for whatever reason, or (2) these students, because they spend most or all of their library time reading newspapers, tend to have little direct contact with library staff, which increases their anxiety levels. (p. 383)

Also noted by these researchers was that students who use the library for social purposes tend to experience high anxiety levels associated with knowledge of the library. The authors asserted that this result might occur because these socially oriented students spend little time getting familiar with the library. Returning books also is a situational variable inasmuch as it predicts library anxiety associated with affective barriers. Interestingly, whereas using the library to read books on reserve is related significantly to higher levels of mechanical barriers, it increases the students' comfort with the library. Finally, obtaining material in the library for a term paper is associated negatively with affective barriers. Similarly, Jiao et al. (1996) reported that when library-anxious students visited the library, they tended to do so either to use the online/computer index, to return a book, to conduct a library search for a thesis/dissertation, to obtain a book or article for an assignment, or to study for a class project. Thus, reasons for using the library clearly represent an important class of situational antecedents.

Jiao et al. (1996) found that the number of library instruction courses undertaken by students was weakly related to levels of library anxiety ($r = -.14, p < .01$). Similarly, Abusin (1998) observed that first-year students enrolled in a university in Malaysia who attended a library instruction course reported statistically significantly lower levels of library anxiety than did students who had not attended such a course. However, again, the effect size was extremely small (Cohen's (1988) $d = 0.05$). Also, Cleveland (2001) found that first-year students attending the University of North Carolina at Chapel Hill who were enrolled in a 30–40 minute bibliographic instruction course reported statistically significantly lower levels of library anxiety than did their counterparts who did not participate in this course, even after controlling for previous library experience and prior knowledge of the library. The Cohen's $d$ effect size was estimated by the present authors to be 0.57, indicating a moderate effect. More specifically, Cleveland (2001) documented that students in the bibliographic instruction group reported statistically significantly lower levels of library anxiety associated with barriers with staff and affective barriers than did the control group. Further, the bibliographic instruction group reported statistically significantly lower levels of library anxiety associated with barriers with staff than did a third group consisting of students who had completed a 30–45 minute computer-assisted tutorial session. Abusin (1998) also found that students who did not like to attend library instruction courses reported higher levels of library anxiety than did their counterparts. On the other hand, Ben Omran (2001) found that the number of bibliographic instruction sessions attended did not predict levels of library anxiety.

Jiao et al. (1996) found a moderately statistically significant negative relationship between the frequency of visits to the library and levels of library anxiety. Consistent with this result, as noted earlier, Jiao and

Onwuegbuzie (2002b) found that high-anxious students are approximately two-and-a-half times less likely to visit the library than are low-anxious students. Although it is likely that this association indicates that students who are the most anxious tend to avoid utilizing the library, it is also possible that this link suggests that avoiding the library results in students not acquiring the necessary library skills, thereby increasing their library anxiety levels (Jiao et al., 1996). The extent to which the latter sequence explains the relationship between frequency of visits and library anxiety justifies classifying visit frequency as a situational variable. The propensity for a student to ask a librarian or a library staff member for help also can be considered a situational antecedent of library anxiety. Indeed, Abusin (1998) reported a statistically significant difference in levels of anxiety between students who do not ask librarians for help and those who do. However, the effect size was small ($d = .26$).

Prior academic achievement in college-level courses can be classified as a situational environment of library anxiety. One of the most comprehensive measures of academic performance is grade point average (GPA). Interestingly, Jiao et al. (1996) found that GPA was a statistically significant predictor of library anxiety. Similarly, Jiao et al. (1996) found that GPA predicted library anxiety associated with comfort with the library and mechanical barriers.

Reading ability is another dispositional antecedent that has been linked to library anxiety. Specifically, Jiao and Onwuegbuzie (2003c) found that reading comprehension and reading vocabulary were related statistically significantly to barriers with staff, comfort with the library, and knowledge of the library. The reading ability and library anxiety dimensions shared 39.4% of the total variance.

Other forms of academic-related, state-based anxiety that are related to library anxiety also can be considered as situational antecedents of the latter. For example, Onwuegbuzie and Jiao (2002b) documented that library anxiety is related to research anxiety (Onwuegbuzie, 1996), statistics anxiety (Cruise & Wilkins, 1980; Cruise, Cash, & Bolton, 1985), and writing anxiety (Daly & Miller, 1975c). Specifically, these researchers found that research anxiety, statistics anxiety, and writing anxiety were each statistically significantly related to the following four dimensions of library anxiety: barriers with staff, affective barriers, comfort with the library, and knowledge of the library. For the most part, these correlations were moderate to large, ranging from .19 to .57.

Consistent with this set of findings, Mizrachi (2000) and Shoham and Mizrachi (2001) reported a statistically significantly relationship between library anxiety and computer attitudes. In particular, all seven dimensions of the Hebrew Library Anxiety Scale were associated statistically significantly with computer anxiety, with correlations ranging from .11 (physical comfort) to .47 (knowledge). These authors also noted that, after applying the Bonferroni adjustment, Staff was related to home usage of computer, work usage of computer, and use of computer games. Knowledge was related to home usage of computer, work usage of computer, use of word processors, use of computer spreadsheets, use of computer games, and use of the Internet. Language was associated with home usage of computer, work usage of computer, use of computer spreadsheet, use of the Internet, and language of computer program. Physical comfort only was related to use of computer games. Library policies/hours was associated with home usage of computer. Further, library computer comfort was related to home usage of computer, use of word processors, and use of computer games. Jerabek et al. (2001) also found levels of computer anxiety to be related to levels of library anxiety for both men and women.

Using a canonical correlation analysis, Jiao and Onwuegbuzie (2003a) documented a multivariate relationship between library anxiety and computer anxiety. The observed squared canonical correlation coefficient indicated that the library anxiety subscale scores and computer anxiety subscale scores shared 40.82% of the common variance. In particular, scores pertaining to all five subscales of the Library Anxiety Scale were related simultaneously to computer liking and computer usefulness. That is, students with the highest levels of library anxiety associated with barriers with staff, affective barriers, comfort with the library, knowledge of the library, and mechanical barriers were less likely to indicate that they liked computers and tended to report the most negative perceptions of the useful of computers.

Similarly, using multiple regression techniques, Collins and Veal (in press) found that two dimensions of library anxiety, namely, knowledge of the library and affective barriers, were statistically significant predictors of students' attitudes toward the educational use of the Internet. These dimensions explained 9% of the variance in respondents' attitudes toward the educational use of the Internet. Specifically, students with the highest levels of library anxiety associated with knowledge of the library and affective barriers tended to have the least positive attitudes toward the educational use of the Internet.

On the other hand, Ben Omran (2001) found no association between library anxiety and frequency of Internet use. Similarly, Onwuegbuzie and Jiao (2002c) documented no relationship between library anxiety and students' attitudes toward the educational use of the Internet, although these investigators noted that students who were connected to the Internet exhibited statistically significantly higher levels of library anxiety than did their counterparts (i.e., small-to-moderate effect size). According to Onwuegbuzie and Jiao (2002c), these results suggest that students who are library anxious are more likely to ensure that they are connected to the Internet to minimize using the library. Also, these researchers documented that students who revealed that if they could obtain all lecture and course information from the Internet, they would still attend class, reported lower levels of library anxiety than did their counterparts.

The final situational antecedent of library anxiety documented in the extant literature is learning style. Abusin (1998) found that students enrolled in a Malaysian university who refrained from asking librarians for help reported statistically significantly higher levels of library anxiety than did their help-seeking counterparts (Cohen's $d = 0.25$). This researcher also noted that students who stopped their computerized library search as soon as they faced a problem tended to exhibit statistically significantly higher levels of library anxiety than did their more persistent peers (Cohen's $d = 0.62$). Abusin (1998) further reported that students who did not utilize computers to undertake library searches tended to record statistically significantly higher levels of library anxiety than did their fellow students (Cohen's $d = 0.53$), although it should be noted that the number of noncomputer users in the sample was small.

The role of learning style in library anxiety also has been studied by Jiao and Onwuegbuzie via a series of studies. First, Onwuegbuzie and Jiao (1998a) found that graduate students with the highest levels of library anxiety tend be those who like structure, who are self-motivated, who lack persistence, and who are peer-oriented learners. Further, they tend to prefer to receive information via the visual mode but not via either tactile or kinesthetic modes. Finally, these students tend to require mobility in learning environments and do not prefer to undertake difficult tasks in the afternoon. In a follow-up inquiry, Onwuegbuzie and Jiao (1998b) found that the following 13 learning modalities were related to one or more of the five dimensions of library anxiety: noise preference, responsibility, persistence orientation, visual orientation, tactile orientation, kinesthetic orientation, multiple perceptual orientation, mobility preference, structure, peer orientation, morning preference, afternoon preference, and evening preference. In the third investigation, Jiao and Onwuegbuzie (1999c) reported that graduate students who prefer to work in quiet surroundings, who like structure, who prefer not to receive information via the tactile mode, who prefer to undertake difficult tasks in the morning, and who prefer not to undertake difficult tasks either in the afternoon or evening tend to have the highest levels of library anxiety associated with affective barriers, comfort with the library, and mechanical barriers. Also, compared to their counterparts, students who prefer to work while surrounded by noise and who require mobility in learning environments tend to have higher levels of library anxiety associated with barriers with staff, affective barriers, knowledge of the library, and mechanical barriers.

Based on the findings from these three studies, the researchers recommended that a learning-style-based (LSB) approach to library instruction be utilized. Such an approach would involve organizing bibliographic instruction around different learning modalities to accommodate the needs of the majority of library users. As asserted by Onwuegbuzie and Jiao (1998a), teaching through learning style strengths would capitalize on the individual differences of library users by providing for the many types of modality learners.

## Environmental antecedents

Unlike the case for dispositional and situational antecedents, the environmental antecedents of library anxiety are not as clear-cut. For example, although Jacobson (1991), Jiao and Onwuegbuzie (1997), and Jiao et al. (1996) found that males have higher levels of library anxiety than do females, Bostick (1992) and Mech and Brooks (1995, 1997) reported no gender differences. To complicate matters further, Mizrachi (2000) and Shoham and Mizrachi (2001) documented that female students enrolled in several teachers' colleges in Israel reported statistically significantly higher levels of library anxiety with respect to the Staff (Cohen's $d$ = 0.34), Language (Cohen's $d$ = 0.34), and Resources (Cohen's $d$ = 0.28) dimensions. Although these effect sizes (not reported but calculated by the present authors) were approaching the moderate range, caution should be exercised in interpreting Mizrachi's (2000) and Shoham and Mizrachi's (2001) findings because despite the large sample size used ($n$ = 664), the overwhelming majority of the study participants were female (88%). Care in generalizing Bostick's (1992) results also is needed because of the relatively small sample size used ($n$ = 69), as well as the fact that only 13 males were involved in the gender comparisons. Similarly, as noted by Jiao et al. (1996), "the small sample size, coupled with the use of a 4-item scale to measure library anxiety, seriously threatens the validity of [Jacobson's (1991)] finding" (p. 153).

Thus, it is likely that low statistical power affected the findings of Bostick (1992), Jacobson (1991), Mizrachi (2000), and Shoham and Mizrachi (2001). In any case, because the studies with the two largest sample sizes found gender differences (although the direction of the differences were contradictory) and because gender differences have been documented in test anxiety (e.g., Biaggio & Nielsen, 1976), mathematics anxiety (Llabre & Suarez, 1985), statistics anxiety (e.g., Benson, 1989; Benson & Bandalos, 1989), and foreign language anxiety (e.g., Onwuegbuzie et al., 1999a), it is reasonable to treat gender as an environmental antecedent of library anxiety.

With respect to age, although McKenzie (2000) did not find a relationship between library anxiety and age, Bostick (1992) found that students more than 50 years old reported higher levels of library anxiety than did their younger counterparts. Further, Ben Omran (2001), Bostick and Onwuegbuzie (2002a), Jiao et al. (1996), and Jiao and Onwuegbuzie (1997) found that library anxiety declines linearly as age increases. Similarly, Mizrachi (2000) and Shoham and Mizrachi (2001) noted that younger students (aged 18–24 years) exhibited statistically significantly higher levels of library anxiety with respect to the Knowledge, Language, Policies/Hours, and Resources factors than did older students (aged 25–55 years). Despite this contradiction, it is clear that age can be treated as an environmental antecedent of library anxiety.

Native language also can be implicated as an environmental antecedent. Specifically, Jiao et al. (1996), Onwuegbuzie and Jiao (1997b), Jiao and

Onwuegbuzie (1997, 2001b), and Liu and Redfern (1997) independently found that nonnative English speakers are more library anxious than are native English speakers. In contrast, Mizrachi (2000) and Shoham and Mizrachi (2001) found that Arabic speakers reported higher levels of library anxiety pertaining to the English language factor than did Hebrew speakers, despite the fact that the language of instruction at the institutions under study was Hebrew. However, these authors noted that Arabic students reported lower levels of library anxiety pertaining to the Knowledge factor than did Hebrew students. Interestingly, Abusin (1998) found that students enrolled in a university in Malaysia who did not shift to another language when facing a problem with the Online Public Access Catalog (OPAC) reported higher levels of library anxiety than did those who did shift to another language (Cohen's $d = .49$). Similarly, Andrews (1991) documented comments made by students at the Manchester Polytechnic Library who expressed anxiety while using OPAC. Andrews attributed these elevated levels of anxiety to user inexperience and catalog inconsistencies. In any case, more research is needed regarding the role of language in the context of library searches.

It is possible that employment status is another environmental antecedent of library anxiety. Indeed, Jiao et al. (1996) found that whether a person was engaged in full-time or part-time employment was a predictor of library anxiety. However, this variable only explained 1% of the variance in library anxiety scores. Further, the fact that this is the only study examining the relationship between employment status and library anxiety suggests strongly that more research is needed before this construct can be declared as an environmental antecedent. Similarly, no regional differences have been found within a country in library anxiety. Specifically, Jiao et al. (1996) found no statistically significant difference in anxiety levels between students enrolled in a university in the northeastern region and those enrolled in a university in a mid-southern state. Also, Mizrachi (2000) and Shoham and Mizrachi (2001) found no regional differences in levels of anxiety between students enrolled in eight universities across Israel. On the other hand, Bostick and Onwuegbuzie (2000b) reported that students enrolled in universities in England reported higher levels of anxiety associated with barriers with staff than did college students in both Ireland and the United States. Thus, although within-country region does not appear to be an environmental antecedent of library anxiety, the country in which the library resides may be; however, much more research involving cross-cultural comparisons are needed before this conclusion can be generalized.

Jiao, Onwuegbuzie, and Bostick (2003) examined racial differences in library anxiety. These authors found that African American students attending a research-intensive institution reported statistically significantly lower levels of library anxiety associated with barriers with staff (Cohen's $d$ = .74), affective barriers (Cohen's $d$ = .88), and comfort with the library (Cohen's $d$ = .40) than did Caucasian American graduate students enrolled at a doctoral-granting institution. However, because the two groups also differed with respect to type of institution, the researchers were unable to conclude whether the difference in anxiety levels, which were moderate to large, were the result of race or educational experience/ aptitude. Thus, these writers declared that it was not clear whether race is an environmental antecedent of library anxiety.

In a follow-up investigation, Jiao and Onwuegbuzie (2003b) also compared the African American and Caucasian American students with respect to library anxiety. However, in an attempt to control for educational background, these two groups were selected from the same institution. A series of independent $t$-tests revealed no statistically significant racial differences in library anxiety for any of the five LAS dimensions. However, across all five library anxiety measures, the African American sample reported lower scores than did the Caucasian American sample. In order to test whether this trend was statistically significant, Onwuegbuzie and Levin's (2003a) test of aggregate $z$-scores was employed. Specifically, for each of the five measures, raw scores were converted to $z$-scores such that each participant had five $z$-scores. These five $z$-scores were then summed for each participant to yield an aggregate $z$-score. Finally, an independent samples $t$-test was conducted to compare the aggregate $z$-scores between the African American and Caucasian American students. This test revealed that the African American students ($M$ = −1.01, $SD$ = 7.74) had statistically significantly ($t$ = 1.67, $p$ < .01) lower $z$-scores than did the Caucasian American students ($M$ = 0.16, $SD$ = 3.94). The effect size, as measured by Cohen's (1988) $d$ was .31, suggesting a small-to-moderate effect. Thus, the test of aggregate $z$-scores revealed that the consistency with which the African American graduate students had lower levels of library anxiety than did the Caucasian American students was both statistically and practically significant.

Because both samples in Jiao and Onwuegbuzie's (2003b) study were from the same institution, these authors concluded that racial differences in library anxiety appear to prevail. Jiao and Onwuegbuzie's (2003b) results, alongside those of Jiao et al. (2003), suggest that race is an environmental antecedent of library anxiety. Nevertheless, more research is needed to determine why African Americans in both studies reported significantly *lower* levels of library anxiety—bearing in mind that African American graduate students typically report *higher* levels of statistics anxiety (Onwuegbuzie, 1999b) and attain *lower* levels of achievement in research methodology courses (Onwuegbuzie, 1999c) than do their Caucasian American counterparts.

Several authors have noted a relationship between library anxiety and year of study. Specifically, Bostick (1992) found that graduate students have higher levels of library anxiety than do undergraduate students and community college students. Similarly, Mech and Brooks (1995) noted that freshmen and sophomores report statistically significantly higher levels of library anxiety than do seniors. Consistent with these results, Jiao et al. (1996) and Onwuegbuzie and Jiao (1997b) observed that library anxiety declines as a function of year of study, with the highest levels of anxiety occurring among freshmen. Similarly, Mizrachi (2000) and Shoham and Mizrachi (2001) documented a general decline as a function of year of study in library anxiety, as measured by the Staff and Knowledge factors. Conversely, these authors noted an inverted "U" shape for library anxiety scores with respect to year of study. In any case, year of study clearly is an environmental antecedent of library anxiety.

## SUMMARY AND CONCLUSIONS

Anyone who has studied or taught at the college level can attest to the overwhelming degree of anxiety experienced by some college students. To date, several forms of academic anxiety have been identified, including computer anxiety, research anxiety, statistics anxiety, mathematics anxiety, writing anxiety, foreign language anxiety, and general test anxiety. Each of these anxiety types has been found to be very pervasive. For example, Onwuegbuzie (in press-a) estimated that between two-thirds and four-fifths of graduate students appear to experience uncomfortable levels of statistics anxiety. Indeed, for many graduate students, statistics is one of the most anxiety-inducing courses in their programs of study (Schacht & Stewart, 1990; Zeidner, 1991). However, whereas most graduate students take one or more statistics courses as part of their degree requirements, many graduate students, for example in education programs, are not compelled to take statistics courses. Similarly, not all students are required to take a college-level foreign language class. On the other hand, virtually every student is expected to utilize the library as a result of course assignments (e.g., term paper), degree requirement (e.g., thesis/dissertation), or some other requirement. Indeed, academic libraries play an important role for the overwhelming majority of students at all colleges in most countries, regardless of degree program. Hence, library anxiety is likely more pervasive than is any other form of academic-related anxiety (Jiao & Onwuegbuzie, 2002a).

In this chapter, the nature and etiology of library anxiety were described. Library anxiety was defined as a negative state-based phenomenon that lies on a continuum, with students experiencing the highest levels being more at risk for exhibiting avoidance behaviors. The major symptoms of library-anxious students that have been identified in the literature were presented. Next, the components of library anxiety were described. These dimensions have been identified via quantitative and qualitative research techniques. Finally, the antecedents of library anxiety were delineated. These antecedents, which are summarized in figure 2.1, were categorized as being either dispositional, situational, or environmental. The array of dispositional, situational, and environmental antecedents described above that place a student at risk for library anxiety demonstrates the diverse nature of library users, as well as illustrates the challenges faced by librarians to meet their needs.

At the time of writing, this chapter has presented a comprehensive and exhaustive review of the published literature on library anxiety. Despite the fact that 75%–85% of undergraduate students experience some form of library anxiety (Mellon, 1986) and that library-anxious students are approximately 2.5 times less likely to utilize the library, only 26 studies have been published on the topic of library anxiety. Further, only a handful of more formal inquiries currently are being undertaken. Thus, clearly, more research is needed in this area. Such research would increase our understanding of the role of anxiety in the library context.

*Chapter Three*

# Conceptual and Research-Based
# Models of Library Anxiety

## OVERVIEW

In the previous chapter, the nature and etiology of library anxiety were described and summarized. Also discussed were symptoms and components of library anxiety. Finally, the antecedents of library anxiety were presented. These antecedents were organized into the following three dimensions: dispositional, situational, and environmental. The results from 26 published research articles and several more unpublished manuscripts in the area of library anxiety were presented.

The purpose of the current chapter is to present five models of library anxiety. The first model presented is Kuhlthau's Model of the Information Search Process (Kuhlthau, 1983, 1985, 1987, 1988a, 1988b, 1989, 1991, 1993, 1994; Kuhlthau et al., 1990). The next four models outlined are the Cognitive-Affective Stage Model of Library Anxiety, the Information Literacy Process Model of Library Anxiety, the Dispositional-Situational-Environmental Model of Library Anxiety, and the Anxiety-Expectation Mediation Model of Library Anxiety. Although Kuhlthau's models have been documented, the latter four models of library anxiety have not previously been presented. Moreover, the latter two models represent the first attempts to use structural equation modeling techniques in the field of library and information science research. The structural equation modeling techniques are deemed among the most sophisticated statistical methods (Bollen, 1989; Browne & Cudeck, 1993; Hu & Bentler, 1999;

Onwuegbuzie & Daniel, 2003; Schumacker & Lomax, 1996; Thompson, 1997, 2000). It should be noted that Mellon's (1986) theory of library anxiety is not included in this chapter because it does not represent a model but a theory. Indeed, a model is "a schematic description of a . . . theory . . . that accounts for its properties and may be used for further study of its characteristics" (*The American Heritage College Dictionary,* 1993, p. 876).

## KUHLTHAU'S MODEL OF THE
## INFORMATION SEARCH PROCESS

As described in chapter 2, research in the area of library anxiety suggests that library anxiety is related to a myriad of variables. Unfortunately, because of the correlational nature of all these studies, the causal direction of these associations has not been clearly identified. Specifically, whereas some of these variables may induce library anxiety, other variables may be exacerbated by library anxiety. That is, library anxiety may serve as a causal agent for some variables and as an effect, at least in part, of other variables. Still other constructs may be related to library anxiety in a bidirectional or reciprocal manner. For instance, in observing a relationship between levels of academic procrastination and library anxiety, Onwuegbuzie and Jiao (2000) concluded the following:

> Perhaps it is most likely that a bidirectional relationship exists between academic procrastination and library anxiety, with each affecting the other. If this is true, it would indicate that academic procrastination and library anxiety are intricately intertwined. For example, it is possible that, while engaged in the research process, high-procrastinating graduate students experience extreme elevations in library anxiety. Individuals who experience increases in levels of library anxiety are more likely to postpone using the library and performing library tasks. In any case, this cycle of procrastination and library anxiety is likely to continue until levels of both are maximized. Where for some students the procrastination component of the cycle is likely to stem from a fear of failure, for others the driving force is task aversiveness. (p. 51)

To understand better the causal nature of library anxiety, models of library anxiety are needed that can be tested using quantitative and qualitative techniques. Kulthau's Model of the Information Search Process (ISP) is one such model.

According to Kuhlthau (1991), the ISP involves the following three domains: the cognitive (i.e., thoughts), the physical (i.e., actions), and the affective (i.e., feelings). That is, the information search represents a process of constructing meaning from the information they encounter that involves thoughts, actions, and feelings, which represent the whole experience of the individual (Kuhlthau, 1991). Kuhtlhau (1988a) developed a six-stage process of the ISP. These stages are task initiation, topic selection, prefocus exploration, focus formulation, information collection, and search closure.

During the task initiation stage, the goal is to recognize the need for information. Cognitions involve contemplating the problem, understanding the task, and linking the problem to existing knowledge and experience. Actions typically entail discussing possible topics and strategies with peers, mentors, instructors, and/or other professionals. Feelings encompass uncertainty and anxiety that occur when individuals first become cognizant of their lack of knowledge, awareness, or understanding (Kuhtlhau, 1988a; Westbrook & DeDecker, 1993).

The next stage is topic selection. During this phase, the goal is to identify and to select the general topic area to be researched and/or the strategy to be followed. Thoughts involve weighing the various options in light of personal experience and interest, assignment requirements, the information available, and the amount of time available. The consequence of selecting each option is predicted and the topic or strategy deemed to have the greatest likelihood of success is selected. Actions involve conferring with peers, mentors, and instructors. Some individuals may undertake an initial, informal search of the information available, and search for a synopsis of alternative topics. Feelings of anxiety often decrease after selection has been made. However, they are exacerbated if selection is delayed or postponed. In fact, these feelings typically heighten until the selection is made (Kuhlthau, 1988a).

The third stage of the ISP is prefocus exploration. The task here is for individuals to research information on the general topic selected in the previous stage in order to increase their understanding. Thoughts surround becoming adequately informed about the topic to form a focus. Actions center around locating information about a general topic, reading to expand existing knowledge, and linking new information to what is already known. Reflecting on interesting ideas is likely a useful strategy at this stage. Because information found rarely is sufficiently compatible with previous knowledge and information from different sources often appear to contradict one another, library users may find this stage frustrating and threatening, resulting in confusion, uncertainty and, moreover, anxiety. In fact, this stage often is the most anxiety-producing stage in the process. Utilizing strategies that attempt to secure a premature closure culminates in heightened anxiety and may even lead some library users to abandon the search completely (Kuhlthau, 1988a).

Focus formulation represents the fourth stage of the ISP. The goal in this phase is to develop a focus from the information that emerges in the previous stage(s). Thoughts involve identifying and choosing ideas contained in the information in order to obtain a focused perspective of the topic. The individual takes more ownership over the topic if construction takes place at this stage. Although a focus may emerge at a moment's instance, it is more likely to develop gradually as constructs become clearer. According to Kuhlthau (1993), focus formulation represents a turning point in the ISP because during this period, feelings become more positive, with anxiety levels decreasing as confidence increases alongside a sense of clarity. However, if the entire research process is completed without a clear focus, the paper that ensues will lack clarity and coherence and the new mental constructs fail to emerge.

Information collection, the fifth stage, is the process whereby the quality of the interaction between the library user and the information system is maximized. At this phase, the goal is to collect information pertaining to the focused topic. Thoughts involve defining, extending, and supporting the focus. Actions center around selecting information pertinent to the focused perspective of the topic and taking detailed and comprehensive notes on the focused information, as opposed to taking notes on general information, which is no longer relevant after the formulation stage. The library user at this stage, armed with a clearer sense of direction and more focus, is in a position to request relevant, focused information from library staff and systems that facilitate a comprehensive search of all accessible resources. Confidence continues to increase and anxiety levels decrease as more information is extracted.

The search closure represents the sixth and final stage of the ISP. The goal in this stage is to terminate the search and to prepare to present or to utilize the findings. Thoughts involve organizing a synthesis of the topic, weighing the completeness of the information available, the time and energy needed to complete the process, and the likelihood of success of additional energy expended. Actions center around an information search in which the amount of relevant information extracted decreases and the amount of redundant information increases. That is, saturation point is reached. The end of the search is characterized by feelings of relief and substantial anxiety reduction if the search has been successful and feelings of elevated anxiety levels if the search has not been productive (Kuhlthau, 1991).

In sum, according to Kuhlthau (1983, 1985, 1987, 1988a, 1988b, 1989, 1991, 1993, 1994; Kuhlthau et al., 1990), library anxiety can occur at any one of the six stages of the ISP. Although the stages of Kuhlthau's model are presented in a sequential manner, in reality, students typically progress in an iterative manner (Kuhlthau, 1991). However, episodes of anxiety tend to be more prevalent in the early stages of the ISP, although anxiety levels can be more pervasive and debilitative at the latter stages of the process if the search terminates unsatisfactorily or is abandoned. Interestingly, college students tend to be less confident and to display higher levels of anxiety at the initiation stage than do public library users. Apparently, the situation is reversed at closure, with college students exhibiting more favorable affective outcomes than do high school students (Kuhlthau, 1991). In any case, "The series of stages offers a way to communicate an approximation of common experiences which users have readily acknowledged as accurately describing their process" (Kuhlthau, 1991, p. 370).

## COGNITIVE-AFFECTIVE STAGE
## MODEL OF LIBRARY ANXIETY

A second model that describes students' experiences in the library context is the Cognitive-Affective Stage (CAS) Model of Library Anxiety. This model is designed to describe the thoughts and behaviors of students before, during, and after using the library. The implication of this model is that students can exhibit behaviors and experience cognitive interference and arousal patterns that are indicative of library anxiety during the following three stages of the library-task cycle: library preparation, library use, and library reflection.

## Library Preparation Stage

Library anxiety can manifest itself during the library preparation stage in a myriad of ways. Moreover, library anxiety is related to several constructs that have been found to culminate in performance decrements and failures. Indeed, many of the dispositional, situational, and environmental antecedents of library anxiety identified in chapter 2 have been linked to various achievement outcomes. For example, library anxiety is related to academic procrastination in general, as well as academic procrastination resulting from both fear of failure and task aversiveness in particular (Onwuegbuzie & Jiao, 2000). Academic procrastination, which is experienced by as many as 95% of college students (Ellis & Knaus, 1977), is defined as the pertinacious and unnecessary delay in beginning or completing assignments and responsibilities (Ellis & Knaus, 1977; Rothblum, Solomon, & Murakami, 1986). Apparently, a significant proportion of college students report problems with procrastination on academic tasks such as writing term papers, studying for examinations, and keeping up with weekly readings. According to Rothblum et al. (1986), academic procrastination includes the self-reported tendency nearly always or always to experience problematic levels of anxiety associated with this procrastination.

Disturbingly, academic procrastination has been found to be associated with negative academic outcomes such as missing deadlines for submitting assignments, delaying the taking of self-paced quizzes, low course grades, and course withdrawal (Beswick, Rothblum, & Mann, 1988; Rothblum et al., 1986; Semb, Glick, & Spencer, 1979). Thus, to the extent that worry and emotionality lead to academic procrastination and other avoidance behaviors, library anxiety during the library preparation stage threatens students' ability to complete the task or to complete it successfully. This is because procrastination reduces the amount of time a student has to complete the task. Unfortunately, delaying or postponing the task at the library preparation stage not only affects the future outcome but also further heightens library anxiety levels, such as those that occur at the task initiation and topic selection stages of the ISP (Kuhlthau, 1988b, 1991, 1993). Thus, a negative cycle of elevated library anxiety levels and procrastination levels may ensue, further threatening the students' ability to reach search closure and the like at subsequent phases of the library-task process.

Another variable that appears to play a role in the library preparation stage is study habits, a dispositional antecedent of library anxiety. Jiao and Onwuegbuzie (2001a) found that study habits are significant predictors of library anxiety, with library-anxious students tending to be those with the poorest study habits. Researchers have documented that students with high levels of academic-related anxiety typically anticipate that they will attain poor educational outcomes (Hunsley, 1987; Onwuegbuzie & Daley, 1996). Unfortunately, such expectations tend to interfere with task preparation. This interference may take the form of avoidance behaviors (Onwuegbuzie, 2004, Onwuegbuzie & Collins, 2001; Onwuegbuzie & Jiao, 2000; Rothblum et al., 1986), attention to information and material that is irrelevant to the task (Wine, 1980), and diminished information processing capacity due to preoccupation with negative self-defeating thoughts (Kuhlthau, 1991, 1993; Tobias, 1985). Thus, the relationship between study habits and library anxiety has the potential to affect task performance at the library preparation stage.

Similarly, perfectionism, another dispositional antecedent of library anxiety, may play a central role in the library preparation stage, as reflected by the relationship documented between levels of socially prescribed perfectionism and library anxiety (Jiao & Onwuegbuzie, 1998). As noted by Jiao and Onwuegbuzie (1998), the relationship between socially prescribed perfectionism and library anxiety is consistent with the findings of Mellon (1988) that anxious library users tend to feel that other students are adept at using the library, whereas they alone are inept, and that their incompetence is a source of embarrassment and, consequently, should be kept hidden. These socially prescribed perfectionists likely are reluctant to seek help from librarians for fear of having their perceived ignorance exposed. As such, these students are more apt to delay entry into the library-use stage (i.e., Stage 2) of the library-task process and are more prone to experience a difficult transition from the library preparation stage to the library use stage of the cycle. Socially prescribed perfectionism also may play an adverse role in the library preparation stage because it can lead to learned helplessness due to an incongruity between an individual's expected performance and the perceived unrealistic standards prescribed by others (Hewitt & Flett, 1991a).

Self-esteem, self-concept, and self-perception (dispositional antecedents) also may play important roles in the library preparation stage. A student who lacks any of these qualities is likely to experience some form of academic-related anxiety. Indeed, levels of self-perception have been found to predict library anxiety (Jiao & Onwuegbuzie 1999b). According to Pyszczynski and Solomon (1986), students with low self-esteem and self-concept often are unable to increase their ability to cope with anxiety-producing situations. Further, Greenberg et al. (1992) have postulated a terror management theory whereby "people are motivated to maintain a positive self-image because self-esteem protects them from anxiety" (p. 913). Thus, low self-esteem, self-concept, and self-perception likely increase library anxiety levels in the library preparation stage.

Hope is another dispositional variable that may come to the fore during the library preparation stage. Consistent with this prediction, Onwuegbuzie and Jiao (1998c) reported that students who have the poorest sense of successful determination in relation to their goals and the least positive appraisals of their ability to generate ways to overcome goal-related obstacles and to reach their goals tend to have the highest level of library anxiety. It is likely that low levels of hope affect students negatively in the library preparation phase by unduly increasing their levels of library anxiety.

Social interdependence is an additional potentially influential dispositional variable that may come to the fore at the library preparation stage. Interestingly, in their award-winning article, Jiao and Onwuegbuzie (2002a) found that students with the least cooperative orientation tend to have the highest levels of library anxiety. Therefore, it is likely that students who are not comfortable learning in cooperative groups are more likely to have problems at the library preparation phase.

Finally, the reason that a student needs the library to undertake the task is a situational antecedent that plays a role in the library preparation stage. Both Jiao et al. (1996) and Onwuegbuzie and Jiao (2002a) found that students' reasons for using the library can be predicted by their levels of library anxiety. Moreover, the more complex the library task, the more anxiety threatens its chances of it being completed. However, even routine tasks such as returning library books can induce anxiety, which can lead to procrastination and subsequent library fines.

Situational variables that may affect the quality of preparation in the first stage of the library-task process include learning style. Onwuegbuzie and Jiao (1998b) found a link between library anxiety and learning style (i.e., noise preference, responsibility, persistence orientation, visual orientation, tactile orientation, kinesthetic orientation, multiple perceptual orientation, mobility preference, structure, peer orientation, morning preference, afternoon preference, and evening preference). Felder and Henriques (1995) described learning styles as the manners in which individuals typically acquire, retain, and retrieve information. Cornett (1983) theorized that each person is born with certain proclivities toward particular learning styles that are subsequently influenced by culture, personal experiences, maturation, and development. Further, learning styles have been referred to as an individual's typical way of reacting to and utilizing stimuli in the context of learning (Claxton & Ralston, 1978). For the overwhelming majority of college students, the library represents an essential learning context. Consequently, some learning style profiles may cause students unique problems at the library preparation stage. Similarly, students' perceptions of the size, layout, and décor of the library; their knowledge of the library; and their knowledge of library procedures, as well as the number of library instruction courses taken and how frequently they visit the library, all may affect how they prepare to use the library in the second stage of the process.

Environmental antecedents that potentially play an important role in the library preparation phase include a student's employment status. This variable has been found to be related to library anxiety, with students who engage in full-time employment being more at risk for anxiety (Jiao et al., 1996). Full-time employment competes with the time students have to prepare to utilize the library, thereby increasing library anxiety levels at this stage. Similarly, a student's age and year of study, also environmental predictors of library anxiety (Jiao et al., 1996), likely make a difference in the library preparation stage, with young and first-year students being more likely to experience problems at this juncture.

## Library Use Stage

The debilitative effect of library anxiety has been most extensively addressed in the library use stage (e.g., Kuhlthau, 1991, 1993; Onwuegbuzie, 1997a), which represents the time period during which the student completes the task. Whereas the library preparation stage tends to include Kuhlthau's (1988b, 1991, 1993) first two phases (task initiation and topic selection) of the ISP, the library use stage typically encompasses the last four stages (prefocus exploration, focus formulation, information collection, and search closure). The anxiety generated at any one of these four stages can prevent a library search task from being completed. Moreover, the anxiety at one stage typically is carried into the remaining stages of the process.

The perceived threat induced by the library also becomes pertinent during the library use stage, over and above the expectations the student maintained prior to entering the library in the library preparation stage. As soon as library-anxious students set foot inside the library, their levels of worry and emotionality increase (Mellon, 1986, 1988; Onwuegbuzie, 1997a). It is at these early formative moments that such at-risk students form impressions of the difficulty imposed by the task (Onwuegbuzie, 1997a). Library users with the highest levels of library anxiety, particularly those who encountered high levels of library anxiety in the library preparation phase, often have their initial judgments of the task distorted. These students quickly conclude that the task is too difficult for them to complete effectively (Onwuegbuzie, 1997a), culminating in task-irrelevant thoughts and negative self-defeating deliberations that prevent them from focusing adequately on the task itself.

One possible explanation for the impact of library anxiety on task performance in the library use stage is that library-anxious students tend to have the worst coping strategies (Onwuegbuzie, 1997a). Indeed, the difference in performance of library tasks (e.g., library searches) between high- and low-anxious students manifests itself in the amount of attention focused on task-relevant behavior. Students having high levels of library anxiety attend more to task-irrelevant responses, culminating in a decrease in task performance (Onwuegbuzie, 1997a; Onwuegbuzie & Daley, 1996). In turn, the reduction in task performance ensures incongruity between effort and success. The greater this gap, the higher the subsequent levels of library anxiety.

Interestingly, inadequate coping strategies can affect a variety of cognitive activities, such as the capacity to encode a limited set of relevant information (Nottleman & Hill, 1977); to use appropriate techniques for retaining, storing, and retrieving information from both long- and short-term memory (Mueller, 1979); and to use a myriad of logical rules and procedures related to higher-order, conceptual processes (Meyers & Martin, 1974). Thus, it is likely that library anxiety adversely impedes students' ability to complete tasks, such as reaching search closure.

All the dispositional, situational, and environmental variables that induce library anxiety at the library preparatory stage also remain at the library use stage. Variables that induce library anxiety at the library preparation phase are likely to remain at the library use stage, probably at exacerbated levels. For example, if low self-perception increases a student's anxiety levels at the library preparation stage, then it is likely to cause the student problems at the library use stage.

## Library Reflection Stage

The library reflection stage involves the period after the library task has been completed or abandoned. Thus, for example, this stage would begin immediately after the search closure phase, Kulthau's sixth and final stage of the ISP. Interestingly, library reflection tends to occur regardless of the difficulty of the library task; consequently, even returning a library book or making photocopies in the library induces library reflection (Onwuegbuzie, 1997a).

Library anxiety during the library reflection stage is mediated by students' attributional biases that affect future library-related perceptions, attitudes, behavior, and outcomes. Academic-related anxiety is often associated with cognition about causes of failure. Many high-anxious students tend to attribute failure to internal deficiencies (i.e., internal attributions), to believe that failure is likely to recur in the future (i.e., global attributions), and to view their situations as unchangeable (i.e., stable attributions) (Weiner, 1966; Weiner & Schneider, 1971).

One of the earliest studies on academic-related anxiety and attributions demonstrated that students with high levels of test anxiety tended to blame themselves more for failure than did students with low anxiety (Doris & Sarason, 1955). Similarly, Arkin and Schumann (1984) found that high-anxious students perceived themselves to be less able (i.e., internal attribution) and the task more difficult (i.e., external attribution). Sappington (1987) found that students returning to nontraditional degree programs attributed their feelings of anxiety more often to external rather than to internal sources. These external sources included lack of time to accomplish their learning goals, failure to realize the high expectations they had of themselves, and fear concerning the impact that returning to school would have on their interpersonal relationships.

Hunsley (1985) reported that test and mathematics anxiety tended to influence students' cognitive processes, including their appraisals, thought contents during examinations, and several types of causal attributions. Further, Arkin, Kolditz, and Kolditz (1983) contended that unsuccessful, highly test-anxious students blamed their personality, as opposed to their behaviors or the environment, for their failure. In other words, they made internal, global, and stable attributions for their lack of success. In contrast, Wahl and Besag (1986) found that low-anxious students attributed their success to their own effort and ability (i.e., internal), while attributing failure to characteristics of the task (i.e., external).

It has also been found that there is a "pervading asymmetry" (Geen, 1980, p. 43) in the contrasting effects of success and failure on the performance of students with high and low anxiety. Research indicates that, following failure, students with high levels of test anxiety have a tendency to perform less well, whereas low-anxious students tend to increase their performance levels. Following success, the reverse is likely to occur. That is, students with high levels of anxiety perform better, whereas their counterparts perform worse (Wine, 1980).

Attribution theory suggests that low library-anxious students may attribute failure to an unstable internal factor (e.g., lack of effort; "I'm not trying hard enough"), causing them to work harder in the future to complete the library task. Conversely, it is likely that high library-anxious students attribute failure to a stable internal factor (e.g., lack of ability; "I'm not good enough"); consequently, they give up and disengage from future library tasks. Indeed, as noted by Mellon (1986, 1988), students with high levels of library anxiety typically believe that other students are competent at using the library, whereas they alone are inept, and that their ineptness is a source of shame and guilt and thus should be kept hidden.

Research indicates that both success and failure have greater impact on the subsequent performance of high-anxious students than on the achievement of those with low anxiety (Weiner, 1966; Weiner & Schneider, 1971). Therefore, library anxiety evokes attributional biases at the library reflection stage. One likely process through which these biases affect future performance is through reduced self-concept and self-esteem that occur in response to failure. In particular, students who fail typically experience a loss of self-esteem due to the high premium that is placed on achievement and success in the educational context. Unfortunately, by internalizing the failure experience with an attribution centering around ability, the library-anxious student likely will avoid future attempts to engage fully in library tasks (Elliott & McGregor, 1999). This, in turn, would threaten successful completion of the library preparation and library use stages.

As the library user experiences more and more situations in which attributions for failure are internally based, the likelihood also increases that future library tasks will be considered ego threatening rather than merely challenging (Schwarzer & Jerusalem, 1992). In other words, these students will go from a stage in which every attempt is made to complete the library task (e.g., to reach search closure) to a stage wherein feelings of threat are commonplace and library anxiety likely becomes debilitating. Further, in situations where the students acquire external attributions, learned helplessness ensues, culminating in disengagement from the task and subsequent failure (Schwarzer & Jerusalem, 1992). Moreover, because there is no discrete transition point from the library reflection phase to the next library preparation phase, the longer students fixate on their failure and display attributional biases, the less likely they are to negotiate successfully their next library preparation phase (Covington, 1985).

All the dispositional, situational, and environmental variables that induce library anxiety at the library preparatory and library use stages also prevail at the library reflection stage, probably at elevated levels. Moreover, any antecedents that are transferred to the library reflection stage interact with their existing attributional biases, distorting these biases to an even greater degree. Thus, dispositional, situational, and environmental antecedents of library anxiety generate a cycle of increased worry, emotionality, attributional biases, and performance decrements in the library context.

## Relationship among the Three Stages

Although the library preparation, library use, and library reflection stages of the CAS Model of Library Anxiety have been presented in a linear manner, these stages often are cyclical. That is, a student may go through many cycles, especially when the task is complex. For example, students engaged in writing dissertations will go through each of the three stages on multiple occasions. At the same time, students may terminate the task at any stage of the process, depending on their levels of motivation and persistence (Abusin, 1998; Onwuegbuzie, 1997a; Onwuegbuzie & Jiao, 1998a, 1998b). Alternatively, students experiencing a failure at one stage may return to an earlier stage. Each failure increases levels of library anxiety as the amount of time available to complete the task is reduced.

# INFORMATION LITERACY PROCESS
# MODEL OF LIBRARY ANXIETY

The amount of information available in the world has grown and continues to grow exponentially. The available information has become more "fragmented into different formats and media, and duplicated in multiple physical locations" (Ercegovac & Yamasaki, 1998, p. 1). To access and use the myriad sources of information effectively, people must become information literate (Ercegovac & Yamasaki, 1998). According to the final report of the American Library Association Presidential Committee on Information Literacy, "to be information literate, a person must be able to recognize when information is needed and have the ability to locate, evaluate, and use effectively the needed information" (1989, p. 1). Here, the needed information "applies to more than just the printed word. Other literacies such as visual, media, computer, network, and basic literacies are implicit in information literacy" (Plotnick, 2000, p. 27). Indeed, it has been argued that "information literacy goes beyond the skills and knowledge involved in information seeking and retrieval, and strives for higher levels of understanding regarding the context of information in today's society" (Brandt, 2001, p. 74). Thus, information literacy "is both a keystone of lifelong learning and a basic skill essential to the 21st century workplace" (Young, 1999, p. 8). Those who do not possess information literacy tend to be overwhelmed by the deluge of new information and knowledge that they encounter (Amstutz & Whitson, 1997), leading to high levels of library- and other information-based anxieties (Onwuegbuzie, 1997a).

Information literacy is a learning process by which a person learns first to identify a need or to define a problem and then to seek applicable resources, to locate sources and find information within those sources, to analyze and interpret the information, and finally to synthesize and effectively communicate the information to others. At the microlevel of the information literacy process, once the target information has been located via a search, whether online or in print material, the person has to manage this information on three fundamental levels. These levels are input, processing, and output. This is the essence of the Information Literacy Process (ILP) Model of Library Anxiety.

According to the ILP model, library anxiety interferes with information literacy on three distinct levels: input, processing, and output. Firstly, library anxiety occurs at the input phase, which is when the library user initially encounters the stimulus (i.e., the target information). At this point, anxiety inhibits the efficient preprocessing of this new information. For example, the library user may have difficulty mentally extracting the literature found. The level of anxiety at this stage depends on the user's ability to recognize, attend to, concentrate on, and encode external stimuli. Moreover, high levels of anxiety at this stage may diminish the proportion of stimuli that remains in memory for processing or later retrieval, which, in turn, impedes the user's information literacy.

Anxiety produced at the input phase likely will reduce the effectiveness of input. This may occur when the library-anxious user's ability to attend to the new information presented is impaired and nominal stimuli become ineffective due to an inability to represent input internally (Tobias, 1977). Library users with high levels of anxiety at this phase often attend more to task-irrelevant information and material, thereby minimizing the capacity to receive input (Onwuegbuzie & Daley, 1996). Library users with high levels of anxiety at the input phase may have to reread the extracted material on several occasions to compensate for missing or inadequate input.

Secondly, library anxiety interferes with processing, which can be described as the application of new understanding to the task (e.g., information search). The user may understand the new information but be unable to apply the new knowledge to a specific problem (e.g., writing a literature review). Furthermore, library anxiety at the processing phase denotes the apprehension experienced when cognitive operations are performed on the external stimuli—that is, when library users usually are striving to organize and to retain input. The amount of anxiety involved at this phase appears to depend on the complexity of the information extracted, the extent to which memory is needed, and the degree to which the material is organized in a way that is compatible with the user's learning style (e.g., linear, systematic). Anxiety at this stage can debilitate information literacy by interfering with the processes that transform the input material and generate a solution to the task at hand. In other words, library anxiety may reduce the efficiency with which memory processes are utilized to complete the task (e.g., library search). Moreover, high levels of library anxiety associated with processing may reduce a user's ability to make sense of the information extracted or to relate the new information to what is already known.

Thirdly, library anxiety interferes with the output of a response. Library anxiety at the output phase involves the apprehension experienced when users are required to demonstrate their ability to produce previously learned material. In particular, anxiety at this phase involves interference that appears after information processing has been completed but before it has been reproduced effectively as output. High levels of library anxiety associated with output might hinder users' ability to present or to use the information. It should be noted that other forms of academic-related anxieties, representing situational antecedents, often exacerbate the output levels of library anxiety. For example, if the goal of an information search is to obtain literature to write a paper, then writing anxiety likely will interact with the library anxiety experienced at this stage (Onwuegbuzie, 1997a). Because library anxiety often induces a writing block (Onwuegbuzie, 1997a, 1998a, 1999a; Onwuegbuzie & Collins, 2001; Rose, 1984), the anxiety experienced at the output phase will be exacerbated, which subsequently will threaten the quality of the paper. Similarly, levels of research anxiety probably will increase the initial interference that occurs (Onwuegbuzie, 1997a, 1997b, 1997c, 1997d).

It should be noted that the ILP model builds on the framework conceptualized by Tobias (1977). According to Tobias (1977, 1986), academic-related anxiety interferes with learning and performance in three ways.

First, anxiety inhibits the efficient preprocessing of new information. For example, the user may have difficulty organizing study material. Second, anxiety interferes with processing, which Tobias (1977) describes as the application of new understanding to the solution of a problem. The user may understand the new material but is unable to retrieve the information or apply the new knowledge to a specific problem. Third, Tobias (1977) suggests that anxiety interferes with the output of a response. The correct answer may be grasped and then lost before the user verbalizes or records. The ILP model also parallels that of MacIntyre and Gardner (1994a). These investigators have conceptualized foreign language anxiety as occurring at each of the following three stages: input, processing, and output (see also, MacIntyre & Gardner, 1994b; Onwuegbuzie, Bailey, & Dailey, 1999b, 1999c). Similarly, Onwuegbuzie (2002b) theorized that statistics anxiety occurs at the input, processing, and output stages of the learning process in college-level research methodology and quantitative-based courses.

The ILP model has an advantage in that it incorporates anxieties that occur during any part of literature or information search. That is, this model not only attempts to account for debilitative levels of anxiety that occur while users are using the library, but it is also pertinent when users are conducting information literature searches outside libraries (e.g., while using the Internet at home). As such, the ILP model appears to represent an expansion of the current theories of library anxiety, helping to increase our understanding of the difficulty that users face in their quest to become information literate for lifelong learning.

Although the ILP model theorizes library anxiety as occurring at three distinct stages of the information literacy process (i.e., input, processing, and output), the term *stage* should not be taken to mean that literacy occurs in discrete sections. Nevertheless, the interdependence of these three phases does not preclude conceptualizing library anxiety as occurring at these phases. Currently, Onwuegbuzie, Jiao, and Bostick (2002) are seeking to test the ILP model empirically.

## DISPOSITIONAL-SITUATIONAL-ENVIRONMENTAL MODEL OF LIBRARY ANXIETY

In chapter 2, library anxiety was described as being either dispositional, situational, or environmental. Specifically, 8 sets of constructs were classified as dispositional antecedents, 17 were delineated as representing situational antecedents, and 7 were categorized as environmental antecedents (see figure 2.1). Based on this conceptualization, using structural equation modeling techniques, Onwuegbuzie and Jiao (2002d) posited that the following dispositional antecedents were directly or indirectly related to library anxiety: self-perception, academic procrastination, level of perfectionism, hope, and social interdependence. Also, they hypothesized that learning style and GPA, both situational antecedents, were related to library anxiety. Finally, they predicted that gender and age, two environmental antecedents, are directly related to library anxiety.

Initial research determined that a few of the hypothesized paths were not statistically significant. These paths were removed and a subsequent final model was tested (Onwuegbuzie & Jiao, 2002d). This led to the final structural equation model displayed in figure 3.1. This model is called the Dispositional-Situational-Environmental (DSE) model of library anxiety. It can be seen from this figure that there is a direct (negative) path from self-perception to library anxiety and a direct (positive) path from academic procrastination to anxiety and from age to library anxiety. Interestingly, the relationship between hope and library anxiety was mediated by self-perception and academic procrastination. Also, the association between perfectionism and library anxiety was mediated by academic procrastination. That is, hope and perfectionism were indirectly related to library anxiety.

The fit indices (i.e., indices that facilitate the assessment of statistical and practical significance, such as the chi-square value and path coefficients, respectively) reported by Onwuegbuzie and Jiao (2002d), although marginal, provide partial support for the DSE model. In this model, self-perception and academic procrastination appear to play a central role in moderating students' level of library anxiety. More specifically, students' level of library anxiety is mediated by their perceived academic competence, intellectual competence, and overall self-worth, alongside their levels of academic procrastination stemming from fear of negative evaluation and aversive tasks. These set of constructs moderate the extent to which library anxiety is affected by students' (a) sense of successful determination in relation to their goals (i.e., agency); (b) degree of positive appraisals of their ability to generate ways to overcome goal-related obstacles and to reach their goals (i.e., pathways); and (c) levels of self-oriented

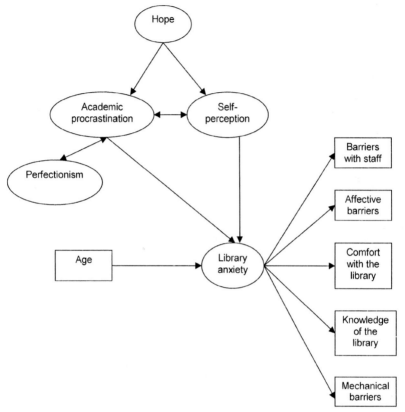

**Figure 3.1**   **The Dispositional-Situational-Environmental (DSE) model of library anxiety.**

perfectionism, other-oriented perfectionism, and socially prescribed perfectionism.

As noted by Onwuegbuzie and Jiao (2002d), the DSE model, at least in part, is consistent with Kuhlthau's (1991, 1993, 1994) ISP model, inasmuch as the two pivotal variables in the DSE model, namely, academic procrastination (i.e., prolonging library tasks) and self-perception (i.e., confidence) also play a central role in the ISP model. For example, at Kuhlthau's topic selection stage, anxiety is increased and confidence (i.e., self-perception) decreased if selection is delayed or postponed (i.e., procrastination).

## ANXIETY-EXPECTATION MEDIATION
## MODEL OF LIBRARY ANXIETY

As reported in chapter 2, levels of library anxiety have been found to have moderate-to-large relationships with other levels of academic-related anxiety, including research anxiety, statistics anxiety, and writing anxiety (Onwuegbuzie & Jiao, 2002d). It is feasible that one or more of the models of anxiety that have been conceptualized in these academic-related areas are pertinent to library anxiety. Indeed, because it can be contended that learning how to conduct library searches and the like, for many students, is similar to learning a foreign language (Onwuegbuzie, 1997a), it is likely that Onwuegbuzie et al.'s (in press) Anxiety-Expectation Mediation (AEM) model of foreign language achievement can be used as a basis for modeling behavior in the library milieu.

Onwuegbuzie et al. (2002) used path analysis techniques to develop their AEM model of foreign language achievement. According to this model, one cognitive variable (i.e., anxiety) and one affective variable (i.e., expectation of foreign language achievement) are related to each other in a reciprocal manner. That is, anxiety and achievement play a role in the foreign language learning context such that a change in either one would culminate in changes in the other in order to reestablish the equilibrium. Also in the AEM model, anxiety and foreign language achievement are reciprocally related—with a direct negative path from anxiety to achievement and a similar direct negative path from achievement to foreign language anxiety. Additionally, there is a direct positive path from expectation to achievement. As such, anxiety and expectation serve as factors that mediate the relationship between foreign language acquisition and other cognitive, personality, and demographic variables.

In a follow-up study, Onwuegbuzie (in press-b) found that the AEM model also transfers to the context of learning statistics. This model consists of a direct negative effect of statistics anxiety on statistics achievement, as well as a direct positive effect of expectation on statistics achievement. Further, statistics anxiety and expectation are reciprocally related. The model also contains a direct negative path from course load to statistics achievement. Finally, statistics anxiety mediated the relationship between statistics achievement and the following variables: number of college-level statistics courses taken, study habits, research anxiety, and course load, whereas expectation reciprocally mediated the relationship between statistics achievement and research anxiety.

Using Onwuegbuzie et al.'s (in press) and Onwuegbuzie's (in press-b) model, Onwuegbuzie and Jiao (in press) have arrived at what they call the AEM Model of Library Anxiety. This model contains variables that are directly or indirectly related to research performance, as measured by students' score on their research proposals. Onwuegbuzie and Jiao's (in press) final AEM model is presented in figure 3.2. This figure reveals a direct (negative) path from library anxiety to research performance, as well as a direct (negative) path from research performance to library anxiety. That is, library anxiety and research achievement are reciprocally

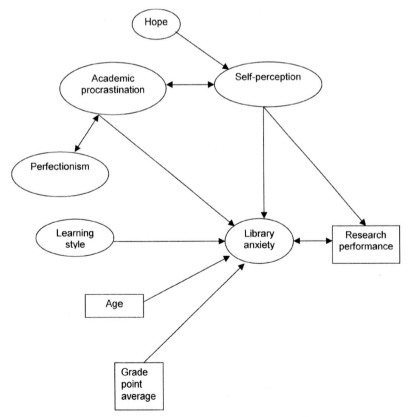

Figure 3.2  The Anxiety-Expectation Mediation model of library anxiety.

related. Furthermore, anxiety mediates the relationship between research performance and the following variables: age, academic achievement (i.e., GPA), learning style, academic procrastination, and self-perception. The path diagram also shows a direct (positive) path from self-perception to research performance. In addition, self-perception moderates the relationship between research achievement and academic procrastination, perfectionism, and hope.

In sum, the AEM model of library anxiety indicates that library anxiety and self-perception serve as factors that mediate the relationship between performance in writing a research proposal and other cognitive, personality, and demographic variables. As such, this model is consistent with the AEM models in both the foreign language (Onwuegbuzie et al., in press) and the statistics (Onwuegbuzie, in press-b) learning context.

The central role of library anxiety in the AEM model suggests that Wine's (1980) Cognitive-Attentional-Interference theory can be applied to the library setting, as it can be to the foreign language and statistics-learning context. Under the present framework, Wine's theory would predict that library anxiety interferes with students' ability to perform library information search task by impeding their ability to become information literate. Additionally, it is likely that library anxiety reduces the efficiency with which memory processes are employed while striving to receive, to encode, and to process new information, making it difficult to reach a successful search closure.

The importance of self-perception in the AEM model suggests that the social cognition theory (Bandura, 1977, 1986) in general, and the self-efficacy theory in particular (Bandura, 1977, 1982, 1986, 1997), are relevant to the underlying library information seeking processes because self-perception is a manifestation of self-efficacy. Self-efficacy theory posits that individuals' belief systems affect their behaviors, amount of effort invested, levels of persistence, and task success in the library context (Bandura, 1977, 1982, 1986, 1997). Furthermore, the finding that self-perception predicts research achievement suggests that a self-fulfilling prophecy prevails, in which students who have low academic self-competence and who believe that they are inept in using the library (Mellon, 1986, 1988) exhibit behaviors that culminate in underachievement. The present results suggest that interventions designed at reducing students' levels of library anxiety, as well as improving self-perceptions of their ability to undertake effective library research, may have direct positive educational outcomes.

## SUMMARY AND CONCLUSIONS

The present chapter outlined five models of library anxiety. The first model presented was Kulthau's Model of the Information Search Process (ISP) (Kuhlthau, 1983, 1985, 1987, 1988a, 1988b, 1989, 1991, 1993, 1994; Kuhlthau et al., 1990). This model incorporates six stages of the search process during which affective variables play a central role throughout. These variables can range from anxiety and feelings of ineptness at the early stages to confidence and a sense of achievement or heightened anxiety and disappointment at the end of the search process. Perhaps the most useful aspect of the ISP model is that it describes cognitions, actions, and emotions that underlie the ISP at distinct stages. Kracker (2002) and Kracker and Wang (2002) demonstrated the utility of the ISP model. These researchers found that a 30-minute presentation of Kuhlthau's six-stage ISP model reduced students' anxiety levels and increased their awareness of affective components related to research and writing. Findings from these studies help identify the causal processes that underlie the ISP model.

The second model delineated was the Cognitive-Affective Stage (CAS) Model of Library Anxiety. Of the five models presented in this chapter, this model represents the most macro in nature. Indeed, whereas the ISP model and ILP model pertain to the task of conducting library and information searches, the CAS model incorporates all library tasks, from returning books to studying for a class project to undertaking an extensive literature search. The CAS model characterizes library anxiety during the three stages of the library-task cycle: library preparation, library use, and library reflection.

The third model presented was the Information Literacy Process (ILP) Model of Library Anxiety. This represents a more micro model than Kulthau's model, inasmuch as it describes how library anxiety interferes with information literacy on three distinct levels: input, processing, and output. Although these levels are distinct, they are also interdependent such that anxiety that prevails at any of the three levels affects the anxiety experienced at subsequent levels. The utility of the ILP model is that it applies to both library and other information searches.

The fourth model discussed was the Dispositional-Situational-Environmental (DSE) Model of Library Anxiety. The DSE model illustrates the pivotal role that self-perceptions and academic procrastination play in the formation of library anxiety. Both of these variables represent dispositional antecedents, which suggests that this class of antecedents might be more important than are situational and environmental antecedents in the library anxiety process.

The fifth and final model presented was the Anxiety-Expectation Mediation (AEM) Model of Library Anxiety. According to this model, library anxiety and self-perception play a crucial role in mediating the relationship between performance in writing a research proposal and other cognitive, personality, and demographic variables. Like the DSE model, the AEM model has important counseling and instructional implications. In particular, the AEM model suggests that interventions designed at reducing students' levels of library anxiety, as well as improving their self-perception of their ability to utilize the library, may have a direct positive effect on academic performance.

The models presented in this chapter offer five possible realizations of the library anxiety context. These representations suggest that library anxiety is an extremely complex phenomenon. It is hoped that future studies subject these models to rigorous tests using both quantitative and qualitative methods in the same vein as those by Kracker (2002) and Kracker and Wang (2002). Undoubtedly, other realizations of library anxiety exist. Thus, we hope that researchers and practitioners from the library and information science field continue to study this construct until successful search closure is reached.

# Chapter Four

# Framework for Conducting Multimethod Research: Research Design/Data Collection Stage

## OVERVIEW

Research has played a critical role in the study of human behavior. In some cases, it has led to the development of theory; in other cases, research has led to theory testing, theory comparison, theory confirmation, or theory modification. As such, research has played a major part in influencing and informing practice and policy. The last decade has seen an exponential increase in the number of articles published in academic journals. A vast majority of these have involved either original or replication studies. Further, the researchers involved in these investigations utilized previous research in developing their conceptual and theoretical frameworks, as well as in providing qualitative (e.g., content analyses) and quantitative (e.g., meta-analyses) reviews of the literature in which the key findings are summarized. Published articles that have not represented research studies typically have represented opinion papers. Nevertheless, the authors of these essays typically have relied on research articles to form their opinions.

Over the decades, a myriad of published works have been the basis of educational, political, economic, or social reform in a multitude of settings (Onwuegbuzie & Daniel, 2003). As a result, there has been a call from many sectors (e.g., industry) for individuals graduating from colleges with an advanced degree (e.g., Masters degree, Doctoral degree) to be trained to be research literate. Many graduate students are now required to enroll in one or more research-based courses, including statistics and qualitative research classes, as a part of their degree programs. Students' experiences in these courses may permanently shape their attitudes toward the field of research and thus determine whether they become consumers of research in the future (Onwuegbuzie et al., 1997; Ravid & Leon, 1995). However, although the goal of many research methodology instructors is to produce students with research consumer skills (i.e., the ability to read, to interpret, to synthesize, and to utilize research) and research production skills (i.e., the ability to design and to implement original research studies) (Ravid & Leon, 1995), many students who have completed research-based courses report being inadequately prepared either to understand or to conduct research (Fleming, 1988; Green & Kvidahl, 1990; Rackliffe, 1988). Additionally, a vast majority of students typically experience lower levels of performance in these courses than in their other graduate-level classes. As a result, these students often view research methodology courses as merely a hurdle that they must overcome to obtain their degrees (Onwuegbuzie, 1998b). Anxiety is thus prevalent in these courses (Onwuegbuzie, 1997a, 1997b, 1997c, 1997d, in press-a; Onwuegbuzie & Wilson, 2003; Onwuegbuzie et al., 1997; Roberts & Bilderback, 1980; Schacht & Stewart, 1990; Zeidner, 1991).

The negative experiences, coupled with the relatively low levels of performance, in research methodology courses dissuade many graduates from conducting research studies in their chosen fields. Further, many practitioners who do attempt to undertake research studies experience problems at one or more stages of the research process (i.e., research design/data collection, data analysis, data interpretation). These problems often culminate in findings, interpretations, and conclusions that are seriously flawed (Daniel, 1998c; Hall, Ward, & Comer, 1988; Keselman et al., 1998; Onwuegbuzie, in press-a; Thompson, 1998a; Vockell & Asher, 1974; Ward, Hall, & Schramm, 1975; Witta & Daniel, 1998). These problems are then exacerbated by the fact that, in conducting literature reviews, researchers use these flawed findings to develop their conceptual and theoretical frameworks, mistakenly assuming that the documented findings are trustworthy.

The overwhelming majority of these analytical and interpretational flaws have stemmed from graduate-level research methodology instruction in which research techniques are taught as a series of routine steps instead of as a holistic, comprehensive, reflective, and integrative process (Kerlinger, 1960; Newman & Benz, 1998); from graduate programs that utilize curricula that minimize students' exposure to quantitative and qualitative research techniques (Aiken et al., 1990; Thompson, 1998a); from propagation of various inaccurate and misleading "mythologies" about the nature of research (Daniel, 1997; Kerlinger, 1960); from an increasing proportion of research methodology instructors unqualified to teach research-based courses; and from a failure, reluctance, or even refusal to concede that research techniques that previously were deemed appropriate are subject to extreme criticism by the bulk of the research community (Schmidt & Hunter, 1997).

In the library and information science field, as is the case for all social and behavioral disciplines, all research questions can be addressed using either quantitative, qualitative, or mixed-methodological research techniques. The most basic distinction between these three sets of techniques centers on the type of data that are primarily of interest. For the most part, quantitative research involves the collection, analysis, and interpretation of numbers. For example, a library researcher might be interested in determining the prevalence of library anxiety among high school students or may be interested in comparing levels of library anxiety between middle school and high school students. On the other hand, qualitative inquiry involves the collection, analysis, and interpretation of words, observations, and/or experiences. For instance, a library researcher might want to describe the experiences of high school students as they use academic or public libraries. Finally, as its name suggests, mixed-methodological studies involve the collection, analysis, and interpretation of both numbers and words/observations/experiences, either simultaneously or in a sequential manner. For example, a library researcher might be interested both in determining the prevalence rate of library anxiety among high school students and describing their experiences in libraries within the same study.

Regardless of the research technique used (quantitative, qualitative, mixed-methodological), all research studies involve the following three major stages: research design/data collection, data analysis, and data interpretation/validation. The research design/data collection stage involves both planning (research design phase) and implementing (data collection phase) a study that addresses the underlying research questions and/or tests the hypotheses of interest. The data analysis stage entails analyzing the data collected in the previous stage. Finally, the data interpretation/validation stage encompasses interpreting data that have been analyzed and assessing the extent to which the data appear to be valid and the interpretation legitimate. It should be noted that while these three stages typically occur in a linear fashion in quantitative studies (Onwuegbuzie, 2003a), these stages are cyclical and interactive in qualitative (Onwuegbuzie, 2000b) and mixed-methodological studies (Onwuegbuzie & Johnson, in press; Onwuegbuzie & Teddlie, 2003). That is, in qualitative and mixed-methodological research, either the data analysis stage or data interpretation/validation stage may be followed by more data collection, and so forth, until the research question is appropriately addressed.

Thus, as can be seen, researchers have an array of tools at their disposal for advancing our knowledge base. Unfortunately, in the library and information science field, most graduate students are underprepared to conduct research studies, whether quantitative or qualitative. Indeed, the majority of library science programs require only one or two research methodology courses. So, it should not be surprising that the library science field is underrepresented with respect to the number of formal research investigations that appear in the literature. More specifically, as noted in chapter 2, scant research has been undertaken in the area of library anxiety, with only 26 studies published on this topic in the last three decades. In fact, it has been recently noted that "while the idea of library anxiety has been around since 1972, and has existed as a theory since 1986, the amount of research that has been conducted leaves something to be desired" (Anonymous, n.d., para. 2).

Therefore, the purpose of the present section of this book is to provide a framework for conducting quantitative, qualitative, and mixed-methodological studies at the three major stages of the research process (research design/data collection, data analysis, and data interpretation). In this chapter, a definition and a description of the goal of quantitative, qualitative, and mixed-methodological studies are presented. Included in this description is a delineation of the major steps involved in the quantitative, qualitative, and mixed-methodological research process. The chapter also contains a brief outline of the various types of research designs and data collection methods that fall under each of these three research paradigms.

Chapter 5 presents a framework for conducting quantitative, qualitative, and mixed-methodological data analyses. With respect to quantitative (i.e., statistical) analyses, recommendations for good practices, based on the literature, are provided for each of the major data-analytic techniques including: bivariate correlational analyses, multiple regression, analysis of variance, analysis of covariance, multiple analysis of variance, multiple analysis of covariance, discriminant analysis, exploratory factor analysis, confirmatory factor analysis, structural equation modeling, and hierarchical linear modeling. With regard to qualitative and mixed-methodological data analytic techniques, suggestions are made that stem from the most recent literature. Throughout chapter 5, examples from the library anxiety literature are offered to provide the reader with practical applications of each data-analytical technique. In the few cases where specific examples do not exist from the library anxiety literature, examples of viable future studies in this area are presented.

In chapter 6, the major interpretational errors that occur in published research are discussed. In particular, the concept of validity is presented within the quantitative, qualitative, and mixed-methodological research paradigms. A model for assessing the trustworthiness of the findings is presented for each of these paradigms

It is hoped that this section of the book will motivate more librarians and library educators to conduct research in the field of library science in general and library anxiety in particular. Furthermore, it is hoped that authors, as well as editorial board members, article reviewers, and editors of journals from the library and information science field use these chapters to design the most appropriate studies that address their research questions, with a view to maximizing the knowledge gleaned and determining the most beneficial practices and policies to adopt that stem from this knowledge base.

## QUANTITATIVE RESEARCH PARADIGM

### Research Designs

There are five major objectives in social and behavioral science research (Gay & Airasian, 2000; Johnson & Christensen, 2000). These objectives are exploration, description, explanation, prediction, and influence. Specifically, exploration fundamentally utilizes inductive methods to explore a concept, construct, phenomenon, or situation with the intent of developing tentative hypotheses or generalizations. Description entails identifying and describing the nature and characteristics of a phenomenon. Explanation involves the development of a theory with the goal of clarifying the relationships among phenomena and ascertaining reasons for occurrences of events. Prediction involves using previously acquired information to determine what will occur at a later point in time. Finally, influence encompasses the manipulation of the variable or situation in an attempt to produce a desired outcome.

The research purpose, which identifies the phenomenon or phenomena that will be studied, stems directly from the research objective. For example, in Jiao and Onwuegbuzie's (2003c) study, the purpose was to determine whether reading ability predicts library anxiety. As such, their research objective was predictive, as indicated by their title.

Once the research objective and research purpose have been specified and the research questions and/or hypotheses matched to the research objective and purpose, the researcher's first major task is to determine the most appropriate research design to use and to decide how to collect the data. The remainder of this chapter outlines the different research designs that are available for quantitative, qualitative, and mixed-methodological research paradigms. In addition, the major components of research designs will be identified and discussed—specifically, methods of data collection, comprising sampling and instrumentation.

The quantitative paradigm is regarded commonly as the traditional, the positivist, the experimental, or the empiricist paradigm. Individuals who classify themselves as quantitative researchers view reality as "objective" and independent of the researcher. These objective phenomena are measured via the use of questionnaires, cognitive measures, and so forth. In an attempt to control for bias, quantitative researchers are supposed to be distant and independent of what is being researched. As such, they attempt to keep their values out of the study by using impersonal language in reporting the facts and by making their conclusions follow as closely as possible from the evidence gathered in the investigation.

In quantitative studies, the problem typically evolves from the literature, insofar as a body of literature exists on which the researcher can build. Variables often are known, and theories may exist or are developed by the researcher, which need to be tested and verified. Quantitative researchers tend to use a more deductive form of logic vis-à-vis testing hypotheses in a cause-and-effect order. Concepts, variables, and hypotheses often are chosen prior to the study and remain fixed throughout the study (i.e., static design). One does not venture beyond these predetermined hypotheses (i.e., research is context free). The aim is to develop generalizations that contribute to the theory and facilitate better prediction, explanation, understanding, and/or control of some phenomenon.

Broadly speaking, a quantitative research study involves the collection, analysis, and interpretation of numeric data (i.e., numbers). As noted by Schwartz, Slate, and Onwuegbuzie (1999), quantitative research involves an eight-step cyclical process involving: (a) identifying an issue or problem to investigate; (b) gathering and reviewing relevant literature; (c) formulating research questions and/or hypotheses; (d) developing a research plan of action; (e) implementing the research plan; (f) analyzing the data and interpreting the findings; (g) communicating the findings; and (h) repeating the cycle with a modified problem or strategy derived from what was learned in the previous cycle (i.e., problem redefinition) until the research question is addressed in its entirety.

As can be seen from Schwartz et al.'s (1999) conceptualization, the quantitative research process is cyclical. Simply put, one study is *never* enough to address a research question or to test a hypothesis. For example, although Onwuegbuzie and Jiao (2000) found a relationship between academic procrastination and library anxiety, several replications are needed to assess the generalizability of this result. Because probabilities (i.e., *p*-values) were used by Onwuegbuzie and Jiao (2000) to determine whether this association exists, it is possible that this result represents a false positive or, in the words of statisticians, a Type I error. On the other hand, the link found by Onwuegbuzie and Jiao (2000) may actually understate the true relationship. Both types of inaccuracies often stem from sampling error, which is the difference between the information gleaned from the sample and that which would have been obtained if the total population had been used. This is why the Food and Drug Administration requires that numerous multicenter, multicountry replications be made before a drug is ratified. Unfortunately, in the social and behavioral sciences, some researchers would like to believe that one well-designed study, which they call a "definitive study," containing a large random sample and utilizing sophisticated statistical techniques, is sufficient to make firm conclusions about a phenomenon. This could not be further from the truth. That is, attempting to conduct a definitive study is an elusive and futile goal.

As noted by Gay and Airasian (2000), there are five distinct quantitative methods of research, or research designs. These designs are historical, descriptive, correlational, quasi-experimental (i.e., causal-comparative), and experimental. Each of these designs is discussed below.

*Historical research*

Historical research involves studying, understanding, and explaining past events. Historical research differs from other research designs inasmuch as the phenomenon of interest must already have occurred. As such, historical research designs are used much less than are other quantitative research designs, namely: (a) definition of a problem, (b) formulation of hypotheses/research questions, (c) systematic collection of data, (d) objective evaluation of data, and (e) confirmation or disconfirmation of hypotheses. A literature review tends to be much broader in a historical study and refers to all sorts of written communication, including legal documents, records, minutes of meetings, letters, and other documents that are not normally indexed alphabetically by subject, author, and title in a library.

The purpose of historical research designs is to arrive at conclusions concerning causes, effects, or trends of past events that may help explain present events and predict or control future events. The steps involved in conducting a historical study are similar to those involved in other quantitative studies. That is, historical research can involve just describing a past phenomenon (i.e., historical descriptive), determining the relationship among two or more variables that were measured in the past (i.e., historical correlational), or comparing two or more groups on one or more past outcomes (i.e., historical quasi-experimental). However, a historical research design can never be experimental because none of the variables can be manipulated since they have occurred already.

The data that are acquired usually are already available. These sources of data either are primary or secondary. Primary sources are more reliable but are more difficult to obtain, especially in historical research. Thus, authenticity (external criticism) and accuracy (internal criticism) are key issues. In determining the accuracy of documents, at least four factors must be considered: (a) knowledge and competence of the author, (b) the time delay between the occurrence and recording of events, (c) biased motives of the author, and (d) consistency of the data.

Examples of historical data in the library and information science field include comparing the number of users of academic libraries between the 19th century and 20th centuries. Another example is examining the trends in expenditure of public or academic libraries over the last few decades.

## Descriptive research

Descriptive research involves the depiction or account of characteristics of a particular individual, group, or situation. These studies are a means of discovering new meanings, describing what exists, determining the frequency with which a phenomenon occurs, and/or categorizing information. In descriptive research, the researcher often uses structured observations and/or self-report instruments (e.g., questionnaires) to describe the underlying phenomenon. Descriptive studies, which predominantly utilize descriptive statistics (e.g., means, proportions, percentages, totals, standard deviation), provide the knowledge base needed to conduct the other types of quantitative research.

Descriptive research involves collecting data in an attempt to answer research questions that relate to the current status of the participants in a study. The descriptive researcher has no control over what is and can only measure what already exists. Moreover, results of a descriptive research study are not generalized beyond the sample. In descriptive studies, data usually are collected via questionnaire, surveys, interviews, or observations. Instruments often are constructed especially for the study. Such instruments need to be field tested and revised until they yield scores that are reliable and valid. Descriptive studies often involve one or both of the following: (a) self-report or (b) observation. Self-report studies include survey research, developmental research, follow-up research, sociometric studies, questionnaire studies, and formal and informal interviews.

Survey research, involving either a sample or census, is probably the most used type of descriptive research. Most sample surveys are cross-sectional inasmuch as they collect information from individuals at one point in time. However, longitudinal surveys, in which responses are tracked over time, are not unusual. Examples of a survey research study in the library and information science field include determining the proportion of students with debilitative levels of library anxiety (cross-sectional) or monitoring library anxiety levels of one or more library users over time (longitudinal).

Developmental studies, for the most part, are concerned with behavioral variables that differentiate children at different levels of age, growth, or maturation with respect to various factors such as intellectual, physical, emotional, or social development. For example, a researcher could try to determine the onset of library anxiety among children. Developmental studies also can be cross-sectional or longitudinal.

Follow-up studies are conducted to monitor an individual or a group of interest after some period of time. For example, one or more individuals can be tracked to determine the effect of bibliographic instruction on library anxiety after a period of time has elapsed. Sociometric studies are undertaken to assess and analyze interpersonal relationships within a group of individuals. This type of research involves asking each member to indicate with which peers he or she would most like to engage in a particular activity. The choices made by the group can be graphically depicted as a sociogram that plots which individuals chose whom. A sociogram will identify stars (members who are chosen the most often), isolates (members not selected by anyone), and cliques (small subgroups of members who mutually select each other). Sociometric techniques are used by both researchers and practitioners.

Questionnaire studies involve the use of questionnaires. Questionnaires, if used properly, are more efficient than many other methods of collecting data in quantitative research studies because they require less time, are less expensive, and permit data collection from a much larger sample than do other methods. In descriptive research, most questionnaires primarily comprise closed-ended items (i.e., structured items) that are easier to code, score, and analyze. In constructing a questionnaire, the researcher should (a) avoid asking leading questions; (b) avoid asking sensitive questions unless absolutely necessary; (c) refrain from asking questions from which the identity of the respondent will be revealed; (d) field test the questionnaire; (e) include a cover letter explaining purpose and importance of study, a commitment to share the results, an endorsement of a respected person or organization, a guarantee of anonymity and confidentiality, deadline dates, and a stamped, addressed envelope (if mailed); (f) send reminder postcards, when applicable; (g) send a second set of questionnaires, with a new cover letter reminding them of the purpose and significance of the study; (h) use follow-up telephone calls if possible; and (i) randomly select a subset of nonrespondents and try to find out whether their responses would have been typical of the responders. When presenting results, researchers always should report the total sample size and response rate.

Interviews also can be used to administer questionnaires. In descriptive research, these questionnaires, which are called interview schedules, tend to involve structured questions for which counts can be obtained from participant responses. Interviews are often preferable to mailed questionnaires or questionnaires administered to groups because they are more personable and flexible; produce more in-depth data; facilitate the asking of unstructured questions; facilitate rapport and, consequently, may increase the item response rate and the propensity for honest responses; facilitate clarification of items, resulting in more accurate responses; and facilitate follow-up and probing questions to incomplete responses. However, interviews are more time consuming and expensive and, therefore, typically lead to smaller samples than for questionnaires administered by other means. Also, interviews may invoke interviewer bias, especially when the interviewer is not very experienced.

## Correlational research

Correlational research involves collecting data to determine whether, and to what degree, a relationship exists between two or more quantifiable variables. Regardless of whether a relationship is causal, the existence of a strong relationship facilitates accurate prediction. Correlational studies may be used either to determine which variables from a set are related or to test hypotheses regarding expected relationships. Variables to be included should be selected on the basis of theory—either deductively or inductively.

Correlational research helps identify important and unimportant variables. In this respect, this research design helps to give direction to subsequent causal-comparative and experimental studies. For instance, unimportant variables can be removed from subsequent studies, whereas important variables can be manipulated (if possible) in an attempt to establish causality. Also, variables that are important but not of interest, can be controlled for, in order to minimize their confounding effects on the relationship between the dependent variable(s) and independent variable(s)

When the relationship between two variables is of interest, a correlation coefficient is used as a measure of the degree of the association. A correlation coefficient is a decimal number between $-1.00$ and $+1.00$, inclusive. Correlation coefficient values near $+1.00$ indicate a strong positive correlation (relationship). Conversely, correlation coefficient values near $-1.00$ indicate a strong negative (inverse) correlation (relationship). Correlation coefficient values near 0.00 indicate no correlation (relationship). The further away from 0.00 the coefficient is, in either direction (toward -1.00 or $+1.00$), the stronger the relationship.

*Pearson's product moment correlation coefficient* (Pearson's $r$) is used if both variables represent interval data (i.e., continuous scores with no true zero, such as scores on the LAS) or ratio data (i.e., continuous scores with a true zero, such as time spent in the library), whereas *Spearman's rho* is used if at least one of the variables represent ordinal data (i.e., ranked/ordered data such as ordering of library anxiety scores from least anxious to most anxious). *Chi-square techniques* are used when both variables are categorical (e.g., high-anxious vs. low-anxious). Regardless of which technique is used to compute a relationship, correlation coefficients tend to be lowered (i.e., attenuated) when measures are used that generate less-than-perfectly-reliable scores. Correlation coefficients also tend to be attenuated when scores on the two variables represent a restricted range. Although corrections to correlation coefficients can be made in both cases (i.e., a correction for attenuation and a correction for restriction of range), caution should be exercised when interpreting these corrected values because they do not represent what was actually found.

A correlation coefficient often is interpreted in terms of both its statistical significance and its practical significance (e.g., effect size). Statistical significance refers to whether we can infer that the correlation coefficient is really different from zero and reflects a true relationship, *not merely a chance relationship*. The decision regarding statistical significance is made at a given level of probability, usually at a 5% level. A hypothesis regarding whether there is a relationship between two variables can either be supported or not supported. A researcher cannot *prove* or *disprove* the hypothesis, just as the court of law does not set out to prove or disprove that someone is guilty but rather to find evidence that supports or does not support a guilty verdict. Thus, the researcher's aim is to provide evidence beyond reasonable doubt (e.g., 95% confidence level or 5% rate of error) that the correlation coefficient is (statistically) significantly different than zero. To do this, researchers use statistical tables. Specifically, to determine statistical significance, researchers use a table that indicates how large a coefficient has to be in order to be (statistically) significant at a given probability level and given size of sample.

Authors of research methodology textbooks (e.g., Creswell, 2002; Gay & Airaisian, 2000, 2003) generally consider 30 participants to be the minimum acceptable sample size for correlational research. However, a minimum sample size of 82 is desirable in order to attain sufficient statistical power (i.e., .80) to detect a moderate relationship (i.e., $r = .30$) between two variables (i.e., statistical significance) at the 5% level of significance (Erdfelder, Faul, & Buchner, 1996).

With respect to practical significance, according to Cohen (1988), correlations around .1 or −.1 are considered small, correlations around .3 or −.3 are considered medium or moderate, and correlations around .5 or −.5 or higher are considered large. To determine the common variance shared by two variables, one should square the correlation coefficient representing their relationship. For example, if the correlation between library anxiety and GPA is 0.5, then because $(0.5)^2 = 0.25 = 25\%$, it can be stated that 25% of the common variance of anxiety and academic achievement is shared. Alternatively, in this example, if the researcher was using anxiety scores to predict or to explain academic achievement, it can be stated that 25% of the variance in GPA scores is explained by library anxiety level. Also, in this example, if using GPA to predict anxiety, it can be stated that 25% of the variation in library anxiety level is explained by GPA. However, unless it is an experimental study, it can neither be stated that academic achievement *causes* library anxiety nor that library anxiety *causes* academic performance.

The following two observations help explain the relationship among the sample size, size of the correlation coefficient, and level of statistical significance (i.e., alpha level). First, keeping the probability level constant, the *smaller* the sample size, the *larger* the correlation coefficient has to be in order to be considered statistically significant. That is, the researcher is less unsure (i.e., more confident) in a correlation based on 100 participants than in one based on 10 participants only. This is because the larger the sample, the more closely it likely approximates the population from which it came and, therefore, the greater the probability that a given coefficient represents a true relationship.

Second, for a given sample size, as we *reduce* our level of uncertainty and subsequently increase our level of certainty (confidence) that a correlation coefficient represents a true relationship, we must *increase* the correlation coefficient. That is, as the level of confidence increases, the $p$-value decreases. For example, a 95% level of confidence corresponds to a *p-value* of $100\% - 95\% = 5\%$ or 0.05. Thus, if we wanted to be 95% confident that a Pearson's correlation coefficient is different than zero (i.e., a true relationship) with a sample size of 20 participants, the $p$-value would be .05 and the correlation must be greater than or equal to .4227. If we want 95% confidence (i.e., 5% error rate) with 100 participants, then the correlation coefficient must be at least .1946, which is much less than the previous coefficient (i.e., .4227). On the other hand, if we wanted to be 99% confident (i.e., 1% error rate) that our correlation coefficient is different than zero (i.e., a true relationship) with a sample size of 20 participants, the $p$-value would be .01 and the correlation must be greater than or equal to .5368, which is larger than the 95% confident correlation coefficient of .4227 obtained with 20 participants. If we want 99% confidence with 100 participants, then the correlation coefficient must be at least .254, which is larger than the 95% confident coefficient obtained from a sample of 100 participants (i.e., .1946). Usually, in the social and behavioral sciences, including library and information science, we use a 5% error rate.

It should be noted that the more variables that are tested for statistical significance at any one time, the more chance that incorrect conclusions will be reached for some of them regarding their levels of statistical significance. For example, if a researcher uses a 5% error rate and tests 100 correlations for statistical significance, the researcher should expect to conclude incorrectly that 5 of these correlations are statistically significantly different than zero. Thus, library researchers and other researchers alike should use theory to select the variables to be studied. A small number of carefully selected variables is always preferable to a large number of carelessly selected variables. Further, the population *must* be one for which data on each of the identified variables can be collected, and one whose members are available to the researcher.

If two variables are related highly, then scores on one variable can be used to predict scores on the other variable (e.g., library anxiety predicting academic performance). This is called *simple linear regression.* The variable on which the prediction is made is called the *predictor* or *independent* variable, while the variable predicted is called the *criterion* or *dependent* variable. Here, it is assumed that the independent variable (e.g., library anxiety) precedes the dependent variable (e.g., academic performance) in time. Similarly, if a dependent variable is related to more than one independent variable, then a prediction based on a combination of those variables would be more accurate than a prediction based on any one of them. Using a combination of variables to predict one (dependent) variable is called *multiple regression.* Any prediction equation should be validated with at least one other group, and the variables that are no longer found to be related to the criterion measure should be taken out of the equation. This procedure is referred to as *cross-validation.*

In a prediction study, statistical significance is secondary to the value of the coefficient in facilitating accurate predictions. Regardless of how many variables are used to predict an outcome, and regardless of the sophistication level of the statistical analysis used, a researcher cannot assert that correlation equals causality. That is, *correlation does not imply causation.*

Scientific experiments can frequently make a strong case for causality by carefully controlling the values of all variables that might be related to the ones under study. Then if the $y$ (i.e., dependent) variable is observed to change in a predictable way as the value of $x$ (i.e., independent variable) changes, the most plausible explanation would be a causal relationship between $x$ and $y$. In the absence of such control and ability to manipulate the independent variable $(x)$, as is the case in correlational studies, the researcher must admit the possibility that at least one more unidentified variable is influencing both the variables under investigation.

This does not mean that correlation analysis may never be used in drawing conclusions about causal relationships. A large correlation in many uncontrolled studies carried out in different settings *can provide support for causality*—as in the case of library anxiety and procrastination—*but establishing causality in uncontrolled studies is often a very elusive and futile task.*

In sum, correlational research involves the systematic investigation of relationships among two or more quantifiable variables. If the relationship exists, the researcher determines the type (positive or negative) and the degree or strength of the relationships (i.e., effect size). The primary intent of correlational studies is to explain the nature of relationships in the real world, not to determine cause-and-effect associations. However, correlational studies often provide a basis for generating hypotheses that guide (future) experimental studies, which do focus on cause-and-effect relationships. Also, correlational research can be used to make predictions. Most of the quantitative research described in chapters 2 and 3 involves correlational research, in which the relationships between library anxiety and an array of cognitive, affective, personality, and demographic variables are explained.

## Quasi-experimental (causal-comparative)

This type of research describes conditions that already exist, attempting to determine reasons for the differences between groups of individuals that exist with respect to a variable(s). Thus, the basic causal comparative approach begins with an effect and tries to identify possible antecedents. Alternative names include *ex post factor* research and *retrospective* research. A variant of the basic approach is *prospective* research, which starts with a hypothesized cause and investigates its effect on one or more variables. Quasi-experimental or causal comparative research designs do not involve manipulation. Rather, this design uses groups that are formed already. Causal-comparative studies involve the use of a variety of descriptive and inferential statistics.

Independent variables in causal-comparative studies involve variables that (a) cannot be manipulated (e.g., gender); (b) should not be manipulated (e.g., amount of library anxiety); and (c) are not manipulated but could be (e.g., methods of bibliographic instruction). Thus, causal comparative research allows investigation of a number of variables that cannot be studied experimentally, such as organismic variables, ability variables, personality variables, and family- and school-related variables. Causal-comparative studies also identify relationships that may lead to experimental studies. However, because independent variables are not controlled in causal-comparative studies, extreme caution must be exercised in interpreting results.

As noted above, the basic causal-comparative design involves selecting two or more groups differing on some independent variable and then comparing them on one or more dependent variables. The groups may differ in the following ways: (a) one group possesses a characteristic or experience that the others do not have or (b) one group possesses more of one characteristic than do the other groups. The characteristic or experience differentiating the groups must be defined clearly and operationally because each group will represent a different population.

There are four major quasi-experimental/causal-comparative research designs. These are (a) the nonequivalent control group design, (b) time series design, (c) multiple time series design, and (d) the counterbalanced design. The nonequivalent control group design, perhaps the most common quasi-experimental/causal-comparative research design, involves comparing one or more experimental groups (i.e., a group that has the treatment/condition of interest) to one or more control groups (i.e., a group that does not have the target treatment or condition). These groups are not formed by the researcher; rather, they represent intact groups. That is, they are either preexisting groups or they formed themselves.

In nonequivalent control group designs, both the experimental and control groups are given a pretest prior to receiving the treatment. These pretests should then be compared to determine how similar the two groups are with respect to this variable. Sometime after the pretest has been administered, the experimental group is given the target treatment/intervention, whereas the control group is given the comparison treatment/intervention (this treatment often represents an existing intervention). After an appropriate period of time, a posttest is given to both groups. This posttest typically is identical to the pretest. In such cases, the pretest is subtracted from the posttest to form a difference score for each student within both groups. The mean difference score for the experimental group is then compared to the mean difference score for the control group at a specified level of significance (e.g., 5%) using a paired-samples $t$-test, also known as a dependent samples $t$-test. If the two means are statistically significantly different in favor of the experimental group, then the researcher can at least rule in the possibility that the intervention may be responsible for this difference. However, strong causal statements can never be made with this or any other type of quasi-experimental design.

An example of a nonequivalent control group design is Kracker's (2002) study of the effect of teaching Kuhlthau's ISP model (Kuhlthau, 1983, 1985, 1987, 1988a, 1988b, 1989, 1991, 1993, 1994; Kuhlthau et al., 1990) on students' levels of research anxiety and perceptions of research. The author called her design an experimental one, which was not technically accurate because the groups used were intact. Thus, her study was quasi-experimental. (Nevertheless, her study was extremely well designed and makes an important contribution to the library anxiety literature.) In Kracker's (2002) investigation, an experimental group and a control group of students were given premeasures of library anxiety and self-perceptions. The two experimental groups then received a guest presentation of Kulthau's ISP model, whereas the two control groups heard a different guest speech about career experiences as a technical writer. Both sets of groups then were given the same instruments that they were given at the pretest stage (i.e., postmeasures of the same instruments). The two conditions were then compared with respect to these measures.

Zahner (1993) provides the only other example of a nonequivalent control group design used in library anxiety research. Zahner (1993) compared the effects of two methods of academic library instruction on research process orientation. The two procedures represented a traditional treatment and a cognitive strategies treatment. The traditional condition involved resource-oriented instruction, consisting of lectures and demonstrations that presented the basic tools and technologies used in library research. The cognitive strategies intervention was process oriented, being based on and emphasizing the research process itself rather than concentrating on specific information sources. Both conditions received pre- and postmeasures of research process orientation, general attitudes toward library instruction, and library anxiety.

The second type of quasi-experimental design is the time series design. In this design, a group containing one or more individuals receives several pretest measures (i.e., baseline measures) followed by the intervention, and then followed by several posttest measures. The pretest and posttest measures can then be plotted on a graph and examined for trend. If the trend improves after the intervention has been administered in a favorable direction, then the researcher might rule in the intervention as possibly being responsible for this. Complicated statistical time series analyses (e.g., ARIMA models) can be used to examine this trend more formally. Such models could then be used to predict outcomes over time. A time series design could be used to examine several interventions over time or the same intervention administered at several time points. In fact, a time series design does not even have to involve any interventions; landmarks (e.g., grade level or year of study in college) can be compared instead. An example of such a design would be to examine library anxiety administered at multiple regular/irregular intervals (e.g., at different grade levels) or to track library anxiety over a long period of time after an intervention (e.g., bibliographic instruction) has been given.

A multiple time series design, the third type of quasi-experimental research design, is identical to the time series design described above, except two or more groups are involved. Specifically, the time series design pertaining to both experimental and control groups are compared using statistical techniques such as repeated measures designs. For example, a group of sophomores that receives bibliographic instruction can be compared to a group that does not receive any type of bibliographic instruction over a period of time, in which at least one premeasure is taken and at least two postmeasures are administered.

The final type of quasi-experimental research design is the counterbalanced design. In this design, there are two or more groups with each receiving two or more interventions. However, these interventions are counterbalanced. That is, the order in which the interventions are administered to the groups are sequentially or randomly different. Suppose a researcher is interested in comparing the effect of bibliographic instruction and anxiety management training in reducing levels of library anxiety. One group could receive bibliographic instruction first, followed several days/weeks later by an anxiety management workshop; the other group could receive the anxiety management workshop first, followed by bibliographic instruction. Such a design would eliminate order of administration as a confounding variable. Indeed, research has shown that some individuals are more influenced by the *recency* effect (i.e., they tend to pay more attention to the treatment/intervention that they received most recently, which induces biased responses) or the *latency* effect (i.e., they tend to pay more attention to the treatment/intervention that they received first, which also induces biased responses). Thus, if the same intervention is provided first for both groups, then any differences found between the groups may be indicative of the ratio of study participants who are influenced more by the recency effect to those influenced more by the latency effect across both groups.

At this point, brief mention also should be made about preexperimental research designs. There are three types of preexperimental research designs: (a) one-shot case study; (b) one-group pretest-posttest design; and (c) static group comparison. The one-shot case study, considered the weakest preexperimental design, involves giving an intervention to a group of participants and then measuring the outcome. For example, in the library context, this could take the form of bibliographic instruction administered to a group of high school students, after which the LAS is administered. One problem with this design is that because there is no pretest administered, it cannot be determined whether any changes in library anxiety levels took place directly as a result of the intervention. Another problem is that because no control group is used, it cannot be ascertained whether the library anxiety observed after the bibliographic instruction had been administered is typical.

The one-group pretest-posttest design is a slight improvement over the one-shot case study, inasmuch as the group is given both a pretest and posttest. In the previous example, the group of high school students would be given the LAS both before and after the bibliographic instruction. However, although changes in outcome before and after the intervention can be compared, it cannot be determined whether any pretest-posttest differences observed are the result of time (i.e., maturational effects) or any other confounding variables.

The static group comparison involves two intact groups that are given an intervention and then postmeasured. This design clearly provides more information than does the one-shot case study. Also, this design is superior to the one-group pretest-posttest design inasmuch as a group control is used for comparative purposes; at the same time, though, it is inferior to the one-group pretest-posttest design insofar as no pretest is administered. Moreover, it should be noted that all three preexperimental designs are extremely weak in establishing causality. Indeed, these designs only should be used where neither quasi-experimental designs nor (true) experimental designs can be employed.

Quasi-experimental research designs do not have to involve comparing an experimental group to a control group. In fact, many quasi-experimental studies involve comparing two groups or subgroups. For example, comparing males and females, different age groups, different years of study, different ethnic groups, or individuals with different levels of perfectionism (e.g., high vs. low) with respect to library anxiety, all represent quasi-experimental designs. Clearly, (true) experimental research designs cannot be used for these comparisons because these variables cannot be manipulated. Because of the lack of manipulation, when using quasi-experimental research designs, many textbook authors (e.g., Creswell, 2002; Gay & Airasian, 2000, 2003) recommend using at least 30 participants per group. However, a sample size of 30 often will be too small to detect a statistically significant difference of moderate size. That is, a sample size of 30 typically will yield statistical power that is too low to detect a moderate difference between two groups.

Therefore, we recommend that *at least 64 participants per group be used* if the researcher is testing a two-tailed hypothesis (i.e., hypothesizes that a difference between the two groups exists but does not specify the exact nature of that difference) and at least *51 participants per group be used* if the researcher is testing a one-tailed hypothesis (i.e., hypothesizes that the scores of one group, on average, are statistically significantly higher than are scores of the other group). These sample sizes will provide a probability of at least 80% (i.e., .80) that the researcher identifies a moderate difference as being statistically significant if such a difference really exists. In other words, sample sizes of 64 and 51 for two-tailed and one-tailed hypotheses involving two groups, respectively, using a 5% level of significance, yields a statistical power of .80 or greater for detecting a moderate difference (Erdfelder et al., 1996). Group sizes of 30 only yield a statistical power of .61 for detecting a moderate difference, which is inadequate because statistical power values lower than .80 typically are deemed inadequate (Cohen, 1965; McNemar, 1960; Onwuegbuzie & Leech, in press).

The way in which the groups are defined will affect the generalizability of the results. If samples are to be selected from the defined population, random selection generally is the preferred method of selection. As with experimental studies, the goal is to have groups that are as similar as possible on all relevant variables except the independent variable. In order to determine equality of groups, information on a number of background and current status variables should be collected.

A final type of quasi-experimental design is the single-subject design. This design also involves the study of a single individual. As such, this design also is called "n = 1 design," "within-subjects design," and "behavior analysis." Although a single-subject study might include several individuals, each person is studied individually. In one realization of this design, the behavior of the "participant" (i.e., "subject") is studied over a baseline period, followed by an intervention, which is then followed by an observation period after the intervention to determine if the treatment affects the outcome. As such, the subjects become their own control in the quasi-experiment. This is called an A-B design. A variant of this design is the A-B-A design, or reversal design, in which the researcher documents the baseline behavior, then administers the intervention, then withdraws or fades out the intervention, and then determines if the behavior has returned to baseline level. The number of baseline periods and intervention periods can be extended (e.g., A-B-A-B design). Multiple baseline designs involve each participant receiving an experimental treatment at a different time (i.e., multiple baselines). Finally, an alternating treatment design is a single-subject design in which the researcher compares the effects of two or more interventions in order to determine which intervention is the most effective with respect to the desired outcome.

The weaknesses of quasi/experimental/causal-comparative research designs include lack of randomization, lack of manipulation, and lack of control. There are a number of control procedures available to the researcher to promote equality of groups with respect to extraneous variables or to correct for identified inequalities (*extraneous variables*). A common method is matching. Here, every participant in one group is paired with one participant within the other group who has the identical or very similar score on the control variable. A problem with this technique is that if a participant does not have a suitable match she or he is eliminated from the study/analysis. Alternatively, groups can be controlled by comparing homogeneous groups or subgroups (e.g., females with low levels of library anxiety and females with high levels of library anxiety with respect to frequency of library visits) at different levels of the independent variable.

Third, if this question is of interest, the best approach is not to do several separate analyses but to build the control variable right into the design and to analyze the results with a statistical technique called *factorial analysis of variance* (ANOVA). ANOVA allows the researcher to determine the effect of the independent variable and the control variable, both separately and in combination. That is, it allows the researcher to determine whether there is an interaction between the independent variable and the control variable such that the independent variable operates differently at different levels of the control variable.

A fourth way to control variables is via an *analysis of covariance* (ANCOVA). This is a statistical method that can be used to equate groups on one or more variables. It adjusts scores on a dependent variable for initial differences on some other relevant variable. ANCOVA is most appropriate for (true) experimental studies (Henson, 1998).

## Experimental research

Experimental research involves a systematic, controlled investigation for the purpose of predicting and controlling phenomena. The overall objective of this type of research is to examine causality. Experimental research is considered the most powerful quantitative method because of the rigorous control of variables. Moreover, this design is considered the only quantitative research design for which causality can be established. Experimental studies always involve a manipulation of the treatment (i.e., independent) variable. In other words, in experimental research, the alleged *cause* (independent variable) is manipulated.

The most common way that manipulation of the independent variable takes place is via randomization. Specifically, participants are randomized to groups. Experimental research designs are similar to causal-comparative designs inasmuch as one or more experimental groups are compared to one or more control groups. However, the major difference is that, whereas in causal-comparative research designs the groups formed themselves or are preexisting (i.e., intact), in experimental research designs the groups are formed randomly by the researcher. Thus, the researcher has maximum control over the formation of the groups in experimental studies. By randomizing participants to groups, the chances are maximized that the groups do not differ significantly on any important variables except for the treatment. If statistically and practically significantly better outcomes are observed for the experimental group(s) than for the control group(s), then the researcher can conclude with confidence that the experimental treatment *caused* this result.

As is the case for quasi-experimental studies, in experimental studies, more control can be obtained via matching, comparing homogeneous subgroups, building the control variable right into the design and using ANOVA techniques to analyze the data, and controlling for a confounding variable by utilizing ANCOVA techniques. However, none of these techniques, per se, justify causal conclusions being made—only randomization provides this justification.

Because experimental studies result in the maximum amount of control, some textbook authors (e.g., Creswell, 2002; Gay & Airasian, 2000, 2003) say that as few as 15 participants per group is considered sufficient to detect true differences between the experimental group(s) and the control group(s). However, we believe that this recommendation is flawed because it typically leads to inadequate statistical power (i.e., < .80). Assuming that the treatment/intervention truly is effective, when randomization takes place, it is reasonable to expect a large difference to be found between the experimental and control groups. However, *at least 21 participants per group* are needed to yield a statistical power of .80 or greater for detecting a large (one-tailed) difference at the 5% level of significance (Erdfelder et al., 1996). Group sizes of 21 only yield a statistical power of .69 for detecting large differences pertaining to a one-tailed hypothesis (i.e., declaring that the experimental group is superior to the control group). Thus, we recommend that group sizes of 21 or greater always be used in experimental studies.

For example, if a researcher wanted to determine whether a learning-style based bibliographic instruction *causes* levels of library anxiety to reduce, a researcher would need to conduct an experiment. Once she had chosen her sample of, say, 42 freshmen students, she would then randomly select (i.e., randomize) 21 students to a treatment condition in which a learning-style based bibliographic instruction is implemented (i.e., experimental group) and the remaining 21 students to a treatment condition in which bibliographic instruction takes place with no learning style information included (i.e., control group). It is essential that the bibliographic instruction in both groups is identical except for the inclusion of learning-style information in the experimental group. In so doing, the effect of the learning-style component of the bibliographic instruction is isolated.

The two most popular experimental research designs are the pretest-posttest control group design and the posttest-only control group design. In the pretest-posttest control group design, the selected participants would be randomized either to the experimental or control group. Both groups would then be pretested. The experimental group would then receive the target intervention, whereas the control group would receive the comparison intervention. On completion of the intervention, both groups would then be posttested. The pretest-posttest differences would then be compared to determine if statistically significant differences prevail. If differences are found in favor of the experimental group, then the intervention could be attributed as the cause of this discrepancy. The pretest-posttest control group design is similar to the nonequivalent control group design, except in the former case, randomization occurs. It is this randomization that enables cause-and-effect statements to be made.

The posttest-only control group design is identical to the pretest-posttest control group design, except that no pretest is given to either group. Again, because participants are randomized to groups, causal statements can be proffered. It should be noted that for a design to be experimental, the randomization must take place at the *individual* level. Consequently, randomizing intact groups to interventions, as was the case in Kracker's (2000) study, does not render a design experimental and, as such, cannot justify causal statements. This is because the intact nature of the groups likely makes them different on one or more confounding variables, which would distort the findings.

In sum, experimental designs represent the apex of research among quantitative researchers. As appealing as experimental research designs are, to date, no experimental study has been undertaken in the area of library anxiety. Before firm conclusions can be made about any library-based interventions, experimental designs are needed.

## Methods of Data Collection

Alongside selecting the research design, researchers must determine the methods to be used in collecting the data. Regardless of the quantitative research design chosen, researchers must decide who to select for the study, as well as what information to collect from each participant and how to collect it. The decision about whom to select is a sampling issue, whereas the decision about what to collect and how to collect the data is an instrumentation issue.

## Sampling

Before deciding who to select for the study and how to select this sample, the population first must be identified. A (target) population is the group of individuals of interest (e.g., college library users) to whom the results are to be generalized. Unfortunately, in the overwhelming majority of studies, because of insufficient time, money, and resources, it is not realistic to study the whole population. Therefore, researchers typically select a sample, which is a subset of the target population. The goal is to select a sample from the sampling frame (i.e., the target population) that is representative of the population. Selecting a representative sample offers the best chance of generating findings that can be validly inferred to the population. Indeed, the more representative the sample, the smaller the sampling error will be. Sampling error is the difference between the sample value (i.e., statistic) and the population value (i.e., parameter).

A sample can be selected using one of the two classes of sampling: probability sampling and nonprobability sampling. In probability sampling, the researcher attempts to select members of the population that are representative of that population. On the other hand, in nonprobability sampling, the researcher chooses sample members from the population because they are accessible, available, convenient, and represent the characteristic of interest.

## Probability sampling

Probability sampling, also called random sampling and scientific sampling, comprises the following five basic types: sample random sampling, stratified random sampling, cluster sampling, systematic sampling, and multistage random sampling. In simple random sampling, individuals are selected in such a way that everyone in the population (i.e., sampling frame) has the same probability of being selected, and the selection of one person does not affect selection of any other individual (i.e., independence). In other words, in simple random sampling everyone in the sampling frame has an equal and independent chance of being selected.

Stratified random sampling represents a sampling scheme that attempts to divide a population into subpopulations such that members of each subpopulation are relatively homogeneous with respect to the variable of interest and relatively heterogeneous from members of other subgroups. In order to obtain a stratified random sample, the sampling frame is first divided into subpopulations, called *strata*, then a random sample is selected from each strata. The aim of stratified random sampling is to select a sample in such a way that identified subgroups on the population are represented in the sample in the same proportion that they exist in the population. That is, the aim of stratified random sampling is to guarantee desired representation of relevant subgroups. For example, a researcher who is interested in studying the role of race in library anxiety might use stratified random sampling techniques to select a sample whose racial groups are distributed in a similar way to the population.

Cluster random sampling is a method of sampling wherein clusters (i.e., intact groups) instead of individuals are randomly selected. For example, rather than randomly selecting all graduate students at a university, a library researcher could randomly select graduate classes and then select all students in each class. Cluster sampling is most appropriate when the population is very large or geographically spread out.

Systematic sampling is a method of sampling in which persons are selected from a list by choosing every *kth* sampling frame member, where $k$ represents the population size divided by the desired sample size. Thus, for example, if a researcher was interested in selecting 10 faculty members from a college containing 100 faculty members using systematic sampling, then $k = 100/10 = 10$. Therefore, the researcher would select every 10th faculty member on the list.

Finally, multistage random sampling involves selecting a sample in two or more stages because either the population is very large or its members cannot easily be identified. In multistage random sampling, the first stage typically involves cluster sampling, whereas subsequent stages involve simple random sampling, stratified sampling, cluster sampling, and/or systematic sampling. For instance, a researcher interested in studying library anxiety among high school students might utilize a multistage random sampling method by first selecting several high schools in a target school district at random (Stage 1: Cluster sampling), then classrooms in the selected schools at random (Stage 2: Cluster sampling), and then selecting every fifth student from each of the selected classrooms (Stage 3: Systematic sampling).

## Nonprobability sampling

It is desirable to use one of the five types of probability sampling techniques presented above because these sampling schemes tend to reduce the sampling error. Another desirable feature of probability samples is that the exact probability of selecting each sample member is known. For example, if 25 students are selected via simple random sampling from a sampling frame of 100 students, then the probability of each person being selected is .25 (i.e., 25/100). Unfortunately, in the social and behavioral sciences, which involve human participants, it is difficult to utilize probability sampling schemes. In fact, the majority of studies in the social and behavioral sciences do not utilize random samples (Leech & Onwuegbuzie, 2002; Shaver & Norton, 1980a, 1980b). Thus, researchers typically are forced to resort to the use of nonprobability sampling—also called nonrandom sampling and nonscientific sampling. Nonprobability sampling approaches include convenience sampling, purposive sampling, quota sampling, and network sampling. Convenience sampling, also called accidental sampling and haphazard sampling, involves selecting whomever happens to be (conveniently) available and willing to participate at the time. This is by far the most common sampling technique in the social and behavioral sciences. However, because sample members are not selected randomly, the probability of selection cannot be computed. Moreover, a researcher cannot be as confident that convenience samples are as representative of the population as are probability samples. Indeed, this is a weakness of virtually all research undertaken thus far in the area of library anxiety research.

In purposive sampling, also called judgmental sampling, the researchers use their experience and knowledge of the members of the sampling frame to identify criteria for selecting sample members. A major limitation of purposive sampling stems from the potential for inappropriateness in the researchers' criteria and subsequent unrepresentative sample selections.

In quota sampling, the data collectors are provided with specific characteristics and quotas of sample members to be selected. As its name suggests, once the quota has been met, no more individuals are selected. A main weakness of this form of sampling is that only those who are accessible at that time have a chance of being selected, culminating in those who are less accessible being underrepresented. For instance, if a researcher incorporated quota-sampling techniques by standing outside a library and selecting for the study the first 100 students entering the library, then the time of day the researcher selects this sample will render a significant proportion of sampling frame members inaccessible.

Network sampling, also called snowball sampling, involves the researcher asking already selected participants to identify other individuals to become members of the sample. This technique often is used when the researcher needs to select individuals from populations that are difficult to identify (e.g., individuals who are HIV positive) or when no sampling frame is available. When researchers use this sampling method, they have less control over who is selected for the study than they do when using any other sampling technique.

## Sample size

In addition to selecting a sampling scheme, researchers must decide how large their samples should be. Earlier in this chapter, we provided minimum sample sizes for correlational, quasi-experimental, and experimental studies. These recommendations stemmed from power analyses. However, we suggest that researchers select as large a sample as possible (over and above the power-driven minimum sample sizes) because, in general, larger samples culminate in smaller sampling errors. Further, large sample sizes can help to compensate, at least to some degree, for a lack of random sampling.

## Instrumentation

Library researchers have a myriad of methods of collecting research data in their arsenal. These methods include cognitive tests, affective measures, personality inventories, interest inventories, quantitative observational instruments, quantitative interviews, and secondary data (Creswell, 2002; Gay & Airasian, 2003; Johnson & Christensen, 2000). It should be noted that in any study, more than one method of data collection may be used. Each of these methods of data collection is discussed briefly below.

## Cognitive tests

Cognitive tests typically measure either aptitude or achievement. Aptitude tests are measures of someone's potential, predicting how well a person is likely to perform on a future occasion. These tests include intelligence tests. Conversely, achievement tests are constructed to provide information about how well examinees have learned the material covered by the test. If an achievement test represents a standardized measure, then an individual's performance on the test can be compared to a normative group, comprising a national group of students in the person's age or grade level who took the same test. In such cases, the test is referred to as a norm-referenced test. Alternatively, scores from a standardized test can be compared to a cut-off score to determine whether or not the person has obtained a passing score. If a passing score has been attained, then the person involved is deemed to have met the criterion. As such, these tests typically are called criterion-referenced tests. When states use a criterion-referenced test to make decisions about children, it is often referred to as a high stakes test. Both norm-referenced and criterion-referenced tests can measure a single subject area (i.e., construct) or multiple curricula areas. The latter class of tests thus contains two or more subtests.

## Affective measures

Affective measures are designed to assess a person's perceptions, beliefs, feelings, values, and attitudes toward self, others, and a variety of activities, institutions, locations, and contexts (Gay & Airasian, 2003). Affective measures can be projective or nonprojective. Projective instruments represent a class of measures that yield information whose meaning might not be directly obvious to anyone except an analyst who has received extensive training for administration and interpretation. These instruments typically yield data that are unlikely to be elicited directly. The overall goal of these instruments is to eliminate some of the problems associated with self-report measures, such as giving "socially desirable" responses. Because the purpose of such instruments is ambiguous, conscious dishonesty is reduced, and the respondents are able to *project* their true feelings. In contrast, nonprojective instruments are self-report measures.

There are at least nine ways to measure affect: rating scales, Likert-format scales, semantic differential scales, checklists, Thurstone scales, Guttman scales, magnitude scaling, Q-sort, and the Delphi technique. A rating scale is a continuum of response options that participants are instructed to use indicating their responses. A *numerical rating scale* consists of a set of numbers and "anchored" endpoints. An example of a numerical rating scale is as follows:

How do you rate your college library?

| 1 | 2 | 3 | 4 | 5 | 6 | 7 |
|---|---|---|---|---|---|---|
| Poorly | | | | | | Highly |

The above example represents a seven-point rating scale. Another type of rating scale is a *fully anchored rating scale*, which has all points anchored with descriptors. An example of such a scale is as follows:

I really like my college library.

| 1 | 2 | 3 | 4 | 5 |
|---|---|---|---|---|
| Strongly agree | Agree | Neutral | Disagree | Strongly disagree |

The above scale represents a five-point rating scale. It should be noted that the above example still represents a five-point scale even if only the descriptors are present (i.e., the numbers are excluded). According to some pscyhometricians (e.g., McKelvie, 1978), rating scales should have between 4 and 11 points, inclusive. According to these individuals, rating scales with fewer than 4 points can yield scores that are not reliable, while rating scales with greater than 11 points can be overwhelming.

Likert-format scales ask participants to indicate the extent to which they agree or disagree to a series of statements. These categories often take values from "1" to "5" either in ascending or descending order. Likert-format scales that contain an odd number of response options (e.g., five-point and seven-point Likert-format scales) include a "neutral" or "uncertain" category that typically is located in the middle—giving a *forced choice* scale. Likert-format scales differ from numerical rating scales and full anchored rating scales because whereas rating scales are analyzed item-by-item, Likert-format scales are composed of multiple items that are constructed to measure the same construct. Usually some of the statements in a Likert-type scale are expressed positively and some expressed negatively in order to avoid inserting a bias into the responses (*response set*). Scale values of negatively expressed items must be reversed prior to analysis. After key reversing has taken place, scores for each statement are summed to obtain a single score, which is then interpreted. Although values obtained of each item technically represent ordinal-level data, the summed scores usually are treated as interval-level data, thereby allowing more sophisticated statistical analyses. The LAS is an example of a five-point Likert-type instrument.

The *semantic differential,* developed by Osgood, Suci, and Tannenbaum (1957), is a scaling procedure used to ascertain the meaning that respondents attach to the subject of the attitude scale on a number of bipolar adjectives such as good-bad and positive-negative. Respondents indicate the point on the continuum that contains endpoints that are bipolar opposites. Total scores are used to indicate whether the respondent has a positive or negative attitude. Semantic differential scales usually have five to seven intervals, with a neutral attitude being assigned a score value of 0.

Checklists represent a list of response categories such that participants are asked to check all responses that apply to them. That is, multiple responses are permitted. An example of a checklist is as follows:

What do you use the library for? (Please check all categories that apply to you.):

_____ To study for a test
_____ To read books on reserve
_____ To read current newspapers
_____ To check out books
_____ To use the computerized indexes and on-line databases
_____ To use the copy machine
_____ Other (please specify): _____

*Thurstone scales* ask respondents to select from a list of statements that represent different points of view on a particular topic. Each item has an associated point value that ranges from 1 to 11. For each item, point values are determined by averaging the values of items assigned by a team of judges such that a person's attitude score represents the average point value of all the statements checked by that individual.

In contrast, the goal of *Guttman scales* is to determine whether an attitude is unidimensional. A scale is unidimensional if it yields responses such that individuals who agree with a specific statement also agree with all related preceding statements. For instance, if individuals agree with the fourth statement, then they would also agree with the first three statements.

*Magnitude scaling* represents scales containing lines that are 100 mm in length. The extremes of the stimuli are placed at each end of the line. Participants are asked to place a mark through the line to indicate the intensity of the stimuli. The analyst then uses a ruler to measure the distance between the left end of the line and the mark placed by the respondent. This measure is the value of the stimuli, which facilitates an array of statistical analyses.

*Q-sort* is a technique of comparative rating. This method utilizes cards to indicate the importance placed on various words or phrases in relation to other words or phrases in the list. Each phrase is placed on a separate card. Participants are asked to place the cards in a designated number of piles. The Q-sort method can be used to determine the priority of the most important items to include in the development of a scale.

The *Delphi technique* is used to measure the judgments of a selected group of experts, to express priorities, or to make predictions. This procedure offers a means to obtain the opinions of a wide variety of experts in order to provide feedback without the necessity of meeting together. By giving responses without the presence of other group members, the opinions of individuals cannot be altered by the persuasive behavior of others. To implement the technique, a panel of experts is first identified. Next, a questionnaire is developed with primarily, closed-ended questions, which address topics of concern. The completed questionnaires are then returned to the researcher, and the responses summarized. This summary is returned to the panel of experts, along with a second questionnaire. Respondents with extreme responses to the first round of the questions

may be asked to justify their responses. The second round of questionnaires is returned to the researcher for analysis. The procedure is repeated
until the data reflect a consensus among the panel members.

## *Personality inventories*

Personality inventories present statements or questions that describe
behaviors that typify underlying personality traits. Respondents indicate
the degree to which each statement is indicative of them. Some personality inventories contain checklists, wherein the respondents check items
that they feel represent them well. Other personality inventories contain
rating scales or Likert-format items.

## *Interest inventories*

Interest inventories ask respondents to indicate their likes and dislikes,
such as the types of activities they prefer (Gay & Airasian, 2003). An
individual's responses typically are compared to known interest patterns.
That is, responses are compared to the patterns of persons who best represent the underlying interest.

## *Quantitative observations*

An alternative way of collecting data is via quantitative observations, also
called structured observations. Here, the researcher observes behavior and
records scores on a checklist, scoring sheet, or rating scale. Quantitative
observations may involve observational sampling techniques. Two such
techniques are time-interval sampling and event sampling. Time interval
involves checking for events during time intervals that are specified prior
to the actual collection of data, whereas event sampling involves making
observations only after a specific event has taken place. An important
advantage of observational instruments is that participants' actual behavior can be identified, instead of their perceptions, beliefs, feelings, values,
or attitudes. However, relative to self-report measures, collecting quantitative observations can be time consuming and expensive. Also, some
types of observations are difficult to quantify.

## Quantitative interviews

Quantitative interviews denote structured interviews. Interview schedules or protocols are used for these interviews. These schedules essentially represent a script written by the interviewee.

## Secondary data

Secondary data are data that were originally collected and recorded at an earlier occasion, often by a different researcher(s), and typically for a different purpose than the current research problem of interest. In quantitative research, secondary data can be virtually any kind of empirical information or qualitative information that can be quantified in a reliable manner. These data can be extracted from official documents and personal documents. Secondary data also can be extracted via archival data sets, which abound.

## Scales of measurement

All the instruments discussed above generate response options to questions or statements that measure (or observe) variables in one of the following four units: nominal, ordinal, interval, or ratio. These units are called scales of measurement. Nominal scales, which are the simplest form of measurement, categorize persons or objects into two or more categories such that each category is exclusive and exhaustive, and such that members of a given category have a common set of characteristics. The categories, which differ in quality but not quantity, can represent either true categories (naturally occurring classifications, e.g., gender) or artificial categories (categories operationally defined by researcher; e.g., anxious: high vs. low). Nominal scales are useful for identification; however, these scales cannot be added, subtracted, divided, or multiplied. Nor can they be ranked.

Ordinal scales classify and rank persons or objects with respect to the degree to which they possess a characteristic. Interval scales allow the researcher to rank order participants. However, because the intervals between ranks are not equal, ordinal scales do not indicate how much higher one data point is than is any other data point. Although it is a more precise measurement than is a nominal scale, it often does not allow the level of precision desired in a research study.

Interval scales have all the characteristics of a nominal and ordinal scale, but also are based on predetermined equal intervals between adjacent numbers. Simply put, interval scales imply that the difference between any two adjacent numbers on the scale is equal to the difference between any two other adjacent numbers. However, interval scales do not have a true zero point (e.g., temperature); rather, there is an arbitrary minimum and maximum point. Therefore, a score of zero does not indicate an absence of the characteristic or attribute being measured. Interval-scale scores can be added or subtracted, but cannot be multiplied or divided. More specifically, ratios cannot be computed from interval scales.

Ratio scales are the highest and most precise levels of measurement. Such scales have all the advantages of the other types of scales and, in addition, they have a meaningful true zero point (e.g., height, weight, time, distance, and speed). Therefore, a score of zero indicates an absence of the characteristic or attribute being measured.

An important feature of these four scales of measurement is that they are hierarchical with respect to levels of precision. As such, a higher-level scale can be converted easily to a lower-level scale; however, the converse is not true. For example, a set of heights measured in inches or centimeters (i.e., ratio scale) can be converted to an ordinal scale (by ranking the heights) or to a nominal scale (by classifying the heights; e.g., tall, medium, short). However, knowledge that a person is tall does not provide information about the person's height. This implies that higher scales of measurements provide more information than do their lower-level counterparts. Moreover, it should be noted that when analyzing data, a statistic (e.g., rank) that is appropriate for a lower level of measurement (e.g., ordinal) can be applied to data representing a higher level of measurement (e.g., ratio). However, the reverse is not true. Therefore, a researcher should attempt to collect data using the highest scale of measurement.

## Psychometric properties of instrument

Whatever quantitative measure is used for a study, researchers always should assess its psychometric properties for the underlying sample. More specifically, researchers should assess the validity and reliability of scores yielded by *every* sample.

## Score validity

As noted in chapter 1, validity entails the appropriateness of interpretations made from instrument scores. Thus, researchers always should look for evidences of score validity every time an instrument is used. The three main evidences of validity are (a) content-related validity (i.e., the degree to which an instrument measures an intended domain of interest), comprising face validity (i.e., the extent to which the instrument appears relevant, important, and interesting to the respondent), item validity (i.e., the extent to which instrument items are relevant to measurement of the domain of interest), and sampling validity (i.e., how well the instrument samples the domain being measured); (b) criterion-related validity (i.e., the extent to which instrument scores predict scores on another measure either in the approximate present [i.e., concurrent validity] or in the future [i.e., predictive validity]); and (c) construct-related validity (i.e., the degree to which scores represent the underlying construct). These three evidences of validity were described in more detail in chapter 1 when we examined the psychometric properties of the Library Anxiety Scale.

## Score reliability

In quantitative research, reliability refers to "the repeatability of the behavior elicited by the test and the consistency of the resultant scores" (American Educational Research Association, American Psychological Association, and National Council on Measurement in Education [AERA/ APA/NCME], 1999, p. 30) or the degree to which scores yielded by an instrument administered to certain individuals at a specific point in time and under certain conditions are reproducible (Allen & Yen, 1979; Crocker & Algina, 1986; Onwuegbuzie & Daniel, 2002b, in press). The four most common methods of estimating a reliability coefficient are (a) administering an instrument to the same group of individuals on two or more occasions and correlating the paired scores (i.e., *test-retest reliability*, or *stability reliability*); (b) administering two different measures of a construct at essentially the same time to the same group of individuals and then correlating the paired scores (i.e., *equivalence reliability*, or *alternate forms reliability*); (c) administering two different measures of a construct at two separate occasions to the same group of individuals and then correlating the paired scores (i.e., *coefficient of stability and equivalence*); and (d) estimating the reliability of scores based on alternate configurations of the items across one administration of the instrument (i.e., *coefficient of internal consistency*). As many of these methods of estimating score reliability as appropriate should be assessed every time an instrument is administered. In any case, because the reliability index is based on one administration (i.e., one set of scores), score internal consistency always should be computed and reported for rating scales, Likert-format scales, and the like. For quantitative observational measures, either score interrater reliability estimates (i.e., reliability of scores from two or more raters) or score intrareliability estimates (i.e., reliability of two or more ratings of the same individuals by the same rater) should be documented. (For more discussion of score reliability, the reader is referred to chapter 1 and chapter 5.)


## QUALITATIVE RESEARCH PARADIGM

### Research Designs

The qualitative paradigm is regarded as the constructivist or naturalistic approach (Lincoln & Guba, 1985), the interpretative approach (Smith & Heshusius, 1986), or the postpositivist or postmodern perspective (Wolcott, 1990). For qualitative researchers, the only reality is that which is constructed by the individuals involved in the research process. Thus, multiple realities exist in any given situation. The researcher needs to report honestly and comprehensively these realities and to rely on the interpretations of informants. Qualitative researchers interact with those they study, often seeking to minimize the distance between themselves and the object of research.

Qualitative researchers admit the value-laden nature of the study and actively report their values and biases, as well as the value nature of the information gathered from the research. The language of the study is often written in the first person and is much more personal than empirical reports. Qualitative researchers often use different terminology than do quantitative researchers. In qualitative studies, the research problem needs to be explored because little information exists on the topic. The variables are largely unknown, and the researcher wants to focus on the context that may shape the understanding of the phenomenon being studied. In many qualitative studies, a theory base does not guide the study because those available are inadequate, incomplete, or simply missing. Qualitative researchers tend to use a more inductive form of logic. This type of reasoning provides *context-bound* information leading to patterns or theories that help to explain a phenomenon. Broadly speaking, qualitative research is the collection, analysis, and interpretation of words and observations. Qualitative studies are conducted in order to increase insights and generate meaning for whole situations and abstract concepts. The outcome of qualitative research is the development or expansion of theory.

Creswell (1994) divides the qualitative research process into the introduction and procedure components. According to this conceptualization, the introduction component, the initial stage of the qualitative process, involves the following elements: the statement of the problem, purpose of the study, the grand tour question and subquestions, definitions, delimitations and limitations, and the significance of the study. The procedure section involves the following: assumptions and rationale for a qualitative design, the type of design used, data collection procedures, data analysis procedures, methods for verification, and the outcome of the study and its relation to theory and literature. As noted by Creswell (1994), the major types of qualitative research are *historical, case study, phenomenological, ethnographic, and grounded theory.* Each of these will be described in turn.

## Historical research

Historical research is a narrative description or analysis of events that occurred in the remote past. Historical research is useful because it often develops from an attempt to prevent past mistakes from being repeated, as well as helping our understanding of present situations. Data are obtained from records, artifacts, or verbal reports. The reader may recall that historical research was one of the five quantitative research designs and may wonder whether that design is different from the design presently being discussed. Actually, historical research under the quantitative paradigm is different than historical research under the qualitative paradigm. With the former, the focus is on the collection of numerical data, typically to test hypotheses about relationships or differences. Indeed, quantitative historical research designs also are called historiography. On the other hand, qualitative historical research involves the collection of events, biographies, and the like.

## Case studies

Case studies represent an exploration of a single entity or phenomenon (i.e., "case") characterized by time and activity (Creswell, 2002; Gay & Airasian, 2000; Johnson & Christensen, 2000). The case could be an event, a process, a program, an institution, an individual, or a particular group. In case studies, detailed information about the case is collected using a variety of data-collecting procedures during a sustained period of time. A case may be studied because it is unusual and therefore of particular interest (i.e., an intrinsic case). Alternatively, a case may be selected from among other cases to provide an example of the underlying issue (i.e., an instrumental case). Multiple cases may be used to provide further insight into a topic (i.e., a collective case study) (Creswell, 2002).

## Phenomenological research

Phenomenological research is inductive, descriptive research that attempts to understand the response of the whole human being, not just understanding specific parts or behaviors (Creswell, 1994). The aim of phenomenological research is to describe an experience as it is lived by the individual. As a method, the procedure involves studying a small number of participants through persistent observation, prolonged engagement, and triangulation to develop patterns and relationships of meaning (Lincoln & Guba, 1985). Through this process, the researcher uses his or her experiences to understand those of the informants. An example of a phenomenological research is the qualitative component of Onwuegbuzie's (1997a) study. Onwuegbuzie (1997a) attempted to study the whole experience of graduate students as they undertook their research proposals.

## Ethnographic research

Ethnographic research is the investigation of cultures through an in-depth study of the members of the culture (the term *culture* is being used generically). This type of research attempts to study an intact cultural group in a natural setting during a prolonged period of time by collecting, primarily, observational data (Creswell, 1994, 1998, 2002; Gay & Airasian, 2000; Johnson & Christensen, 2000). The research process is flexible and typically evolves contextually in response to lived realities encountered in the field setting. According to Creswell (2002), ethnographic research designs typically include the following characteristics: (a) exploration of cultural themes drawn from cultural anthropology; (b) investigation of a culture-sharing group; (c) study of shared patterns of behavior, attitudes, beliefs, and language; (d) collection of data through fieldwork activities; (e) identification, description, and analysis of themes about the culture-sharing group; (f) presentation of themes and interpretation within the context, setting, or time of the group; and (g) reflexivity by the researcher about her or his influence on the study site and on the cultural group and its responses.

## Grounded theory research

Grounded theory research is an attempt to construct a theory by using multiple stages of data collection and the refinement and interrelationship of categories of information (Strauss & Corbin, 1990). Creswell (2002) defines a grounded theory as "a systematic, qualitative procedure used to generate a theory that explains, at a broad conceptual level, a process, an action, or interaction about a substantive topic" (p. 439). Two primary characteristics of this design are the constant comparison of data with emerging categories, and theoretical sampling of different groups in order to maximize the similarities and the differences of information (Lincoln & Guba, 1985). Creswell (2002) outlined the following characteristics of grounded theory designs: (a) studying a process related to an important issue, (b) sampling theoretically involving simultaneous and sequential data collection and data analysis, (c) constantly comparing data with an emerging theory, (d) selecting a core category as the central phenomenon for the theory, and (e) generating a theory that explains the observed process.

According to Creswell (2002), there are three major grounded theory designs, namely: the systematic design, the emerging design, and the constructivist design. The systematic design is the most rigorous type of design that emphasizes the use of the data analysis steps open coding (i.e., forming initial categories of information about the underlying phenomenon by segmenting information); axial coding (i.e., selecting one open coding category, positioning it at the center of the process being studied, and relating other categories to it); and selective coding (developing and writing a theory from the relationships found among the categories in the axial coding stage). The emerging design, in contrast to the systematic design, involves allowing a theory to emerge from the data instead of using specific, preset categories such as that used in the axial coding stage. Finally, the constructivist design focuses on the views, attitudes, beliefs, values, feelings, philosophies, and assumptions of individuals rather than concentrating on facts and describing behavior. The grounded theory researcher should decide beforehand which type of design is the most appropriate for his or her particular study.

Creswell (2002) identified eight steps of grounded theory designs: (a) deciding if a grounded theory design best addresses the research problem, (b) identifying a process to investigate, (c) seeking approval to conduct the study and access to the study site, (d) conducting theoretical sampling, (e) coding the data, (f) using selective coding and developing the theory, (g) validating the emergent theory, and (h) writing a grounded theory research report.

Grounded theory methodology emphasizes observation and the development of practice-based intuitive relationships between variables. The research process involves formulation and the testing and redevelopment of propositions until a theory evolves. As such, the theory derived in this type of design is a process theory. An excellent example of a grounded theory design is Mellon's (1986) landmark study of library anxiety described in previous chapters.

## Methods of Data Collection

In addition to selecting the research design, qualitative researchers must determine the methods to be used in collecting the data. As is the case in quantitative studies, regardless of the qualitative research design chosen, researchers must decide who to select for the study, what information to collect from each participant, and how to collect these data. Even though the goal of qualitative research often is not to generalize samples to the population but to capture the voice of each participant (Connolly, 1998), the decision about whom to select still represents a sampling issue. In fact, decisions about whom to select is just as important in qualitative studies as it is in quantitative investigations. At the same time, interpretivists also have to decide on what information to collect and how to collect the data.

## Sampling

Before deciding whom to select for the study and how to select this sample, the qualitative researcher must decide what the objective of the study is. If the objective of the study is to generalize the findings to a population (i.e., confirmatory), then the researcher should strive to select a sample that is both random and large, and the section on sampling in the quantitative research section above becomes very pertinent. Conversely, if the intent is not to generalize to a population but to obtain insights into processes (e.g., educational, psychological, sociological) that prevail within a specific location, as will typically be the case, then the qualitative researcher purposefully selects individuals, groups, and settings. Moreover, in these instances, the qualitative researcher attempts purposively to select individuals, groups, and settings that maximize understanding of the underlying phenomenon. As such, sampling in qualitative research is referred to as purposeful sampling. Here, individuals, groups, and settings are considered for selection if they are "information rich" (Patton, 1990, p. 169).

Miles and Huberman (1994) have identified 16 strategies for purposive sampling. These strategies are differentiated with respect to whether they are used before data collection has started or after data collection begins (Creswell, 2002). Also, the appropriateness of each strategy is dependent on the research objective and research question. The 16 strategies are maximum variation sampling, homogeneous sampling, critical case sampling, theory-based sampling, confirming and disconfirming cases sampling, snowball/chain sampling, extreme case sampling, typical case sampling, intensity sampling, politically important cases sampling, random purposeful sampling, stratified purposeful sampling, criterion sampling, opportunistic sampling, mixed purposive sampling, and convenience sampling. Each of these strategies is discussed below.

### Maximum variation sampling

The first type of purposive sampling is called maximum variation sampling. In this method, a wide range of individuals, groups, and settings is purposively selected such that all or most types of individuals, groups, and settings are chosen for the study. In this way, multiple perspectives of individuals can be presented that exemplify the complexity of the world (Creswell, 2002). For example, a library researcher might first identify the number of languages spoken by students at a particular college, and then purposively select a sample such that every language is represented.

### Homogeneous sampling

In stark contrast to maximum variation sampling, homogeneous sampling involves sampling individuals, groups, or settings because they all possess similar attributes or traits. Participants are selected for the study based on membership in a subgroup or unit that has specific characteristics. This approach is often used to select focus groups.

### Critical case sampling

In critical case sampling, individuals, groups, or settings are selected that accentuate the phenomenon of interest such that the researcher can learn much more about the phenomenon than would have been learned without including these critical cases. For example, in studying burnout among librarians, a researcher might select a library that has an extremely large staff turnover.

### Theory-based sampling

In theory-based sampling, individuals, groups, or settings are selected because they assist the qualitative researcher to generate or to expand a theory. For example, Mellon (1988) selected a theory-based purposive sample in order to develop her theory of library anxiety.

## Confirming and disconfirming cases sampling

This form of sampling often is used after data collection has begun. Confirming and disconfirming cases sampling is a purposeful strategy that is utilized during the research process to follow up on specific cases in an attempt to explore or to confirm initial findings. The former (i.e., exploration) tends to improve interpretation of the findings, whereas the latter (i.e., confirmation) tends to assist in data validation.

## Snowball sampling

This sampling approach is identical to network sampling used by quantitative researchers. As is the case for quantitative research, snowball sampling is a method of purposive sampling that usually comes to the fore after data collection has begun. Snowball sampling involves asking participants who have already been selected for the study to recruit other participants.

## Extreme case sampling

In extreme case sampling, an outlying case or one that exhibits some extreme characteristic(s) is studied. The procedure is to select extreme cases and then to compare them. For example, a researcher might compare an extremely large library and a very small library. Or a researcher can compare students with extremely high levels of library anxiety and those with little or no anxiety with respect to thoughts, feelings, perceptions, and/or behaviors. The logic behind this strategy is that extreme cases may yield thick and rich data.

## Typical case sampling

In typical case sampling, the researcher studies an individual, group, or setting that is typical or average. The challenge is to determine what a typical case is. The researcher should consult several experts in the area of study to obtain a consensus as to what example(s) is typical of the phenomenon and should, therefore, be studied (Johnson & Christensen, 2000). For example, a researcher could study a librarian who has worked at the institution for an average number of years, as determined by local norms.

## Intensity sampling

In intensity sampling, the researcher studies individuals, groups, or settings that manifest the phenomenon intensely but not extremely. For example, an investigator might study several individuals who have levels of library anxiety that are high but not unusual so.

## Politically important cases sampling

In politically important sampling, the researcher selects salient informants who may need to be included/excluded because they connect with politically sensitive issues expected in the analysis (Miles & Huberman, 1994). For instance, an investigator might select a library director for study.

## Random purposeful sampling

In random purposeful sample, the researcher chooses cases at random from the sampling frame of purposefully selected sample. That is, the researcher first obtains a list of individuals of interest for study (i.e., purposeful sampling frame) and then randomly selects a desired number of individuals from this list for the investigation. Although not stated by Miles and Huberman (1994) or other qualitative methodologists, when selecting a random purposeful sample, the researcher can use any of the random sampling techniques discussed in the section of quantitative sampling techniques: simple random sampling, stratified random sampling, cluster random sampling, systematic random sampling, and multi-stage random sampling. According to Miles and Huberman (1994), random purposeful sample "adds credibility to sample when potential purposeful sample is too large" (p. 28).

## Stratified purposeful sampling

Stratified purposeful sampling is similar to stratified random sampling inasmuch as the sampling frame is divided into subgroups such that members of each subgroup are relatively homogeneous with respect to the variable of interest and relatively heterogeneous from members of other subgroups. To obtain a stratified purposeful sample, the sampling frame is first divided into subpopulations, called *strata*; then a purposeful sample is selected from each strata. The goal of stratified purposeful sampling is to obtain desired representation of relevant subgroups. Such a sampling scheme can facilitate group comparisons (Miles & Huberman, 1994). For example, a researcher who is interested in studying the role of language in library anxiety might use stratified purposeful sampling techniques to select a sample whose language is distributed in a desired manner.

## Criterion sampling

In criterion sampling, individuals, groups, or settings are selected that meet some criterion. For example, a researcher can select students who have attended at least one bibliographic instruction course. According to Miles and Huberman (1994), this sampling technique typically is used for quality assurance.

## Opportunistic sampling

In opportunistic sampling, the researcher capitalizes on opportunities during the data collection stage to select important cases. These cases could represent typical, negative, extreme, or critical cases (Johnson & Christensen, 2000). Thus, opportunistic sampling takes place after the study begins in order to take advantage of developing events. As such, the sample emerges during the study. This form of sampling is particularly useful when the researcher is unable or unwilling to declare in advance of the inquiry every case that will be included in the study. In using this technique, the researcher must be careful not to be distracted away from the original research objective and purpose. However, opportunistic sampling can lead to useful and surprising findings. For example, in studying library anxiety, a researcher might begin by selecting a random purposeful sample of library users. During the course of data collection, the researcher identifies a library-anxious student who has found a way to manage her or his anxiety levels. Because a study of this person could provide new insights about how students can cope with high levels of library anxiety, the researcher studies this individual in an in-depth manner.

## Mixed purposeful sampling

This method of sampling involves the mixing of more than one sampling strategy. For instance, a researcher might begin by selecting two samples: one via extreme case sampling and the other via typical case sampling. The researcher could then compare the results emerging from both samples. Consequently, mixed purposeful sampling can help to triangulate data (Miles & Huberman, 1994).

## Convenience sampling

Convenience sampling techniques used by qualitative researchers is the same as those used by quantitative researchers. That is, convenience sampling involves selecting individuals or groups that happen to be (conveniently) available and are willing to participate at the time.

## Sample size

In addition to selecting a sampling scheme, qualitative researchers must decide how large their samples should be. As presented earlier, quantitative researchers have guidelines for selecting their samples. In particular, they can conduct a priori power analyses to determine an appropriate minimum sample size. However, rules for selecting samples in qualitative research are less clearly stated. Lincoln and Guba (1985) suggest that the foremost criterion of sample size is redundancy of information. In other words, Lincoln and Guba (1985) recommend that sampling should be terminated when no new information is extracted from new units. That is, a sample size is adequate in qualitative research if additional units yield data saturation (Lincoln & Guba, 1985, p. 202).

Unfortunately, for many beginning qualitative researchers, the sample size recommendations provided by Lincoln and Guba (1985) are not explicit enough to be truly helpful. As such, Onwuegbuzie and Leech (2003a) outline how to conduct what they term *qualitative power analyses*. These authors build on Onwuegbuzie's (in press-c) argument that in qualitative research, words that arise from individuals, or observations that emerge from a particular setting, can be treated as sample units of data that represent the total number of words/observations existing from that sample member/context. That is why methodologists recommend *persistent observations* and *prolonged engagement* in qualitative studies (e.g., Lincoln & Guba, 1985). Moreover, Onwuegbuzie (in press-d) contends that in interpreting data, qualitative researchers generalize the *sample* of words and observations that arise in the study to the *population* of words/observations (i.e., the *truth space*) representing the underlying context.

Therefore, Onwuegbuzie and Leech (2003a) recommend that before deciding on an appropriate sample size, qualitative researchers should identify a corpus of interpretive studies that used the same design as in the proposed study (e.g., grounded theory, ethnography) in which data saturation was reached. The researcher should then examine the sample sizes used in these studies with a view to selecting a sample size that is within the range used in these investigations. In addition, when observations or interviews are the data collection methods of choice, Onwuegbuzie and Leech (2003a) contend that researchers should use the extant literature to determine an appropriate number of observations/interviews that are needed and an adequate length of time for each observation/interview that would satisfy Lincoln and Guba's (1985) criteria of persistent observation and prolonged engagement, respectively.

More specifically, some methodologists have provided more explicit guidelines for selecting samples in qualitative studies. In particular, Creswell (2002) has recommended that qualitative researchers should:

- study one cultural-sharing group in an ethnography
- examine three–five cases in a case study
- interview 15–20 people during a grounded theory study
- explore the narrative stories of one individual in narrative research (p. 197)

In addition, Creswell (1998) recommend interviews with up to 10 people in phenomenological research and interviews with 20–30 people to achieve detail in grounded theory. Johnson and Christensen (2000) suggest that focus groups usually contain 6–12 individuals. Finally, although typically not the case, if the qualitative researcher's goal is to make generalizations beyond the sample, then as large a sample as possible should be selected using random sampling techniques where possible. Unfortunately, too many qualitative researchers find it difficult to refrain from making inferences to the population based on a small sample (Onwuegbuzie & Daniel, 2003).

## Instrumentation

Qualitative forms of research data can be classified as being one of the following four types: (a) observations, (b) interviews, (c) documents, and d) audio-visual materials. Observation represents the process of collecting firsthand information by observing individuals, groups, and settings. In contrast to quantitative researchers, interpretivists typically do not use instruments that were developed by other researchers. Rather, they tend to design their own data-collecting tools. Effective observing involves careful attention to detail and good listening skills, as well as management of threats to trustworthiness of the data such as deception of observees (Hammersley & Atkinson, 1995). Researchers can assume the role of participant observer or nonparticipant observer. Participant observers take part in activities in the setting that they observe such that they assume the role of "insider" observer. While participating in activities, participant observers record observations. Conversely, nonparticipant observers record observations without becoming involved in the activities and, as such, serve as "outsider" observers. Observations that are recorded during an observation are called field notes.

An interview is the process wherein researchers ask one or more individuals selected for the study to respond to a series of generally open-ended questions and then record their answers. This information is then transcribed into a data file for subsequent analysis. Interviews can be structured, unstructured, or semistructured. In structured interviews, primarily closed-ended responses are of interest. On the other hand, in unstructured interviews, open-ended answers are sought. Finally, in semistructured interviews, both closed- and open-ended responses are elicited. Interviews can involve one-on-one interviews, focus group interviews, telephone interviews, or e-mail interviews. One-on-one interviews consist of interviews conducted one person at a time. These are the most labor-intensive types of interviews. Focus group interviews represent interviews involving a group of individuals, typically 4–6 (Creswell, 2002) or 6–12 (Johnson & Christensen, 2000) individuals, in which the researcher asks a small number of general questions and elicits responses from all persons in the group. A telephone interview is the process of collecting information using the telephone. Finally, an e-mail interview consists of collecting data through interviews from individuals using websites, listservs, or the Internet.

Documents represent the third source of information. They consist of public and private records to which qualitative researchers have access. These documents include newspapers, personal journals and diaries, official memoranda, letters, jottings individuals write to themselves, e-mail messages, minutes of meetings, records in the public domain, and archival material stored in libraries.

Audio-visual material consists of images or sounds that are collected to help the qualitative researchers understand the underlying phenomenon. These include photographs, digital images, videotapes, pictures, paintings, and physical traces of images (e.g., fingerprints).

## MIXED-METHODOLOGICAL RESEARCH PARADIGM

### Emergence of Pragmatism

The previous two sections have provided a detailed description of the research designs associated with two of the three major research paradigms. Before discussing the third research paradigm, the mixed-methodological paradigm, a little historical context is needed to illustrate how each of these paradigms emerged, as well as their primary similarities and differences. Since the latter part of the 19th century, a passionate and relentless debate has taken place regarding the quantitative and qualitative research paradigms. From these arguments, purists have emerged on both sides: quantitative purists and qualitative purists. Quantitative purists express assumptions that are consistent with a positivist philosophy, whereas qualitative purists (e.g., postpositivists, poststructuralists, and postmodernists) categorically reject positivism.

Prior to the turn of the 20th century, within the physical sciences, as well as within other fields, research evolved from the ontological, epistemological, axiological, rhetorical, and methodological assumptions of logical positivism, a philosophy of science that championed the cause of the pursuit of knowledge. Logical positivism soon took a leading role in the field of science, wherein "hard" data were collected formally and systematically and validated objectively. Mathematical and statistical procedures were developed for analyzing these data using probabilistic and inferential models in an attempt to explain, predict, and control phenomena.

By the beginning of the 20th century, social scientists began to question seriously whether they were justified in using the scientific method of the physical sciences to study human behavior (Smith & Heshusius, 1986). In particular, Auguste Comte, the French philosopher and founder of positivism, and Wihlem Dilthey, the German philosopher, emerged at the extreme ends of the continuum. Whereas Comte's positivistic philosophy represented the most ardent support for the use of the scientific method, Dilthey's interpretive/hermeneutical approach to science is recognized as the first serious challenge to positivism (Smith, 1983).

Comte believed that human behavior should be treated as entities in much the same way as physical scientists treated physical phenomena. He asserted that the observer could be separated from the target that was being observed. That is, he contended that the role of the behavioral and social scientist was independent of the observable reality. Those who agreed with Comte further argued that social science research was value-free, that time- and context-free generalizations were feasible, and that real causes to behavioral and social scientific outcomes could be ascertained reliably and validly. As such, social science researchers should attempt to extricate their biases, move beyond common-sense preconceptions, and not become emotionally involved with the object of study (Smith, 1983). Social science positivists called for value-free scientists who were neutrally rhetorical. According to this position, dissemination of findings should involve an exclusively formal writing style using the impersonal voice and specific terminology, in which the discovery of social laws was the major focus.

Dilthey challenged the core ideology of positivism, proposing an alternative methodology for the behavioral and social sciences. He noted that whereas the physical sciences dealt with inanimate objects that could exist independently of human beings, the behavioral and social sciences focused on the processes and products of the human mind (Ermarth, 1978; Hodges, 1944, 1952). Consequently, Dilthey contended that research into human behavior should not be performed with the methods of the physical sciences due to a fundamental difference in object of study. He further contended that no objective social reality existed. Unfortunately, he faced a dilemma that he was unable to solve. That is, Dilthey reasoned that if meaning depends on the context and if multiple realities existed such that understanding was hermeneutical, then interpretation would depend on the reality of the interpreter. Given this situation, Dilthey questioned whether an optimal interpretation would exist and, if so, how one best interpretation could be derived. Thus, he was caught between assumptions that were epistemologically antifoundational and a desire for criteria that were foundational (Smith, 1983). Unfortunately, Dilthey was not able to find a solution to this dilemma (Hughes, 1958).

German sociologist Max Weber was greatly influenced by Dilthey. However, Weber disagreed with Dilthey in important ways. In particular, he believed that the physical sciences and behavioral and social sciences differed not because of an inherent discrepancy in subject matter but rather because of a different interest taken in the subject matter (Smith, 1983). Nevertheless, Weber believed that both quantitative and qualitative research paradigms had important limitations. Specifically, Weber contended that positivism could not attach meaning to a behavioral and social reality, whereas idealism did not acknowledge the possibility that a social reality might be the prevailing reality. Weber's solution to Dilthey's problem, therefore, was to attempt to unify the positivist and interpretivist perspectives (Outhwaite, 1975). Unfortunately, Weber failed in his task of bringing together quantitative and qualitative paradigms (Outhwaite, 1983). Therefore, shortly after the turn of the 20th century, these two paradigms were in direct opposition to one another. This polarization continued beyond World War II.

During the 1950s and 1960s, *postpositivism* emerged (e.g., Hanson, 1958; Popper, 1959). Postpositivism represented a compromise between quantitative and qualitative paradigms. For example, postpositivists believed that reality is constructed and that research is influenced by the values of investigators, while, at the same time, they believed that some

lawful, reasonably stable relationships among behavioral and social phenomena exist. Nevertheless, advocates of this school of thought tended to
utilize deductive logic, with much of their research being influenced by
hypotheses and theories, which were reflected in a predominantly formal
writing style using the impersonal voice.

Soon after, postpositivism gave rise to more radical paradigms (e.g.,
*constructivism, interpretivism, naturalism*). Many theorists representing
these new iconoclastic paradigms began to argue for the superiority and
exclusiveness of poststructuralism, postmodernism, and the like. These
idealists contended that multiple-constructed realities (i.e., *relativism*)
abound, that time- and context-free generalizations cannot be proffered,
that research is value bound, that logic flows from specific to general, that
it is impossible to distinguish between cause and effects, that the observer
and object of observation are connected, and that knower and known are
inseparable. One of their trademarks became their informal writing style
using personal voice and minimal definitions. The extreme relativists, like
positivists, believed in the purity of their paradigm, advancing the *Incompatibility Thesis* (Howe, 1988), which posited that paradigms and methods could not and should not be mixed.

The multitrait-multimethod approach to validating psychological traits
developed by Campbell and Fiske (1959) provided the impetus for the
*pragmatist* movement. Campbell and Fiske (1959) advanced a process
whereby researchers would collect multiple measures of multiple traits,
and then evaluate each measure by at least two methods. Scores were then
correlated and placed into what was called a multitrait-multimethod
matrix. A researcher could then ascertain whether the trait was valid by
examining this matrix and determining whether the measures of the trait
correlated higher with each other than they did with measures of different
traits using different methods. The information extracted from these
correlations provided evidence about different types of validity (e.g., criterion-related validity, construct-related validity). This multitrait-multimethod technique today is used routinely by instrument developers.

As a result of Campbell and Fiske's (1959) initiative, in the 1960s,
pragmatists began to advocate the use of mixed methodologies (i.e., combining quantitative and qualitative research designs). Mixed methods
became very popular in the 1980s. In the 1990s came the emergence of

mixed-model studies (i.e., combining quantitative and qualitative techniques within various stages of the research process) (Tashakkori & Teddlie, 1998), with the most recent development in this school being the elaboration of a comprehensive framework for conducting mixed-methodological data analyses (Onwuegbuzie & Teddlie, 2003).

Pragmatists entertained the existence of causal relationships, but stated that it may not be possible to pin down many of these causal links. Further, pragmatists accepted external reality and believed that values played a role in the interpretation of findings. However, they believed in the existence of both subjective and objective perspectives. Contending that research is influenced by theory/hypothesis and by observations, facts, and evidence, pragmatists utilized both inductive and deductive reasoning, using explanations that best yielded desired outcomes, and integrating formal and informal writing styles that used both the personal and impersonal voice.

The pragmatist philosophy was congruent with the *Compatibility Thesis* (Howe, 1988; Reichardt & Rallis, 1994), which posited that quantitative and qualitative research traditions were neither mutually exclusive nor interchangeable. Rather, the actual relationship between the two paradigms was one of isolated events lying on a continuum of scientific inquiry (Howe, 1988; Reichardt & Rallis, 1994). Moreover, pragmatists asserted that the logic of justification did not prevent researchers from combining quantitative and qualitative research designs. In other words, pragmatists asserted that a false dichotomy exists between quantitative and qualitative approaches, and that researchers should make the most efficient use of both paradigms in order to understand behavioral and social phenomena.

Thus, as noted by Rossman and Wilson (1985), three major schools of thought prevail with respect to the relationship between quantitative and qualitative research. *Purists* assert that paradigms and methods should not be mixed and promote mono-method studies. *Situationalists* contend that specific methods are more appropriate for certain situations. Finally, *pragmatists* attempt to combine methods within a single study (Creswell, 1994; Tashakkori & Teddlie, 1998), or across a series of studies (Onwuegbuzie & Teddlie, 2003; Tashakkori & Teddlie, 1998). The difference between these three perspectives relates to the extent to which each believes that quantitative and qualitative approaches coexist and can be combined (Onwuegbuzie, 2002c). Indeed, as noted by Onwuegbuzie (2002c), these three camps can be conceptualized as lying on a continuum, with purists and pragmatists lying on opposite ends, and situationalists lying somewhere between purists and pragmatists.

## Misconceptions Held by Purists and Situationalists

As noted by Onwuegbuzie (2002c), many of the differences that are perceived to prevail between quantitative and qualitative research stem from the misconceptions and flawed claims of proponents of both camps. On the positivist side of the spectrum, the barriers that they have built arise from their narrow definition of the concept of "science." In particular, positivists claim that the essence of science is objective verification, and that their methods are objective. However, positivists overlook the fact that many research decisions are made throughout the research process that precede objective verification decisions. For example, in developing instruments that yield empirical data, psychometricians select items in an attempt to represent the content domain adequately (Onwuegbuzie & Daniel, in press). Yet, choosing these items is a subjective decision at every stage of the instrument-development process. Therefore, although the final version of the instrument can lead to objective scoring, because of the subjectivity built into its development, any interpretations of the scores yielded cannot be 100% objective. Thus, as is the case for qualitative research, subjectivity is inherent in quantitative studies.

Moreover, although in the physical sciences, many properties of objects can be measured with near-perfect reliability, in the social sciences, the vast majority of measures yield scores that are, to some degree, unreliable. This is because constructs of interest in the social science fields typically represent abstractions (e.g., personality, achievement, intelligence, motivation, locus of control) that must be measured indirectly (Onwuegbuzie & Daniel, 2002b, in press). Failure to attain 100% score reliability implies measurement error, which, in turn, introduces subjectivity into any interpretations.

Onwuegbuzie (2002c) provides other examples of subjectivity that prevail in quantitative research, including the lack of random sampling prevalent in social and behavioral science research that limits the extent to which findings can be generalized to the population, the obsessive use of the 5% level of significance to test null hypotheses, and the fact that variables can explain as little as 2% of the variance of the dependent variable to be considered statistically significant. Thus, total objective verification is not possible in quantitative research. As such, in the behavioral and social science field, at least, the techniques used by positivists are no more inherently scientific than are the procedures utilized by interpretivists.

Interpretivists also deserve criticism. In particular, their claim that multiple, contradictory, but valid accounts of the same phenomenon always prevail is extremely misleading, inasmuch as it leads many qualitative researchers to adopt an "anything goes" relativist attitude, thereby not paying adequate attention to legitimizing interpretations of their data (Onwuegbuzie, 2000c). That is, many qualitative methods of analyses "often remain private and unavailable for public inspection" (Constas, 1992, p. 254). Yet, without rigor, when do we know whether what we know is trustworthy?

## Similarities between Quantitative and Qualitative Research Approaches

There is little doubt that the most disturbing feature of the paradigm wars is the relentless focus on the differences between the two schools of thought. For some researchers and theorists, this focus has been pursued obsessively. As noted by Onwuegbuzie (2001, p. 4), "much of the quantitative-qualitative debate has involved the practice of polemics, which has tended to obfuscate rather than to clarify, and to divide rather than to unite educational researchers." In fact, the two major research paradigms have culminated in two research subcultures, "one professing the superiority of 'deep, rich observational data' and the other the virtues of 'hard, generalizable' survey data" (Sieber, 1973, p. 1335).

Yet, there are overwhelmingly more similarities between quantitative and qualitative approaches than there are differences. First and foremost, both quantitative and qualitative methods involve the use of observations to address research questions. As declared by Sechrest and Sidani (1995, p. 78), both methodologies "describe their data, construct explanatory arguments from their data, and speculate about why the outcomes they observed happened as they did."

Not acknowledged by purists on either side of the fence is the fact that both quantitative and qualitative researchers employ techniques that are relatively analogous at some level of specificity. In particular, both quantitative and qualitative researchers incorporate safeguards into their research in order to minimize confirmation bias and other sources of invalidity that have the potential to exist in every research study (Onwuegbuzie, 2000b; Sandelowski, 1986). For instance, both quantitative and qualitative researchers routinely attempt to triangulate their data. Additionally, like interpretivists, to some degree, quantitative data analysts attempt to provide viable explanations for their findings, and to make interpretive, narrative conclusions pertaining to the implications of their results (Dzurec & Abraham, 1993).

According to Dzurec and Abraham (1993), meaning is not directly dependent on the type of data collected (i.e., quantitative vs. qualitative). Rather, meaning results from the interpretation of data, whether represented by numbers or words. Whereas quantitative researchers use statistical procedures and subjective inferences to make decisions about what their data mean in the context of an a priori theoretical or conceptual framework, qualitative researchers utilize phenomenological procedures and their worldviews (Dzurec & Abraham, 1993).

Both sets of researchers select and use analytical techniques that are designed to extract maximum meaning from their data and manipulate their data so that findings have utility with respect to their respective views of reality (Dzurec & Abraham, 1993). Moreover, both types of investigators attempt to explain complex relationships that prevail in the social and behavioral science field. As such, quantitative researchers utilize multivariate techniques (Elmore & Woehlke, 1998), whereas qualitative researchers incorporate the collection of rich, thick data into their design via prolonged engagement, persistent observation, and other strategies (Lincoln & Guba, 1985).

Additionally, both quantitative and qualitative investigators use techniques to verify their findings. Quantitative researchers incorporate a variety of control procedures and random sampling techniques to maximize internal and external validity findings, respectively (Onwuegbuzie, 2003), while qualitative researchers employ a myriad of methods for assessing the truth value, credibility, verisimilitude, auditability, authenticity, or legitimacy of qualitative research. Such techniques include prolonged engagement, persistent observation, triangulation, member checking, and obtaining feedback from informants (Onwuegbuzie, 2000b).

Interestingly, data reduction typically is an essential part of the data analysis process for both quantitative and qualitative researchers. Whereas statisticians use data-reduction methods such as factor analysis and cluster analysis, interpretivists conduct thematic analyses and content analyses (Onwuegbuzie, in press-c). Thus, factors that emerge from multivariate analyses are analogous to emergent themes from thematic analyses. In fact, Onwuegbuzie (in press-c) demonstrates how themes emerging from qualitative data analyses can be factor analyzed to obtain what he termed meta-themes that subsume the original themes, thereby describing the association among these themes. Additionally, the popularization of complex multivariate analyses (e.g., path analysis, structural equation modeling, and hierarchical linear modeling), coupled with the increased emphasis on generalizability theory, allow quantitative researchers better to contextualize their findings than previously has been the case.

As noted by Newman and Benz (1998), rather than representing bipolar opposites, quantitative and qualitative research represent an interactive continuum. More specifically, the role of theory is central for both paradigms. Specifically, in qualitative research, the most common objectives are that of theory initiation and theory building, whereas in quantitative research, the most typical objectives are that of theory testing and theory modification (Newman & Benz, 1998). Clearly, neither tradition is independent of the other, nor can either school represent the whole research process. Thus, both quantitative and qualitative studies are needed to gain a more complete understanding of phenomena (Newman & Benz, 1998).

As discussed above, many similarities exist between quantitative and qualitative research. Regardless of paradigms, all research in the behavioral and social sciences is an attempt to understand human beings and the world around them. Thus, it is clear that although, presently, certain methodologies are more often associated with and utilized by one particular research tradition or the other, as contended by Dzurec and Abraham (1993, p. 75), "the objectives, scope, and nature of inquiry are consistent across methods and across paradigms." Indeed, the purity of a research paradigm is a function of the extent to which researchers belonging to that camp are prepared to conform to its underlying assumptions. If discrepancies prevail between quantitative and qualitative researchers, these differences do not stem from different goals but because these two groups of researchers have operationalized their strategies differently for reaching these goals (Dzurec & Abraham, 1993). This suggests that methodological pluralism should be promoted. The best way for this pluralism to occur is for as many researchers as possible to combine both quantitative and qualitative techniques within a single study.

## Mixed-Methodological Research Designs

As noted above, Campbell and Fiske (1959) are credited with providing the impetus for using multiple research methods. A few years later, Webb, Campbell, Schwartz, and Sechrest (1966) coined the phrase *triangulation*. Nevertheless, it was Denzin (1978) who first outlined how to triangulate. Denzin (1978, p. 291) defined triangulation as "the combination of methodologies in the study of the same phenomenon." Further, Denzin outlined the following four types of triangulation: (a) data triangulation (i.e., use of a variety of sources in a study), (b) investigator triangulation (i.e., use of several different researchers), (c) theory triangulation (i.e., use of multiple perspectives to interpret the results of a study), and (d) methodological triangulation (i.e., use of multiple methods to study a research problem).

Additionally, Denzin distinguished *within-methods* triangulation, which refers to the use of multiple quantitative or multiple qualitative approaches, from *between-methods* triangulation, involving both quantitative and qualitative approaches. He expressed a clear preference for between-methods triangulation, contending that (a) by utilizing this mixed-methods approach, "the bias inherent in any particular data source, investigators, and particularly method will be canceled out when used in conjunction with other data sources, investigators, and methods" (p. 14) and (b) "the result will be a convergence upon the truth about some social phenomenon" (p. 14). According to Denzin, three outcomes stem from triangulation: convergence, inconsistency, and contradiction. Whichever of these outcomes prevail, the researcher can construct good explanations of the observed behavioral or social phenomena.

Similarly, although recognizing that triangulation may not be appropriate for all research purposes, Jick (1979) noted the following advantages of triangulation: (a) it allows researchers to be more confident of their results; (b) it stimulates the development of creative ways of collecting data; (c) it can uncover contradictions; (d) it can lead to thicker, richer data; (e) it can lead to the synthesis or integration of theories; and (f) by virtue of its comprehensiveness, it may serve as the litmus test for competing theories.

Morse (1991) presented two types of methodological triangulation: simultaneous or sequential. According to this methodologist, simultaneous triangulation represents the simultaneous use of quantitative and qualitative methods in which there is limited interaction between the two sources of data during the data collection stage, but the findings complement one another at the data interpretation stage. Conversely, sequential triangulation is utilized when the results of one approach are necessary for planning the next method.

Sieber (1973) provided several reasons to combine quantitative and qualitative research. He outlined how such a combination can be effective at the research design, data collection, and data analysis stages. For instance, at the research design stage, quantitative data can assist the qualitative phase by identifying representative sample members, as well as outlying (i.e., deviant) participants. At the data collection stage, quantitative data can play an important role in providing baseline information and helping to avoid "elite bias" (talking only to high-status individuals). During the data analysis stage, quantitative data can facilitate evaluation of the extent to which the qualitative data are generalizable and, thereby, shed new light on qualitative findings.

On the other hand, at the design stage, qualitative data can assist the quantitative component of a study by assisting with conceptual and instrument development. Also, at the data collection stage, qualitative data can facilitate the data collection process. Finally, during the data analysis stage, qualitative data can play a crucial role by interpreting, clarifying, describing, and validating quantitative results, as well as through the modification of theory.

Rossman and Wilson (1985) identified the following three reasons for combining quantitative and qualitative research: (a) to enable confirmation or corroboration of each other through triangulation; (b) to enable or to develop analysis in order to provide richer data; and (c) to initiate new modes of thinking by attending to paradoxes that emerge from the two data sources. Expanding on Rossman and Wilson's (1985) conceptualization, Greene, Caracelli, and Graham (1989) outlined the following five broad purposes of mixed-methodological studies: (a) triangulation (i.e., seeking convergence and corroboration of results from different methods studying the same phenomenon); (b) complementarity (i.e., seeking elaboration, enhancement, illustration, clarification of the results from one method with results from the other method); (c) development (i.e., using the results from one method to help inform the other method); (d) initiation (i.e., discovering paradoxes and contradictions that lead to a reframing of the research question); and (e) expansion (i.e., seeking to expand the breadth and range of inquiry by using different methods for different inquiry components).

After reviewing 57 mixed-method evaluation studies and using their definition of these procedures, Greene et al. (1989) concluded that expansion (41%) was the most common purpose, followed by complementarity (33%), development (11%), and initiation (7%), and triangulation (7%), respectively. Greene et al. (1989) also outlined design elements that influence the selection of a particular mixed-methods design, which they categorized as (a) methods, (b) the paradigmatic framework, (c) the phenomena under investigation, (d) the relative status of the different methods, and (e) criteria for implementation.

Creswell (1994), in his influential book, described the following five types of mixed-method designs: (a) two-phase studies, in which the researcher first conducts a quantitative phase of a study followed by a qualitative phase, or vice versa (the two phases are separate); (b) parallel/simultaneous studies, in which the researcher conducts the quantitative and qualitative portions of the study simultaneously; (c) equivalent status designs, in which the investigator conducts a study using both the quantitative and the qualitative approaches approximately equally; (d) dominant-less-dominant studies, in which the inquirer conducts the investigation within a single dominant design, complemented to a small degree by a component representing the alternative paradigm; and (e) mixed-methodology designs, which represent the highest degree of methodological mixing in which the researcher combines quantitative and qualitative researchers at many or all stages of the research process.

Tashakkori and Teddlie (1998) added a sixth type of mixed-method design to Creswell's (1994) list, namely: designs with multilevel use of approaches, in which researchers utilize different types of methods at different levels of data aggregation. Further, these methodologists renamed Creswell's "mixed-methodology design" as "mixed-model studies," which they defined as "studies that are products of the pragmatist paradigm and that combine the qualitative and quantitative approaches within different phases of the research process" (p. 19).

Creswell (2002) defined the following three types of mixed-methods designs: (a) the triangulation design, (b) the explanatory design, and (c) the exploratory design. The purpose of the triangulation design is to collect both quantitative and qualitative data simultaneously, merge the data, and use the results to maximize understanding of the research problem. The explanatory design involves first collecting quantitative data and then collecting qualitative data to facilitate understanding of the quantitative data. Finally, the exploratory design consists of first collecting qualitative data and then collecting quantitative data to facilitate understanding of the qualitative data.

Tashakkori and Teddlie (1998) differentiated two major methods of mixed research: mixed-model research and mixed-method research. According to these theorists, mixed-model research involves mixing components or stages from qualitative and quantitative research. Conversely, in mixed-method research, the investigator systematically uses one approach for one phase of a research study and the other paradigm for another phase of the research study. In contrast to mixed-model research, in mixed-methods research, the qualitative and quantitative phases are kept intact and separate from each other. Thus, in mixed-method research the qualitative and quantitative research components are undertaken as part of a larger, overall study. In mixed-methods research, the "mixing" generally is undertaken at the interpretation stage of the process.

Onwuegbuzie and Johnson (2004) identified two classes of mixed-model research: within- and across-stage mixed-model research. Within-stage mixed-model research involves the researcher combining quantitative and qualitative research approaches at one or more of the three major research stages (i.e., research objective, data collection, data analysis). Such research involves mixing within at least one of the research stages of a single study. For instance, a researcher could mix within the research objective stage by designing a research study to answer one or more research questions that incorporate both exploration (qualitative) and confirmation (quantitative). Alternatively, the researcher could mix within the type of data stage by collecting both qualitative and quantitative data (e.g., administering a questionnaire that contains open- and closed-ended items). Finally, the researcher could mix within the type of analysis stage by analyzing narrative data both qualitatively (e.g., identifying emergent themes) and quantitatively (e.g., determining how frequently key words occur) or by analyzing numeric data both quantitatively (e.g., computing descriptive statistics) and qualitatively (e.g., forming categories based on the descriptive statistics) (Onwuegbuzie & Johnson, 2004).

Across-stage mixed-model research involves the researcher combining quantitative and qualitative research approaches across at least two of the three research stages in a single research study. For example, a researcher could use a confirmatory approach as the research study's objective (quantitative), collect qualitative data (qualitative), but then analyze the data using quantitative techniques (quantitative) (Onwuegbuzie & Johnson, 2004).

Most recently, Onwuegbuzie (2003b) classified mixed-methods designs according to the following three dimensions: (a) level of mixing (partially mixed vs. fully mixed); (b) time orientation (concurrent vs. sequential); and (c) emphasis of approaches (equal status vs. dominant status). Level of mixing refers to whether the mixed research is partially mixed (i.e., both the quantitative and qualitative elements are conducted either concurrently or sequentially in their entirety before being mixed at the data interpretation stage) or fully mixed (i.e., mixing of quantitative and qualitative techniques within one or more stages of the research process or across these stages). Time orientation refers to whether the qualitative and quantitative phases of the study occur at approximately the same point in time (i.e., concurrent) or whether these two elements occur one after the other (i.e., sequential). Finally, emphasis of approach pertains to whether both qualitative and quantitative phases of the study have approximately equal emphasis (i.e., equal status) with regard to answering the research question(s) or whether one phase clearly has more weight than the other phase (i.e., dominant status).

Onwuegbuzie (2003b) outlined a 2 (partially mixed vs. fully mixed) $\times$ 2 (concurrent vs. sequential) $\times$ 2 (equal status vs. dominant status) matrix that was derived by crossing the three dimensions—yielding the following eight types of mixed research designs: (a) *partially mixed concurrent equal status design* (involving studies with two phases that occur concurrently, such that the quantitative and qualitative phases have approximately equal weight); (b) *partially mixed concurrent dominant status design* (involving studies with two phases that occur concurrently, such that either the quantitative or qualitative phase has the greater emphasis); (c) *partially mixed sequential equal status design* (involving studies with two phases that occur sequentially, with the quantitative and qualitative phases having equal weight); (d) *partially mixed sequential dominant status design* (involving studies with two phases that occur sequentially, such that either the quantitative or qualitative phase has the greater emphasis); (e) *fully mixed concurrent equal status design* (involving studies that mix qualitative and quantitative research within one or more or across the three components in a single research study, with the quantitative and qualitative phases being mixed concurrently at one or more stages or across the components and with both elements being given approximately equal weight); (f) *fully mixed concurrent dominant status design* (involving studies that mix qualitative and quantitative research within one or more or across the three components in a single research study, with the quantitative and qualitative phases being mixed concurrently at one or more stages or across the stages and with either the quantitative or the qualitative phase being given more weight); (g) *fully mixed sequential equal status design* (involving studies that mix qualitative and quantitative research within one or more or across the three stages of the research process, with the quantitative and qualitative phases occurring sequentially at one or more stages or across the stages and being given approximately equal weight); and (h) *fully mixed sequential dominant status design* (involving studies that mix qualitative and quantitative research within one or more of or across the stages of the research process, with the quantitative and qualitative phases occurring sequentially at one or more stages or across the stages and with either the quantitative or the qualitative phase being given more weight).

To date, only two mixed-methods studies have been conducted in the area of library anxiety. Specifically, Onwuegbuzie (1997a) utilized what Creswell (1994) would term an equivalent status design, what Creswell (2002) would regard as a triangulation design and what Onwuegbuzie (2003b) would term as a partially mixed concurrent equal status design.

The purpose of Onwuegbuzie's (1997a) research was complementarity. Specifically, this researcher sought to elaborate, enhance, and clarify the results from one research method with results from the other method (Greene et al., 1989). The goal of the quantitative component of Onwuegbuzie's study was to determine which components of library anxiety and other academic-related anxieties (i.e., statistics anxiety and writing anxiety) best predict students' ability to write a research proposal. The objective of the qualitative component of Onwuegbuzie's investigation was to examine the components of the anxiety experienced by students while they are engaged in writing a research proposal.

Kracker and her colleague (Kracker, 2002; Kracker & Wang, 2002) conducted a two-part investigation to test the applicability of Kulthau's ISP model (Kuhlthau, 1983, 1985, 1987, 1988a, 1988b, 1989, 1991, 1993, 1994; Kuhlthau et al., 1990), as described in chapter 3. Similar to Onwuegbuzie (1997a), Kracker's study represented an equivalent status design (Creswell, 1994), a triangulation design (Creswell, 2002), and a partially mixed concurrent equal status design (Onwuegbuzie, 2003b), in which the purpose of the research was complementarity. Indeed, Kracker and Wang (2002) noted, "The study integrates quantitative and qualitative designs to collect complimentary data" (p. 295). The quantitative part of the study (Kracker, 2002) was a quasi-experimental study investigating the effect of teaching Kulthau's ISP model on upper division undergraduate students' (a) awareness of thoughts associated with the research process, (b) awareness of feelings associated with the research process, (c) anxiety associated with undertaking research, and (d) satisfaction with the research process. The qualitative component involved a content analysis of these participants' descriptions of (a) a past memorable experience of writing a research paper (collected at the beginning of the semester) and (b) current research paper experience for the course (collected at the end of the semester).

## Methods of Data Collection

Along with selecting the research design, mixed-methods researchers must determine the methods to be used in collecting the data. Regardless of the research design chosen, mixed-method researchers must make decisions about the sampling scheme, sample size, and instruments to be used.

## Sampling

Mixed-methods researchers have the advantage that they can select any of the sampling schemes associated with the quantitative and qualitative paradigms that were outlined above. Indeed, as noted by Onwuegbuzie and Leech (2003b), after eliminating redundancies (i.e., convenience sampling, purposeful sampling, network sampling), mixed-method researchers have 22 sampling designs at their disposal. These 22 designs comprise 5 probability sampling schemes (four random + multistage sampling), and 17 nonprobability sampling schemes (16 schemes presented above + quota sampling) as follows: random sampling, stratified random sampling, cluster random sampling, systematic random sampling, multistage sampling, quota sampling, maximum variation sampling, homogeneous sampling, critical case sampling, theory-based sampling, confirming and disconfirming cases sampling, snowball/chain sampling, extreme case sampling, typical case sampling, intensity sampling, politically important cases sampling, random purposeful sampling, stratified purposeful sampling, criterion sampling, opportunistic sampling, mixed purposive sampling, and convenience sampling.

Consistent with Onwuegbuzie and Leech's (2003b) conceptualization, Kemper, Stringfield, and Teddlie (2003) subdivided mixed-methods sampling techniques into probability and purposive techniques. Moreover, Kemper et al. indicated that multilevel mixed-methods studies, typically "call for probability samples for at least one level and purposive samples for at least one level" (p. 286). As noted by these methodologists, "the understanding of a wide range of sampling techniques in one's methodological repertoire greatly increases the likelihood of one's generating findings that are both rich in content and inclusive in scope" (p. 292).

## Instrumentation

With respect to data collection strategies, Johnson and Turner (2003) distinguished intramethod mixing from intermethod mixing. According to these authors, intramethod mixing involves the concurrent or sequential use of a single method of data collection (e.g., questionnaires) that includes both quantitative and qualitative component. For example, in constructing a questionnaire to determine library user habits, the data collection strategy would be labeled as being intramethod if the instrument either involved the concurrent use of open- and closed-ended items on a single form or the sequential use of an open-ended questionnaire and a closed-ended questionnaire in a single research inquiry. In any case, intramethod mixing must involve either a combination of quantitative and qualitative approaches within a single method or a strategy that is neither purely quantitative nor purely qualitative (Johnson & Turner, 2003).

Conversely, intermethod mixing consists of concurrently or sequentially mixing two or more methods. For instance a library researcher might administer a test and conduct interviews on the same or different sample members within the same framework. Intermethod mixing dictates that multiple (i.e., different) methods be employed in a single study. These multiple methods can reflect only quantitative approaches, only qualitative methods, only mixed methods, or a combination of quantitative and qualitative approaches. As noted by Johnson and Turner (2003), "In many cases, the mixing of quantitative and qualitative methods will result in the most accurate and complete description of the phenomenon under investigation" (p. 299), and "often results in more thorough information, corroboration of findings, and overall a much more trustworthy research study" (p. 316).

Johnson and Turner (2003) discussed six major data collection strategies in mixed-methods research. These six methods are (a) mixture of open- and closed-ended items on one or more questionnaires (Johnson & Turner refer to this as Type 2 data collection style); (b) mixture of depth and breadth interviewing (Type 5); (c) mixture of 'a priori' and 'emergent/flowing' focus group strategies (Type 8); (d) mixture of standardized open- and closed-ended predesigned tests (Type 11); (e) mixture of standardized/confirmatory and less structured/exploratory observation, alternating between participatory and nonparticipatory researcher roles (Type 14); and (f) mixture of nonnumeric and numeric documents, consisting of archived data based on open- and closed-ended items (Type 17).

With respect to Type 2 data collection, a researcher utilizing an intramethod mixed questionnaire would administer a survey that includes both open- and closed-ended items. Alternatively, an item can be mixed, for example, by combining a fixed-response options (e.g., specific racial categories) with an open-response option (e.g., "other" category). An intermethod mixed questionnaire could first conduct interviews and then use the findings to construct questionnaires. This would be an example of a sequential intermethod mixing (Johnson & Turner, 2003).

Type 5 intramethod data collection involves the use of a standardized open-ended interview. This method of interviewing is based on conducting an open-ended interview that generates qualitative data; however, at the same time, neither the wording nor the sequence of the questions on the interview protocol is varied such that the presentation is constant across interviews. Alternatively, researchers could include both open- and closed-ended items in a single interview protocol or in two or more protocols that are used in a single investigation. In intermethod mixing, interviews can be combined with other data collection methods. For example, a library researcher could combine an open-ended interview with a (primarily) closed-ended questionnaire.

Type 8 intramethod data collection involves the mixed type of focus group, which, according to Johnson and Turner (2003), is the most common type of focus group. Here, the researcher/moderator would ask both open- and closed-ended questions. The moderator allows the group to digress into related areas but also tries to keep the participants focused, guiding them back to the central topic when necessary. Focus groups also can be used in intermethod mixing by combining a focus group with other forms of data collection. In particular, focus groups can be used (a) for exploration objectives to determine the beliefs, perceptions, and/or attitudes of group members regarding a research topic; (b) to inform the development of questionnaires and interviews in quantitative research (i.e., *development*; Greene et al., 1989); (c) to provide poststudy feedback after quantitative data collection (e.g., via an experiment); (d) to provide legitimization of quantitative data that were collected beforehand; and (e) to increase inference quality by assisting in the interpretation of findings stemming from other data collection methods (Johnson & Turner, 2003).

Type 11 intramethod data collection involves the administering of mixed tests. According to Johnson and Christensen (2000), mixed tests refer to tests that contain a combination of open- and closed-ended items. For example, such a test might include both multiple-choice items and essay items. Tests also can be used in intermethod mixing by combining a test with other types of data collection. For instance, a test could be administered alongside an open-ended survey that elicited information about the participants' attitudes toward the test.

With respect to Type 14 intramethod data collection, a researcher conducting an intramethod mixed observation would mix aspects of quantitative and qualitative observation. For example, the researcher might combine an a priori observation protocol with extensive field notes at different points of the observation period. Alternatively, a researcher could conduct separately a quantitative observation session and a qualitative observation session within a single research study. With regard to intermethod mixed observation, an investigator can combine observations using standardized closed-ended protocols with self-reports from the individuals being observed.

Finally, Type 17 intramethod data collection involves the use of secondary data (e.g., archival data, personal documents, physical data) that combine numeric and nonnumeric information. Secondary data also can be used in intermethod mixing by combining archival data with other types of data collection. For example, a library researcher could administer a knowledge test at the end of a bibliographic instruction session (primary data) and then compare the results to findings from previous administrations of the test that have been archived (secondary data).

## SUMMARY AND CONCLUSIONS

The current chapter has presented a typology of research designs that are associated with the quantitative, qualitative, and mixed-methodological research paradigms. With respect to the quantitative research paradigm, the following five research designs were outlined: historical, descriptive, correlational, causal-comparative (i.e., quasi-experimental), and experimental. With regard to the qualitative research paradigm, the following five research designs were described: historical, case studies, phenomenological, ethnographic, and grounded theory. Concerning the mixed-methodological (i.e., pragmatist) research paradigm, the following research designs were identified: two-phase studies, parallel/simultaneous studies, equivalent status designs, dominant-less-dominant designs, mixed-methodological designs, mixed-model studies, within-stage mixed-model designs, across-stage mixed-model designs, partially mixed concurrent equal status designs, partially mixed concurrent dominant status designs, partially mixed sequential equal status designs, partially mixed sequential dominant status designs, fully mixed concurrent equal status designs, fully mixed concurrent dominant status designs, fully mixed sequential equal status designs, and fully mixed sequential dominant status designs.

Additionally, the major components of research designs were identified and discussed. In particular, the methods of collecting data were described, comprising sampling and instrumentation. For quantitative studies, five probability sampling designs (i.e., simple, stratified, cluster, systematic, multi-stage) and four nonprobability sampling (i.e., convenient, purposive, quota, network) were outlined. For qualitative studies, the following 16 purposive sampling designs were presented: maximum variation sampling, homogeneous sampling, critical case sampling, theory-based sampling, confirming and disconfirming cases sampling, snowball/chain sampling, extreme case sampling, typical case sampling, intensity sampling, politically important cases sampling, random purposeful sampling, stratified purposeful sampling, criterion sampling, opportunistic sampling, mixed purposive sampling, and convenience sampling. These sampling schemes for both quantitative and qualitative research were combined to form a total of 22 unique sampling strategies for mixed-methodological research.

With respect to instrumentation, the quantitative-based methods of data collection discussed were cognitive tests (aptitude tests, achievement tests, norm-referenced tests, criterion-referenced tests); affective measures (i.e., rating scales, Likert-format scales, semantic differential scales, checklists, Thurstone scales, Guttman scales, magnitude scaling, Q-sort, Delphi technique); personality inventories; interest inventories; quantitative observational instruments; quantitative interviews; and secondary data. In addition, the psychometric properties of quantitative instruments were described, namely, score validity (i.e., content-related validity, criterion-related validity, construct-related validity) and score reliability (i.e., test-retest reliability, equivalence forms reliability, coefficient of stability and equivalence, coefficient of internal consistency). With respect to qualitative research, the following four kinds of research data were delineated: observations, interviews, documents, and audio-visual materials. Finally, with respect to mixed-methodological research, the following six major data collection strategies were presented: mixture of open- and closed-ended items on one or more questionnaire (Type 2); mixture of depth and breadth interviewing (Type 5); mixture of "a priori" and "emergent/ flowing" focus group strategies (Type 8); mixture of standardized open- and closed-ended predesigned tests (Type 11); mixture of standardized/ confirmatory and less structured/exploratory observation, alternating between participatory and nonparticipatory researcher roles (Type 14); and mixture of nonnumeric and numeric documents, consisting of archived data based on open- and closed-ended items (Type 17).

As such, the present chapter has provided library researchers with a comprehensive framework for designing studies that fall under each of the three research paradigms. With the numerous research designs, sampling techniques, and instruments available, library investigators are faced with an array of decisions to make. However, these decisions are made easier if the library researchers keep in mind the five major research objectives available to them: exploration, description, explanation, prediction, and influence. This is because the underlying research objective, coupled with the research purpose, drives the research paradigm and, in turn, the research design. The research objective and purpose also help the library researcher to select the most appropriate sampling scheme to use, once the research paradigm and research design have been chosen. Finally, the research objective and purpose assist in the identification of the appropriate instrument(s) to utilize. Data extracted from the instrument(s) are then subjected to one or more of the myriad of analytical techniques available. It is to these data analytical methods that we now turn.

# Chapter Five

# Framework for Conducting Multimethod Research: Data Analysis Stage

## OVERVIEW

In chapter 4, we provided a framework for undertaking the first major stage of the research process, namely, the research design/data collection. Once data have been collected, the researcher's next step is to analyze these data. Quantitative, qualitative, and mixed methods researchers have a myriad of techniques at their disposal for analyzing data. The challenge for these three sets of researchers is to select analyses that are consistent with the data type and, at the same time, most appropriately address the research questions and/or test the hypotheses. As such, it is vital that every analyst checks the assumptions that underlie the selected analytical method. Unfortunately, for reasons identified in chapter 4 (e.g., incompetent research methodology instructors, inadequate graduate-level curricula), a large proportion of researchers do not check these analytical assumptions, culminating in analyses and, subsequently, findings that are erroneous, invalid, and misleading (Daniel, 1998c; Hall et al., 1988; Keselman et al., 1998; Onwuegbuzie, in press-a; Thompson, 1998a; Vockell & Asher, 1974; Ward et al., 1975; Witta & Daniel, 1998).

Thus, the purpose of this chapter is to identify and summarize the most predominant and pervasive data analytical errors that occur in qualitative, quantitative, and mixed-methodological research. A second goal is to disseminate the best data analytic practices that stem from the extant literature. As such, this chapter summarizes and extends the work of Onwuegbuzie and Daniel (2003), who have provided "the most wide-ranging discussion of analytical and interpretational errors in educational research to date" (para. 3). In fact, this chapter appears to be the first piece of literature to provide guidelines for conducting qualitative, quantitative, and mixed-methodological data analysis techniques within the same framework.

## QUANTITATIVE RESEARCH PARADIGM

In quantitative research, data analysis techniques can be classified as falling into one of two types: descriptive statistics or inferential statistics. Descriptive statistics are methods that organize and summarize data that aid in effective presentation and increased understanding. Descriptive statistics include measures of central tendency (e.g., mean, median, mode); measures of dispersion/variability (e.g., range, standard deviation, variance, interquartile range); measures of position (e.g., percentile rank, $z$-scores, $t$-score, stanine); and measures of distributional shape (e.g., skewness, kurtosis). Inferential statistics involve making judgments/inferences about a population based on the properties of a sample obtained from the population (i.e., generalizing findings from a sample to a population from which the sample was selected). Each of these classes of statistics is presented below.

### Descriptive Statistics

Descriptive statistics essentially represent single-number summaries that help organize and summarize data, leading to effective presentation and increased understanding of the underlying sample. As recommended by the American Psychological Association (APA, 2001), whether or not the quantitative study necessitates the testing of hypotheses, library researchers always should report descriptive statistics in empirical investigations:

> Be sure to include sufficient descriptive statistics (e.g., per-cell sample size, means, correlations, standard deviations) so that the nature of the effect being reported can be understood by the reader and for future meta-analyses.

This information is important, even if no significant effect is being reported. When point estimates are provided, always include an associated measure of variability (precision), specifying its nature (e.g., the standard error). (p. 22)

## Correlation Coefficient

Although correlation coefficients can be used as descriptive statistics, typically they are used for inferential purposes. Indeed, Onwuegbuzie and Jiao (1997a, 1998a, 1998b, 2000) have reported correlation coefficients in virtually all of their published studies on library anxiety. Disturbingly, many researchers do not appear to realize that all parametric analyses (i.e., univariate and multivariate techniques), with the exception of predictive discriminant analyses, are subsumed by a general linear model (GLM), and that, as such, *all* analyses are correlational (Cohen, 1968; Knapp, 1978; Thompson, 1998a). Moreover, numerous investigators are not cognizant of the fact that because correlation coefficients represent the simplest form of the GLM, they are bounded by its assumptions (Onwuegbuzie & Daniel, 2002a, 2003).

When utilizing correlational coefficients, library researchers always should check statistical assumptions underlying these indices. In particular, normality of both the independent and dependent measures involved in the bivariate relationships always should be assessed. If both sets of scores appear to be normally distributed, then Pearson's product-moment correlation coefficient should be used; if nonnormality is indicated, then nonparametric techniques such as Spearman's rho and Kendall's tau should be used (Onwuegbuzie & Daniel, 2002a). Additionally, when computing more than one correlation coefficient, library researchers always should control for Type I error. A common way of controlling for Type I error is via the Bonferroni adjustment (Onwuegbuzie & Daniel, 2002a). Here, the level of significance, typically 5%, is divided by the number of bivariate relationships tested. For example, if five correlation coefficients are of interest, .05 should be divided by 5, yielding .01. Then, each of the five correlation coefficients should be tested at the 1% level of significance.

Most importantly, whenever a statistically significant relationship is found, library researchers always should report the effect sizes of correlation coefficients (Onwuegbuzie, 2001; Onwuegbuzie, Daniel, & Roberts, in press). Undoubtedly, the most popular method of reporting effect sizes is using Cohen's (1988) criteria. The $r$-value can be interpreted by using Cohen's (1988) criteria of .1 for a small correlation, .3 for a moderate correlation, and .5 for a large correlation. Reporting effect sizes should lead to the elimination of inappropriate language such as "highly significant," "nearly significant," and "approaching significance," and may result in the regular use of the phrase's "statistically significant" and "not statistically significant" to denote the result of a null hypothesis significance test (NHST) (Daniel, 1988, 1998a, 1998b; Onwuegbuzie & Daniel, 2002a; Thompson, 1998b). As recommended by Onwuegbuzie and Levin (in press), when reporting effect sizes, library researchers always should delineate as many design, analysis, and psychometric characteristics as possible to help subsequent researchers ascertain the extent to which they can compare their effect sizes with previous indices. Simply put, library researchers always should contextualize their effect sizes; that is, they should interpret their effect sizes within the study's specific parameters (Onwuegbuzie & Levin, 2003b).

Investigators in library and information science research should always consider the power of tests of hypotheses. That is, researchers should try to use power tables (e.g., Cohen, 1988) to ensure that the sample size is large enough to detect a true relationship. For example, Table 3.3.5 on pages 92–93 of Cohen's (1988) book reveals that in order to test a two-tailed nil null hypothesis (i.e., a hypothesis of zero correlation for a Pearson product-moment correlation), using a level of significance of .05 and a power of .80, a sample size of 26 is needed to detect a large correlation [i.e., $r = |.5|$], and a sample size of 82 is needed to detect a moderate correlation [i.e., $r = |.3|$]). For a one-tailed test (e.g., statistically significant positive or negative $r$), a sample size of 21 is needed to detect a large correlation (i.e., $r = |.5|$), and a sample size of 64 is needed to detect a moderate correlation (i.e., $r = |.3|$). Because most researchers conduct two-tailed tests of bivariate relationships, perhaps the most notable number from Cohen's (1988) table is that a minimum sample size of 82 is required to detect a moderate relationship with statistical power of .80 and with 95% confidence (i.e., two-tailed $\alpha = .05$). Thus, when interested in determining the relationship between two variables, library researchers should strive to obtain at least 82 cases whenever a two-tailed test is needed. Obviously, the more bivariate relationships are tested, the bigger the sample size should be.

Onwuegbuzie and Daniel (2002a) made the following 10 recommendations for utilizing and interpreting correlation coefficients:

1. Always assess statistical assumptions *before* using Pearson's *r* to conduct tests of statistical significance, as well as *after* the correlation has been computed. Use a nonparametric correlation index (e.g., Spearman's rho) if the normality assumption is not met.
2. Always adjust for the Type I error rate when conducting multiple null hypothesis significance tests (NHSTs) of correlations.
3. Always be aware of the statistical power of NHSTs of correlations, preferably before the data collection stage and, at the very least, at the data analysis stage.
4. When a statistically significant correlation coefficient is found, always interpret the effect size.
5. Do not test whether reliability and validity coefficients are statistically significantly greater than zero.
6. Do not report disattenuated correlation coefficients without also presenting the raw coefficients.
7. Do not correlate variables without a theoretical framework.
8. Do not infer causation from a correlation coefficient, regardless of how large the effect size is.
9. Do not use Hotelling's *t*-test when comparing correlated correlation coefficients.
10. Conduct external replications when possible and, in their absence, always undertake internal replications.

## Reliability of Scores

Reliability, which typically ranges from 0 (measurement is all error) to 1 (no error in measurement), is the proportion of variance in the observed scores that is free from error. (Reliability coefficients also can be negative.) As noted by Onwuegbuzie and Daniel (2002b, in press), score reliability affects the statistical power of NHST.

Unfortunately, as noted by several researchers (Onwuegbuzie, 2002a; Vacha-Haase, Ness, Nilsson, & Reetz, 1999), relatively few researchers in all fields report reliability coefficients for data from their own samples, with as many as 86.9% of authors not presenting any score reliability information for the underlying data. The trend of not reporting current-sample reliability coefficients stems, in part, from a failure to realize that reliability is a function of scores, not of instruments (Thompson & Vacha-Haase, 2000). Similarly, in assessing score reliability of the Library Anxiety Scale across studies, Jiao and Onwuegbuzie (2002c) found that score reliability of the LAS has not always been reported. The dearth in the reporting of reliability estimates led the American Psychological Association (APA) (2001) to recommend the reporting of these indices.

Without information about score reliability, it is impossible to assess accurately the extent to which statistical power is affected. Therefore, library researchers always should report reliability coefficients for the underlying data. Moreover, the use of confidence intervals around reliability coefficients is advocated because reliability coefficients represent only point estimates. In fact, confidence intervals around reliability coefficients can be compared to coefficients presented in test manuals to assess generalizability (Onwuegbuzie & Daniel, 2002b).

When current-sample reliability coefficients are not available, library researchers, at the very least, should compare the sample composition and variability of scores of the present sample with those of the inducted (i.e., norm) group (Vacha-Haase, Kogan, & Thompson, 2000). The results of these comparisons should be discussed. Specifically, as noted by Vacha-Haase et al. (2000), assuming that previously reported reliability coefficients generalize to the present sample is only marginally justified if the compositions and the score variabilities (i.e., standard deviation) of the two samples are similar.

## Independent/Dependent Samples *t*-Test

When library researchers are interested in comparing two independent samples, assuming normality, they must choose between the pooled and nonpooled *t*-test. This choice depends on whether or not the variances are equal or unequal, respectively. When equality of variances can be assumed, the pooled *t*-test should be used. Conversely, when the variances are unequal, or when there is doubt about their equality, the nonpooled *t*-test should be employed. Under the assumption of variance homogeneity, the pooled *t*-test is only slightly more powerful (i.e., smaller Type II error probability) than is the nonpooled *t*-test. At the same time, in the presence of variance heterogeneity, using the pooled *t*-test can increase greatly the chances of an invalid conclusion, especially when the sample sizes are also unequal. Thus, the pooled *t*-test should only be used when prior knowledge, experience, or theory suggests that the population variances are approximately equal. If there is any doubt about the equality of the variances, as is typically the case, library researchers should use the nonpooled *t*-test. For example, Onwuegbuzie and Jiao (1997b) used a series of independent samples *t*-tests, assuming unequal variances, to compare native English speakers and nonnative English speakers with respect to library anxiety and other library-related variables (e.g., frequency of library visits). (A criticism of Onwuegbuzie & Jiao [1997b] here is that they did not specify that unequal variances were assumed.) These comparisons revealed a number of differences between these two samples.

## Analysis of Variance Tests

Analysis of variance (ANOVA) has been found to be the most popular statistical procedure for conducting null hypothesis statistical significance tests among behavioral and social science researchers (Elmore & Woehlke, 1998; Goodwin & Goodwin, 1985; Onwuegbuzie, 2002a). Unfortunately, the ANOVA test is often misused. In particular, not realizing that the ANOVA test represents the general linear model, many researchers inappropriately categorize variables in nonexperimental designs using ANOVA, in an attempt to justify making causal inferences. Yet, by categorizing continuous variables, all that is accomplished is a discarding of relevant variance (Cliff, 1987; Pedhazur, 1982; Prosser, 1990; Thompson, 1986, 1988a, 1992a). Interestingly, Cohen (1983) estimated that the Pearson product-moment correlation between a variable and its dichotomized version (i.e., divided at the mean) was .798, which suggests that the cost of dichotomization is approximately a 20% reduction in the correlation coefficient. More recently, Peet (1999) found that for the one-way ANOVA context, as the number of categorized groups decreases (minimum number = 2), less variance in the dependent variable is explained by the categorical variable, compared to the continuous variable. For instance, Peet observed that with four groups, almost 90% of the variance accounted for by the continuous variable was explained by the categorical variable; however, with two groups, only approximately 50% of the original variance accounted for was explained by the categorical variable. It follows that with factorial ANOVAs, when artificial categorization occurs, even more power is sacrificed.

Therefore, as recommended by Kerlinger (1986), library researchers should refrain from artificially categorizing continuous variables unless the data suggest that this is reasonable (e.g., bimodal). In fact, rather than categorizing independent variables, in many cases, library researchers should use regression techniques (e.g., multiple regression) because they have been shown consistently to be superior to ANOVA methods (Daniel, 1989a; Kerlinger & Pedhazur, 1973; Lopez, 1989; Nelson & Zaichkowsky, 1979; Thompson, 1986).

When using ANOVA, library researchers always should check its assumptions, which include normality and homogeneity of variance. Unfortunately, nonnormality and variance heterogeneity lead to a distortion of Type I and/or Type II error rates, particularly if the group sizes are very different (Keselman et al., 1998). In particular, if the normality assumption is not met, analysts should use nonparametric equivalents, namely, the Mann-Whitney $U$ test (for the two-group case) or the Kruskal-Wallis test (when three or more groups are being compared). When the homogeneity of variance assumption is violated, techniques such as Welch, James, and Brown and Forsythe tests should be utilized because they are reasonably robust when heterogeneity of variance prevails (Maxwell & Delaney, 1990). Jiao et al. (1996) used ANOVA to examine library anxiety as a function of year of study. These researchers used the Shapiro-Wilk test (Shapiro & Wilk, 1965; Shapiro, Wilk, & Chen, 1968) to conclude that the distribution of library anxiety scores was nonnormal, thereby justifying use of ANOVA.

## Analysis of Covariance Tests

Most comparisons made in educational research involve intact groups that may have preexisting differences. Unfortunately, these differences often threaten the internal validity of the findings (Gay & Airasian, 2000; Johnson & Christensen, 2000). Thus, in an attempt to minimize this threat, some analysts (i.e., 4%) utilize analysis of covariance (ANCOVA) techniques, wherein there is an attempt to control statistically for preexisting differences between the underlying groups (Elmore & Woehlke, 1988; Goodwin & Goodwin, 1985; Willson, 1980). Unfortunately, in most of these cases, ANCOVA has been used inappropriately because one or more of the assumptions have either not been assessed or met—particularly the homogeneity of regression slopes assumption (Glass, Peckham, & Sanders, 1972). As noted by Maxwell and Delaney (1990), ANCOVA represents an ANOVA after adjusting for a covariate. That is, the goal of an ANCOVA is to allocate a percentage of the variance in the dependent variable, that would otherwise have been attributed to error in a regular ANOVA, to a potentially confounding variable (i.e., the covariate). As such, the error term in ANCOVA should be smaller than the error term in ANOVA. To the extent that this is the case, the subsequent decrease in error in the ANCOVA model helps to clarify the relationship between the independent and dependent variables (Loftin & Madison, 1991).

The crucial assumption that must be met for ANCOVA to be justified is homogeneity of regression slopes. This assumption implies that the covariate must be highly correlated with the dependent variable but not related to the independent variable. However, as noted by Henson (1998), few covariates exist in the behavioral and social sciences that meet these criteria—especially when study participants are not randomly assigned to groups (i.e., in quasi-experimental designs), which is typically the case. Unfortunately, if an appreciable relationship prevails between the covariate and the independent variable, as is often the situation, then the covariate also can *reduce* the variance in the independent variable—culminating in reduced power and effect size. Thus, the homogeneity of regression assumption means that the regression slopes of the covariate and the dependent variable in each group must be identical, or at least similar, if the single pooled regression slope can be used accurately with all groups.

To the extent that the individual regression slopes are different, the pooled regression slope will not provide an adequate representation of some or all of the groups. In this case, the ANCOVA will introduce bias into the data instead of providing an adjustment for the confounding variable (Loftin & Madison, 1991). Ironically, ANCOVA typically is appropriate when used with randomly assigned groups (i.e., experimental studies); however, it is typically not justified when groups are not randomly assigned (i.e., quasi-experimental studies) (Henson, 1998). Most importantly, library researchers should never use ANCOVA as a substitute for not incorporating a true experimental design (Henson, 1998; Thompson, 1994a). Simply put, statistical analyses, however sophisticated, do not correct for methodological design flaws.

Another argument against the use of ANCOVA is that after using a covariate to adjust the dependent variable, it is not clear whether the residual scores are interpretable (Thompson, 1992b). Thus, library researchers should avoid using ANCOVA. When this technique is employed, extreme caution must be exercised. Further, an assessment of the homogeneity of regression assumption always must be undertaken and documented. If the data are shown to violate this assumption (e.g., via a statistically significant Levene test result), the researcher will make a serious mistake in undertaking an ANCOVA.

## Multiple Regression

According to Elmore and Woehlke (1998), multiple regression is the third most popular statistical (inferential) technique used. Unfortunately, the vast majority of researchers use multiple regression in inappropriate and invalid ways. In particular, many of these analysts incorrectly use stepwise regression procedures (i.e., forward selection, backward selection, stepwise selection). In fact, the use of stepwise regression in behavioral and social research is rampant (Huberty, 1994), probably due to its widespread availability on statistical computer software programs. Disturbingly, because of the extensive use of stepwise regression, as stated by Cliff (1987, pp. 120–121), "a large proportion of the published results using this method probably present conclusions that are not supported by the data."

Several statisticians (Beasley & Leitner, 1994; Davidson, 1988; Edirisooriya, 1995; Huberty, 1989; Lockridge, 1997; Moore, 1996; Thompson, 1994a, 1995, 1998a, 1999; Thompson, Smith, Miller, & Thomson, 1991; Welge, 1990) have identified three problems associated with stepwise regression. First, at every step of the stepwise regression analysis, statistical programs use incorrect degrees of freedom in computing the $p$-values. Unfortunately, these incorrect degrees of freedom typically bias statistical significance tests in favor of deeming trivial effects to be statistically significant. Second, not only does conducting $k$ steps of analysis not necessarily lead to the best predictor set of size $k$, it is very possible that none of the predictors entered in the first $k$ steps are even among the best predictor set of size $k$. Third, because the order in which the independent variables are entered in the regression model is affected by sampling error, which, at any step, can lead to misspecification of the model, and because stepwise regression typically involves several steps, this technique often produces results that are very difficult to validate (Thompson, 1995). A fourth problem identified by Onwuegbuzie and Daniel (2003) is that because stepwise regression utilizes a series of statistical significance tests, it is subject to inflated Type I error rates.

Further, it should be noted that stepwise regression, more than any other regression procedure, tends to capitalize on chance, often culminating in an overfitting of data (Tabachnick & Fidell, 1996) and yielding results that are based on randomness rather than theoretical models selected via the extant literature (Huberty, 1989; Thompson et al., 1991).

Therefore, as advocated by Thompson (1995), instead of conducting a stepwise regression analysis, an *all-possible subset* (APS) (i.e., *setwise*) multiple regression analysis should be undertaken. Using this technique, all possible models involving some or all of the independent variables are analyzed and compared. Indeed, in APS regression, separate regressions are computed for all independent variables singly, all possible pairs of independent variables, all possible trios of independent variables, and so forth, until the best subset of independent variables is identified according to some (practical significance) criterion such as the maximum proportion of variance explained ($R^2$), which provides an index of effect size (Cohen, 1988).

Unfortunately, statistical software programs such as the Statistical Package for the Social Sciences (SPSS; SPSS Inc., 2001) do not allow analysts to conduct APS regression analyses directly, although the Statistical Analysis System (SAS Institute Inc., 1999) does permit such an analysis. It should be noted that both APS regression analyses represent exploratory model-building tools, as opposed to a model-testing procedures (Tabachnick & Fidell, 1996). As such, APS regression models should never be treated as definitive. Indeed, APS regression models routinely should be tested via internal (e.g., cross-validation) and external replications (Thompson, 1994b). For an example of an APS multiple regression in the area of library anxiety research, see Jiao et al. (1996), Jiao and Onwuegbuzie (1997, 1999c, 2001a), and Onwuegbuzie and Jiao (1997a, 1998a).

Other acceptable linear regression methods are hierarchical (i.e., sequential) multiple regression and standard multiple regression. In hierarchical multiple regression, independent variables are entered into the regression equation in an order specified a priori by the analyst. Each independent variable is then assessed with regard to its own contribution to the model at its own point of entry. Independent variables can be entered one at a time or in blocks in a specified order based on the researcher's theoretical considerations (Tabachnick & Fidell, 1996). Standard multiple regression involves entering all variables into the regression equation simultaneously and evaluating the contribution of each (via partial and semipartial correlations) as if it had been entered into the model after all other variables had been entered. Alternatively stated, standard multiple regression involves determining the contribution of each variable in the presence of other variables. Both hierarchical multiple regression and standard multiple regression represent model-testing approaches (Onwuegbuzie & Daniel, 2003), and thus library researchers should use these for confirmatory purposes.

Regardless of the technique employed (i.e., APS regression, hierarchical regression, standard regression), it should be noted that the selection of regression variables is just as crucial as with any other regression technique. Moreover, the variables that are selected for the initial multiple regression model must be based on theoretical, conceptual, and/or practical considerations.

In summarizing the results of a multiple regression model, library researchers should report unstandardized and/or standardized regression coefficients ($b$ or ß weights), as well as regression structure coefficients (Thompson & Borrello, 1985). The former typically is reported; however, the latter usually is omitted from the analysis. Yet, structure coefficients, which describe the relationship between scores on an observed variable with the scores on a given latent (i.e., synthetic) variable, when analyzed alongside standardized weights, can provide vital information about the relative importance of each of the regression variables (Courville & Thompson, 2001). Specifically, the extent to which the standardized weights and the structure coefficients are identical for each variable indicates how correlated the predictor variables are (Thompson, 1998a). Second, if both standardized and structure coefficients of a variable are trivial (i.e., near-zero), the variable is not a practically significant predictor of the outcome measure. Third, a variable with a near-zero standardized coefficient coupled with a relatively large structure coefficient suggests that this variable plays a role in explaining the dependent variable but that this variable is collinear with at least one additional predictor variable. Finally, a variable with a near-zero structure coefficient combined with a large standardized coefficient indicates that the variable is a suppressor variable. Suppressor variables are variables that help in the prediction of dependent variables (i.e., they increase the effect size) on account of their correlation with other independent variables (Tabachnick & Fidell, 1996). Specifically, suppressor variables improve the predictive power of the other independent/predictor variables in the model by suppressing variance that is irrelevant to this prediction as a result of the relationship of the suppressor variable to the other independent variables.

Library researchers should not only report the proportion of variance explained (i.e., $R^2$) but also the adjusted estimate of explained variance (adjusted $R^2$) (Leach & Henson, 2003; Snyder & Lawson, 1993; Yin & Fan, 2001). The adjusted $R^2$ index helps to reduce the positive bias that is inherent in $R^2$ (Ezekiel, 1930; Wherry, 1931) when the sample size is small, correlation is small, or the number of predictor variables is large. Additionally, library researchers should examine the residuals pertaining to the selected multiple regression model to assess the extent to which this model meets the assumptions of normality and homoscedasticity of variance.

When conducting multiple regression analyses, library researchers should strive for an adequate case-to-independent variable ratio. In particular, Green's (1991) criteria could be used for determining an appropriate sample size for a multiple regression analysis that takes into account the effect size. According to Green, the sample size should be greater than or equal to $(8 / F^2) + (V - 1)$, where $V$ is the number of predictor variables, $F^2 = R^2/(1 - R^2)$, and $R^2$ is the proportion of variance in the dependent variable explained by the set of predictor variables. Green (1991) recommends that the sample size should exceed this value if the dependent variable is skewed, if one or more of the variables yield low score reliability, or if a cross-validation technique is needed to test the generalizability of the selected regression model.

Data analysts from the field of library and information science also should examine influence diagnostics to determine whether any observations exert an undue amount of influence on the regression results (Fox, 1997). Such outlying information provides valuable information to the researcher. As noted by Myers (1986), these influence diagnostics include the following: (a) the number of estimated standard errors (for each regression coefficient) that the coefficient changes if the $i$th observation was set aside (i.e., DFBETAS); (b) the number of estimated standard errors that the predicted value changes if the $i$th point is removed from the data set (i.e., DFFITS); and (c) the reduction in the estimated generalized variance of the coefficient over what would have been produced without the $i$th data point (i.e., COVRATIO). (For an example of the use of influence diagnostics, see Onwuegbuzie et al., 2000)

Further, library science researchers should assess the extent to which multicollinearity prevails among the regression variables in the selected model. Multicollinearity leads to excessively large regression coefficients. Techniques for assessing multicollinearity include (a) *variance inflation factors* (VIFs), which indicate the extent to which the variance of an individual regression coefficient has been artificially inflated by the presence of collinearity, and (b) *condition numbers*, which represent the ratio of the largest to the smallest eigenvalues based on a principal components analysis of the regression coefficients yielded by a given analysis and which serve as measures of the strength of linear dependency among the regression variables (Sen & Srivastava, 1990). VIFs and condition numbers less than 10 indicate that multicollinearity is not a serious threat to the accuracy and stability of the regression coefficient (Fox, 1997; Myers, 1986).

## Multivariate Analysis of Variance/Covariance

Multivariate analysis of variance (MANOVA) has been found to be a popular statistical technique (Elmore & Woehlke, 1998; Onwuegbuzie, 2002a). Unfortunately, several flaws are associated with use of MANOVA. In particular, many researchers conduct a MANOVA followed by a univariate analyses (i.e., a MANOVA-univariate data analysis strategy). However, as noted by Keselman et al. (1998, p. 361), "there is very limited empirical support for this strategy." Indeed, Keselman et al. (1998) stated the following:

> If the univariate effects are those of interest, then it is suggested that the researcher go directly to the univariate analyses and bypass MANOVA. . . . Focusing on results of multiple univariate analyses preceded by a MANOVA is no more logical than conducting an omnibus ANOVA but focusing on the results of group contrast analyses. (pp. 361–362)

Furthermore, because this technique relies on a statistically significant MANOVA omnibus test as a gatekeeper to using ANOVA on a posthoc basis, the incompatibility of MANOVA and ANOVA, due to the differences in their respective mean square errors and error degrees of freedom, results in a posthoc ANOVA test that has lower statistical power than if the MANOVA had been bypassed and the ANOVA test used exclusively.

Thompson (1999) also admonished researchers who perform a series of univariate analyses to analyze multivariate data. He contended that because univariate analyses can be viewed as assessing the contribution of one or more predictor variables to a single dependent variable, it typically does not honor, in the optimal sense, the nature of reality that most researchers are interested in examining. This is because most phenomena involve multiple variables. Therefore, library researchers should avoid using the MANOVA-ANOVA analytical strategy and focus instead on conducting analyses that most adequately reflect the underlying multivariate reality of interest. (For a more extensive discussion of MANOVA versus multiple ANOVAs, see Huberty and Morris, 1989.)

Another common mistake made by researchers employing MANOVA techniques is the failure to report the criteria used for determining statistical significance. These criteria include Wilk's Lambda, Hotelling's trace criterion, Pillai's criteria, and Roy's *GCR* criterion. Under certain conditions (e.g., when the independent variable has two levels), the first three criteria yield identical $p$-values. However, there are times when these techniques will yield different $p$-values. Thus, library researchers always should specify which criteria were used. Interestingly, no study was found in the area of library anxiety in which MANOVA techniques were employed. A possible application of MANOVA would be to determine the effect of two or more nominal-scaled independent variables (e.g., gender, ethnicity) on the five dimensions of library anxiety, as measured by the LAS. Such an analysis would allow assessment of interaction effects (e.g., gender x ethnicity), which are seriously lacking in behavioral and social science research (Onwuegbuzie, 2003a).

Finally, as for the case of ANCOVA, library researchers should avoid using MANCOVA. This is because MANCOVA is subject to the same assumptions as is ANCOVA. However, not only is MANCOVA based on the multivariate normal distribution, but also it is assumed that the regression between covariates and the dependent variables in one group is the same as the regression in all other groups (i.e., homogeneity of regression), such that using the mean regression to adjust for covariates in all groups is appropriate and meaningful (Tabachnick & Fidell, 1996). This is an extremely difficult assumption to meet.

### Discriminant Descriptive Analysis/Predictive Discriminant Analysis.

According to Huberty and his colleagues (Huberty, 1994; Huberty & Barton, 1989; Huberty & Wisenbaker, 1992), descriptive discriminant analysis (DDA) describes the differences on two or more interval- or ratio-scaled dependent variables with respect to group membership, a nominal-scaled variable. Conversely, predictive discriminant analysis (PDA) involves predicting group membership from response variables that are interval- or ratio-scaled. In PDA, the percentage of correct classification is of particular interest, whereas in DDA, the function and structure coefficients are the major foci, with the hit rate being irrelevant (Thompson, 1998a). Also, as Thompson (1998a) surmised, whereas DDA is a member of the general linear model (GLM), PDA is not a direct member of the GLM family. One of the biggest flaws in interpreting DDA results is a failure to interpret both the discriminant function coefficients and the structure coefficients.

Whether DDA or PDA is being used, library researchers must report the criteria employed for statistical significance (e.g., Wilk's Lambda, Pillai's criteria, Hotelling's trace criterion, and Roy's *GCR* criterion). In addition, analysts must refrain from conducting stepwise discriminant analysis procedures because they contain serious flaws, as is the case with stepwise multiple regression. Indeed, stepwise discriminant analysis should *never* be used. Instead, standard discriminant analysis, canonical discriminant analysis, or hierarchical discriminant analysis should be utilized. An example of standard discriminant analysis can be found in the study by Onwuegbuzie and Jiao (1997b). These investigators used discriminant analysis to determine which reasons for using the library (all dichotomous variables) best predict students' native language status (dichotomous variable; English speaker vs. non-English speaker).

Both PDA and DDA are subject to the assumption of multivariate normality. As best as possible, this assumption always should be assessed. If there is reason to believe that this assumption is violated, logistic regression could be used (Tabachnick & Fidell, 1996). Logistic regression is more versatile than is discriminant analysis because it makes no assumptions about the distributional properties of the regression variables—in particular, the predictors do not have to be multivariate normally distributed, nor do they have to linearly relate or to have equal variances within each group. Further, the regression variables can be discrete, continuous, or represent a combination of the two. It is thus surprising how infrequently logistic regression is used in the behavioral and social science field in general and by library researchers in particular—despite its popularity in the health sciences. In fact, to date, no study in the field of library and information science field appears to exist in which logistic regression has been used. Because logistic regression is a discrete response-variable analog to multiple regression, the recommendations made above for the latter (e.g., nonuse of stepwise methods, checking assumptions, and conducting internal replications) are pertinent for using the former.

## Canonical Correlation Analyses

Canonical correlation analysis is used to examine the relationship between two sets of variables, whereby each set contains more than one variable (Cliff & Krus, 1976; Darlington, Weinberg, & Walberg, 1973; Thompson, 1980, 1984). In fact, as stated by Knapp (1978, p. 410), "virtually all of the commonly encountered tests of significance can be treated as special cases of canonical correlation analysis." In other words, canonical correlation analysis can be used to undertake all the parametric tests that canonical correlation methods subsume as special cases, including

Pearson's *r*, *t*-tests, multiple regression, ANOVA, ANCOVA, MANOVA, and MANCOVA (Henson, 2000; Thompson, 1988b).

As recommended by Thompson (1991) and reiterated by Humphries-Wadsworth (1997), when performing a canonical correlation analysis, above all else, library researchers should report (a) both the *p*-values pertaining to canonical functions and the squared canonical correlation coefficients (i.e., effect sizes) and (b) both the canonical function coefficients and the canonical structure coefficients, along the lines outlined above for multiple regression and discriminant analysis. Examples of canonical correlation analyses can be found in the studies conducted by Jiao and Onwuegbuzie (1998, 1999b, 1999c, 2002a) and Onwuegbuzie and Jiao (1998c, 2000).

## Principal Component Analysis and Factor Analysis

Principal component analysis (PCA) and factor analysis (FA) are statistical procedures that are performed on a set of variables to determine which variables in the set form logical subsets or factors that are statistically independent from each other. Specifically, variables that are statistically related with each other but statistically independent from other subsets of variables are combined into components/factors. These components or factors thus are assumed to represent the underlying phenomena that are responsible for the observed relationships among the variables.

The overall goals of both PCA and FA, which are the two most popular techniques for factor extraction, are to summarize patterns of correlations among the observed variables, to reduce the dimensionality of the set of variables, to describe an underlying process via the observed relationships among variables, or to test theories about the nature of underlying processes or constructs (Tabachnick & Fidell, 1996).

There are two major types of FA: exploratory FA and confirmatory FA. Exploratory FA represents an analytic technique conducted in the early stages of the research process with the goal of reducing a larger set of variables into a smaller, interpretable set, based on the observed relationships among the underlying variables. The researcher hopes to maximize understanding the internal structure of an instrument or a data set using the minimal number of dimensions. In other words, exploratory FAs are based on mathematical solutions and do not test any hypotheses (Daniel,

1989b). Conversely, confirmatory FAs usually occur in the latter stages of the research process to test a theory about the latent processes (Kieffer, 1999).

Many researchers use too small a sample to justify a FA. That is, they use an inadequate participant-to-variable ratio. As recommended by Onwuegbuzie and Daniel (2003), at a bare minimum, library researchers should use 5 participants per variable. However, they should aim for at least 10 participants per variable, where possible (Gorsuch, 1983). When library researchers use case-to-variable ratios that are less than 5, this should be readily acknowledged in the report as providing a threat to internal validity.

The difference in PCA and FA is that the former uses the total variance of each variable to determine the shared variation among the variables. That is, PCA uses "ones" on the diagonal of the correlation matrix that is factor analyzed. Conversely, FA uses estimates of common variance or score reliability on the main diagonal. It is likely that FA better reflects reality to a more appropriate degree than does PCA because the latter assumes that each variable has perfect score reliability (Kieffer, 1999). Regardless, analysts of library-related data should specify which extraction method they have used and provide a rationale for their choice.

When undertaking an oblique rotation (i.e., rotation of the factors in the factor space such that the angle between the factors is different than 90 degrees), library researchers should report both the factor pattern matrix and the factor structure matrix (Hetzel, 1996; Thompson, 1997). The rationale for this is the same as that provided above for interpreting both standardized coefficients and structure coefficients in multiple regression and discriminant analysis. Reporting only one of these two matrices provides incomplete information (Thompson, 1997). In contrast, when varimax rotation (i.e., orthogonal rotation of the factors in the factor space such that all factors are at 90-degree angles to each other) is used, the factor pattern matrix and the factor structure matrices are identical. Thus, only the factor structure matrix should be reported.

When performing confirmatory factor analyses, library researchers should analyze the variance-covariance matrix instead of the correlation matrix (Thompson & Daniel, 1996). Using correlation matrices with confirmatory factor analyses is tantamount to utilizing a variance-covariance matrix wherein the manifest variables have been standardized to unit variance (Bollen, 1989), which likely does not reflect reality.

When exploratory factor analysis is being undertaken, researchers always should include as many of the following statistics as possible: the sample size, initial number of variables, correlation matrix (for replication purposes), method of factor extraction, criteria used for selecting the number of factors to be extracted, procedure for factor rotation, eigenvalues, correlation matrix of the extracted factors, final communality estimates, estimates of reliability, rotated factor pattern matrix, and rotated factor structure matrix (if oblique rotation is utilized) (Kieffer, 1999).

An example of exploratory factor analysis with a varimax rotation is Bostick (1992) and Jerabek et al. (2001). However, these authors did not present all relevant statistics. Thus, for a complete model of factor analysis see Witcher, Onwuegbuzie, and Minor (2001), Kieffer (1999), and Henson and Roberts (in press).

For confirmatory factor analyses, effect sizes should be reported alongside chi-square ($\chi^2$) values because the latter is influenced heavily by the sample size (Schumacker & Lomax, 1996). Also, because there is no universally agreed-on index for assessing model adequacy, library researchers should report several fit indices (i.e., effect size measures), such as the ratio of chi-square to degrees of freedom ($\chi^2/df$), the Adjusted Goodness-of-Fit Index, the relative fit index (RFI), the incremental fit index (IFI), the Tucker-Lewis index (TLI), the comparative fit index (CFI); and the root mean square error of approximation (RMSEA) (Bentler, 1990; Bentler & Bonett, 1980; Bollen, 1986, 1989; Browne & Cudeck, 1993; Schumacker & Lomax, 1996; Steiger, 1990). Cut-off values between .90 (e.g., Bentler & Bonett, 1980) and .95 (Hu & Bentler, 1999) have been recommended for demonstrating model adequacy. For RMSEA indices, a cut-off value of .06 has been suggested (Hu & Bentler, 1999). Finally, with respect to the $\chi^2/df$ ratio, values less than 2.00 should be indicative of adequate fit (Byrne, 1989). The one example of confirmatory factor analysis in the library anxiety field is Onwuegbuzie and Jiao (2002e).

## Path Analysis and Structural Equation Modeling

Path analysis was developed in the 1920s by Sewall Wright to gain a better understanding of genetic theory. This method of analyzing data became popularized in the behavioral and social sciences in the 1960s (Schumacker & Lomax, 1996). Path analysis is a method for examining the direct and indirect effects of variables on one of more outcomes. Direct effects involve two latent variables that are connected by a single directional path, whereas indirect effects occur between two unobserved (i.e., latent) variables when no single straight arrow connects them but when the second latent variable can be reached by the first latent variable through one or more other latent variables via their paths. Conveniently, the path coefficients that are estimated in path models represent Pearson's product-moment correlation coefficients or standardized partial regression coefficients. Moreover, the paths indicate whether the dependent variables are related to correlated *effects*, mediated *effects*, and/or independent *effects*. Further, unlike multiple regression analyses, path analysis models permit researchers to hypothesize the type of relationship among the independent variables when predicting one or more dependent variables.

Path analysis involves partitioning or decomposing the correlation matrix and then comparing original coefficients with the path coefficients computed on the basis of the path model. Correlations between any two variables are decomposed into simple and complex paths (Schumacker & Lomax, 1996). Path coefficients can be tested for statistical significance (e.g., using *t*-values). Also, the overall path model can be tested for statistical significance via goodness of fit tests (e.g., chi-square tests). Unfortunately, because statistically significant chi-square values suggest that a model does not fit the underlying data, sample sizes greater than 200 have a tendency to reject models, as is the case for CFA (Schumacker & Lomax, 1996).

## Structural Equation Modeling

A structural equation model differs from a path analysis model in that the former uses latent variables rather than observed variables, and combines a measurement model (i.e., confirmatory factor analysis) with a structural model (i.e., path analysis) to test theory (Schumacker & Lomax, 1996). By using multiple observed variables in defining a particular latent variable or hypothesized construct, measurement error can be estimated and, as such, measurement properties (i.e., structural-related validity) can be assessed via parameter estimates.

As with confirmatory factor analysis, library researchers who utilize structural equation modeling techniques should report several fit indexes simultaneously (Thompson, 2000) because there is "no *single* statistical test of significance that identifies a correct model given the sample data" [emphasis in original] (Schumacker & Lomax, 1996, p. 120). However, it should be noted that even though SEM analyses often lead to models that more closely reflect reality, no causal statements should be made from the selected model. In fact, structural equation modeling is no less correlational in analytical framework than is any other member of the general linear model. Examples of structural equation models have been provided in chapter 3 (i.e., Onwuegbuzie & Jiao, 2002d).

## Hierarchical (Multilevel) Linear Modeling

Hierarchical Linear Modeling (HLM) is an analytical technique that is designed to analyze data that are structured hierarchically. Indeed, HLM has been found to be particularly relevant to studies of the educational context because students typically are clustered together within classes, classes are clustered within levels, levels are clustered together within institutions, institutions are clustered together within systems, systems are clustered within regions, and so forth (Bryk & Raudenbush, 1992; Goldstein, 1987, 1995; Gray & Wilcox, 1995; Kreft & De Leeuw, 1998). As HLM software has become more readily available, this method of data analysis is increasing in popularity (Onwuegbuzie, 2002a). However, due to its relative complexity, relatively few researchers use HLM.

In HLM, models contain one or more variables measured at different levels of the hierarchy. Models can have as few as two levels (e.g., students nested within bibliographic instruction courses) or many more than two. The lowest level measurements are referred to as being at the *micro level*, whereas all higher-level measurements are deemed to be at the *macro level*. Because HLM models are generalizations of multiple regression models (Kreft & De Leeuw, 1998), the same assumptions associated with multiple regression not only prevail when using HLM, but they are even more complex. Further, when one or more of these assumptions are violated, Type I and Type II errors can be severe.

As admonished by Kreft and De Leeuw (1998), HLM should not be used for data exploration. In fact, such exploration should be undertaken prior to the HLM stage. Additionally, when using HLM, library researchers should not test models that are too complex—that is, models that contain many independent variables, that are measured at all levels of the hierarchy, and/or that include many cross-level interactions (Kreft & De Leeuw, 1998). Such models should be avoided not only because they are sensitive to subtle changes in the system and thus contain unstable parameter estimates but also because these models are much more difficult to interpret, as well as to replicate from one sample to the next and from one context to the next. Not surprisingly, no study was identified in library and information science that has used HLM. However, it is only a matter of time before this technique is employed in this field. For example, library researchers could use HLM techniques to examine the relationship between library anxiety and a selection of cognitive, affective, personality, and demographic variables simultaneously at the individual (i.e., library user) level (i.e., Level 1) and at the group (e.g., library institution) level (i.e., Level 2).

## Nonparametric Statistics

When analyzing data, particularly at the univariate level, library researchers can use either parametric or nonparametric techniques. Whether parametric or nonparametric procedures are more appropriate to test a specific hypothesis depends on the assumptions that underlie the data at hand. Disturbingly, many researchers do not check data assumptions (Leech & Onwuegbuzie, 2002). Instead, they routinely conduct parametric analyses even if the parametric assumptions (e.g., normality) are grossly violated. Unfortunately, most data in the social and behavioral sciences fail to meet the assumptions needed to justify utilization of parametric statistics (Micceri, 1989).

Using parametric techniques when the normality assumption is seriously violated can have dire consequences (Siegel, 1956). In particular, large skewness and kurtosis coefficients affect Type I and Type II error rates. For example, a nonnormal kurtosis coefficient characterized by distributional shapes that are either more peaked (i.e., leptokurtic) or less peaked (i.e., platykurtic) than the normal distribution often produces an underestimate of the variance of a variable, which, in turn, increases the Type I error rate (Tabachnick & Fidell, 1996). Further, although the parametric *t*-test usually is robust with respect to Type I error when subgroups are large and equal, this test does not yield adequate statistical power when data are positively or negatively skewed. In fact, under skewed conditions, the Wilcoxon Rank Sum test, a nonparametric counterpart of the *t*-test can be three to four times more powerful (Blair & Higgins, 1980; Bridge & Sawilowsky, 1999; Nanna & Sawilowsky, 1998)—a finding of which many researchers appear to be unaware.

Because many researchers do not check their analytical assumptions and because incorrect use of parametric analyses can have serious consequences, it is possible that a significant proportion of the extant literature is based on findings that stemmed from the invalid use of parametric statistics. Therefore, to reverse this trend, library researchers always should check their analytical assumptions. In particular, library researchers should assess the extent to which the normality assumption holds.

Nonparametric statistics represent a class of statistical methods that have specific "desirable properties that hold under relatively mild assumptions regarding the underlying populations(s) from which the data are obtained" (Hollander & Wolfe, 1973, p. 1). Further, Bradley (1968) defined a nonparametric test as being a "distribution-free test . . . which makes no assumptions about the precise form of the sampled population" (p. 15). Alternatively stated, nonparametric methods often are called distribution free because they can be used for variables whose joint distribution represents any specified distribution, including the bivariate normal, or whose joint distribution is not known and therefore is unspecified (Gibbons, 1993). Therefore, when the normality assumption is not met, nonparametric techniques represent a more appropriate choice (Leech & Onwuegbuzie, 2002).

Onwuegbuzie and Daniel (2002a) have provided simple, objective criteria for evaluating the assumption of normality. Specifically, these authors stated the following:

> Additionally, for adequate sample sizes, a formal test of statistical significance can be conducted by utilizing the fact that the ratio of the skewness and kurtosis coefficients to their respective standard errors (i.e., standardized skewness and standardized kurtosis coefficients) are themselves nor-

mally distributed. Most other statistical packages print as options skewness and kurtosis coefficients but not their standard errors. However, these standard errors can be approximated manually (the standard error for skewness is approximately equal to the square root of $6/n$, and the standard error for kurtosis is approximately equal to the square root of $24/n$, where $n$ is the sample size). For both small and large sample sizes, rather than conducting a test of statistical significance, criteria can be used for assessing whether the standardized skewness and/or kurtosis coefficients are unacceptably large. One rule of thumb that we offer is that (a) standardized skewness and kurtosis coefficients which lie within (2 suggest no serious departures from normality, (b) coefficients outside this range but within the $\pm 3$ boundary signify slight departures from normality, and (c) standardized coefficients outside the $\pm 3$ range indicate important departures from normality. Using such a rule provides an objective method of assessing normality that is based on effect sizes (i.e., standardized coefficients). (p. 75)

The use of nonparametric methods offers many advantages. Hollander and Wolfe (1973) outlined six reasons for using nonparametric techniques. Specifically, they posited that nonparametric procedures (a) require few assumptions about the underlying population from which the data are collected; (b) do not require the assumption of normality; (c) are often easy to understand; (d) are typically easier to apply than are their parametric alternatives; (e) are appropriate when parametric methods cannot be used; and (f) are only slightly less efficient than are parametric methods under normality, while being more efficient under nonnormality.

Siegel (1956) also outlined six main advantages of nonparametric techniques. According to this methodologist, the first advantage is that the "accuracy of the probability statement does not depend on the shape of the population" (p. 32). Second, the size of the sample is not as important for nonparametric statistics as it is for parametric statistics because small sample sizes will not cause the results to be misleading to the extent that small samples unduly affect parametric tests. Third, nonparametric statistics can be utilized when data come from several different populations. Fourth, nonparametric techniques can be used with data that are ordinal, as well as with interval- and ratio-scaled data. Fifth, nonparametric statistics can be used with nominal data as well. Finally, nonparametric statistics can be easily learned and applied by most researchers, at least at the univariate level. Indeed, many statistical computer software packages, such as the Statistical Package for the Social Sciences (SPSS; SPSS Inc., 2001) and the Statistical Analysis System (SAS Institute Inc., 2002), include nonparametric statistics.

McSeeney and Katz (1978) identified several reasons for using nonparametric statistics. These include (a) nonparametric statistics have fewer assumptions, (b) nonparametric statistics can be used with rank-ordered data, (c) nonparametric statistics can be used with small samples, (d) data do not need to be normally distributed, and (e) nonparametric analyses remain appropriate in the presence of outliers.

Moreover, when approximate normality is met, nonparametric tests are still relatively efficient. In fact, the asymptotic relative efficiency of nonparametric tests with respect to parametric tests can be as high as 95.5% (Gibbons, 1993; Hollander & Wolfe, 1973). That is, in many instances, library researchers would only have to sample an additional 5 participants for every 100 sample members for nonparametric tests to have the same statistical power as their parametric counterparts. Therefore, for the most part, researchers are not taking undue risks by using nonparametric tests if the distribution is normal. Further, if the distribution is not normal, tests based on nonparametric tests likely are more efficient than are their parametric alternatives. As noted by Leech and Onwuegbuzie (2002), it is thus surprising that more researchers do not use nonparametric techniques. In fact, nonparametric statistics infrequently appear in published research articles, including those appearing in the most reputable journals (Elmore & Woehlke, 1996; Jenkins, Fuqua, & Froehle, 1984). Further, many researchers do not report whether assumptions were checked or whether their data fit the assumptions. For example, Keselman et al. (1998) reported that less than one-fifth of articles (i.e., 19.7%) "indicated some concern for distributional assumption violations" (p. 356). Similarly, Onwuegbuzie (2002a) found that only 11.1% of researchers discussed the extent to which the assumptions underlying analysis of variance, analysis of covariance, multivariate analysis of variance, or multivariate analysis of covariance were violated.

Numerous nonparametric statistics exist for conducting distribution-free tests. Conveniently, the overwhelming majority of these tests are readily available from the major statistical software (e.g., SPSS, SAS). A selection of some of the most common tests is provided in table 5.1. As noted by Leech and Onwuegbuzie (2002), parametric tests and their non-

**Table 5.1 Typology of nonparametric statistics.**

| Method | Test |
|---|---|
| *Measures of Association:* | |
| Spearman's Rank Correlation Coefficient | consistency |
| Kendall's Rank Correlation Coefficient | consistency |
| Chi-Square Test of Independence | concordance/discordance |
| Tau | consistency |
| Theil Test | slope of regression line |
| Cochran Test | consistency |
| Fisher's Exact Test | relationships |
| *Single Population Tests:* | |
| Binomial | proportions |
| Kolmogorov-Smirnov Goodness-of-Fit Test | goodness of fit test for continuous data |
| Sign Test | paired replicates |
| Wilcoxon Signed Rank Test | symmetry and equality of location |
| Gupta Test | symmetry |
| Hodges-Lehman One-Sample Estimator | median |
| *Comparison of Two Populations:* | |
| Chi-Square Test of Homogeneity | differences in proportions |
| Wilcoxon (Mann-Whitney) Test | differences in location and spread |
| Kolmogorov-Smirnov Two-Sample Test | differences between population distributions |
| Rosenbaum's Test | differences in location |
| Tukey's Test | differences in spread |
| Hodges-Lehman Two-Sample Estimator | difference in medians |
| Savage Test | differences in spread when medians equal |
| Ansari-Bradley Test | differences in dispersion |
| Moses Confidence Interval | differences in location |
| *Comparison of Several Populations:* | |
| Kruskal-Wallis Test | symmetry and equality of location |
| Friedman's Test | symmetry and location (two-way data) |
| Terpstra-Jonckheere Test | medians equals vs. changing median |
| Page's Test | ordered alternatives |
| The Match Test for Ordered Alternatives | medians equal vs. medians ordered |
| Miller's Jackknife Test | unknown squared ratio of scale differs from 1 |
| Hollander Test | X and Y variables are interchangeable |

parametric counterparts do not test strictly the same hypotheses. For instance, whereas parametric independent *t*-tests test the null hypothesis that two population *means* are equal, nonparametric independent *t*-tests (e.g., Mann-Whitney's $U$) test the null hypothesis that the two samples are from the same population against the location alternative hypothesis that one sample is shifted by a specific amount (i.e., difference in *medians* between the two populations). Nevertheless, both techniques test whether both samples are from the same population, which typically is the ultimate interest of library researchers.

Further, nonparametric procedures can be employed to calculate *exact* probability levels, especially when sample sizes are small. Indeed, exact probability (nonparametric) tests represent the most reliable methods of testing hypotheses. Therefore, library researchers should use nonparametric exact tests whenever possible. For example, Fisher's exact test of the equality of proportions in two populations, which utilizes hypergeometric probabilities, is more accurate than are any of its large-sample approximation counterparts, such as the chi-square statistic, which requires that the expected counts be greater than 5. Fisher's exact test can be undertaken using many of the leading statistical software (e.g., SPSS, SAS).

Reporting and interpreting effect sizes is no less essential for statistically significant nonparametric results than it is for statistically significant parametric findings. Indeed, statistically significant nonparametric statistics *always* should be followed up by some measure of effect size. However, it should be noted that just as parametric tests are adversely affected by violations to GLM assumptions, so too are parametric effect sizes (e.g., Cohen's *d*). For example, as noted by Onwuegbuzie and Levin (2003b), parametric effect sizes are affected by nonnormality and heterogeneity of scores. Therefore, whatever assumptions were violated that led to the use of nonparametric methods also would distort the parametric effect size. Consistent with this assertion, Hogarty and Kromrey (2001), using Monte Carlo methods, demonstrated that the most frequently used effect-size estimates (e.g., *d*) are extremely sensitive to departures from normality and homogeneity.

Consequently, where possible, library researchers should follow up statistically significant nonparametric *p* values with nonparametric effect sizes. Nonparametric effect sizes include Cramer's *V,* the phi coefficient, and the odds ratio. These effect size indices, which are appropriate for chi-square analyses, can be readily accessed via SPSS and SAS.

## Significance of Observed Findings

Thus far in this book, two types of significance have been described and advocated: statistical significance and practical significance. An observed finding is judged to be statistically significant when it is "significantly" larger than or smaller than would be expected by chance (Cohen, 1994). The $p$-value represents the probability of observing a finding as extreme or more extreme, assuming that the null hypothesis is true. However, $p$-values do not indicate the size or importance of the effect (APA, 2001; Wilkinson & the Task Force on Statistical Inference, 1999). Historically, statistical significance has been the only type of significance reported in most journal articles (Thompson, 2002). Unfortunately, use of statistical significance testing has many drawbacks, including that it is unduly affected by sample size; the larger the sample is, the easier it is to find statistical significance (Abelson, 1997). More specifically, a $p$-value tends to be underinterpreted when the sample size is small and the corresponding observed finding is large. On the other hand, a $p$-value tends to be overinterpreted when the sample size is large and the associated observed finding is small (Daniel, 1998a, 1998b).

The second type of significance mentioned throughout this book is practical significance. The $p$-value only indicates how likely it is that the result might occur, it does not address the amount of importance (i.e., practical significance) of the result. Yet, the practical significance of the finding also needs to be reported (Thompson, 2002). Practical significance represents the importance a finding has (Kirk, 1996). Alternatively stated, practical significance represents the size of the relationship or difference. Although useful in interpreting the meaningfulness of an observed result, like $p$-values, effect size indices have several limitations. Onwuegbuzie and Levin (2003b) identified the following nine limitations of effect size indices: (a) effect sizes vary as a function of research objective (i.e., theory application or effects application); (b) effect sizes vary as a function of research design; (c) many researchers do not specify the effect size index used; (d) guidelines for interpreting effect sizes are inconsistent and generally arbitrary; (e) effect sizes vary as a function of sample size and sample variablity; (f) effect sizes are sensitive to departures from normality and homogeneity of variance; (g) effect sizes vary as a function of score variability of the measure of interest; (h) effect sizes vary as a function of score reliability; and (i) effect sizes vary as a function of scale of measurement used (i.e., nominal, ordinal, interval, ratio).

Clinical significance is the third type of significance that has been suggested to be routinely reported (Thompson, 2002). Kazdin (1999) defines clinical significance as "the practical or applied value or importance of the effect of the intervention—that is, whether the intervention makes a real (e.g., genuine, palpable, practical, noticeable) difference in everyday life to the clients or to others with whom the client interacts" (p. 332). According to Kazdin, clinical significance can be found even in the absence of practical significance. In the library context, an intervention designed to reduce library anxiety might have no appreciable impact with respect to making study participants (statistically significantly or practically significantly) distinct in anxiety scores from control group members who did not receive the treatment. Notwithstanding, the intervention may be effective in helping students cope better when their library anxiety levels are elevated. In such cases, the intervention would be deemed to have generated clinically significant findings. Thus, library researchers should consider supplementing reporting of statistical significance (i.e., *p*-values) and practical significance (e.g., effect size) indices with measures of clinical significance. Unfortunately, it should be noted that clinical significance is often difficult to estimate due to its qualitative nature.

Very recently, Leech and Onwuegbuzie (2003) contended that the three types of significance available for social and behavioral science researchers do not convey all the information needed to make policy decisions. Therefore, they proposed a fourth type of significance, *economic significance,* which they maintained has a greater chance of driving policy in an objective manner. According to Leech and Onwuegbuzie, economic significance refers to the economic value of the effect of an intervention. For example, if an intervention prevents a child from dropping out of school, then the economic significance could represent that child's economic contribution to society, weighted by the probability of selected risk factors (e.g., probability of no future incarceration).

Leech and Onwuegbuzie (2003) provided a framework for conducting economic significance analyses. They discussed economic significance analyses and economic significance indices. An economic significance analysis (ECA) can be defined broadly as the derivation, computation, and use of a broad set of cost-based indices that facilitate evaluation and decision making. Economic significance indices (ECIs), which are based on ECAs, can be utilized to supplement or to complement any of the three existing types of significance, or it can be used alone. Leech and Onwuegbuzie presented a typology of ESIs, comprising measures of cost-effectiveness, cost-benefit, cost-utility, cost-feasibility, and cost-sensitivity. According to these methodologists, *cost-effectiveness ESIs* provide information about the effectiveness of an intervention per level of cost or the cost per level of effectiveness. That is, cost-effectiveness ESIs take into account both the cost and effect. *Cost-benefit ESIs* yield estimates that allow comparisons of costs and benefits. *Cost-utility ESIs* provide information about the cost of the interventions relative to the estimated utility of their observed outcomes. *Cost-feasibility ESIs* provide information about the cost of an intervention in order to determine whether it is within boundaries of the budget or other available resources. Finally, *cost-sensitivity ESIs* represent estimates of economic significance that incorporate uncertainty into the estimate of effectiveness, cost, benefit, utility, and/or feasibility. All of these classes of ESIs provide indices based on monetary units. Further, Leech and Onwuegbuzie discussed several indices for each of these five classes of ESI. For instance, with respect to cost-effectiveness ESIs, Leech and Onwuegbuzie defined *cost/effect-size indices,* expressed in pecuniary terms, as the ratio between the cost of the intervention and the effect size. Additionally, Leech and Onwuegbuzie outlined how to construct confidence intervals around ESIs.

As noted by Leech and Onwuegbuzie (2003), economic significance provides a fourth type of significance that is more readily understood by policy makers and stakeholders than are the three other measures of significance, thereby having great potential for significantly impacting policy. Thus, library researchers should consider computing and reporting measures of economic significance. Indeed, in an era of increasing library budget cuts, and librarians being required to justify their roles to a much greater extent than previously, economic significance indices could be used to address a myriad of important research questions, including the following: What is the economic benefit to society of good library skills? What is the economic impact of academic librarians? What is the economic significance of a $1,000 increase/decrease in the library budget? To date, no study in the area of library anxiety has included measures of economic significance. As such, economic significance indices should be a subject of future library anxiety research.

## QUALITATIVE RESEARCH PARADIGM

### Describing Data-Analytical Techniques

As noted by Onwuegbuzie and Teddlie (2003), qualitative researchers tend to present their results in a sociocultural context to a greater extent than do their quantitative counterparts. Moreover, interpretivists by collecting richer, thicker data, typically are able to extract more meaning from their analyses than are statisticians.

However, while providing meaning to a set of findings is a particular strength of qualitative research, specifying information about the analytical methods used and the major features of the analysis is a particular weakness (Constas, 1992; Onwuegbuzie & Teddlie, 2003). For instance, while Mellon's (1986) seminal study provided important implications information for the library science and information field, scant details were presented about how the journals were analyzed. In particular, it was not clear how the themes emerged. In particular, no account was furnished as to how Mellon arrived at the four causes that emerged for students feeling lost when using the library. Similarly, Onwuegbuzie (1997a), in conducting a thematic analysis of graduate students' journals, provided insufficient information about how the emergent themes were developed.

To help qualitative researchers provide more information about the analytical methodology used, Constas (1992) outlined a framework for describing typology development (i.e., the creation of themes). According to Constas (1992), in creating a typology, at least five sources can be utilized. These five loci of origination are *investigative* (constructed directly by the researcher), *literature* (derived from findings and conclusions documented in the extant literature), *participants* (participants themselves identify categories), *interpretative* (developed from a preexisting set of analytical concepts), and *programs* (constructed from a set of goals or objectives stated in program manifesto). The qualitative researcher should decide before data are analyzed where the responsibility or authority for the typology development resides. Once a decision has been made, library researchers conducting qualitative analyses should delineate which source was used in the final report.

In addition, library researchers should decide on the source of the names used to identify a given category, theme, or typology. As is the case for loci of origination, the source of names used to identify a category comprise the following: *investigative* (provided directly by the researcher), *literature* (existing theories from the literature lead to the naming of categories), *participants* (participants themselves name the categories), *interpretative* (names derived from a preexisting set of analytical concepts), and *programs* (derived directly from programmatic objectives).

After a typology has been developed via a qualitative data analysis, the library researcher should attempt to justify its construction. According to Constas (1992), at least six sources of justification are at the analyst's disposal: *empirical* (verifies a typology by examining the coverage, uniqueness, and exclusivity of the categories that underlie it), *rational* (using logic and reasoning to justify a given typology), *technical* (employs language, ideas, and concepts used by researchers to verify a typology, such as interrater reliability), *participative* (participants are asked to review, and then to verify or to modify one or more categories), *referential* (using research findings or theoretical frameworks to justify, through corroboration, a particular typology), and *external* (employing a panel of experts not connected to the study to verify and to substantiate a given typology). It should be noted that the library science researcher could use simultaneously more than one of these sources to verify a typology.

Temporal designation refers to the temporal characteristics of the data analysis process. With respect to this element, the library science researcher should decide whether typology development would occur *a posteriori, a priori*, or iteratively (Constas, 1992). In the *a posteriori* case, categories are created after all qualitative data have been collected. In the *a priori* case, categories are created before data are collected. Finally, in the iterative scenario, categories are created at different phases of the qualitative research process.

In summary, to make qualitative data analysis more of a "public event" (Constas, 1992), library researchers should provide the reader with as much information as possible about the source of typology development, the nomination source for typology development, the verification source for typology development, and the temporal designation for the data-analytic procedures. Such details would lead to the improvement of the reporting practices of library researchers conducting qualitative inquiries. An excellent example of a qualitative study in which the typology development was described is Kracker and Wang (2002).

## Generalizing Findings beyond Sample

Typically, the overall goal of qualitative research in the study of human behavior is to obtain insights into particular behavioral, social, educational, and familial processes and practices that exist within a specific location (Connolly, 1998). Moreover, in qualitative research, the aim typically is not to make broad generalizations of the findings but to maximize the information extracted from each person. In such cases, compared to quantitative research designs, qualitative inquiries use a relatively small number of participants. Further, random samples are rarely ever taken, with qualitative researchers often preferring to select purposive samples.

As such, the sample used in qualitative investigations routinely is not designed to be representative of a larger population from where the sample was taken. Therefore, it is very disturbing that many qualitative researchers attempt to generalize their findings (e.g., thematic representations) beyond the sample to the underlying population (Onwuegbuzie, in press-c; Onwuegbuzie & Teddlie, 2003). In fact, it is only when relatively large representative samples are used that it is fully justified for researchers to generalize findings from the sample to the population. For example, Mellon (1986) was justified in generalizing her results to the population because she obtained qualitative data from an extremely large sample of 6,000 undergraduate students. Even though a nonrandom sample was selected, it is very likely that such a large sample was representative of undergraduate students in general. Interestingly, although qualitative in nature, Mellon's (1986) study, by far, involved the largest sample used in the area of library anxiety research. This is why it is widely recognized that Mellon has made a unique contribution to this field.

## Failure to Estimate and Interpret Effect Sizes

The latest edition (version 5) of APA's publication manual (APA, 2001) stipulated that the reader should be provided "not only with information about statistical significance but also with enough information to assess the magnitude of the observed effect or relationship" (p. 26). In addition, APA (2001) stated the following: "For the reader to fully understand the importance of your findings, it is almost necessary to include some index of effect size or strength of relationship in your Results section" (p. 25). Clearly, these stipulations were made for quantitative data. Yet, as articulated by Onwuegbuzie (in press-c) and Onwuegbuzie and Teddlie (2003), effect sizes also should be reported and interpreted when analyzing qualitative data. According to Onwuegbuzie (in press-c), reporting effect sizes for qualitative data often leads to the enhancement of meaning. Apparently, the failure to utilize effect sizes by qualitative researchers stems, at least in part, from researchers associating effect sizes with the quantitative paradigm (Onwuegbuzie, in press-c).

Onwuegbuzie (in press-c) presented a typology of effect sizes for qualitative data, which was further expanded by Onwuegbuzie and Teddlie (2003). The typologies presented by these methodologists were classified as either *manifest effect sizes* (i.e., effect sizes pertaining to observable content) and *latent effect sizes* (i.e., effect sizes referring to nonobservable, underlying aspects of the phenomenon being studied). Onwuegbuzie (in press-c) noted that, when conducting thematic analyses, qualitative researchers typically only classify and describe emergent themes. However, he contended that much more information could be determined about these themes. Specifically, these themes can be quantitized (i.e., quantified) by counting the frequency of occurrence (e.g., least/most prevalent theme) and intensity of each identified theme. That is, for each study participant, a score of "1" is given for a theme if it represents a significant statement or observation pertaining to that individual; otherwise, a score of "0" is given. For each sample member, each theme is *binarized* to a score of "1" or "0." Accordingly, this binarization culminates in the formation of matrices that Onwuegbuzie (in press-c) called an *interrespondent matrix* (*participant x theme matrix*) and an *intrarespondent matrix* (*unit x theme matrix*). These matrices can be used to determine the frequency of occurrence and to ascertain the order of prevalence.

Onwuegbuzie (in press-c) demonstrated how exploratory factor analyses, typically undertaken by quantitative researchers, could be performed on these matrices such that the hierarchical structure of the themes (i.e., *meta-themes*) and their interrelationships can be identified. Onwuegbuzie also illustrated how effect sizes (e.g., eigenvalues, trace, and proportion of variance explained by each theme) pertaining to the thematic structure and relationships among themes and metathemes could be estimated.

Onwuegbuzie (in press-c) and Onwuegbuzie and Teddlie (2003) discussed the concept of *adjusted effect sizes* in qualitative research, in which the frequency and intensity of themes are adjusted for the time occurrence and length of the unit of analysis (e.g., text, observation, interview). For example, with respect to the length of unit analysis, library researchers could divide the frequency of the emergent theme by the number of words, sentences, paragraphs, and/or pages analyzed. As contended by Onwuegbuzie (in press-c), such adjusted effect sizes help minimize bias that is inherent in the data. Although they did not term it as such, Kracker and Wang (2002) provided several measures of effect size for their qualitative data. For instance, these researchers reported the following:

> Along the cognitive dimension (Table 2), all categories were mentioned by at least six participants. The categories most often mentioned, with 60 or more mentions, include: task initiation (ISP stage 1 mentioned by 59% of participants), overall aspects (ISP model; 55% participants), information collection (ISP stage 5; 47% participants), and writing (not addressed explicitly in the ISP; 42% participants). (p. 299)

## Failure to Use Computerized Data Analysis Tools

Although quantitative researchers virtually always use computers to analyze empirical data, computer software has been severely underutilized by qualitative researchers (Creswell, 1998). Yet, as stated by Creswell (1998), when the text database is large, computers offer many advantages over the traditional, manual data analysis. These benefits include the fact that qualitative computer programs provide electronic data that can be accessed quickly and easily. However, qualitative computer programs should never be used as a substitute for a comprehensive reading of the text in order to maximize meaning. Choice of the most appropriate type of qualitative software to use depends on the experience of the analyst with computers, whether single or multiple cases are used, whether the data are structured or unstructured, whether the data are fixed or evolving, and the size of the database (Miles & Huberman, 1994). As noted by Miles and Huberman (1994), selection of qualitative software also depends on whether the intended data analysis is exploratory or confirmatory, whether the coding scheme is fixed or evolving, whether single or multiple coding is being utilized, whether the data analysis is iterative, the level of interest in the context of the data, the specificity of the analysis, and the level of sophistication needed for the data display. In any case, Kracker and Wang (2002) should be applauded for their use of a computerized data analysis (i.e., QSR NUD*IST; Richards & Richards, 1994) of their qualitative data.

## MIXED-METHODOLOGICAL
## RESEARCH PARADIGM

Onwuegbuzie and Teddlie (2003) defined the "*fundamental principle of mixed methods data analysis* as the use of quantitative and qualitative analytical techniques either concurrently or sequentially, at some stage beginning with the data collection process, from which interpretations are made either in a parallel, integrated, or iterative manner" (p. 352). According to these authors, mixed-methodological data analyses provide researchers with the opportunity to address the relative weaknesses of quantitative and qualitative research combining the strengths of data analysis techniques typically associated with both paradigms. However, before library researchers should conduct mixed-methodological analyses, they must be cognizant of the important considerations that underlie such class of procedures.

Over the last decade, procedures for conducting mixed-method data analyses have emerged. In particular, Caracelli and Greene (1993) summarized the following mixed data analysis strategies used in the behavioral and social sciences: (a) data transformation (i.e., the transformation of one data type into another in order that both data can be analyzed simultaneously); (b) typology development (i.e., the analysis of one type of data yields a typology that is subsequently used as a framework applied in analyzing and contrasting the data types); (c) extreme-case analysis (i.e., extreme cases identified from the analysis of one data type and pursued via additional data collection and data analysis of data of the other type, with the goal of examining and modifying the initial explanation for the extreme cases); and (d) data consolidation/merging (i.e., the joint review of both data types to create new or combined variables or data sets, which can be expressed in either quantitative or qualitative form that are used in future analyses).

Similarly, Tashakkori and Teddlie (1998) identified (a) concurrent mixed-data analyses, comprising parallel mixed analysis (i.e., triangulation), concurrent analysis of the same qualitative data using both quantitative and qualitative techniques, and concurrent analysis of the same quantitative data using both quantitative and qualitative techniques; and (b) sequential analyses, consisting of qualitative data analysis followed by confirmatory quantitative data collection and analysis and quantitative data analysis followed by qualitative data collection and analysis.

As noted by Onwuegbuzie and Teddlie (2003), library researchers should consider the following 12 decisions before undertaking a mixed-methods data analysis: (a) the purpose of the mixed-methods research; (b) whether a variable- or a case-oriented analysis should be conducted; (c) whether to utilize exploratory or confirmatory data-analytic techniques, or both; (d) which data types (i.e., quantitative or qualitative) should be utilized; (e) what the relationships are between quantitative and qualitative data types, if both types are used; (f) what data-analytic assumptions underlie the analyses; (g) what the source of typology development is; (h) what the nomination source for typology development is; (i) what the verification source for typology development is; (j) what the temporal designation for the data-analytic procedures is; (k) whether computer software should be used to analyze the data; and (l) what process of legitimation should be used. Addressing these 12 considerations would provide a framework for the library researcher's qualitative data analysis.

Onwuegbuzie and Teddlie (2003) identified seven stages of the mixed-methodological data analysis process as follows: (a) data reduction, (b) data display, (c) data transformation, (d) data correlation, (e) data consolidation, (f) data comparison, and (g) data integration. Data reduction, the first stage, involves reducing the dimensionality of the quantitative data (e.g., via descriptive statistics, exploratory factor analysis) and qualitative data (e.g., via exploratory thematic analysis, memoing). The second stage is data display, which involves describing pictorially the quantitative data (e.g., tables, graphs) and qualitative data (e.g., matrices, charts, graphs, networks, lists, rubrics, and Venn diagrams). This is followed by data transformation, the third stage, in which qualitative data are converted into numerical codes that can be represented statistically (i.e., *quantitized*; Tashakkori & Teddlie, 1998) and/or numerical data are converted into narrative data that can be analyzed qualitatively (i.e., *qualitized*; Tashakkori & Teddlie, 1998). The fourth stage is characterized by data correlation, in which the quantitative data are correlated with the qualitized data. This is followed by data consolidation, the fifth stage, wherein both quantitative and qualitative data are combined to create new or consolidated variables or data sets. The sixth stage, data comparison, involves comparing data from the quantitative and qualitative data sources. Data integration characterizes the seventh stage of Onwuegbuzie and Teddlie's model, whereby both quantitative and qualitative data are integrated into a coherent whole or two separate sets (i.e., quantitative and qualitative) of coherent wholes. Onwuegbuzie and Teddlie (2003) conclude, however, that although these seven stages are somewhat sequential, they are not linear. In both Onwuegbuzie's (1997a) and Kracker's (Kracker, 2002; Kracker & Wang, 2002) mixed-methodological studies, the quantitative and qualitative data underwent the following steps: data reduction, data display, data transformation, data comparison, and data integration.

## SUMMARY AND CONCLUSIONS

The present chapter provided a framework for conducting quantitative, qualitative, and mixed-methodological data analyses. With regard to quantitative data analyses, recommendations for good practices, based on the extant literature, were provided for each of the major data-analytic techniques, including the following: bivariate correlational analyses, multiple regression, analysis of variance, analysis of covariance, multiple analysis of variance, multiple analysis of covariance, discriminant analysis, exploratory factor analysis, confirmatory factor analysis, and structural equation modeling, as well as hierarchical linear modeling. In addition, recommendations for reporting score reliability and effect sizes were provided. Further, the use of nonparametric statistics was promoted.

With respect to qualitative data analyses, a framework was outlined (i.e., Constas, 1992) to help library researchers to provide more information about the analytical methodology used. This included a conceptualization of how to describe the typology development, the source of the names used to identify a given category, the basis for the development of the typology, and the temporal characteristics of the data analysis process. In addition, a typology of effect sizes for qualitative data were presented.

With regard to mixed-methodological data analytic techniques, 12 pre-analysis decisions were presented. Specifically, it was recommended that library researchers make the following 12 considerations before undertaking a mixed-methods data analysis: (a) the purpose of the mixed-methods research; (b) whether a variable-oriented or a case-oriented analysis should be conducted; (c) whether to utilize exploratory or confirmatory data-analytic techniques, or both; (d) which data types (i.e., quantitative or qualitative) should be utilized; (e) what the relationships are between quantitative and qualitative data types, if both types are used; (f) what data-analytic assumptions underlie the analyses; (g) what the source of typology development is; (h) what the nomination source for typology development is; (i) what the verification source for typology development is; (j) what the temporal designation for the data-analytic procedures is; (k) whether computer software should be used to analyze the data; and (l) what process of legitimation should be used. Furthermore, Onwuegbuzie and Teddlie's (2003) seven-stage mixed-methodological data analysis process was summarized. These steps were data reduction, data display, data transformation, data correlation, data consolidation, data comparison, and data integration.

Finally, four types of significance were discussed. In particular, it was recommended that library researchers compute, report, and interpret economic significance indices whenever possible. According to Leech and Onwuegbuzie (2003), economic significance provides indices that are more easily understood by policy makers and stakeholders than are the three other measures of significance, thereby having great potential for significantly impacting policy.

The data-analytic recommendations provided throughout this chapter were extremely up-to-date and cutting-edge. Therefore, the current chapter has provided library researchers with a comprehensive framework for conducting quantitative, qualitative, and mixed-methodological data analyses. Just as choice of the research paradigm, research design and data collection strategies should stem from the research objective and research purpose, so should the selection of data-analytic procedures. However, regardless of the level of complexity or sophistication, it is imperative that library researchers exercise extreme caution when undertaking quantitative, qualitative, and mixed-methodological data analyses. In fact, as noted by Onwuegbuzie and Daniel (2003), use of complex and sophisticated data analytical techniques and computer software should never serve as a substitute for really getting to know the underlying data and carefully checking all analytical assumptions.

*Chapter Six*

# Framework for Conducting Multimethod Research: Data Interpretation Stage

## OVERVIEW

In chapter 5, we provided a framework for undertaking the second major stage of the research process, namely, the data analysis stage. Once data have been analyzed, the next step in the quantitative, qualitative, and mixed-methodological research process is to interpret the data. Part of interpretation includes assessing the validity or truth value of the findings. While using an appropriate data analysis technique is extremely important, legitimation of the data is even more crucial because however appropriate or sophisticated the analysis used, if the data are invalid, then any interpretations are invalid.

Thus, the purpose of this chapter is to discuss the major interpretational errors that occur in published research. In particular, the concept of validity is presented within the quantitative, qualitative, and mixed-methodological research paradigms. A model for assessing the trustworthiness of the findings is presented for each quantitative and qualitative paradigm.

## QUANTITATIVE RESEARCH PARADIGM

In quantitative research, researchers strive to maximize internal and external validity. Indeed, achieving this goal is considered essential before findings can be called scientific. Gay and Airasian (2000, p. 345) define internal validity as "the condition that observed differences on the dependent variable are a direct result of the independent variable, not some other variable." Therefore, internal validity is threatened when plausible rival hypotheses cannot be eliminated. Johnson and Christensen (2000, p. 200) define external validity as "the extent to which the results of a study can be generalized to and across populations, settings, and times."

Internal validity and external validity are very distinct concepts. A finding that has high internal validity does not necessarily have high external validity. In other words, even if a particular finding possesses high internal validity, this does not mean that it can be generalized outside the study context. For example, a finding from a carefully controlled experimental study in a small, rural university revealing that bibliographic instruction significantly reduces levels of library anxiety is likely not generalizable to other tertiary institutions—especially to large urban universities.

Similarly, a result with high external validity does not necessarily have high internal validity. For example, a finding from an investigation conducted over a four-year period (high external validity) revealing that library anxiety reduces over time may be low in internal validity because it lacks sufficient control (i.e., the researcher has no control over unforeseen events that take place during the four-year observation that might influence library anxiety). In fact, to some extent, internal validity and external validity are inversely related, inasmuch as the more the researcher controls the study (i.e., increases internal validity), the less likely the condition/setting is to reflect the normal state of affairs (i.e., decrease in external validity). The converse also is true: increasing generalizability (i.e., increase in external validity) likely leads to less control by the researcher (i.e., decrease in internal validity).

The groundbreaking works of Donald Campbell and Julian Stanley (Campbell, 1957; Campbell & Stanley, 1963) provide the most authoritative source pertaining to threats to validity. Campbell (1957) and Campbell and Stanley (1963) identified eight threats to internal validity pertaining to experimental studies: history, maturation, testing, instrumentation, statistical regression, differential selection of participants, mortality, and interaction effects (e.g., selection-maturation interaction). Building on the works of Campbell (1957) and Campbell and Stanley

(1963), Smith and Glass (1987) classified threats to external validity relating to experimental investigations into three areas: population validity (i.e., selection-treatment interaction); ecological validity (i.e., experimenter effects, multiple-treatment interference, reactive arrangements, time and treatment interaction, history and treatment interaction); and external validity of operations (i.e., specificity of variables, pretest sensitization).

Extending Campbell and Stanley's (Campbell, 1957; Campbell & Stanley, 1963) framework of sources of invalidity, Onwuegbuzie (2003a) presented 50 threats to internal and external validity that occur at the research design/data collection, data analysis, and/or data interpretation stages of the quantitative research process. These threats are presented in figure 6.1. It can be seen from this diagram that Onwuegbuzie's (2003a) model is more comprehensive than its predecessors. Each of these threats is summarized below.

## Internal Validity at the Research Design/Data Collection Stage

From Figure 6.1, it can be seen that 22 threats to internal validity occur at the research design/data collection stage. These threats comprise Campbell and Stanley's (1963) 8 threats to internal validity, plus an additional 14 threats. Each of these threats is discussed below.

*History* refers to the occurrence of events, conditions, or dispositions that are unrelated to the intervention but that occur at some point during the study to yield changes in the outcome measure. *Maturation* involves processes that function within a study participant as a result of the passage of time. These processes lead to physical, emotional, mental, and intellectual changes such as aging, fatigue, motivation, boredom, learning, and illness that can be incorrectly attributed to the independent variable. *Testing*, also labeled as *pretesting* and *pretest sensitization*, encompasses changes that may occur in participants' scores obtained on the second administration or postintervention instrument as a result of having taken the preintervention measure. That is, being admitted a preintervention measure may improve scores on the postintervention measure whether or not the intervention took place in between these two measures. *Instrumentation* occurs when scores yielded from an instrument lack adequate relia-

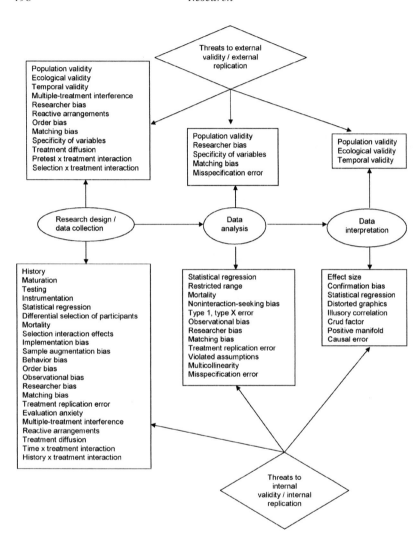

**Figure 6.1   Threats to internal and external validity.**

bility and validity (i.e., inadequate content-, criterion-, and/or construct-related validity). *Statistical regression* often occurs when study participants are chosen on the basis of their extremely low or extremely high scores on some preintervention instrument. This threat pertains to the tendency for extreme scores to regress, or move toward, the mean on subsequent administrations of the measure. It should be noted that many library researchers study special groups of persons such as library users with high levels of library anxiety. These special subgroups typically are identified by library researchers because of their extreme scores on some measure (e.g., the Library Anxiety Scale). Thus, a researcher cannot be certain whether any observed postintervention differences are real or whether they stem from statistical artifacts.

*Differential selection of participants*, also known as *selection bias*, refers to important differences that prevail between two or more of the comparison groups prior to the implementation of the intervention. This threat usually comes to the fore when intact (i.e., already-formed) groups are compared. Group differences may occur that give the false impression that they were caused by the intervention, when, instead, they were actually the result of cognitive, affective, personality, and/or demographic differences between the experimental and control groups. *Mortality,* also called *attrition*, refers to the situation in which participants who have been selected to participate in a research study either fail to take part at all or do not participate in every phase of the inquiry (i.e., drop out of the study). Mortality, per se, does not necessarily confound the findings. Such a bias occurs when participants dropping out of the study leads to discrepancies between the groups that cannot be attributed to the intervention. This is often the case when the rate of attrition is significantly higher for one group than for the other group(s). *Selection interaction effects* involve the interaction of any of the above threats to internal validity with the differential selection of participants threat (e.g., selection x mortality, selection x maturation), which produces an effect that resembles the intervention effect. For instance, a selection by mortality interaction threat can arise if one group experiences a significantly higher rate of attrition than do the other group(s), such that any differences found between the groups reflect, at least to some extent, the differential attrition. Similarly, a selection by maturation interaction threat prevails if one group has a higher rate of maturation than does the other group(s).

Onwuegbuzie (2003a) outlined 14 more threats to internal validity at the data collection stage. According to Onwuegbuzie (2003a), *implementation bias* is one of the most frequent and pervasive threats to internal validity at the data collection stage in intervention studies. Implementation bias stems from the protocol designed for the intervention not being followed sufficiently. It often arises from *differential selection of instructors* who administer the intervention to groups. Onwuegbuzie (2003a) notes that as the number of instructors (e.g., bibliographic instructors) involved in an innovative intervention increases, so does the likelihood that at least some of the teachers will not implement the initiative to its fullest extent. Such lack of adherence to the intervention protocol on the part of some instructors might stem from lack of time, energy, motivation, training, or resources; insufficient knowledge or ability; low perceived self-competence; implementation anxiety; intransigence; or poor attitudes (Onwuegbuzie, 2003a).

Whatever the cause, implementation bias leads to the protocol designed for the intervention not being implemented in the intended manner (i.e., *protocol bias*). For example, poor attitudes of some librarians toward a new bibliographic instruction course may lead to the intervention protocol being violated, which is then transmitted to the prospective library users taking the course, culminating in the true difference between the experimental and control group being masked. An especially common aspect of the implementation threat that prevails is related to time. Many studies involve the assessment of an innovation after a short period of time (e.g., after a one-hour or shorter bibliographic course), which does not offer a realistic chance to observe positive gains (Rogers, 1995). A difference in the experience of the library educators between instructors participating in the intervention and nonintervention groups is another way that implementation bias may pose a threat to internal validity.

*Sample augmentation bias*, essentially the opposite of mortality, occurs when one or more persons join the intervention or nonintervention groups after the study has begun (e.g., children transferring from a school not involved in the study to a school that is serving either as the experimental or control group). *Behavior bias* takes place when an individual has a strong personal bias in favor of or against the intervention prior to the beginning of the study. *Order bias* occurs when multiple interventions are being compared in a study such that all participants are exposed to and measured under each and every intervention condition. Order bias threatens internal validity when the effect of the order of the intervention conditions cannot be separated from the effect of the intervention conditions.

*Observational bias* occurs when the data collectors did not obtain a sufficient sampling of the behavior(s) of interest. It occurs when the researcher's data collection did not involve persistent observation and/or prolonged engagement (Lincoln & Guba, 1985). *Researcher bias*, which can be active (e.g., statements or mannerisms made by the researcher that makes clear his or her biases) or passive (e.g., personality traits or attributes of the researcher), may occur during the data collection stage when the researcher has a personal bias in favor of one intervention over the remaining technique(s). When such a bias exists, the researcher might subconsciously influence the study findings. *Matching bias* occurs when individuals from the sampling frame for whom a match cannot be found are excluded from the study, such that any difference between those selected and those excluded may lead to a statistical artifact.

*Treatment replication error* comes to the fore when researchers collect data that do not represent the correct unit of analysis (e.g., an intervention is administered once to each group of participants, yet only individual outcome data are collected) (McMillan, 1999). Such a practice seriously violates the assumption that outcome scores of every individual, regardless of group, is independent of all other individuals. This is because individuals within a group typically influence one another in a group context, confounding the findings (Onwuegbuzie, 2003a). *Evaluation anxiety*, which is experienced by many library users, threatens internal validity by introducing systematic error into the measurement. *Multiple-treatment interference* takes place when the same participants are exposed to more than one intervention during the course of the study. In such cases, carryover effects from one or more of the earlier interventions may render it difficult to determine the effectiveness of subsequent interventions, culminating in the findings being confounded (i.e., rival hypotheses).

*Reactive arrangements* (i.e., *Hawthorne effect*, *John Henry effect*, *resentful demoralization*, *novelty effect*, and *placebo effect*) pertain to changes in individuals' responses that can occur as a direct result of being aware that one is participating in a research study. The *Hawthorne effect* occurs when persons interpret their receiving an intervention as receiving special attention, making it difficult to separate their responses from the true effects of the intervention. The *John Henry effect*, or *compensatory rivalry*, is the result of study participants selected for the control group deciding to compete with the new intervention administered to members of the experimental group by expending extra effort during the study. This effect tends to reduce the observed difference between the experimental and control groups because of the extra effort expended by control group members. Conversely, *resentful demoralization* is the result of study participants selected for the control group becoming resentful about not being administered the intervention, resulting in a loss of morale and effort expended. As such, the difference between the experimental group and control group is inflated. The *novelty effect* refers to participants experiencing increases in motivation, effort, or interest in participation merely because the study involves a different or novel task or intervention. The novelty effect threatens internal validity because reactions to the novel task cannot be separated from the true responses to the intervention. The *placebo effect* occurs when individuals in the control group attain more favorable outcomes (e.g., lower anxiety levels, higher levels of performance) merely because they believed that they were in the intervention group. This effect tends to reverse the difference between the experimental and control groups in a manner that contradicts the underlying theory.

*Treatment diffusion*, also known as the *seepage effect*, prevails when members from different intervention groups communicate with each other during the course of the investigation, such that some of the treatment *seeps* out into the control group. Therefore, treatment diffusion reduces the difference between the experimental and control groups because some of the control group members are actually receiving some of the intervention. *Time x treatment interaction* refers to individuals in one group being exposed to an intervention for a longer period of time than are individuals receiving another intervention, in such a way that this differentially affects group members' responses to the intervention. Finally, *history x treatment interaction* occurs when the groups being compared experience different history events, such that these events differentially affect group members' responses to the intervention.

## External Validity at the Research Design/Data Collection Stage

According to Onwuegbuzie (2003a), the following 12 threats to external validity occur at the research design/data collection stage. *Population validity* refers to the extent to which results are generalizable from the study participants to the population from which the sample members were selected. Using nonrandom or small samples tends to reduce the population validity of the findings. *Ecological validity* refers to the extent to which results from an investigation can be generalized across settings, conditions, variables, and contexts. Limiting a study to one setting, condition, variable, or context tends to reduce ecological validity. *Temporal validity* refers to the extent to which research findings can be generalized across time. Failure to consider the role of time in generating the results can threaten the researcher's ability to generalize. *Multiple-treatment interference*, as noted above, occurs when the same research participants are exposed to more than one intervention. The specific order that the interventions are administered reduces the generalizability of the findings.

*Researcher bias*, also known as experimenter effect, threatens external validity because the results may be dependent, at least in part, on the attributes and values of the researcher. *Reactive arrangements*, as described above in the section on internal validity, is more traditionally viewed as a threat to external validity. Indeed, the five components of reactive arrangements (i.e., *Hawthorne effect*, *John Henry effect*, *resentful demoralization*, *novelty effect*, and *placebo effect*) reduce external validity because results become a function of which of these components prevail. *Order bias*, as is the case for reactive arrangements, poses a threat to external validity because in its presence, observed findings would depend on the order in which the multiple interventions are administered. Thus, findings could not necessarily be generalized to conditions in which the order of administration of the treatment was different.

*Matching bias* is a threat to external validity to the degree that results from the matched participants could not be generalized to the findings that would have occurred among persons in the accessible population for whom a match could not be obtained—that is, those in the sampling frame who were not selected for the study. *Specificity of variables* is a threat to external validity in almost every study. Indeed, the more unique the participants, context, conditions, time, and variables, the less generalizable the findings will be. *Treatment diffusion* threatens external validity because it results in the intervention being diffused to other treatment conditions, thereby threatening the researcher's ability to generalize the findings. *Pretest x treatment interaction* refers to situations wherein the administration of a pretest increases or decreases the participants' responsiveness or sensitivity to the intervention, thereby rendering the observed results of the pretested group unrepresentative of the effects of the independent variable for the unpretested population from which the study participants were chosen. In such cases, the researcher can generalize findings to pretested groups but not to unpretested groups. Finally, *selection x treatment interaction* is similar to the differential selection of participants threat to internal validity inasmuch as it arises from important pre-intervention differences between intervention groups, differences that come to the fore because the intervention groups are not representative of the same underlying population. Thus, it would not be possible to generalize the results from one group to another group.

## Internal Validity at the Data Analysis Stage

As illustrated in figure 6.1, the following 21 threats to internal validity occur at the data analysis stage. *Statistical regression* can occur at the data analysis stage when researchers attempt (a) to statistically equate groups, (b) to analyze difference scores, or (c) to analyze longitudinal data. All of these techniques affect internal validity because they are susceptible to regression toward the mean. *Restricted range* occurs typically when researchers artificially categorize continuous variables, leading to a loss in statistical power. In fact, artificially categorizing participants to groups often leads in a degree of misclassification, which threatens internal validity. Moreover, internal validity is increasingly threatened as the number of categorized groups decreases, such that dichotomizing a continuous variable often provides the biggest threat to internal validity. *Mortality* occurs when researchers discard some of the participants' scores from their final data sets in an attempt to analyze groups with equal or approximately equal sample sizes (i.e., to undertake what is called a "balanced" analysis). *Noninteraction seeking bias* stems from researchers' failure to examine the presence of interactions when testing hypotheses. Neglecting interaction effects might underrepresent the true relationship.

*Type I to Type X errors* refer to 10 errors identified by Daniel and Onwuegbuzie (2000) associated with statistical significance testing that distort the findings. The first four errors are labeled by statisticians as Type I (falsely rejecting the null hypothesis), Type II (incorrectly failing to reject the null hypothesis), Type III (incorrect inferences about result directionality), and Type IV (incorrectly following-up an interaction effect with a simple effects analysis). The following six additional statistical errors were identified by Daniel and Onwuegbuzie (2000): (a) Type V error—internal replication error—measured via incidence of Type I or Type II errors detected when conducting internal replications (i.e., resampling the same data to assess the stability of coefficients); (b) Type VI error—reliability generalization error—measured via linkages of statistical results to characteristics of scores on the measures used to generate results (a particularly problematic type of error when researchers fail to consider differential reliability estimates for subsamples within a data set); (c) Type VII error—heterogeneity of variance/regression—measured via the extent to which data treated via analysis of variance/covariance are not appropriately screened to determine whether they meet homogeneity assumptions prior to analysis of group comparison statistics; (d) Type VIII error—test directionality error—measured as the extent to which researchers express alternative hypotheses as directional, yet assess results using two-tailed tests; (e) Type IX error—sampling bias error— measured via discrepancies in findings generated from numerous convenience samples across a multiplicity of similar studies; and (f) Type X error—degrees of freedom error—measured as the tendency of researchers using certain statistical procedures (chiefly stepwise procedures; cf. Chapter 5) erroneously to compute the degrees of freedom utilized in these procedures.

*Observational bias* occurs whenever interrater reliability of the coding scheme is less than 100%. *Researcher bias,* specifically the *halo effect,* prevails when researchers are evaluating open-ended responses and allow their prior knowledge of the participants to influence the scores given. *Matching bias* occurs when groups are matched after the data on the complete sample have been collected. Bias is introduced as a result of omitting participants who were not matched, thereby threatening internal validity. *Treatment replication error* occurs when researchers utilize an inappropriate unit of analysis even though data are available for them to engage in a more appropriate analysis. *Violated assumptions* pose as a threat to internal validity at the data analysis stage when researchers do not adequately check the underlying assumptions (e.g., normality) associated with a particular statistical test. *Multicollinearity* is a threat when two or more independent variables are so related to one another that they confound the researcher's attempt to predict the dependent variable(s).

Finally, *misspecification error* involves omitting one or more important variables from the final model, which often stems from a weak or non-existent theoretical framework for developing and testing a statistical model.

## External Validity at the Data Analysis Stage

As illustrated in figure 6.1, the following five threats to external validity occur at the data analysis stage. *Population validity* occurs every time researchers analyze a subset of their data sets, making results emerging from this subset less generalizable than are those that would have arisen if the total sample had been analyzed. *Researcher bias*, such as the halo effect, not only affects internal validity at the data analysis stage but also poses as a threat to external validity at this stage because the particular type of researcher might be so unique as to make the findings ungeneralizable. *Specificity of variables* can be an external validity threat by the way in which the independent and dependent variables are operationalized (e.g., using local norms). *Matching bias* provides a threat to external validity at the data analysis stage if participants not selected for matching from the data set are in some important way different than those who are matched, such that the results from the selected individuals may not be generalizable to the unselected individuals. Finally, *misspecification error* involves omitting, deliberately or otherwise, one or more important variables (e.g., interaction terms) from the analysis. Although a final model selected may have acceptable internal validity, such omission reduces the external validity of the findings because it is not clear whether the results would be identical if the omitted variable(s) had been included.

## Internal Validity at the Data Interpretation Stage

As illustrated in figure 6.1, the following eight threats to internal validity occur at the data interpretation stage. *Effect size* occurs when researchers interpret statistical significance without taking into account the practical significance (i.e., effect size). As noted in chapter 5, lack of consideration of practical significance can lead to overinterpretation of statistically significant findings, as well as an inability to place findings in an appropriate context. *Confirmation bias* represents the tendency for interpretations and conclusions based on new findings to be overly consistent with preliminary hypotheses. Accordingly, confirmation bias is more likely to occur when researchers are attempting to test theory than when they are attempting to generate theory because testing a theory can "dominate research in a way that blinds the researcher to potentially informative observation" (Greenwald, Pratkanis, Leippe, & Baumgardner, 1986, p. 217). When research hypotheses are not supported, analysts with confirmation bias often proceed as if the theory underlying the hypotheses is still likely to be correct. In proceeding in this manner, these analysts fail to realize that their research methodology no longer can be deemed to be theory testing but theory confirming (Onwuegbuzie, 2003a).

Nevertheless, confirmation bias, per se, does not necessarily pose a threat to internal validity. It only threatens internal validity at the data interpretation stage when one or more plausible rival explanations to the underlying findings prevail that might be demonstrated to be superior if given the opportunity. On the other hand, when no rival explanations exist, confirmation bias helps to provide support for the best or sole explanation of the findings (Greenwald et al., 1986). However, because rival explanations are commonplace in the field of behavioral and social science research, library researchers should be aware of the role that confirmation bias plays in reducing the internal validity of the findings at the data interpretation stage.

*Statistical regression* arises from regression toward the mean, which could affect interpretations. *Distorted graphics* stem from an inappropriate interpretation of graphs from which misinterpretations can ensue. *Illusory correlation* represents a tendency to overestimate the relationship among variables that are only slightly related or not related at all, threatening internal validity at the data interpretation stage. *Crud factor* involves rejecting null hypotheses in the presence of trivial relationships. This typically happens when both the number of relationships examined and the sample size are large. This crud factor results in some analysts identifying and interpreting relationships that are not real but represent statistical artifacts, posing a threat to internal validity at the data interpretation stage. *Positive manifold* refers to the phenomenon that individuals who perform well on one ability or attitudinal measure tend to perform well on other measures in the same domain. This occurrence could lead to overinterpretation of findings. Finally, *causal error* refers to inferring a cause-and-effect relationship from nonexperimental studies. Clearly, such inferences represent a threat to internal validity at the data interpretation stage.

## External Validity at the Data Interpretation Stage

As illustrated in figure 6.1, three threats to external validity occur at the data interpretation stage. *Population validity, ecological validity,* and *temporal validity* typically occur from small and/or nonrandom samples. Thus, library researchers should be very careful not to overgeneralize their conclusions. Instead, they always should compare their results to the literature base as comprehensively as is possible, so that their findings can be interpreted in a more realistic context. Moreover, library researchers should focus more on recommending external replications and on providing directions for future research than on making definitive conclusions (Onwuegbuzie, 2003a).

## QUALITATIVE RESEARCH PARADIGM

## Validity Orientations in the Qualitative Context

According to Denzin (1994), a crisis of legitimation prevails in qualitative research. Denzin says that this crisis requires an answer to the question of how qualitative research findings should be evaluated. Over the last several decades, within the social sciences, four schools of thought have emerged with respect to the legitimation crisis. These schools of thought primarily have at their roots positivism, postpositivism, poststucturalism, or postmodernism.

Researchers who interpret result validity in qualitative research using a positivistic framework, apply the same criteria as are used by quantitative researchers. Specifically, these proponents evaluate qualitative research findings with respect to internal validity and external validity. For instance, Miles and Huberman (1984), who deemed themselves to be "right-wing qualitative researchers" and "soft-nosed positivists" (p. 23), declared that "internal validity issues [are] primary" (p. 22). In addition to evaluating internal and external validity, these methodologists assess qualitative research findings with regard to reliability and objectivity.

Simply put, the positivist view of validity in qualitative research is the belief that the same set of criteria be applied to all social and behavioral science research, regardless of whether it represents quantitative or qualitative research.

Postpositivism is the second legitimation orientation in qualitative research. Postpositivists assert that a set of validity criteria unique to the qualitative paradigm should be utilized. In reality, however, these criteria usually have represented positivist criteria modified for the qualitative research context. In particular, members of this camp contend that the validity of qualitative research findings should be assessed via its ability to generate theory, to be empirically based, to be scientifically credible, to yield generalizable results, and to be internally reflexive inasmuch as the effects of the researcher and the research methodology on the findings are examined (Denzin, 1994).

The third legitimation orientation in qualitative research is poststructuralism. Poststructuralists believe that an entirely new set of criteria need to be developed, criteria that are completely separate from the influence of positivists and postpositivists. Denzin (1994, p. 298) stated that these criteria should involve "stressing subjectivity, emotionality, feeling, and other antifoundational criteria." Denzin surmised that politics is an important impetus for framing validity. To this end, Lather (1986) defined *catalytic validity* as the extent to which a particular research study empowers and liberates a research community. Still within this context, Lather (1993) described the following four types of validity: *ironic, paralogical, rhizomatic,* and *voluptuous* legitimation. Ironic legitimation relies on the assumption that multiple realities of the same phenomenon exist such that the truth value of the research depends on its capacity to reveal co-existing opposites. Paralogical legitimation represents that aspect of validity that identifies paradoxes. Rhizomatic legitimation stems from mapping data and not merely from describing data. Voluptuous legitimation, also referred to as *embodied validity* or *situated validity*, is interpretive in nature. This form of legitimation assesses the degree to which the researcher's level of interpretation exceeds her or his knowledge base arising from the data. In summary, Lather's (1993) four types of validity provide a framework for representing truth that rejects correspondence theories of truth (Newman & Benz, 1998).

The fourth legitimation orientation is postmodernism. Postmodernists seriously question whether criteria can be developed for assessing the validity of qualitative research findings. According to this school of thought, the idea of assessing qualitative research is "antithetical to the nature of this research and the world it attempts to study" (Denzin, 1994, p. 297). As such, many postmodernists believe that validity and qualitative research is an oxymoron. However, some postmodernists believe that criteria are needed, although they advocate criteria that are drastically different than in quantitative research (e.g., internal validity, external validity). For instance, critical theorists believe that control over who to study, what to study, how to undertake the investigation, and the relationship of the researcher to the participant(s) is determined with regard to the power relations representing society at large, unless steps are taken to guarantee that inquiries are designed in a democratic manner. Therefore, the goal of critical theorists is to "democratize" research (Eisenhart & Howe, 1992). Further, feminist researchers maintain that studies with valid findings are represented by those in which (a) the lived experiences of the participants being studied are portrayed, (b) participants are able to understand and to transform their subordinate experiences, (c) the discrepancy between the participants' accounts of their experiences and the researcher's description is minimized, and (d) the researcher's prior theoretical and political commitments are allowed to be informed and transformed by the knowledge and understanding that emerge from the participants' experiences (Roman & Apple, 1990).

Kvale (1995) also outlined a postmodernist view of validity. Interestingly, Kvale termed his view of validity as representing "moderate postmodernism" or an "affirmative post-modernism" (p. 21). According to Kvale, knowledge stemming from qualitative research is the result of a social construction. Consequently, he rejected the idea of universal truth, at the same time acknowledging the possibility of specific local, personal, and community dimensions of truth, which have a focus on everyday life and local narrative.

Kvale (1995) labels his validity components as *investigation validity*, *communicative validity*, and *action validity*. Investigation validity is the quality of craftmanship, wherein validity represents the researcher's quality control. Accordingly, validity not only is a function of the methods used, but also of the researcher's attributes, personality traits, and ethicalness. That is, instead of denoting some final decision, validity is a verification process built into the research study involving continual checks of trustworthiness, credibility, and plausibility. Moreover, each step of the research process encompasses a specific aspect of validity. As a result, the investigative concept of validity is inherent in grounded theory (Glaser & Strauss, 1967). Kvale's investigation validity pertains to how theories are derived from the underlying data, as well as how researchers should conceptualize their research topics. This form of validity implies that the extent to which theory is consistent with the research objective, purpose, and data indicates the degree of validity.

Kvale's (1995) communicative validity involves assessing the validity of knowledge claims in a discourse. Alternatively stated, findings have communicative validity if they are agreed on by the community of researchers. Kvale contended that "a construct and its measurement are validated when the discourse about their relationship is persuasive to the community of researchers" (p. 22). Finally, with regard to Kvale's action validity, justification of the validity of the research depends on whether or not it works—that is, whether or not the research findings are used by decision makers and other stakeholders. In summary, Kvale's three-dimensional conceptualization of validity involves questioning, theorizing, and checking.

At the most extreme end of the postmodernist school of thought lie constructivists such as Wolcott (1990), who question whether validity is appropriate, legitimate, or even useful in qualitative inquires. Moreover, Wolcott declares that validity does not capture the essence of what he seeks and, therefore, "validity neither guides nor informs" his research (p. 136). Instead, for Wolcott, validity interferes with his goal of understanding the underlying phenomenon. However, Wolcott does not dismiss validity completely but rather places it within a more general context. In particular, he seeks to identify "critical elements" and to write "plausible interpretations from them" (p. 146). Wolcott notes that understanding is a more fundamental concept for qualitative research than is validity. Thus, he strives to understand what is occurring rather than to convince his audience about his findings.

## Quest to Establish Legitimacy

According to Eisenhart and Howe (1992), the following three major responses emerged from the quest to establish legitimacy in qualitative research: (a) adoptions of the conventional approach, (b) alternatives to the conventional approach, and (c) eclecticism. As noted above, some qualitative researchers adopted the conventional approach, namely, the positivist or empiricist conceptualization of internal and external validity. For instance, Denzin (1989), who compared seven research methodologies (i.e., experiments, participant observations, surveys, unobtrusive methods, life histories, interviewing, and filming), used Campbell and Stanley's (i.e., Campbell, 1957, 1963a, 1963b; Campbell & Stanley, 1963) eight threats to internal validity and four threats to external validity as a basis for comparison. Denzin demonstrated that each of these designs had relative strengths and weaknesses in terms of minimizing threats to internal and external validity, with experiments and participant observations being rated as representing the most robust design. However, Denzin noted that threats to validity are not minimized in the same manner in each research design.

Goetz and LeCompte (1984) also discussed validity in qualitative research within the framework of conventional threats to internal and external validity, as well as with respect to construct-related validity. Goetz and LeCompte contended that attributes of a good qualitative research include completeness, clarity, appropriateness, comprehensiveness of scope, credibility, and significance. However, whereas Denzin (1989) considered how various research designs, when used together within the same framework, meet the requirements of the conventional approach, Goetz and LeCompte translated the conventional meanings of validity into qualitative vernacular (Eisenhart & Howe, 1992).

The second response to the challenge of validity in qualitative research under Eisenhart and Howe's model represented alternatives to the conventional (positivist) conception of validity. This position was characterized by extreme skepticism (e.g., Erickson, 1986) or outright refutation (e.g., Lincoln & Guba, 1985) of the claim that the conventional definitions of validity can be transferred to qualitative research. Erickson (1986, p. 119) declared that the "basic validity criterion" of qualitative research is "the *immediate and local meanings of actions*, as defined from the actors' point of view" [emphasis in original]. According to Erickson, the crucial aspect of validity in ethnographic studies is the manner in which the story is told and evidence for its truth value is provided. Erickson also contended that legitimation in qualitative research also relates to how the findings will be understood and used by various audiences.

Lincoln and Guba (1985) took an even more extreme position with respect to validity in qualitative research, advocating the development of an entirely different set of standards than that employed by quantitative researchers. Lincoln and Guba's stance is similar to that of Ely, Anzul, Friedman, Garner, and Steinmetz (1991), who declared that using quantitative vernacular tends to be a defensive measure that results in holding quantitative research as a standard by which qualitative research is evaluated.

Lincoln and Guba (1985) concluded that meeting the standards involves (a) conducting qualitative research in such a way as to increase the likelihood that the categories pertaining to the participants rather than to the researcher will emerge, and (b) having participants approve the researchers' interpretations. These interpretive theorists also promoted the use of persistent observation, prolonged engagement, and triangulation as methods of assessing trustworthiness of data. Lincoln and Guba referred to four types of trustworthiness in qualitative research, which, ironically, are analogous to Campbell and Stanley's (1963) major concepts. Specifically, Lincoln and Guba's (1985) elements of trustworthiness, namely, truth value, applicability, consistency, and neutrality, are similar to Campbell and Stanley's (1963) concepts of internal validity, external validity, reliability, and objectivity, respectively (Eisenhart & Howe, 1992). Other terminology used by Lincoln and Guba to discuss validity in qualitative research includes credibility, dependability, confirmability, and transferability. Again, however, these concepts are parallel to the concepts of internal validity, reliability, objectivity, and external validity, respectively, advanced by quantitative researchers (Daniel & Onwuegbuzie, 2002).

Rather than using the term validity, Eisner (1991) discussed the credibility of qualitative research. He outlined standards such as *structural corroboration, consensual validation*, and *referential adequacy*. In structural corroboration, qualitative researchers use multiple types of data to support or to contradict the interpretation. Eisner called this form of triangulation "confluence of evidence" (p. 110). Consensual validation originates from the opinion of others, with "an agreement among competent others that the description, interpretation, and evaluation and thematics of an educational situation are right" (p. 112). Finally, referential adequacy high-lights the importance of criticism. According to Eisner, the goal of criticism is to emphasize the subject matter, from which a more complex level of *verhesten* emerges.

The third and final response to the challenge of validity in qualitative research under Eisenhart and Howe's model represented what they called eclecticism. This form of criteria incorporates ideas stemming from both quantitative and qualitative orientations of validity. Apparently, eclectics believe that criteria generally can be applied to all research designs. Consequently, this form of legitimation is the most inclusive. An example of an eclectic conceptualization of validity is Maxwell (1992), who identified five types of validity, which he labeled as *descriptive validity, interpretive validity, theoretical validity, generalizability*, and *evaluative validity*. Descriptive validity pertains to the factual accuracy of the account as documented by the researcher. As noted by Johnson (1999), the key questions addressed in descriptive validity include: Did what was reported by the researcher as occurring in the group being studied actually take place? Did the researchers accurately document what they observed, saw, and heard? That is, descriptive validity refers to the accuracy in reporting descriptive information (e.g., description of peoples, statements, objects, events, behaviors, settings, places, and time). According to Maxwell (1992), descriptive validity can involve both errors of omission and commission. Descriptive validity can also refer to statistically descriptive aspects of accounts (Maxwell, 1992).

Maxwell (1992) defines interpretive validity as the extent to which a researcher's interpretation of an account represents an understanding of the perspective of the group under study and the meanings attached to their words and actions. That is, interpretative validity refers to the degree to which the study participants' voices (e.g., viewpoints, beliefs, thoughts, intentions, feelings, intentions, experiences, actions) are accurately understood by the researcher and captured in the research article. Understanding participants' inner (i.e., phenomenological) worlds is central to interpretive validity, which refers to the accuracy in depicting these inner worlds (Johnson, 1999).

Theoretical validity represents the extent to which a theoretical explanation developed from research findings fits the underlying data and, therefore, is credible, trustworthy, and defensible (Johnson, 1999). Maxwell (1996) deems theoretical validity to be the most serious threat to validity. According to Maxwell (1996), threats to theoretical validity occur when a researcher does not collect or pay attention to discrepant data or does not consider all rival explanations of the underlying phenomena.

Generalizabilty, the fourth type of validity discussed by Maxwell (1992), refers to the extent to which a researcher can generalize the account of a particular behavior, situation, or population to other individuals, groups, times, settings, or context. Maxwell distinguishes internal generalizability from external generalizability. The former (i.e., internal generalizability) refers to how generalizable a conclusion is within the setting or group studied, whereas, the latter (i.e., external generalizability) pertains to the extent to which interpretations can be generalized beyond the group, setting, time, or context. According to Maxwell, internal generalizability usually is more important to qualitative researchers than is external generalizability. Finally, evaluative validity pertains to the degree to which an evaluation framework can be applied to the objects of study rather than a descriptive, interpretive, or explanatory one (Maxwell, 1992).

Eisenhart and Howe (1992) criticize all three approaches to validity (i.e., adaptation of the conventional approach, alternatives, eclecticism) because they promote the belief either that all research, regardless of paradigm, must be evaluated with respect to the same criterion (adaptation) or that there must be different types of validity (alternatives, eclecticism). Conversely, Eisenhart and Howe (1992, p. 656) advance a unitary concept of validity with "different design-specific instances." Moreover, they outline five general standards for conducting social and behavioral research that are relevant for all research designs. Specifically, these five standards are (a) there is an appropriate match among research questions, data collection techniques, and analytical techniques; (b) the application of specific data collection and analysis procedures are appropriate and effective; (c) the research is coherent with respect to previous work; (d) the research represents essential and ethical work; and (e) the research is comprehensive.

With the exception of a few qualitative researchers such as Wolcott (1990), who question whether validity is appropriate or useful in qualitative studies, it appears that the majority of interpretivists acknowledge and accept the legitimacy of the concept of validity. In fact, it is likely that a reason for the rejection of validity by some qualitative researchers stems from their perceptions that the positivist framework of validity (e.g., internal validity, external validity, construct-related validity, structural validity, criterion-related validity) typically is used as the standard against which all other standards are conceptualized and assessed. Therefore, they believe that to reject positivism, they must reject validity. However, this should not be the case. In fact, as observed by Constas (1992, p. 255), unless procedures for examining rival hypotheses in qualitative research are developed, "the research community will be entitled to question the analytical rigor of qualitative research"—where rigor is defined as the attempt to make data and interpretations as public and as replicable as possible (Denzin, 1978).

Unfortunately, too many qualitative researchers adopt an "anything goes" relativist attitude, thereby not paying sufficient attention to providing an adequate rationale for interpretations of their data. For instance, many interpretivists do not sufficiently document how they identify emergent themes. Yet, as contended by Onwuegbuzie (2000b), if there cannot be standards (i.e., validity) for qualitative research, how do editors of qualitative journals determine which studies get published? Surely, editors use criteria for judging the quality of qualitative research articles. Therefore, it is clear that rigor in research always is essential, regardless of whether quantitative or qualitative research techniques are used. With regard to the latter, it is important that qualitative researchers assess the truth value of their findings. This can be accomplished by reframing the concept of validity in qualitative research, for example, by treating validity as an issue of selecting among rival interpretations and of examining and providing arguments for the relative credibility of competing knowledge claims (Polkinghorne, 1983) or by redefining validity as having multi-faceted criteria (e.g., credibility, dependability, confirmability, transferability; Lincoln & Guba, 1985).

## Establishing Design-Specific Legitimacy in Qualitative Research

As noted by Onwuegbuzie and Daniel (2003), one of the most common errors committed by qualitative researchers is a failure, often on philosophical grounds, to legitimize research findings and interpretations through documentation of validity (e.g., credibility, relativism, internal criticism, external criticism) and reliability (e.g., interrater reliability). Although the importance of validity has long been accepted by quantitative researchers, this concept has been the subject of much debate among qualitative researchers. At one end of the qualitative continuum are researchers (e.g., Goetz & LeCompte, 1984; Miles & Huberman, 1984) who contend that validity for qualitative research should be interpreted in the same manner as for quantitative research. At the opposite end of the spectrum are postmodernists (e.g., Wolcott, 1990) who question the rationale for incorporating validity into qualitative research, asserting that the goal of documenting evidences of validity is unrealistic and even unnecessary. Disturbingly, a common definition of validity among relativists is that it represents whatever the research community agrees it should represent. Unfortunately, such a definition is ambiguous and misleading and, consequently, does not help beginning qualitative researchers to design their studies and to evaluate the legitimacy and trustworthiness of their findings.

Yet, for qualitative findings to be taken seriously by stakeholders, as is the case for quantitative researchers, qualitative researchers must be accountable fully at all phases of their research study, including the data collection, analysis, and interpretation stages. Such accountability can only come to the fore by providing evidence of legitimation. Thus, in an attempt to integrate the qualitative field more with respect to legitimation, Onwuegbuzie (2000b) proposed a *Qualitative Legitimation Model*. This model, presented in figure 6.2, attempts to integrate many of the types of validity identified by qualitative researchers. Onwuegbuzie (2000b), like Onwuegbuzie (2003a), conceptualized validity in qualitative research as occurring at the research design/data collection, data analysis, and data interpretation stages of the research process. However, Onwuegbuzie (2000b) noted that the data collection, data analysis, data validation, and data interpretation stages are not linear but represent iterative, cyclical, recursive, and interactive steps in the chain.

The Qualitative Legitimation Model comprises threats to internal credibility and external credibility. Onwuegbuzie (2000b) defined internal credibility as the truth value, applicability, consistency, dependability,

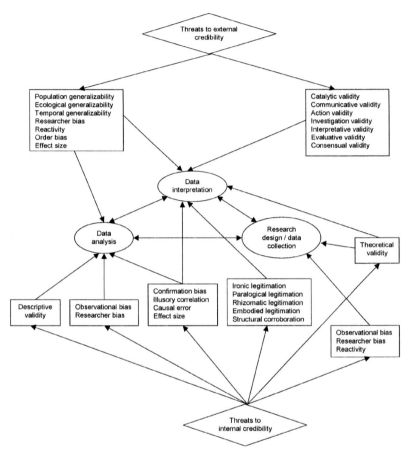

**Figure 6.2  Qualitative legitimation model.**

neutrality, and/or credibility of interpretations and conclusions within the particular setting or group. Internal credibility corresponds to what Onwuegbuzie (2003a) termed internal replication in quantitative research. Conversely, external credibility involves the degree to which findings from a study can be generalized across different populations of persons, settings, contexts, and times. In other words, external credibility pertains to the confirmability and transferability of results and conclusions. All threats identified in the Qualitative Legitimation Model are classified either as threats to internal credibility, external credibility, or both. Each of these threats, presented in figure 6.2, is described below.

## Threats to Internal Credibility in Qualitative Research

As illustrated in figure 6.2, the following threats to internal credibility are pertinent to qualitative research: ironic legitimation, paralogical legitimation, rhizomatic legitimation, voluptuous (i.e., embodied) legitimation, descriptive validity, structural corroboration, theoretical validity, observational bias, researcher bias, reactivity, confirmation bias, illusory correlation, causal error, and effect size. The first seven sources of legitimation have been described in the preceding qualitative sections; the next six sources were discussed in previous quantitative sections in this chapter. The final source, effect size, was described for both quantitative research (in previous quantitative sections of this chapter) and qualitative research (chapter 5).

## THREATS TO EXTERNAL CREDIBILITY IN QUALITATIVE RESEARCH

As presented in figure 6.2, the following threats to external credibility are pertinent to qualitative research: catalytic validity, communicative validity, action validity, investigation validity, interpretive validity, evaluative validity, consensual validity, population generalizability, ecological generalizability, temporal generalizability, researcher bias, reactivity, order bias, and effect size. The first seven sources of legitimation were described in the preceding qualitative sections. The next three sources (i.e., population generalizability, ecological generalizability, temporal generalizability) were discussed for both quantitative research (in previous quantitative sections of this chapter) and qualitative research (chapter 5). The next three threats (i.e., researcher bias, reactivity, order bias) were described in previous quantitative sections in this chapter. The final source, effect size, was described for both quantitative research (in previous quantitative sections of this chapter) and qualitative research (chapter 5).

## A TYPOLOGY OF METHODS FOR ASSESSING
## OR INCREASING LEGITIMATION

As noted by Onwuegbuzie (2000b), a qualitative study cannot be assessed for validity (e.g., truth value, legitimation, credibility, dependability, trustworthiness, generalizability). Rather, validity is "relative to purposes and circumstances" (Brinberg & McGrath, 1987, p. 13). Moreover, assessing legitimation does not lead to a dichotomous outcome (i.e., valid vs. invalid) but represents an evaluation of level or degree.

Although no method is guaranteed to yield valid and dependable data or trustworthy conclusions (Phillips, 1987), nevertheless, it is essential that library researchers assess the procedures used in qualitative studies in order to rule in or to rule out rival interpretations of data. Such strategies either help to evaluate legitimation or to increase legitimation or both (Onwuegbuzie, 2000b). Therefore, what follows is a comprehensive typology and description of methods for assessing the truth value of qualitative research. This list of procedures have been compiled from several researchers (e.g., Becker, 1970; Creswell, 1998; Fielding & Fielding, 1986; Guba & Lincoln, 1989; Kidder, 1981; Lincoln & Guba, 1985; Maxwell, 1996; Miles & Huberman, 1984, 1994; Newman & Benz, 1998; Onwuegbuzie, 2000b; Patton, 1990). The following strategies are described below: prolonged engagement, persistent observation, triangulation, leaving an audit trail, member checking/informant feedback, weighting the evidence, checking for representativeness of sources of data, checking for researcher effects/clarifying researcher bias, making contrasts/comparisons, theoretical sampling, checking the meaning of outliers, using extreme cases, ruling out spurious relations, replicating a finding, referential adequacy, following up surprises, structural relationships, peer debriefing, rich and thick description, the modus operandi approach, assessing rival explanations, negative case analysis, confirmatory data analyses, and effect sizes.

### *Prolonged engagement*

Prolonged engagement refers to undertaking a study for a sufficient period of time to obtain an adequate representation of the "voice" (i.e., "capture the voice") under study. Prolonged engagement includes understanding the culture, building trusts with research participants, and checking for misinformation arising from anomalies introduced by the researcher or the participants (Ely et al., 1991; Glesne & Peshkin, 1992; Lincoln & Guba, 1985).

## Persistent observation

The goal of persistent observation is to identify characteristics, traits, and attributes that are most relevant to the phenomenon under examination and focus on them extensively (Lincoln & Guba, 1985). As stated by Lincoln and Guba (1985, p. 304), persistent observation "adds the dimension of salience to what might otherwise appear to be little more than a mindless immersion." To engage in persistent observation, the library researcher must be able to distinguish and separate relevant from irrelevant observations. Whereas prolonged engagement provides scope, persistent observation provides depth.

Many interpretivists (e.g., Lincoln & Guba, 1985) recommend that persistent observation be combined with prolonged engagement to maximize the credibility of the findings (see Onwuegbuzie et al., 1997). As declared by Fetterman (1989, p. 46), "working with people day in and day out, for long periods of time, is what gives ethnographic research its validity and vitality." However, library researchers should guard against "going native," which occurs when researchers' professional judgments are unduly compromised as a consequence of being in the field too long, such that they become too accepting and appreciative of the culture under investigation (Lincoln & Guba, 1985). Whether using persistent observation or prolonged engagement, the researcher must strike a balance between premature closure and "going native."

## Triangulation

Triangulation involves the use of multiple and different methods, investigators, sources, and theories to obtain corroborating evidence (Ely et al., 1991; Glesne & Peshkin, 1992; Lincoln & Guba, 1985; Merriam, 1988; Miles & Huberman, 1984, 1994; Patton, 1990). Triangulation reduces the possibility of chance associations, as well as of systematic biases prevailing due to a specific method being utilized, thereby allowing greater confidence in any interpretations made (Fielding & Fielding, 1986; Maxwell, 1992). (For more information about triangulation, the reader is referred to the *Framework for Mixed-Methodological Research* section in chapter 4.)

## Leaving an audit trail

Leaving an audit trail involves the researcher collecting and maintaining extensive documentation of records and data stemming from the inquiry. Halpern (1983), in his seminal work, identified the following six classes of raw records: (a) raw data (e.g., videotapes, written notes, survey results); (b) data reduction and analysis products (e.g., write-ups of field notes, summaries, unitized information, quantitative summaries, theoretical notes); (c) data reconstruction and synthesis products (e.g., structure of categories, findings and interpretations, final reports); (d) process notes (i.e., methodological notes, trustworthiness notes, audit trail notes); (e) materials related to intentions and dispositions (e.g., research proposal, personal notes, reflexive journals, expectations); and (f) instrument development information (e.g., pilot forms, preliminary schedules, observation formats, and surveys). Each of these six categories is further subdivided by Halpern to provide examples of the types of evidence that each category of raw data might yield.

Halpern proposed that auditors examine the available categories of raw data to evaluate whether the findings and interpretations are supported adequately by the data. Halpern outlined an algorithm for the audit process itself. This algorithm comprises the following five stages: (a) pre-entry (characterized by a series of discussions between the auditor and auditee that lead to a decision to continue, to continue conditionally, or to discontinue the underlying audit); (b) determination of auditability (involving understanding the study, becoming familiar with the audit trail, and evaluating the study's auditability); (c) formal agreement (involving a written agreement between the two parties on what is to be accomplished by the audit; establishing the time limits, roles to be played by the various parties; determining the logistics; ascertaining the deliverables and format of these products; and establishing renegotiation criteria if the audit trail leads to inconsistencies); (d) determination of trustworthiness (establishing dependability, credibility, and confirmability); and (e) closure (involving feedback, possible renegotiation, and the writing of the final report). Lincoln and Guba (1985) equate the audit trail to a fiscal audit.

## Member checking/informant feedback

Member checking, also referred to as informant feedback, involves systematically obtaining feedback about one's data, analytic categories, interpretations, and conclusions from the sample members (Guba & Lincoln, 1989). Member checking, which occurs throughout the inquiry, can be both formal and informal (Lincoln & Guba, 1985). This type of legitimation can occur at the data collection, data analysis, or data interpretation stages of the qualitative research process. In member checking, the participants are provided with the opportunity to play a major role in evaluating the trustworthiness of the account (Stake, 1995). According to Maxwell (1996), member checking is the most effective way of eliminating the possibility of misrepresentation and misinterpretation of the "voice." Similarly, Lincoln and Guba (1985) rated member checking as being "the most critical technique for establishing credibility" (p. 314). Some researchers (e.g., Stake, 1976) even contend that the justification for member checking is a quasi-ethical one, inasmuch as informants have a right to know the researcher's findings and interpretations. Unfortunately, relatively few interpretivists utilize member checks to check or to establish legitimation (Miles & Huberman, 1994), probably because of the potential time-consuming nature that would be added to an already time-consuming study.

Whereas triangulation is a process undertaken with respect to data, member checking is a process conducted with respect to constructions or interpretations. That is, whereas triangulation pertains to judgments of the accuracy of specific units of data, member checking involves judgment of the overall credibility (Lincoln & Guba, 1985). When used as a follow-up to interviews, member checking can (a) provide the opportunity to evaluate intentionality, (b) provide the respondent with an immediate opportunity to correct factual errors and to challenge the investigator's interpretations, (c) give the respondent an opportunity to clarify any misunderstandings, (d) provide the respondent with an opportunity to present additional information, (e) put the respondent on record as having verified the accuracy of interpretations, and (f) offer an opportunity for the

researcher to capture the "voice" (Lincoln & Guba, 1985). However, as
noted by Lincoln and Guba (1985), more formal member checking is
needed for a researcher to establish a meaningful claim to credibility. This
can take the form of the participants receiving a draft of the research
report and being asked to provide feedback.

## Weighting the evidence

Because the quality of data varies from one sample member to the next,
from one group to the next, and from one study to the next, qualitative
researchers, and quantitative researchers, should give more weight to
stronger data than to weaker data. As described by Miles and Huberman
(1994), the reasons why certain data are stronger than others are linked to
Maxwell's (1992) descriptive and interpretive validity. According to
Miles and Huberman, situations when data typically are stronger include
the following: (a) when they are collected later or are the result of prolonged engagement and persistent observation, (b) when they are
observed or reported firsthand, (c) when the data are collected in informal
settings, and (d) when the fieldworker is trusted.

## Checking for representativeness

Representativeness relates both to Maxwell's (1992) internal and external
generalizability. Miles and Huberman (1994) contend that inaccurate generalizations occur when (a) nonrepresentative informants are sampled,
which often arise from an overreliance on accessible and elite informants;
(b) generalizations are made from nonrepresentative events or activities,
which often stem from the researcher's noncontinuous presence in the
field, as well as from an overrating of striking events; and (c) inferences
are made from nonrepresentative processes, often stemming from nonrepresentative informants and events, holistic biases, overreliance on
plausible interpretations, and an adequate fit of data into emerging interpretations. As is the case for quantitative research, representativeness can
be increased by increasing the number of participants, stratifying the sample, looking purposively for contrasting participants, and obtaining a random sample (Miles & Huberman, 1994).

## Checking for researcher effects/clarifying researcher bias

As noted earlier, researcher bias is an extremely serious threat to validity in qualitative research. Miles and Huberman (1994) identified two sources of researcher bias: (a) the effects of the researcher on the participant(s) (i.e., Bias A); and (b) the effects of the participant(s) on the researcher (i.e., Bias B). These biases may permeate any stage of the research process. According to Miles and Huberman, Bias A occurs when the researcher disrupts or poses a threat to the existing social or institutional relationships. In such cases, the participant(s) typically will "switch into an on-stage role or special persona, a presentation of self to the outsider" (p. 265). Also, informants may tailor their responses to be agreeable and amenable to the researcher (i.e., provide socially desirable responses) and to protect their self-interests. Bias A can also lead to informants implicitly or explicitly boycotting the researcher, who is viewed as a nuisance, spy, unethical, voyeur, or adversary. In addition, Bias A can inhibit informants. Conversely, Bias B can lead to the researcher going native.

Miles and Huberman (1994) surmised that Bias A can be reduced by (a) prolonged engagement, (b) persistent observation, (c) using unobtrusive measures where possible, (d) making the researcher's intentions clear, (e) co-opting an informant, (f) conducting some of the interviewing and focus groups at a neutral site, and (g) being careful not to exacerbate any potential problems. Additionally, Bias B can be minimized by (a) avoiding going native by spending time away from the site, (b) avoiding elite bias by selecting a heterogeneous sample, (c) including nontypical participants, (d) maintaining a conceptual framework, (e) using informants to provide background and historical information, (f) triangulating data, (g) examining potential informant bias, (h) showing field notes to a colleague, and (i) continually keeping the research questions firmly in mind.

Researchers also should examine their own biases from the outset of the study, as well as the ways in which their biases could unduly influence data collection, analysis, and interpretation. Furthermore, researchers should make clear in the final reports their position and any biases, assumptions, experiences, prejudices, and orientations that may have impacted their findings and interpretations (Merriam, 1988).

## Making contrast/comparisons

Although use of control groups is commonly associated with quantitative research, there are some occasions where comparisons in qualitative studies are justified. Here, multigroup studies can be extremely enlightening. For instance, Witcher, Onwuegbuzie, and Minor conducted two qualitative studies to determine preservice teachers' perceptions of characteristics of effective teachers at two different universities (i.e., Minor, Onwuegbuzie, Witcher, & James, 2002; Witcher et al., 2001). The emergent themes from the two investigations were compared. The similarity of these themes helped to increase the credibility of both sets of findings. Qualitative findings also can be compared with the extant literature, as well as with the researcher's experience and knowledge base.

## Theoretical sampling

As advanced by Newman and Benz (1998), theoretical sampling involves the researcher following where the data led and not leading the data. When the goal of the qualitative research is to develop theory, the researcher should "attempt to capture the best theory that explains the data" (p. 53).

## Checking the meaning of outliers

As is the case for quantitative research, it is very common for qualitative data to contain extreme observations. Unfortunately, the temptation of researchers is to ignore these outlying observations or to attempt to explain them away (Miles & Huberman, 1994). Yet, outliers can provide extremely valuable insights into the underlying phenomenon. In particular, a careful examination of the outlying observations, cases, groups, settings, events, or treatments can help strengthen conclusions not only by testing the generality of the findings but also by minimizing confirmation bias, illusory correlations, and causal error (Onwuegbuzie, 2000b). Moreover, scrutinizing outlying results promotes the use of *condition-seeking* methods, wherein a progression of qualifying conditions are made based on existing findings (Greenwald et al., 1986). Indeed, as noted by Onwuegbuzie (2003a), "such condition-seeking methods would generate a progression of research questions, which, if addressed in future studies, would provide increasingly accurate and generalizable conclusions" (p. 87).

## Using extreme cases

As stated by Miles and Huberman (1994), extreme cases can be extremely informative for assessing the validity of interpretations and conclusions. By identifying extreme cases, researchers can then verify whether what is absent in them is present or different in other participants, or vice versa.

## Ruling out spurious relations

As is the case for quantitative research, library researchers should carefully examine whether a relationship between two variables that emerges from the data represents a causal link or whether one or more intervening factors are responsible for the association. The latter scenario implies the existence of an illusory correlation, discussed above. To minimize this occurrence, researchers should proceed with care before deciding whether two variables are causally related. As such, library researchers should consider using a knowledgeable colleague or other nonstakeholder who is not part of the research team to play the role of "devil's advocate" in searching for possible moderating variables.

## Replicating a finding

The greater the extent to which researchers can generalize the account of a particular situation or population to other individuals, times, settings, or context (i.e., internal generalizability; Maxwell, 1992), the more confident they can be about the observed finding and, subsequently, the greater the evidence of legitimation. Similarly, credibility is enhanced if results can be generalized beyond the group, setting, time, or context (i.e., external generalizability; Maxwell, 1992). Thus, where appropriate, qualitative researchers should examine the internal and/or external generalizability of findings, interpretations, and conclusions.

## Referential adequacy

Eisner (1975) is credited for introducing the concept of referential adequacy. This term was originally coined to represent the process of using videotape and audiotape recordings of observations that could be later examined and compared to the critiques that have emerged from all of the data collected. In other words, the recordings are utilized to establish the adequacy of written critiques. Consequently, these recorded supportive materials provide a form of standard against which later data analyses, interpretations, and conclusions (i.e., the critiques) could be assessed for adequacy (Lincoln & Guba, 1985).

Referential materials are not limited to electronically recorded data. Other types of materials could be utilized, such as photographs and text. However, whatever materials are used, it is essential that they represent a component of the raw data that are not analyzed by the researcher for the purpose of data interpretation but are archived for later recall and comparison. Alternatively stated, the referential materials must be reserved exclusively for undertaking an adequacy test. Unfortunately, referential adequacy can pose problems for qualitative researchers because of the difficulty in ensuring that the referential material are representative of the data and that, at the same time, giving up this material for storage does not impede their ability to interpret the data accurately. Notwithstanding, when used appropriately, referential adequacy can help to establish reliability (i.e., demonstrating that different analysts can obtain similar interpretations of the emergent themes) and validity, thereby providing a powerful way of demonstrating the credibility of naturalistic data (Lincoln & Guba, 1985).

## Following up surprises

By its very exploratory nature, interpretivist research lends itself to unexpected findings, some of which may be very surprising to the analysts. Rather than ignoring or dismissing surprising findings, qualitative researchers should explore these surprises further. Miles and Huberman (1994) have identified that following up surprises have the following three components: (a) reflecting on the surprise to surface on the violated theory, (b) considering how to revise the violated theory, and (c) looking for evidence to support revised theory.

## Structural relationships

Newman and Benz (1998) recommend that datasets be compared for consistency. Accordingly, when attempting to interpret data and generate conclusions, constructivists should obtain support for their insights by comparing and contrasting different datasets. These datasets may arise from different orientations that can be compared in much the same manner that findings can be compared with the extant literature, to the researcher's experience, and to the knowledge base, as described above.

## Peer debriefing

Peer debriefing provides an external evaluation of the research process (Ely et al., 1991; Glesne & Peshkin, 1992; Lincoln & Guba, 1985; Maxwell, 1996; Merriam, 1988; Newman & Benz, 1998). This method of validation is essentially another form of interrater reliability—the major difference being that it is not empirically based but logically based. Lincoln and Guba (1985, p. 308) describe the role of the peer debriefer as the "devil's advocate," representing a person who keeps the researcher "honest"; who poses difficult questions about the methods, meanings, interpretations, and conclusions; and who provides the researcher with the opportunity for "carthasis" by being empathetic with the researcher's feelings. The peer reviewer can be a peer or any other person who is not directly involved in the study. Ideally, the peer reviewer should not be a stakeholder, that is, one who depends to some degree on the findings, interpretations, and conclusions. Rather, the peer reviewer should serve as a "disinterested peer" (Lincoln & Guba, 1985, p. 308). Yet, it is important that the peer debriefer be knowledgeable about the substantive area of investigation and be someone who is neither the researcher's junior nor senior in rank. Lincoln and Guba (1985) recommend that both the researcher and peer reviewer maintain written accounts of the debriefing sessions (i.e., audit trail), which they call *peer debriefing sessions.*

When used properly, peer debriefing should lead to researchers' biases being probed, meanings explored, and interpretations elucidated. The major goal of the researchers should be to ensure that the interpretivist is fully aware of their biases. Additionally, peer debriefing typically provides an opportunity for researchers to test initial hypotheses. By attempting to justify these hypotheses to the peer debriefer, researchers should be able to determine their plausibility. As declared by Lincoln and Guba (1985), "debriefing is a useful—if sobering—experience to which to subject oneself; its utility, when properly engaged, is unquestionable" (p. 309).

## Rich and thick description

An important way of providing credibility of results is by collecting rich and thick data, which correspond to data that are detailed and complete enough to maximize the ability to extract meaning. Becker (1970) advocated that such data necessitate verbatim transcripts of interviews, as opposed to selected notes. For observations, detailed, descriptive note taking about specific, explicit events and behaviors underlie rich, thick data. Becker maintained that providing such data minimizes confirmation bias by facilitating the testing of emerging theories rather than merely providing a source of supporting data points. Also, rich, thick description informs the reader about transferability. In other words, with such detailed information, the reader is able to transfer information to other settings and contexts to determine whether the findings can be transferred "because of shared characteristics" (Erlandson, Harris, Skipper, & Allen, 1993, p. 32).

## The Modus Operandi approach

In the modus operandi method, a phrase termed by Scriven (1974), threats to validity are treated as events rather than as elements to be controlled. When using this procedure, analysts search for clues as to whether or not these threats to validity occurred (Maxwell, 1996). Peer reviewers can play an important role here in determining which sources of invalidity might have prevailed.

## Assessing rival explanations

Because of the time-consuming nature of qualitative data analyses, it is challenging for interpretivists to detach themselves from their initial data interpretations. As noted by Miles and Huberman (1994), qualitative researchers tend to "get married to . . . [their] . . . emerging account and usually opt for investing the scant time left to buttress, rather than to unhorse, [their] explanation" (p. 274). Consequently, during the data analysis stage, researchers are too tired to assess rival explanations to their findings. In fact, few naturalists conduct rival hypothesis testing, perhaps also because hypothesis testing is viewed as belonging to the quantitative paradigm and its empiricist ideology.

Yet, rival hypothesis testing, which is central to all types of research, represents an important way to assess the credibility of interpretations and conclusions. In testing rival explanations, qualitative researchers should consider several rival explanations, and perhaps even collect more data, until one explanation emerges as the most compelling. However, rather than comparing and contrasting several *possible* explanations, the researcher should only consider *plausible* explanations. Foreclosing too early on rival explanations leads to confirmation bias in general and illusory correlations and causal error in particular. Conversely, closing too late on alternative interpretations typically culminates in too weak a case being built for the chosen explanation because of the overwhelming amount of rival hypothesis-testing data collected. Thus, rival-hypothesis data collection should cease when saturation point has been reached—that is, when the rival explanations are shown to be either flawed or better than the existing explanations. As recommended by Miles and Huberman (1994), researchers should consider asking colleagues or other nonstakeholders to help them assess rival explanations. Checking the meaning of outliers, using extreme cases, ruling out spurious relations, following up surprises, and negative case analyses are techniques that can be used to assess rival explanations.

## Negative case analysis

Negative case analysis involves continually modifying the emerging hypothesis using past and future observations until all known data are accounted for by the hypothesis (Kidder, 1981; Newman & Benz, 1998). That is, negative case analysis is the process of expanding and revising one's interpretation until all outliers have been explained (Creswell, 1998; Ely et al., 1991; Lincoln & Guba, 1985; Maxwell, 1996; Miles & Huberman, 1994). A single negative (i.e., discrepant) case is sufficient to necessitate the researcher to modify the hypothesis (Kidder, 1981). For any cases that do not fit the final hypothesis or model, Wolcott (1990) recommends that they be documented in the final report to allow readers to evaluate them and to draw their own conclusions. As noted by Lincoln and

Guba (1995), negative case analysis provides a useful way of making data more credible by minimizing the number of negative cases.

## Confirmatory data analyses

As outlined by Onwuegbuzie (2000b), *confirmatory thematic analyses* can be conducted, in which replication qualitative studies are conducted to assess the replicability (i.e., external generalizability) of previous emergent themes (i.e., research driven) or to test an extant theory (i.e., theory driven), when appropriate. Such confirmatory techniques help provide legitimation to previous qualitative findings, interpretations, and conclusions.

For example, as noted earlier, Witcher et al.'s (2001) study identified six characteristics (i.e., themes) of effective teachers noted by preservice teachers (i.e., student-centeredness, enthusiasm for teaching, ethicalness, classroom and behavior management, teaching methodology, and knowledge of subject). In their follow-up study (i.e., Minor et al., 2002), the same six themes were confirmed, with an additional theme emerging, namely personableness. The confirmation of the six themes helped increase their credibility as interpretations of preservice teachers' perceptions regarding competent teachers.

## Effect sizes

As stated by Sechrest and Sidani (1995, p. 79), "qualitative researchers regularly use terms like 'many,' 'most,' 'frequently,' 'several,' 'never,' and so on. These terms are essentially quantitative." In fact, by obtaining counts, qualitative researchers can quantitize such expressions. As noted by Miles and Huberman (1994), in qualitative research, numbers tend to get disregarded. Yet, emergent themes stem from isolating an event, behavior, or word that occurs (a) a specific number of times and (b) consistently in a specific manner (Miles & Huberman, 1994). Both "'number of times' and 'consistency' judgments are based on counting" (Miles & Huberman, 1994, p. 251). These counts form the basis of effect sizes.

The concept of effect sizes in qualitative research was described in chapter 5, using Onwuegbuzie's (in press-c) conceptualization. Interestingly, consistent with Onwuegbuzie's (in press-c) conceptualization of effect sizes in qualitative research, more than 30 years ago, Becker (1970) advanced the use of "quasi-statistics" in qualitative research. According to Becker, quasi-statistics pertain to the use of descriptive statistics that can readily be extracted from qualitative data. Becker (1970, pp. 81–82) asserted that "one of the greatest faults in most observational case studies has been their failure to make explicit the quasi-statistical basis of their conclusions." As noted by Maxwell (1996):

> Quasi-statistics not only allow you to test and support claims that are inherently quantitative, but also enable you to assess the *amount* of evidence in your data that bears on a particular conclusion or threat, such as how many discrepant instances exist and from how many different sources they were obtained. (p. 95) [emphasis in original]

In fact, the qualitative work of Becker, Geer, Hughes, and Strauss (1961/1977) contain more than 50 tables and graphs of the amount and distribution of qualitative data that support their interpretations and conclusions. Moreover, the concept of quasi-statistics can be traced even further back—that is, to the work of Lazarsfeld and Barton (1955)—nearly half a century ago. Effect sizes in qualitative research are not only useful for extracting meaning but also for providing legitimation for interpretations, especially those that involve words such as "important," "significant," "prevalent," "dominant," "recurrent," or the like. According to Miles and Huberman (1994), "there are three good reasons to resort to numbers: to see rapidly what you have in a large batch of data; to verify a hunch or hypothesis; and to keep yourself analytically honest, protecting against bias" (p. 253). Thus, effect sizes represent an extremely powerful method of providing legitimation.

## MIXED-METHODOLOGICAL RESEARCH PARADIGM

Because mixed-methods research combines both quantitative and qualitative techniques, library researchers conducting this form of research should assess the validity and legitimation concepts presented in figures 6.1 and 6.2. Clearly, mixed-methods library researchers have a bigger task

than do quantitative and qualitative researchers. Nevertheless, by conducting a comprehensive legitimation process, not only will mixed-methods
library researchers have thicker, richer data, but they will have findings
that will make the greatest contribution to the field of library and information science.

## SUMMARY AND CONCLUSIONS

The present chapter provided the major interpretational errors that occur
in published research. In particular, the concept of validity was presented
within the quantitative, qualitative, and mixed-methodological research
paradigms.

With respect to quantitative research, several rationales were provided
for identifying and discussing threats to internal and external validity for
all quantitative research designs (i.e., descriptive, correlational, causal-
comparative, and experimental). Next, threats to internal and external
validity were conceptualized as occurring at the three major stages of the
research process, namely, research design/data collection, data analysis,
and data interpretation. Using Onwuegbuzie's (2003a) conceptualization,
a comprehensive model of sources of validity was developed. This model
was represented as a 3 (stage of research process) x 2 (internal vs. external
validity) matrix comprising 50 unique components of internal and external validity threats, with many of the components comprising subcompo-
nents (see figure 6.1).

It is hoped that this model makes it clear that *every* study contains multiple threats to internal and external validity and that library researchers
should be extremely careful when making conclusions based on one or
a few studies. Additionally, it is hoped that this model emphasizes the
importance of assessing sources of validity/invalidity in every research
study and at different stages of the research process.

Although the importance of validity has long been acknowledged and
accepted among quantitative researchers, this concept has been an issue of
contention among qualitative researchers. Thus, the section on qualitative
research provided a comprehensive discussion of the different ways that
validity has been defined. Second, it was contended that in order to be
taken seriously, the onus is on qualitative researchers to be fully account-

able for their data collection, analysis, and interpretive procedures. Moreover, it was argued that rigor in qualitative research is needed and that interpretivists always should assess the truth value of their results. This can be undertaken by reframing the concept of validity in qualitative research, for example, by treating validity as an issue of choosing among rival interpretations and of examining and providing arguments for the relative credibility of competing knowledge claims or by redefining validity as having multifaceted criteria. Third, the *Qualitative Legitimation Model* was introduced, which attempted to integrate many of the types of validity identified by qualitative researchers. Finally, a description of 24 methods for assessing the truth value of qualitative research was provided.

In outlining the Qualitative Legitimation Model, the goal is to facilitate the sharing of standards, as is recommended by a growing number of qualitative theorists (Howe & Eisenhart, 1990; Miles & Huberman, 1994; Williams, 1986). As stated by Maxwell (1992), use of legitimation frameworks, such as the Qualitative Legitimation Model, does not depend on the existence of some absolute truth or reality to which an account can be compared but only on the fact that there exist ways of assessing accounts that do not depend entirely on features of the account itself but in some way relate to those things that the account claims to be about (p. 283).

Although the Qualitative Legitimation Model is relatively comprehensive, it is by no means exhaustive. Also, it should be noted that in any particular qualitative study, not all of the threats contained in the model will be pertinent. Unlike in quantitative research, where the goal is to minimize all sources of invalidity, different validity components of the Qualitative Legitimation Model will be relevant in different qualitative studies. As such, it is extremely flexible. Indeed, as other threats to legitimation in qualitative research are conceptualized, these can be added to the Qualitative Legitimation Model.

The last three chapters have provided a comprehensive framework for conducting quantitative, qualitative, and mixed-methodological studies. Specifically, these chapters attempted to disseminate best practices for conducting all three types of research at the three major stages of the research process: research design/data collection, data analysis, and data interpretation stages. Indeed, it is hoped that these chapters could serve as a miniresearch text, which library researchers can use in their research.

Moreover, these chapters contain a myriad of references, many of which are extremely current, that readers can consult to extend their knowledge of the research process even further. The time is now ripe for more research to be undertaken on library science research in general and library anxiety studies in particular.

*Chapter Seven*

# Prevention, Reduction, and Intervention of Library Anxiety

## OVERVIEW

The research findings reported in preceding chapters indicate that library anxiety is a situation-specific anxiety, which occurs when an individual is using the library or contemplating its use. This indicates that library anxiety transpires in both actual and potential library use situations. Individuals with high levels of library anxiety often exhibit cognitive, affective, and physiological symptoms that may include discomfort, fear, tension, feelings of uncertainty, learned helplessness, self-defeating thoughts, and mental disorganization (Jiao et al., 1996). These symptoms can have such debilitating effects on actual as well as potential users that they direct attention away from these users' intended library tasks, culminating in library avoidance behaviors. These behaviors paradoxically sustain library anxiety through the mechanism of negative reinforcement.

Library-anxious users tend either to overestimate the perceived threat in a library due to their previous negative experiences or to underestimate their ability to cope with the demands of a library task in the information rich library environment. In either case, there is an exaggerated perception of threat or danger in the library environment. Research suggests that library anxiety is a prevalent phenomenon among college students (Mellon, 1986). Although it has not yet been studied extensively in other types of libraries, there has been a recognized need to develop intervention strategies to help users cope with various library anxiety responses (Westbrook & DeDecker, 1993).

One of the most difficult challenges facing librarians over the years is to determine for what anxiety symptoms and for whom the intervention procedures are to be developed. Not every library-related task induces anxiety. Not every user's inquiry runs into a dead end and needs to be mediated. In fact, the most common use of library collection and resources is a self-service that users conduct themselves through the library's existing bibliographic system, tools, and services without any librarian's intervention. During the library visit or in a library search, the user may or may not experience frustration and anxiety. It depends on many factors including the user's prior knowledge, previous experience, search ability, and the difficulty of the task in question. Library use is a personal, dynamic, and complex experience involving a series of feelings, thoughts, and actions (Kuhlthau, 1993). There are various sorts of library use and many levels of library information needs.

How do librarians distinguish those users who are experiencing anxiety from those who are not and then provide the former with necessary treatment in the largely self-service library environment? At what stage of the user's information seeking process do librarians need to intervene? At least, for now, it can be said that librarians do not have the resources and training to deal with library-anxious users the way mental health professionals, such as clinical psychologists and school psychologists, treat their patients suffering from various anxiety disorders. Clinical psychologists are able to offer a wide range of therapies and treatments for anxiety disorders and draw on significant advances in diagnosis and treatment procedures. Without proper means of diagnosis and clinically established procedures, librarians are not in a position to provide medically related procedures for individual library-anxious users, even though library anxiety and other anxiety disorders are considered state anxieties of a treatable nature (Spielberger, 1966).

This has not discouraged conscientious librarians from developing strategies aimed at prevention, reduction, and intervention rather than treatment of library anxiety. The importance of prevention over treatment can be argued by historical examples in medicine, where the greatest advances often were not some treatment breakthroughs but the development of vaccinations. Medical treatment always implies restoring people from sickness to health. Vaccination, on the other hand, implies that people will be kept in a state of good health by developing immunity to the disease or from contracting the disease as a result of the vaccine (Sieber, O'Neil, & Tobias, 1977). Applying the example of vaccination to library anxiety, librarians have proposed and implemented preventive procedures for all users with the goal of restraining anxiety-provoking stimuli and increasing effective library use. This assumption, which is based on research literature and practical experience, is that the majority of users may experience library anxiety at certain stages of their library use or potential use. Because it is not possible in real library situations first to identify and then to classify users by their anxiety level or type, librarians have chosen to implement intervention strategies for all potential users at different stages.

During the past two decades, many library anxiety prevention and intervention programs and procedures have been proposed or implemented in various types of libraries, especially academic libraries. Although different procedures have the same goal of preventing or reducing library anxiety among users, they each have a different focus. Some focus on attempting directly to reduce anxiety responses in the library physical environment. Others focus on cognitive approaches, attempting to enhance users' skills and knowledge of the research process through library education programs. Still others deal with the affective aspects of library anxiety, focusing on better understanding the attitudes, feelings, and anxiety-provoking thoughts via training, instruction, and individualized services. The general goal of these procedures is to instill in anxious library users a sense of confidence that they can cope with a library situation and develop a feeling of personal control over the anxiety responsiveness. The combined effects of these different approaches may reasonably be expected to help prevent or reduce specific aspects of library anxiety and facilitate performance on library use among different types of users.

There are basically three aspects of library anxiety prevention and intervention. One is facility and resource oriented, focusing on ameliorated library ambience and behaviorally functional organization of library collections and resources for self-service. Another is knowledge based, emphasizing enhanced intellectual access to information, search skills and strategies, problem solving, and learning through instruction. The third is human assisted, involving librarians' mediation at certain stages of library use and the information seeking process. This chapter presents and summarizes the existing library-anxiety intervention procedures and strategies around the three aforementioned aspects. The major intervention procedures and strategies also are summarized in table 6.1 for easy and quick reference.

## LIBRARY ANXIETY PREVENTION AND REDUCTION IN THE PHYSICAL ENVIRONMENT

One facet of library anxiety results from the perceived threat in the library's physical environment. In particular, the library building may intimidate potential users due to its size, complexity, and ambiguity (Mellon, 1986, 1988). Users' perceptions of both quantity and ignorance seem to be determinants of anxiety and uncertainty. Perceptions of quantity relate to the physical environment, where the size of the collection and the layout of the facility often are overwhelming and inhibiting (Kuhlthau, 1993). Nearly all reasonably sized libraries induce some feelings and responses that cause disorientation and trepidation among users from the onset. For example, the frustrations of trying to find one's way in the library can diminish the effectiveness of library use. The negative feelings and anxiety of the initial experience may influence the frequency of library visits and the use of its collections, resources, and services (Onwuegbuzie & Jiao, 1997a).

This is very unfortunate because the library facility, collections, and services are designed for patrons to use without much inhibition. Library services and their users are thought of as a system of interacting parts (Smith, 1980). When the user comes to use the library, he or she may interact with one or more parts of the library freely. But that is obviously not the case in a lot of libraries. Many library buildings are rarely given much thought after they have been constructed, even though the lighting, furniture arrangement, collection organization, service points, signs, noise level, ventilation, humidity, and study areas all contribute to a positive learning experience of the users (Bosman & Rusinek, 1997). The burden of adapting to the library environment often falls on users themselves because the architects, through their training and practice, made decisions about the physical design and layout without giving enough consideration of the potential difficulties that might be experienced by the library user.

The finished building has become something to be regretted but tolerated by those who later use it and work in it. The difficulties of users within the library physical environment are of genuine concern to librarians, who have dealt with the problem by using visual guidance and applying tested ergonomic concepts as intervention strategies in an attempt to create comfortable and user-friendly atmospheres.

## Signs and Graphics

A library needs its physical space to house many of its collections, resources, and services. Once inside the library, users need directions to locate the information or services they require. In an ideal situation, there are no physical, technological, or monetary barriers between the user and the information. Although this does not imply that an ideal library represents a self-service orientation, the user does have a right to use the library without having to ask for assistance (Reynolds & Barrett, 1979). In fact, according to Kuhlthau (1993), "many people will use the library as a self-service collection. In most instances, independent access will remain the primary use of the [library] system" (p. 178). If users can tie together an understanding of current location with an understanding of desired designations that are not in the immediate perceptual range, they are believed to be oriented, otherwise they are deemed to be at risk with respect to effective library use (Loomis & Parsons, 1979).

An unfamiliar library environment makes special demands on the users. Even the simple library setting can involve lots of environmental cues that have to be encoded, deciphered, and processed by the user before they become meaningful. The user must select relevant information from an array of architectural cues, signs and other graphic material, human aids, and her or his prior knowledge about using a library and then choose the next course of action (Pollet & Huskell, 1979). Library signs and graphics can help users feel more oriented by funneling information to them in simple forms. They help those unfamiliar with architectural idiosyncrasies of a particular library and with the location of its resources and services. Signs may be used to orient, inform, warn, or even prohibit users. Direct visual information assures library users and encourages them to feel welcome. At the same time, signs enrich the environment in which they are placed and help allay potential building-related anxiety. Signs can also spare people the discomfort in requesting assistance.

According to Swope and Katzer (1972), it is estimated that between three-fifths and two-thirds of all library users hesitate about seeking help from librarians. These users are not sufficiently self-assured to ask questions because they dislike revealing their ignorance (Mellon, 1986) and may even resent the necessity of doing so. The pitfalls in unfamiliar library surroundings threaten library users' self-esteem. Moreover, those with the poorest academic self-concept are likely to be those who would experience more problems in the library (Jiao & Onwuegbuzie, 1999b). Effective signage also helps to reduce valuable librarian's time otherwise spent on directing traffic. As library collections grow in size and services expand in complexity, signs and visual guides become increasingly essential.

Although libraries may have inherent architectural features that can pose many difficulties for installing signs (Van Allen, 1984), librarians can do a lot to make the environment more understandable and accessible to users. Library signs can take many different forms. The major physical orientation device perhaps is a building directory placed at a visible location near the entrance of a library. This directory might contain a floor plan, a simple book stack scheme, and a list of service points. Information about the location of facilities and equipment, such as water fountains, telephones, copy machines, and microfilm readers, should be included in floor plans. Library users frequently mention particular difficulties in finding rest rooms. These facilities should be identified on all floors and locations in the library. Copy machines and change machines often are situated in obscure and unpleasant locations. The location of this equipment must be clearly indicated. The limited numbers of copy machines and a poor state of repair can lead to unpleasant experiences and increase or create anxiety for library users (Bostick, 1992) and may lead to future avoidance behaviors (Onwuegbuzie & Jiao, 1998c).

The function of the directory is to make users aware of the entire library environment in a concise way. It can be mounted on the wall or as a freestanding box. The building directory can be extremely helpful in reducing the initial trepidation and anxiety among users. Similarly, a kiosk, commanding a central point of a library building, also can be very effective as a kind of road sign and central information source. Directional signs that serve to guide users from one decision point to another also are important. They may be mounted on the wall or suspended from the ceiling. Other important signs provide service point identification. These areas are often best served with overhead-suspended signs. Open-stack libraries frequently have no staff assistance in the stack areas. Once users leave a service point, they are on their own to succeed or fail in locating the desired material. In fact, hundreds of individually printed pieces of signs on the book stacks and furniture are needed.

Signs and graphics in the library's physical environment are found to be very important in helping users overcome their initial fears and anxieties. But this finding has not been treated as seriously as it should have been, and the related intervention procedures have not always been met with understanding and support. Some librarians simply do not like visual guidance, such as signs and graphics, in the library. They view signs and graphics as forms of clutter and as a direct attack on the unity of the building design. Often those in charge of the construction and maintenance of library buildings share this aversion of signs in the library. As a result, in some libraries, only the most essential signs required by law, such as EXIT, can be found. In these libraries, no directional or identification signs are available.

Some libraries recognize the need for visual guidance but are unable to afford a professional graphics designer. In the end, they may either use a makeshift sign or else conclude that it is better to have no signs at all than to utilize an unprofessional product. The makeshift signs may even reinforce the user's insecurity if they fail to inform or direct. In other libraries, signs are allowed but a camouflage technique is used. Signs are made with like color or material and affixed to the décor of the building. The message of these signs is difficult to find and, once located, even more difficult to read. Another factor that sometimes makes librarians hesitant to commit resources on developing signs is that the magnitude of the physical orientation problems is difficult to be determined. There has been no agreed-on and direct means of assessing the impact of a library setting on the use of libraries. It is very difficult to ascertain just how threatening a library environment can be for someone with little or no previous experience of library use or for someone with extensive prior knowledge about libraries. Despite all of these concerns and problems about signs and graphics in the libraries, it is important for libraries to continue to find ways of communicating to users in the library spatial context through various visual guidance including signs, graphics, book location charts, building diagrams, and the like. Indeed, research has a vital role to play here. However, balance must be maintained so that the potential effects of clutter or confusion, which defeat the purpose of signs and graphics, can be minimized.

## Space and Layout

The library space arrangement is all too frequently taken for granted by those who manage and maintain it and those who use it. Users generally accept whatever physical and administrative arrangements exist in the library even though these arrangements may be based on the outdated views of user behavior. With or without a conscious philosophy or explicit recognition of the relationship between library space and user behavior, a library interior layout is, in fact, shaping and reshaping the behavior of its users one way or another on a daily basis. In general, a library's physical environment and its services should mirror the educational mission of its parent institution or the interests of the population served. But a library's interior space arrangement, including the location of its furniture, stacks, and equipment, such as computers, copy machines, microfilm readers, and printers, often cause confusion, difficulties, and anxiety among users, which can undermine the mission of the institution. Many libraries do not even have interior walls except for those around the technical processing area, the administrative offices, and the rest room facilities. Furnishings form most of the corridors and walkways, directing users at predictable angles and pathways through the building. By rearranging the furnishings, clear lines of movement can be formed. Space arrangement can make a difference in users' success or failure in locating the proper stack and the desired book(s) within that particular area. Signs and graphics may not provide enough direction, especially in large or complex library buildings.

Librarians have long been aware that users frequently encounter difficulties in finding desired library material. The location of periodicals and books often present great difficulties for both libraries and library users. In many libraries, the distance between the catalog terminals or help desk and the location of periodicals is both a psychological and a spatial barrier to their location and delivery. The perpetual difficulties of finding them either in their loose or bound format demand not only explicit written information about how to locate them in the library but also relocation and rearrangement of the furniture in order to break any barriers. One way to break the perceptual barrier is to arrange each open stack area in the same pattern, or in as few patterns as possible, even though the stack floors are of different sizes and shapes. The result of this arrangement is that even users who do not succeed in developing a cognitive map of the entire building may learn the pattern of a stack area and be able to predict the pattern of other stack areas if the pattern is repeated. Repeating the same stack arrangement in all stack areas is helpful because many users are slow to develop a cognitive map of the library building.

Psychologists have long been incorporating the personal space theory in public-access environments. This theory has been applied to library situations in terms of space design and furniture selection and placement, which are two library anxiety prevention strategies. Personal space is defined as "an area with invisible boundaries surrounding a person's body into which intruders may not come" (Sommer, 1969, p. 26). The invisible boundaries are not necessarily spherical in shape. The personal space is found to be widest to the front, narrowing at the sides and back. Some psychologists claim "people will allow others to come closer if the approach is to the side and the back rather than the front. Anxiety seems to increase distance between people" (Cohen & Cohen, 1979, p. 19). Two users rarely sit on a study table side by side unless they know each other. Strangers tend to sit as far apart from each other as possible and to minimize eye contact. The implication is that the manner in which library study tables, chairs, and couches are placed can either help reduce or increase users' anxiety levels. The size and shape of the furniture also make a difference. Research shows that rectangular tables seem better for work and study. Round tables seem best for conversation and socialization. A user can clearly define his or her territory on a rectangular table, while it is more difficult to mark out the territory from a round table (Cohen & Cohen, 1979). Librarians can apply some of the principle of personal space psychology to rearranging library furniture in order to produce a more welcoming and less stressful library environment.

In general, the type of library and its adopted philosophy of service have a direct bearing on the interior design of its building. Public libraries must cater to users of all ages, cultures, and ethnic groups of a given community. Their interior layout tends to reflect the diversity of information needs and role of community center, as well as the place for finding the recorded knowledge and developing skills. Academic and research libraries tend to have features of traditional library design, which puts emphasis on the physical collection and access to recorded knowledge with plenty of private space for quiet study, as well as features of present-day electronic gateway facilities, such as electronic classrooms for teaching library research skills, wired study carrels, network connections, networked printing, and computer workstations.

In all types of libraries, it is very important for librarians to make efforts to create a pleasant environment and comfortable study space, which requires careful selection and arrangement of furniture, stacks, and equipment using sound ergonomic concepts. It has been found that users' interest in face-to-face interactions does not seem diminished with increasingly fast and effective means of communication via electronic chat, e-mail, and telephone. In fact, "effective research and reference consultation over the phone and through the network only increases the number of users in the physical library building" (LaGuardia, Blake, Farwell, Kent, & Tallent, 1996, p. 9). If the library is to be a pleasant place where opportunity to socialize is expected, space and furnishings should be arranged with that in mind. A combination of small and large round tables should be put intermittently so that some people can talk and be physically close to one another. If the library is intended as a research facility where serious concentration is the goal, the layout should consist primarily of small rectangular tables to help preserve personal space.

In addition to furnishings arrangement, there are many other environmental and policy-related factors that usually cause discomfort and anxiety among library users. Examples include fear for personal safety in the library, fear of "undesirable" loiterers, theft of personal belongings, poor lighting and ventilation, limited parking space, high noise level, insufficient loan period, insufficient availability of staff to assist with computer and equipment problems, insufficient provision of computer workstations, and limited opening hours. These issues have been addressed using a variety of administrative procedures, some of which are effective, others are not quite as successful and need to be modified to better confront the new administrative challenges in the changing environment. For instance, controlling the noise level in the library is one of the old as well new administrative challenges. The fast pace of contemporary life with mobile telecommunication devices has users' cell phones ringing in the library. Despite the policy to get users to turn off their ringers and to ban cellphone buzzing at all times, the use of cell phone has become rampant.

The safety and security policies of a library are also related to users' library anxiety (Bostick, 1992). Some users are concerned about the theft of their personal belongings while away from their seats. Theft represents a common crime in the library setting. It is also very difficult to detect. In addition, thefts are often not taken seriously by law enforcement officials (Allen, 1997). Libraries need to evaluate their existing policies and develop new safety and security policies. Shuman (1997) has recommended many useful steps to establish these policies. Among the recommended steps are evaluation of the library's security personnel, analysis of possible unauthorized access points, distribution of an up-to-date security and safety checklist, staff discussions of potential problem patrons, close cooperation with police departments, and orientation on safety for new employees.

## Cooperative Resource Development

Although a library collection is ordinarily thought of in terms of books and periodicals, it actually contains a very broad range of materials, including microfilms, photographs, paintings, videotapes, movies, recordings, documents, manuscripts, archives, artifacts, numeric data resources, electronic bibliographic and full-text databases, and electronic books and journals. Indeed, a large part of librarians' efforts is spent on this aspect of value-added service, which involves selection, acquisition, organization, preservation, promotion, and access to resources. The assembling of a collection and making it accessible is the first stage of the process of information retrieval for potential library use. Most of the time, the organized collection is for users to access by themselves. However, due to budget constraints in library purchases of print materials over the past decade, multiple-copy buying is almost nonexistent and periodicals must demonstrate their worth by usage before they are acquired.

Providing physical access to monographic books and print journals has become increasingly more challenging for money-strapped libraries. The reduction of local holdings for economic or other reasons creates a bottle-neck of accessibility of library material. The lack of available copies of the desired book or titles of badly needed journals has generated lots of disappointment, frustration, anxiety, and library avoidance behaviors among the loyal users (Onwuegbuzie, 1997a). One workable, but not necessarily economical, solution for the availability problem has been through more efficient document delivery service in the form of interlibrary loan for monographs and print or electronic copies of journal articles. Another solution is through forming various types of library collection sharing consortia, which may encompass on-site as well as borrowing privileges. Resource sharing enables users of one library or library system to use the material at another library.

Interlibrary loan, document delivery, library consortia, and referral services may help reduce users' library anxiety caused by the availability problem to some extent, but they may not be able to deal effectively with the anxiety associated with the urgency of an inquiry. Document delivery methods are getting faster. Users are beginning to realize the efficiency of these e-mail or fax delivery methods. However, there are still many users who are not aware of these document delivery services. New ways of communication need be explored to alert these users of the fast document delivery options.

## Tours and Open House

Studies in academic libraries have found that many college students suffer from library anxiety (Mellon, 1986). As noted by Mellon (1986), these students attributed their anxiety to not knowing where things were located, what to do, and how to begin their library research. Until recently, the library has been considered just a physical entity with its buildings and collections. To be library literate, students need to know how to find the way both through the physical building and through navigating the resources within it (Mardikian & Kesselman, 1995). To a large extent, this is still true, even in the evolving digital library environment where many library collections are located and accessed outside the physical building and services are provided beyond library walls. Indeed, despite the belief that the Internet will eventually take the place of traditional libraries, library leaders see a continuing role for the library building in the evolving digital revolution.

Although information technology has dramatically transformed library activities and functions, the library building as a vital source of "place" is playing an important role in the communities as a gateway to worldwide information and as perhaps the only institution where information is freely available. LaGuardia et al. (1996) notes, "Even if we believe that there will be a day when there are no physical collections to be housed, the library will remain an actual physical building for at least the foreseeable future" (p. 8). When users are contemplating a trip to the library, their hesitation and anxiety are partly due to their ignorance about the library resources and services. Surveys on public library users also indicate that both users and nonusers do not seem to be aware of some of the most basic services the public library offers (Massachusetts Board of Library Commissioners, 1997).

Library tours are potentially useful in preventing and reducing the anxiety associated with ignorance of where things are located and how services are organized for new and future library users. The guided physical tour is probably the most common form of library orientation offered in all types of libraries for a wide range of library users. A knowledgeable and personable tour leader can establish good connections with the group of new users by highlighting the major services and collections of a library. The good impression presented by the library likely will make new users feel comfortable enough to approach a service desk to ask for help with their information needs in their future visits to the library. Oling and Mach (2002) found that "Despite the infiltration of technology into all other areas of the library, the most popular tour continues to be the traditional guided tour" (p. 22). The key to an effective physical tour, however, is to control the amount of information provided and to select motivated and upbeat tour leaders. There is a tendency for the tour leader to offer too much unconnected information and directions within a short period of time. Information overload can actually minimize the gains from a well-intended tour, while an unmotivated tour leader can equally diminish the expected results.

Many libraries offer the self-guided or self-paced tour using printed information, which is an attractively printed handout in all sizes and colors distributed at the library entrance, reference or other service desks, or near information kiosks. Users can give themselves a tour by following the steps listed in the handout. The format of self-guided tours may appeal to those users whose dominant mode of information processing is through learning by doing. Oling and Mach (2002) reported in their survey of over 100 academic libraries that belong to the Association of Research Libraries (ARL) that self-guided tour is the second-most-popular tour option after the guided physical tour. Although videotaped library tours have been reported to be successful in reducing library anxiety (Tidwell, 1994), tours that rely on trendy modern technology, such as audiocassette, slide/tape, CD-ROM, and videotape have "experienced only a brief surge of popularity before being replaced by something else" (Oling & Mach, 2002, p. 22).

Many colleges and universities have comprehensive orientation programs for freshmen and other new students. Some of these programs are voluntary and others mandatory. Some programs contain a session, which includes a tour of the library building, followed by time in an electronic classroom where students are given the opportunity to experiment with the online catalog and listen to an explanation of how to use it and of library services and policies. To make the experience more interesting and rewarding, some librarians have attempted to use cooperative learning approaches by designing various exercises and then pairing students to work on them. Most students enjoy being actively involved in undertaking a meaningful task. And, at the same time, they are able to observe aspects of the library they would not have observed otherwise.

Although not intended to replace the physical tours, most libraries now have created self-guided interactive multimedia virtual tours on their homepages. A virtual tour can be viewed selectively by service points or by following the floors of a library building. The advantage of the virtual tours is that users can take the tour anywhere and anytime. The self-guided virtual tour will lead a person through every floor of the library and provide an overview of important locations of different areas of the physical library building, highlighting the resources, services and collections with panoramic views, graphics, pictures, maps, text information, and, sometimes, multilingual options. The self-guided tours are especially useful in meeting the needs of users at distant locations.

The format of the guided physical tours usually consists of a group of users following a tour guide in a library facility and sometimes crowding around one computer terminal for a demonstration of the available electronic resources. However, these tours tend to be isolated and scratch only the surface of many users' information need. They are not related to a specific inquiry for immediate library use, but designed for possible future use of a library. Despite their lack of any lasting educational experience, tours do make current and potential users comfortable and informed about a library's physical environment. That brief experience can help prevent or reduce possible anxiety induced in library physical environment and make potential users "see the library as a great place with fascinating information and warm, friendly people available to help them" (Mellon, 1986, p. 164).

In addition to tours, a well-designed and well-executed library open house event can be an effective way to educate users about the library physical environment as well as its resources and services. During an open house, the entire library is on display for a few hours, maybe a whole day. An open house provides an opportunity for both new and existing users to experience the library at its best with perhaps eye-catching exhibits, tours, demonstrations, and interactions with librarians.

## Informational Brochure and Handout

Good signage, comfortable space arrangement, and friendly-guided tours are only part of the library anxiety prevention and reduction strategies for the physical environment. The availability of library informational brochures, pamphlets, and handouts also can help reduce the initial anxiety and disorientation of users by providing guidance in the largely self-service environment and by saving them from the frustration of having to search blindly or ask trivial questions. The straightforward provision of information about the library environment may be an overlooked but perhaps a basic ingredient in library anxiety prevention. These publications explain the library in detail, including many of the procedural or policy-related provisions, such as entrance requirements, hours, services, equipment use, floor plans, telephone numbers, personal computers, loan periods, collections, information resources, services, call numbers, special searches, policies for cellular phones, lockers, checkrooms, food and drink, and other rules and regulations. They are meant for users to take home for future reference because these individuals often feel a need for some printed material they can take with them and consult again later. These publications can be distributed at an information desk, at new student orientation sessions, and during guided physical tours, as well as posted on the library homepage, which is becoming indispensable for both remote and on-site users. The library homepage also is used to announce the library's presence, amplifying its image and broadcasting its services.

One of the common sources of frustration and anxiety among users is that their required book, journal, or newspaper is not found in the designated place. Studies conducted in academic libraries have shown that the chance of finding a needed book that is possessed by a library is only around 60% (Buckland, 1974). Therefore, the user needs to know what steps to take if the desired material is not found, whether the item in question is in use elsewhere, and what the waiting period is for the recall of the item. Such information should be clearly stated in the general information brochure.

Some experienced library users are anxious about wasting their valuable time explaining their highly specialized inquiries to "someone unfamiliar with his or her specialty" (Bungard, 1987, p. 146) because they suspect the librarian on duty would not understand them. Therefore, a directory of subject specialists within the library or library consortium who might help with specific or technical problems of research also should be included in the informational brochure to help save time for this type of users, as well as for librarians.

Some library policies or practices that are not in congruence with users' expectations or previous experience can cause potential resentment and anxiety. For example, often library users will come to the library en route to another destination. Some of them expect a safe place to store their belongings while they use the library. Prior knowledge about whether or not the library has a checkroom or lockers would help prevent later frustration. Information about whether the library offers computer nodes for personal laptop connections, scanner, copy service, fax machine, paging service, word-processing facilities, availability of parking space, and policies regarding food and drink, cellular phones, and so forth should be clearly delineated in the brochure. To avoid information overload, the information could be broken down into categories and presented in pamphlet or handout format.

Effective means to assist self-service users in finding their way around the physical library environment calls for a coordinated strategy of effective signage, specific informational brochures and handouts, logical and pragmatic space and furniture arrangement, efficient document delivery service, fully functional library consortia, the appropriate amount of physical tours, and well-executed library open houses. The combination of these elements will greatly enhance users' chances of successfully finding information and preventing or reducing their anxiety levels at a crucial point of their introduction to the library environment.

## LIBRARY ANXIETY PREVENTION THROUGH INSTRUCTION

Much user frustration is a result of knowing that the information needed is available either in the library or from the library networked databases but not knowing how to get it. Lack of information retrieval skills and library research strategies in dealing with the plethora of searching tools and resources is believed to be one of the sources of library anxiety among users. This lack of competency is related to several factors, including absence of previous library experience, ignorance of the capabilities and extent of library information retrieval systems, and inadequate knowledge of subject matter and the library research process (Kuhlthau, 1983, 1985, 1987, 1988a, 1988b, 1989, 1991, 1993, 1994; Kuhlthau et al., 1990). The most commonly used approach to preventing library anxiety resulting from lack of experience and skills is by enhancing users' information retrieval skills and competencies through traditional bibliographic instruction (Zahner, 1993). There are many different kinds of instruction offered by librarians, ranging from quick one-on-one instruction at a reference or information desk to organized group instructional sessions. Although library instruction is offered in all types of libraries, school and academic libraries have given it a priority to develop students' library competence and independent research skills.

Bibliographic instruction is defined as "the intensive process of teaching the efficient and effective use of library by demonstrating library research methodology, search strategy, and the bibliographic structure of a given literature in a discipline" (Roberts & Blandy, 1989, p. 1). Using bibliographic instruction as a library anxiety prevention tool may appear straightforward, but there are many issues and controversies involved that render it very challenging to implement in practice.

If the user experiences library anxiety because he or she fails to retrieve the needed information due to lack of information retrieval skills, the most efficient way to reduce the situational library anxiety is perhaps for the librarian simply to provide the information to the user either at a reference desk or through electronic reference services. Why does the librarian even bother to teach the user how to retrieve the information by him or herself in this case? Librarians have been considered as experts in accessing and retrieving information available from resources both within and outside the library. Users normally expect to get help from the librarian to obtain the needed information so that they can complete their task at hand. Indeed, users rarely expect to get a rushed lesson on how to find the information themselves from the librarian, who sometimes naively believes that the user with a specific information need actually absorbs the contents of the hurried minilesson. How self-reliant does the librarian hope to teach the user to be in most cases? Many users do not desire to learn about the process of searching for information in the library. Some users do not see the problem of inadequate search abilities as their own but rather perceive the situation as the inadequacies in the library's collection (Doyen, 1989). They do not usually relate any difficulties they experience to the need of understanding the search process, but attribute their information-retrieval difficulties to a lack of time, unreasonableness of the task assigned, or inadequate help.

In a survey conducted of different types of library staff, Harris (1992) found that whereas academic librarians were convinced of the need for user education, staff at special libraries was generally opposed to the concept, and public librarians were ambivalent. One public librarian commented, "many patrons like to be informed so that they will bring more skill to their next library visit. However, just as many patrons are not interested in how the library works; they just want the information. I equate this to me and the grocery store: I want to know where the cat food is, not why or how the store decided to put it there" (Harris, 1992, p. 254).

The full-service model adopted by most corporate and special libraries, whereby the primary function is to provide the appropriate information without their users having to do it themselves is not without problems.

There are occasions, for example, in a hospital library where the information needed is urgent but immediate information retrieval by a librarian is not available and the doctor does not have the skills to search for a particular database by him or herself. In academic libraries, reference services are often limited to certain hours. When the librarian is not available for consultation, the student has either to rely on whatever can be extracted or simply to postpone or to give up the information retrieval task altogether. To invest in time to learn the retrieval skills and strategies of library search makes a lot of sense to the student because a large part of his or her study may depend on the quality of information to be gathered.

In spite of the different attitudes toward library instruction in various types of libraries, many librarians and library administrators, especially in academic libraries, believe that the library and information environment has been changed dramatically by the emerging information technologies. Although technology itself is not the reason to provide user instruction because successful bibliographic instruction predates the automated and electronic libraries, information technology has made library instruction more important and visible. Miller (1992) noted, "As collection building becomes less important, it seems inevitable that the notion of the teaching library will become the primary one to which the profession aspires" (p. 153).

Technology has been a driving force for changing attitudes toward library instruction. Academic libraries are compelled by the ever-changing information technologies to create learning opportunities for every user to develop various levels of competencies of acquiring information in any format, even at the expense of tremendous amount of staff time and resources. It is believed that users will enjoy the long-term benefits by extending their current information-retrieval skills to their future questions. Handing the information to the user may very well reduce her temporary anxious state, but it does not effectively prevent or help reduce her future anxiety responses. In the information age, only self-reliant or information-literate users are "able to function more effectively as independent learners, continuing to grow intellectually outside the structure and requirements of formal education" (Tuckett & Stoffle, 1984, p. 59).

The time when library instruction is offered also has many implications. Librarians tend to offer more spontaneous instruction during a reference interview when users come to request assistance. Users generally ask questions because something has caught their interest or they just want to know something. Their "teachable moment" usually begins with a question of intense personal interest and curiosity. Although this moment usually is very brief, it is worth hours of prescribed instruction at a later time and location. The users' receptiveness to learning information retrieval skills often increases when the inquiry is self-generated. School and academic libraries tend to offer both spontaneous instructions as well as planned teaching activities.

There are many occasions when a more organized approach to instruction may be preferable for a group of students who need the same advice or library experience for the requirements of a particular assignment. Effective library instruction is often timed to coincide with heightened student motivation to undertake library research for a term paper or a research project. Coordinating group instruction with imminent demand of library use by students can make the most of the "teachable moment." But students often tend not to participate in library instructional programs that are offered on a voluntary basis and removed from their classroom instruction because they do not see any immediate need. Studies have shown that isolated, skills-oriented instructional sessions are not effective, not even when they are related to a topic of study (see Breivik, 1998; Lechner, 1989; Morrison, 1992; Vincent, 1984). These sessions need to be integrated with classroom instruction in a planned and flexible manner. Information skills should be learned incrementally over time.

The isolated, tool-oriented, one-shot library instruction sessions tend to overwhelm users with sources and overload them with detailed search commands because for most instruction librarians class time may be their only point of contact with these users. According to Hope, Kajiwara, and Liu (2001), "Librarians feel pressure to cover all of the information that students will need for successful research in the limited instructional opportunities available to them" (p. 24). They tend to teach all they know once and for all in a content-packed lecture or demonstration with little time left for questions and answers (Hope et al., 2001) and hope the users will be able to conduct library search independently. The tool-oriented approach to library instruction "has many limitations that may render it ineffective for achieving true user self-reliance" (Tuckett & Stoffle, 1984, pp. 59–60). Although the credit-bearing library courses that are offered as an elective and taught by librarians in some college libraries have the luxury of ample class time to explain in detail the concepts of information structure and the skills of information retrieval, often these courses are taught at different levels. The focused contents and higher expectations of these credited courses may benefit a limited number of dedicated students who need to know their specialized subject information structure and retrieval skills, while leaving other students at a loss.

The question of what is to be taught during a library instruction session also has generated an array of debates and discussions. For some, library instruction should focus on information retrieval skills based on the existing library bibliographic organization, such as how to use online catalogs, print and electronic indexes and abstracts, full-text electronic databases, public web search engines, other relevant bibliographic reference tools, and the basics of classification systems. However, the networked communication technologies have transformed not only the physical space of libraries but also the resources that take place in them. With many library resources migrated to the Internet and more information available from the World Wide Web, including resources and materials not published elsewhere, the role of the library as a repository for printed information is significantly expanding. The library building-centered resources are diminishing in their relevance in the wake of busy lives of many users even though "books remain the most elegant and satisfactory way to present a substantial intellectual product" (Bazillion & Braun, 1995, p. xiii).

The "distinction between 'library information resources' and 'Internet resources' is weak, and weakening, as more and more of our collections and services go online" (Hope et al., 2001, p. 22). In many instances, library users are able to obtain information services without traveling to a particular library location. The library faces the challenge of balancing traditional library services with those demanded by constantly changing technologies. As noted by Hope et al. (2001), "The sheer number and variety of resources in the networked information environment has added considerably to the content that librarians must be prepared to teach" (p. 19). The instruction the users need is increasingly linked to the skills and competencies of accessing virtual resources.

Other librarians believe that library instruction should not be focusing just on the discrete components of library use, whether it is for print or electronic resources "because students are taught only how to use a particular reference tool or tools, they generally are not able to link this random array of sources into a cohesive approach to information retrieval" (Tuckett & Stoffle, 1984, pp. 59–60). To these librarians, tool-based library instructional sessions admittedly can help users to some extent, but they do little to produce an information-literate citizen who is self-reliant to pursue his or her life-long goals in the information society. In addition, the ever-changing electronic information environment presents a new challenge for the tool-oriented library instruction whose usefulness becomes ephemeral. As Sager (1995) writes, "If new technologies have given us new skills to teach, they have also made clear how fleeting the useful shelf life of many of these skills might be" (p. 56). These librarians contend that library instruction should combine both specific skills and abstract concepts by guiding users through the library research process, thereby encouraging lifelong learning.

Users should be taught the concept, structure, role, and organization of information, as well as critical thinking and problem-solving skills during this process, including evaluation of the information found (American Library Association, 1989). Teaching users how to use library resources to solve their immediate problems is generally believed by the knowledge transfer–oriented librarians to be insufficient because the user must return to the librarian for each new question. The short-term gain in specific skills is considered limited in its transferability. Rather, these knowledge transfer–oriented librarians believe that what should be taught are the competencies in users that go beyond the skill needed to decipher a particular reference source (Frick, 1975) or specific skills for searching a particular bibliographic database. Apparently, users should acquire skills that they can recognize as being transferable from one library research problem to another. According to the knowledge transfer–oriented librarians, the aim of library instruction should be to produce independent library users who have developed information competencies and successful library research strategies to enable them to carry on their current, as well as future, information endeavors.

Knowledge transfer–oriented librarians cite the finding that independent library users tend to be the least anxious-prone. It seems that the difference of opinions is just a matter of focusing on short-term need and long-term effect. However, the two elements do not necessarily contradict each other. In fact, both discrete database retrieval skills and abstract critical thinking are important and can and should be taught during library instruction sessions, depending on user needs and the resources available. The components necessary to achieve the long-term information literacy effect include acquiring and cumulating specific short-term skills and knowledge sufficient to enable users to interact successfully with library resources for their immediate information needs and to help them move towards their independency. Successful library research consists of a hierarchy of information problem-solving skills that need to be acquired over an extended period of time through structured curricula of library instruction.

If library instruction is to be effective in developing skills that help reduce anxiety, it has to be designed and presented in a way that allows users to build on their existing knowledge, skills, and affective levels. Users' emotions and feelings are "the first contact points with library, librarians, and the process of finding information" (Vidmar, 1998, p. 75). How users feel initially will ultimately determine the course of action that they will take to carry on their information-seeking tasks. Library instruction that fails to address the "feelings of uncertainty and anxiety as well as attitudes of resistance potentially will fall short of achieving the desired effect" (Vidmar, 1998, p. 75).

Users' emotional readiness to assimilate the knowledge of cognitive-oriented information retrieval skills is an important factor to consider in the design of library instruction. Vidmar (1998) studied the effect of having a short presession of 10–20 minutes prior to the regular 50-minute skills-based library instruction sessions. The presession was simply designed to address the affective states of students through establishing a relationship with them and explaining the typical emotions and feelings during the library search process. It is like preparing students psychologically before teaching them more challenging subjects. Vidmar (1998, p. 76) reported that "students who were exposed to a presession felt better about the librarians and library research in general."

Kracker (2002) and Kracker and Wang (2002) studied the effects of a 30-minute presentation of Kuhlthau's (1993) Information Search Process (ISP) model on college students' perceptions of research anxiety. They found that a 30-minute presentation of the ISP model can substantially increase awareness of the emotional states and affective aspects associated with research and reduce anxiety by a significant amount. Joseph (1991) has argued that, in many cases, helping students foster positive attitudes toward library is more important than teaching them specific information retrieval skills. In fact, Joseph (1991) contended, "Traditional instructional practices can be the vehicle by which student attitudes are influenced" (pp. 112–113). Another strategy to break the ice and reduce library anxiety early on is to use humor to help illustrate library research concepts in class (Sarkodie-Mensah, 1998).

Although there is no one correct way to learn, "there are certain styles that are more appropriate for a given situation. Thus, when an individual learns, the style should be unique to the task or a negative experience may ensue" (Onwuegbuzie & Jiao, 1998a, p. 238). Ideally, library instruction should be oriented toward individual users by helping them to conceptualize their information needs and by training them in continuous self-assessment thinking based on the mode of learning that suits them best. In recent years, there has been increased emphasis on more personalized library instruction through the Internet. Anecdotal experience with these innovative instructional methods indicates that they may have important affective benefits for the learner. Yet, no systematic research has been conducted in this area.

A web-based tutorial program is intended to stand alone as an instructional entity for self-paced learning. A well-designed tutorial program leads the user through the subject matter by presenting concepts of ever-increasing complexity. Some academic libraries have produced flexible and generic research-oriented instruction modules that contain instructional screens featuring text and interactive graphics covering a wide range of topics important to all students who are new to the library research process and who might not have convenient access to on-campus library instruction. Some of these modules enable students to organize and track their experiences and achievements and to reflect critically on their current levels or stages of development by adding an interactive assessment tool to the module. Bowling Green State University Jerome Library's Web tutorial, FALCON, for example, models a standard library instructional session on the use of the library's web-based catalog (Dennis & Broughton, 2000).

Tutorials can be particularly helpful in reaching large numbers of students. The degree of interactivity and the design of a tutorial are dependent on the goals of its creators and the intended audience of the product. Several features make FALCON unique. It is interactive, self-contained, and focuses on a single resource. Interactivity is accomplished without scripts or forms. The tutorial's self-containment, achieved with a complex system of files and with a live catalog connection, enables users to learn how to search the catalog at their own pace, at a time or place of their choosing without the threat of venturing into cyberspace (Dennis & Broughton, 2000).

Cognitive development of users also has practical implications for designing effective library instruction because information processing needs considerable skills in abstraction. To facilitate learning, library instruction needs to be designed as a continuum from concrete search strategies to more flexible and alternative ways of accessing and using information in order to accommodate the different levels of cognitive development. One of the often-cited theories of cognitive development by academic librarians was theorized by William G. Perry, Jr. (1970), who identified a scheme of four basic stages of intellectual and ethical development of college students known as duality, multiplicity, relativism, and commitment.

Mellon (1982) has recapitulated the four stages of development in her publication. According to Mellon (1982), college students in the duality stage tend to look at the world in terms of right or wrong. Library instruction designed for this type of student, therefore, should be simple, straightforward, and easily understood. Although students at the multiplicity stage still believe part of the world remains right or wrong, they are beginning to think that sometimes there is more than one answer or perspective to a problem. Instruction designed for students at this stage can be more complex and abstract, emphasizing problem-solving skills. Students at the relativistic stage become aware that many aspects cannot be known absolutely. This is the stage of abstract thinking and reasoning. They gather information and evidence before forming their opinions and making decisions. They are more willing to take the responsibility for defining their own library research. The instruction for students at this stage should focus on complex information retrieval concepts, comparison and evaluation of various bibliographic or electronic tools available in relation to the information need, and alternative research strategies. At the commitment stage, students come to realize that in this world nothing seems to be certain. In order to progress, they must take a stand or make choices in the relative world of shifting values. Learning at this stage is more personal because the students are ready to make commitments to their own library research strategies that fit the interests and needs of their choices.

Smalley and Plum (1982) compared the structure of literature between the humanities and the natural sciences and concluded that the distinctive characteristics of research processes and the subsequent reporting formats of the disciplines "have significant effects on their literatures and, consequently, on the use of their bibliographic access tools" (p. 141). They proposed a contextual approach to bibliographic instruction, which would be based on the structure of literature of a specific discipline as the teaching framework. This brings up another issue of the subject expertise and preparation of the instruction librarian. Is the generalist librarian prepared to teach the bibliographic structure of the distinctive research literature across disciplinary areas? Or does the library need to hire more subject specialists who are familiar with the distinctive challenges in various disciplines, as the number of reference resources has become more specific and the users more sophisticated? And how does the library handle this with reduced personnel budgets and the rapidly changing information needs?

Bringing all of these issues, arguments, and opinions together, the instruction librarian must face an enormous amount of challenge in designing and implementing library instructional sessions that not only will meet the information needs of users, but also will elevate and optimize their levels of information literacy and will expose them to transferable information-retrieval strategies that best meet their individual modes of learning. But, again, who are these individual library users? Are they distant users who access library databases from a remote location and never walk into the library's physical facilities? Are they typical library users who frequent the library building as well as remotely access the databases and Internet resources? How much do we know about their difficulties, skills, and needs? How will the librarian identify them for instruction?

Library anxiety prevention through instruction, which aims at reaching the wide variety of existing as well as potential users, is very much open to experimentation at present. In spite of what has been known about the significance of information literacy and the importance of collaboration between librarians and teaching faculty in colleges and universities, most libraries for various reasons keep seeking validation for the traditional methods of one-on-one instructional assistance, one-shot lectures and workshops, freshman seminars, course-related sessions, printed guides, and web-based research tutorials. Hope et al. (2001) have pointed out, "Librarians have always known the value of actively engaging with information, but ironically, we have historically been among the worst culprits of the top-down, lecture-driven, one-size-fits-all, Transmission Mode teaching" (p. 24).

As far as library anxiety prevention is concerned, these traditional instructional approaches work more effectively than do the long-range information literacy education because library anxiety is situation specific. It lasts as long as the situation itself is present. While library anxiety can show itself in the thinking processes and judgment, intruding on concentration, and clouding perceptions, it is temporary. It is dealt with more effectively with immediate and specific intervention measures, such as one-on-one instruction at reference desks and one-shot lectures and workshops aimed at developing proficiency in using specific library tools and resources in demand, especially those traditional library resources and effective search strategies.

With the changing demographics and proliferation of computing and telecommunication technologies, library users nowadays are more diverse in terms of their preparedness and skills to use library electronic tools. The perceptions of the library users have changed substantially in the electronic age. Traditionally, bibliographic instruction offered in academic libraries tended to target students by their academic levels or cultural and language backgrounds in the case of international students. Current library instruction initiatives are focusing more on the computer skills and electronic habits of various user groups, regardless of their age, gender, level of study, and socioeconomic backgrounds. There are three potential sources of library anxiety that need to be intervened through library instruction programs. One source is the interface design of the various library subscription databases and other retrieval systems. Another source is the access of traditional print-oriented library materials. And the third is related to the lack of understanding of the library research process.

New technologies and electronic databases in libraries continue to challenge our abilities to adapt. The search interface of various databases is especially confusing and illogical for many users, who are sometimes frustrated and anxious, not because they do not have the mental ability to conduct a basic search but because they cannot tell the differences from the plethora of databases and the seemingly disparate interface designs. They are simply overwhelmed by the choices and do not know where to start. As Sager (1995) noted, "Improvement in interface design has lagged far behind improvements in search engines or improvements in electronic access to and transfer of information" (p. 55).

Traditional bibliographic instruction such as one-on-one instruction at reference or information desks and one-shot lectures and workshops are all good devices for hand-holding users through the maze-like choices of databases and systems and explaining to them the common features that all of them share as well as the unique characteristics associated with individual searching tools. The knowledge gleaned from this instruction can help prevent and reduce potential library anxiety. In the foreseeable future, this type of library system or database-specific instruction will continue to play an intermediary role between the structures of electronic resources and users' information needs. But it will eventually lose its value to the improved database and library system designs that emphasize a consolidated and one-stop solution, which makes it easier for users to acquire information from multiple information databases in a single search interface. As users become accustomed to the improved interfaces, librarians will be "freer to emphasize the concepts over mechanics in instruction" (Hope et al., 2001, p. 23), and "the focus of instruction shifts to content and use of materials" (Tenopir, 1999, p. 278).

Commercial vendors of library bibliographic databases are fully aware of the importance of meeting the end-user needs and preferences with better design and more flexible search commands, such as guided searching and natural language searching. Vendors have integrated their databases with World Wide Web protocols and have them delivered through the Internet. The improvements have narrowed the gap between the users' electronic habits of using Internet search engines and library bibliographic databases. Users are becoming more and more capable of navigating various Internet-based resources than of evaluating and using the information they have found. Increasingly, it is the access of traditional library resources, such as monographs, print journals, microfilm, historical documents, and statistics that cause anxiety and frustration among the new generation of electronic-oriented users. Online catalogs that are favorite tools for librarians are often considered by these users as difficult, confusing, and not as easy to use as commercial databases. Teaching the use of library online catalogs can be traced back to the 1980s. Today, it is still one of the most important components of library instruction in academic libraries. Ironically, after more than 20 years of bibliographic instruction and with so many improvements in the design of library online catalog systems, searching the library online catalog still poses many challenges to users. In teaching the use of traditional library resources, librarians have vast amounts of literature and years of experiences upon which to draw. Preventing library anxiety through bibliographic instruction in the use of traditional library resources is part of the daily lives of many librarians.

Traditional library instruction programs can be very helpful in reducing the participants' anxiety responses related to the unfamiliar search interfaces and remote access procedures of various library databases and systems. However, they may not be effective as a costly information service to tackle the real sources of library anxiety related to users' attitudes, emotions, research strategies, and the use of information during a library research process because users' anxiety is probably at its highest level when they are initially imposed on an unfamiliar task to perform within a limited time frame.

Students at various levels of educational systems face this kind of situation throughout their school years. Indeed, Gross (1998) has identified the school assignment as one of the most common examples of the imposed information seeking behavior in libraries. She has found that the upper-level elementary school children and adolescents showed not only high levels of imposed information seeking behaviors but also a decrease in their library use for self-generated needs (Gross, 1999b). With so many uncertainties and unknowns in the typical library research process, students tend to become very anxious, not only about what to expect but also about where to start and how to proceed. What they need most at this initial stage of imposed information seeking is help with their affective reactions as well as constructive guidance from the librarian.

Instructors give assignments that require students to practice information access and use while exploring and synthesizing new ideas and concepts. The library is considered a logical place for students to work on their term papers and research projects, to examine different viewpoints, and to acquire information literacy skills (McGregor, 1999). However, "many students are intimidated by the demands of a research-based assignment" (McGregor, 1999, p. 30). They do not realize that the anxiety, fear, and feelings of uncertainty they experience are a natural reaction to the unfamiliar and demanding library research process, which involves more than just gathering of information and putting the ideas on paper. Nor do they realize that the process of library research is an important opportunity for them to acquire and practice decision-making, problem-solving, and information-literacy skills, as well as computer competency and socioethical knowledge regarding copyright and plagiarism issues. All of those skills and competences are essential for their life-long learning. Too often, the end product is all that matters for students and for some instructors. Both instructors and librarians tend to ignore what happens during the initial stage of topic exploration and the final stage of making sense of the gathered information.

The beginning and ending stage of a library research-based assignment is usually the time when students struggle the most and experience the highest levels of anxiety (Kuhlthau, 1983, 1985, 1987, 1988a, 1988b, 1989, 1991, 1993, 1994; Kuhlthau et al., 1990). It takes time to explore a topic. It takes even more time to focus and then to decide on a feasible topic on which to work. If students do not form a focus during the initial search process, they will experience difficulty and frustration throughout the remainder of their assignments (Kuhlthau, 1983, 1985, 1987, 1988a, 1988b, 1989, 1991, 1993, 1994; Kuhlthau et al., 1990; Onwuegbuzie, 1997a). Instead of helping students mitigate the common feelings of uncertainty, anxiety, doubt, and tension during the stage of selecting and narrowing a topic by explaining the natural stages of the research process and the associated feelings, some instructors even choose to quantify their research assignments by setting time constraints and checkpoints.

Students must produce a bibliography, an outline, or a draft by a certain date. This practice pressures students to shorten the important stage of thinking and understanding their topics and sends them right to the information-gathering stage (McGregor, 1999), which demands the least amount of critical thinking and problem-solving skills. Many students head straight to the Internet and computer workstations. Also, because of the imposed time constraints, students may not have enough time to digest what they have gathered in a hurry before they throw everything together and submit their final products.

This cycle starts with the instructors who give the library-based research assignment and assume that students either already possess the knowledge of the research process or will learn the research skills by undertaking the task. Some of the instructors have undertaken little preparation themselves or have little experience using research tools. Librarians are eager to assist students with information retrieval and gathering through library and nonlibrary resources. The students are then expected to work on the research assignment independently. Their library research experiences are likely to be remembered as confusing, painful, helpless, but inescapable (Onwuegbuzie, 1997a).

Can librarians intervene during these stages of anxiety and uncertainty through library instructional programs? The answer is an emphatic "yes." How many libraries are actually offering instructional sessions that focus on understanding the various affective reactions during a typical library research process? How many instructional sessions help students evaluate and use the information they gathered for their assignments? The answer to these questions is, probably, "very few." The challenge to provide instruction that addresses students' affective reactions during a typical library-based research process involves developing a proper form of instructional delivery, getting administrative support, and working in collaboration with teaching faculty (Jiao & Onwuegbuzie, 1997).

The more effective way to teach this type of process-oriented and practice-based content is to integrate library instruction with students' classroom instruction. Students need to know that library research is a process that has several stages (Kuhlthau, 1993) and that each stage requires different kinds of skills and generates different feelings and emotions. Anxiety and uncertainty are common feelings at the early stage of the process. Assuming that goals are being met along the way, as they move through the research process, their anxiety will be gradually decreased. They will become more optimistic and confident. Although the emotions and the research process they have undergone are tied to the specific assignment, the skills and feelings they have experienced during the process can apply to other information-seeking situations in their daily lives. This type of instruction needs administrative support from academic departments and the understanding and cooperation of teaching faculty because it takes up class time, and the contents of the instruction are not conventional.

Attitudes and perceptions of teaching faculty toward research process–

oriented instruction are important factors to be considered. Many teaching faculty believe that it is appropriate for librarians to teach information-retrieval skills used for accessing library resources and databases whether it is delivered in their classes or in a library setting, but they may have reservations about sharing their podium with librarians to teach research strategies that help their students to work on the discipline-specific research projects about which they are more knowledgeable and have complete authority. As noted earlier, some teaching faculty assume that students already possess the basic library research skills, and some believe that students will acquire enough skills by working on the research assignments.

Librarians also may have their own reservations about the responsibility of teaching the research process. From the librarian's point of view, the early stage of selecting and focusing on a topic and the later stage of synthesizing and writing up the research report are almost always carried out between students and the teaching faculty. The librarians' role in the process is to help students with the information retrieval and data collection. Teaching faculty should be the ones to teach their students about the process of research and help students synthesize new ideas and concepts. However, the reality is that most teaching faculty do not teach their students the research process. Nor do they help hone the judgment needed to evaluate material gathered from library bibliographic systems.

Thus, it appears that academic librarians are the most concerned with the presence of the research skills in students. And the "practice and teaching of research training has come primarily from librarians" (Frick, 1982, p. 193) who see the disconnection in the educational process every day and realize the necessity to offer help to make the link between students and teaching faculty in the library research process. As noted by Blandy and Libutti (1995), "It is the librarians who may take over as coaches and guides through the thorny process of creating a researched report. It is the librarians who must infer a great deal about the student's ability from evidence such as body language, blank monitor screens, and huge piles of paper" (p. 290). Faculty's overestimation of their students' research skills prevents them from giving the needed guidance that would make their students' research experience more enjoyable, engaging, meaningful, and long lasting. Students' misperceptions about the role of librarians often keeps them from considering librarians as the equals of the teaching faculty. And they tend not to approach librarians for questions concerning their research topic development even though librarians may be willing and capable of providing help. For these and other related reasons, the librarians' offer of instruction is not always met with appreciation from teaching faculty and students. A substantive rather than conceptual partnership between librarians and teaching faculty must be formed in order to address effectively this unintentional disconnection in the educational process. However, for a real partnership to work, library instruction and other information literacy efforts have to be placed within the context of existing campus commitments rather than promoted as a new initiative for faculty to accept. The efforts involve both people and institutional challenges.

A somewhat less challenging approach in terms of dealing with attitudes and perceptions is to introduce the concepts of the research process in the traditional library instructional programs, such as course-related lectures, library workshops, freshman orientation sessions, and credit courses. However, the new contents of strategies, processes, affective reactions, and information use and evaluation will inevitably compete with already limited class time for the existing library curricula that are often based on search techniques and information-retrieval skills of specific library bibliographic tools. A new curriculum needs to be designed to allow room for new content, which requires support of the library administration, as well as librarians.

Notwithstanding, no prescriptive procedures can be given here for obvious reasons. Every library is different. Every instruction librarian is a professional. A lot of support, judgment, and creativity are needed. Students can benefit from instruction as simple as a physical tour of the library to a more advanced session on information retrieval skills and research process. Librarians are playing an increasingly important role as teachers in the information-rich library environment. Those accustomed to teaching users in selecting and using printed and electronically based resources can modify their bibliographic instruction to accommodate the concept and knowledge of the research process.

Library instruction as an intervention for preventing anxiety should not be just focusing on the less anxiety-provoking stage of information gathering but also on the early stage of exploring the subject matter and the later stage of evaluation and use of information. Process-oriented instruction can help change the perceptions of the traditional role of librarians in the research process and make the student's research endeavor a meaning-ful learning experience. Librarians need to be convinced of the impor-tance of their expanding roles as information retrieval professionals, as well as teachers of intellectual use of information. Practical difficulties regarding the means of instructional delivery in each library can be sur-mounted if the librarians are persistent in playing out their greater roles in the information age.

## LIBRARY ANXIETY INTERVENTION THROUGH MEDIATED INFORMATION SERVICES

The library as an institution has existed for many centuries. But compared to the basic bibliographic services of acquiring, preserving, and organizing materials and making them available for library use, personal guidance to users in the United States is a relatively new practice, dating only back to 1876. According to Rothstein (1994), "The generally recognized starting point for the history of reference librarianship is the paper delivered by Samuel Swett Green of the Worcester (Mass.) Public Library in 1876" (p. 541), the year when the American Library Association (ALA) was founded. Green later published his article in the first issue of *American Library Journal*, then official publication for ALA. Green (1876) declared that simply to place reference books at the disposal of library users was not enough. Librarians must, in addition, provide personal service to users. Since then, the theories and practices of personal assistance have evolved from simple help in locating library books to today's multifaceted information services. Librarian-assisted service is so commonplace in today's American libraries that users tend to take them for granted with-out realizing the fundamental change in the range of assistance and levels of help offered. This valuable human intervention helps users prevent and reduce a wide variety of library anxiety responses evoked in the library setting in general and during the library search process in particular. Librarian-mediated service has evolved to become perhaps the most com-prehensive and most effective anxiety intervention procedure because it brings library anxiety intervention down to a personal level.

## Reference Assistance at Public Service Desks

An information, reference, or help desk near the main entrance to or at a central point of the library building offers valuable human assistance to users. The public service desk is often the initial human contact for library users as they enter the library facility. Staffed by professional and sympathetic librarians who are familiar with the workings of the various divisions, collections, and systems of the library, this desk can bridge an important psychological and intellectual barrier between the user and the unfamiliar library setting. Its functions include giving directions, providing answers to specific questions, offering basic research guidance, and assisting with problems of information retrieval systems and equipment.

Although the goal of connecting users with information remains unchanged at public service desks, the proliferation of electronic information technology renders it possible for reference librarians to reach that goal faster and more efficiently. As more users become electronically sophisticated and the technology becomes more usable, traditional librarian-mediated services that focus on helping users locate material within the four walls of the library have shifted toward helping and teaching the access of electronic information in the virtual world. Nonetheless, the complete virtual library is not yet here. Nor will it be here for quite some time. Although many users are becoming more and more competent in accessing virtual information, the complexity of the information environment also is increasing. It is not always obvious to users how to approach the vast resources available electronically as well as in traditional print format. Therefore, the librarian's mediation in the user's process of selecting, retrieving, and evaluating information in all formats is still the most effective way to help them get the information they want in the least stressful manner.

Because every user has his or her particular linguistic, cultural, and technical orientation, as well as a unique conceptual framework to approach the library search process (Onwuegbuzie & Jiao, 1998a), one of the important tasks required of reference librarians is that of translating vague requests into meaningful terms. Librarians at the public service desk are playing a major role of interpreting users' inquiries, identifying the appropriate sources for an answer, teaching and assisting users to find information in library computer workstations and at users' home computers, and deciding whether or not the retrieved information is adequate.

## Reference Roving

In recent years, providing electronic and digitized information has become a desirable part of the mission of a library. Allocations for library technologies, including capital investment in computers and other equipment, are increasing more rapidly than is any other budget area. As a result, more and more special equipment has occupied the library space, such as online public access catalog (OPAC) terminals, networked CD-ROM stations, and computer workstations. Although electronic information carries less constraint with it, meaning that more than one user can use it at the same time in different locations, retrieving machine-readable and digitized information often follows a less predictable manner than that of paper-oriented resources. The user often does not know which electronic tool to use to search for a given topic, what kind of query to form, and which search command to use to produce the desired response in the seemingly quite different electronic information retrieval environment. As a result, reference librarians have experienced increasing demand for services related to library equipment, electronic bibliographic databases, and web-based educational server software.

To be efficient in retrieving library material through library systems, the user must possess certain cognitive as well as psychomotor skills to handle the retrieval process, which may contain diverse levels of access and require different sorts of actions. Library anxiety often occurs when these assumed skills are not present to handle the search task demanded by the system-oriented information-seeking process. There are two major difficulties to remedying the anxiety-provoking situation inherent in various library information retrieval systems. First, librarians are neither in direct control of designing the interface and command languages of the new electronic tools, nor are they in control of how users actually form their queries to the library systems in the self-service environment. Second, it is difficult for librarians to intervene during the search process of individual users unless the user asks for help from a librarian at the reference or information desk. But frequently they do not ask for help (Swope & Katzer, 1972).

Roving can be an effective library anxiety prevention or reduction strategy. Proactive roving calls for librarians actively to seek out those users who may be experiencing difficulties of various kinds by extending a helping hand at their points of need. Unlike approaching the information desk where library staff may be helping others or being occupied with other duties, users tend to feel more comfortable requesting assistance from the rover, who gives an "impression that he or she is not 'bothered' by questions" (Kramer, 1996, p. 68). The spontaneous one-on-one situation helps ease the interpersonal communication between the user and rover. Although roving involves many unsolved operational difficulties, including how properly to identify the rover, the identification of potential users to help, concerns about intrusion of users' privacy, and timing of the offer to help (Ramirez, 1994), it is being used by many libraries as a way of providing good service to users. The effect of proper roving actually helps to prevent or to reduce many users' situational library anxiety responses.

## Individualized Information Services

In recent years, there have been numerous exhortations among academic librarians to individualize library research assistance because the majority of the academic library users have undifferentiated requirements for information. For example, the students may have to write a term paper, a thesis, or to work on a research project. These users are not seeking specific answers or highly technical information but rather a variety of materials at various levels of depth and sophistication to support their purposes. Students initially approach the public service desk for help, but the way a typical public service desk is operated often prevents them from getting more personalized and sustained help. There is a general perception that although librarians are very helpful and knowledgeable at public service desks, they do not have sufficient time to deal fully with users who have in-depth questions. To facilitate students' library research, many academic libraries have established individualized information services. These individualized services carry different names, such as "Student Thesis Assistance" (University of North Carolina at Wilmington Randall Library, 2003); "Research Clinics for Undergraduates" (Bowling Green State University Libraries, 2003); "Individual Research Consultations" (SUNY-Brockport Drake Memorial Library, 2003); and "Student Research Consultation" (Rochester Institute of Technology Libraries, 2003).

Typically, these services take the form of an appointment-based consultation, which allows a user the opportunity to receive individualized instruction and assistance from a professional librarian. It is intended for in-depth analysis of a research problem and one-on-one instruction on the search and use of appropriate information resources. The type of individualization is based on both the librarian's and user's knowledge and experience. The user's level of knowledge and affective reactions are adequately handled during the consultation. As one would expect, these individualized services vary substantially. Truly individualized library research assistance implies that different instructional strategies would be employed to match each student's individual characteristics and information need. However, individualized information service demands that there are well-established research findings documenting the effectiveness of the approach. Unfortunately, to date, there are few empirical data in support of any of these practices except for the plausible reason that undivided attention from the librarian in the one-on-one situation would make the student more comfortable, relaxed, and freer to express himself or herself. The rate at which this individualized assistance proceeds is another variable that may be optimal for library-anxious students. But the subject expertise of the librarian in this individualized service remains a significant variable.

In the individualized consultation situation, students typically may take as much or as little time as they feel necessary in order to get sufficient help in the research process. Students are invited to return periodically until they feel comfortable enough to work on their own. This service is an effective way to instill in students that library research is a time-consuming, constructive, and continuous process, not just the activity of gathering relevant information. There are definite advantages to having the dedicated attention of one librarian. The one-on-one sessions will save valuable research time and provide continuity throughout the research process. The user-oriented, individualized service may have a modest impact on library anxiety because it tends to guide the user in the making of certain kinds of deliberate, task-oriented choices. Generally speaking, students high in library anxiety would improve in their library research skills and attitudes with those services that can be characterized by either a high degree of structure and individuality or by opportunities for them to see the meaningful results in a relatively time-saving and friendly environment. The individualized assistance program is, perhaps, also a good way to foster a positive view of library resources and services among the "at risk" students and to mitigate previous negative experiences and perceptions.

## SUMMARY AND CONCLUSIONS

A variety of library anxiety intervention programs and procedures have been designed and implemented by librarians in many different library and information settings, especially in academic libraries. This chapter has reviewed these programs and procedures in three broad categories with regard to library physical environment, library user education, and mediated information services. These programs and strategies are summarized in table 7.1. The major goal of these seemingly different programs and procedures is to instill in anxious or potentially anxious library users a sense of confidence that they can handle the intricacies and challenges of the library information seeking process. Although the procedures aimed at reducing anxiety responses in a library physical environment are easier to be identified and implemented, effective inter-

Table 7.1  Summary of library anxiety prevention, reduction, and intervention procedures and strategies.

| Intervention Approach | Procedures and Strategies |
| --- | --- |
| Library facilities and resources | Effective signs and graphics<br>Logical space and furniture arrangement<br>Efficient document delivery system<br>Fully functional library consortia<br>Right amount of physical tour<br>Well-executed library open house |
| Library instruction | Teaching information retrieval skills<br>Teaching unfamiliar search interfaces<br>Teaching remote access procedures<br>Teaching research process<br>Conducting presessions for affective reactions |
| Mediated information services | Mediated reference assistance<br>Active reference roving<br>Individualized information consultation |

vention, prevention, and reduction of library anxiety through library instruction or mediated information services are open to experimentation and further research.

One of the major goals for today's libraries is to have professional librarians focus their energies and talents on user-oriented tasks such as individual consultation, point of use instruction, and proactive roving, while leaving routine tasks to various technologies. The potential benefits of moving toward these user-focused services are many, including reduced anxiety level of users, enhanced information literacy skills, increased efficiency of library use, expanded professional pride, and enhanced morale of librarians. During times of shrinking budgets, decreased resources, and increased competition from the library-like information institutions in the private sector, a renewed focus on user-oriented services provides a basis for redefining priorities. Budget reductions each year make it difficult for libraries to keep an adequate number of qualified staff, appropriate level of collections, and information technologies. Therefore, this is an extremely challenging time for libraries and librarians to try to provide quality services, resources, and lifelong learning opportunities to meet the informational, educational, cultural, and recreational needs of a diverse and changing population with less and less money and financial support.

*Chapter Eight*

# Future Research, Issues, and Challenges

## OVERVIEW

Nearly two decades have passed since the influential study conducted by Constance A. Mellon in 1986, which led to the grounded theory of library anxiety (Mellon, 1986). Today, library anxiety research has become an emergent field of study for educators, psychologists, library science researchers, graduate students, and practicing librarians across the United States and in many foreign countries. From the very beginning, the research has been guided by a commitment to "expand the dimensions of the theory of library anxiety" (Mellon, 1986, p. 165) and to produce useful findings for librarians, educators, and administrators in their daily practice of helping anxious users respond adaptively to the information-rich library environment.

During the past few years, we have witnessed unprecedented changes in libraries and the information environment. With the development of the Internet and its wealth of data, advances in digital information, and global networking, both libraries and librarians have opportunities to provide more comprehensive content and broader range of services. Although librarians are still being asked to bring users together with the resources required to meet their information needs, the environment in which they work is becoming ever more complex. The dramatic increase in the capabilities of microcomputers, the growing sophistication of computer software programs, and the equally dramatic reduction in the costs of computer and related hardware equipment have made online systems a staple in almost every library in this country. Libraries nowadays rely more heavily on information technologies to deliver information and services. Both librarians and library users are in a constant process of adapting to this changing information environment. Given the fact that important changes have taken place in the libraries and more changes will arise, does library anxiety research need to be more narrowly focused, shifted, or expanded? Are the research findings mainly from the 1980s and 1990s reported in the preceding chapters still applicable to today's library and information environment? How does the changing library and information landscape impact library anxiety research in the future? What is the goal of library anxiety research now? This chapter highlights the potential areas for future research on library anxiety and also discusses the issues and challenges involved in the research.

## POTENTIAL AREAS FOR FUTURE RESEARCH

If there is one goal of library anxiety research, it has been and will continue to be the promotion of scholarly pursuit of understanding the nature of this prevalent and debilitating phenomenon. This understanding is not simply meant to satisfy scientific curiosity but also to guide library policies and services for helping library users to achieve their immediate and life-long goals. There are two aspects of this goal. One is the basic inquiry into the nature of library anxiety. The other is to use the research findings to develop meaningful policies and programs to improve the conditions that adversely affect the library anxiety experience of users.

The theory-building aspect of library anxiety research has undergone several stages and continues to evolve and expand. The early studies focused on the phenomenological understanding of feelings and emotions of undergraduate students while they were using the physical library collection for various research purposes. Qualitative data were collected from students' personal writing in composition courses. Analyses of these descriptive data led to the discovery of the phenomenon that "many students become so anxious that they are unable to approach the problem logically or effectively" (Mellon, 1986, p. 163). Mellon's (1986) findings resulted in a redesign of the typical 50-minute library instruction session by incorporating information about library anxiety into the presentation and also culminated in "a better professional relationship between librarians and faculty" (p. 164), as teaching faculty began to appreciate the intricacies of the library information–seeking process.

Library anxiety research underwent a significant change after Sharon L. Bostick (1992) developed the Library Anxiety Scale (LAS). The research expanded to measure the five quantitatively constructed dimensions of library anxiety and to predict levels of library anxiety for both undergraduate and graduate students. Later studies shifted toward investigating the relationship between library anxiety and many academic factors, such as academic achievement, course load, computer experience, writing skills, research proposal ability, employment status, number of college credit hours earned, frequency of library use, and native language status. The research gradually focused its attention on the association between the dimensions of library anxiety and various personality and human characteristics. Good progress was made on the analysis of interactions of library anxiety with other personality and individual difference variables. Many studies emerged from this line of research, including those examining the relationship between library anxiety and learning modality preferences (Jiao & Onwuegbuzie, 1999c); learning style (Onwuegbuzie & Jiao, 1998a); perfectionism (Jiao & Onwuegbuzie, 1998); hope (Onwuegbuzie & Jiao, 1998c); academic procrastination (Onwuegbuzie & Jiao, 2000); self-perception (Jiao & Onwuegbuzie, 1999b); study habits (Jiao & Onwuegbuzie, 2001a); and social interdependence (Jiao & Onwuegbuzie, 2002a). These are all important investigations in that they are useful in helping to identify ways to facilitate learning and performance in the library information–search process.

Nevertheless, the application aspect of library anxiety research has advanced comparatively slowly. As we look back to the 1980s and 1990s it becomes difficult to identify library anxiety research that has clearly and directly led to change in a particular library practice. The reasons for that are many, including traditional attitudes among library administrators and librarians toward research, individual library's receptiveness to research findings, and lack of proper mechanism for translating research findings into practical solutions. Yet, it usually takes time for the findings of basic research to infiltrate into the practice of library and information services. As Line (1991, p. 8) stated, "Good research has a gradual impact on thinking and then percolate through into practice, often without the practitioners realizing it." Potential theoretical and applied research areas abound in the investigation of the internal and external conditions of library anxiety, effective intervention procedures, and measurement of the expanding construct domain. Some librarians may think that library anxiety research has reached the point of saturation; yet, the most exciting developments are only beginning to be uncovered.

## Research in Different Library Settings

The library provides services to meet the information needs of all kinds of users with a wide variety of preferences, backgrounds, styles, and expectations. Traditionally, different types of libraries have adopted different service models. For instance, public libraries tend to provide information directly for their patrons. Special libraries (i.e., corporate libraries, medical libraries, law libraries, military libraries, religious libraries, and government agency libraries) offer value-added services by repackaging the existing information to meet their patrons' immediate needs. Most academic and some school libraries tend to be curriculum oriented, following a self-service model where users are expected to be able to find information by themselves or to learn to find information independently. This is one of the reasons why library anxiety has been reported predominately from academic library settings.

However, the information technologies are gradually blurring the distinctive service models among academic, public, and special libraries because the same information products and equipment "are being successfully marketed to what used to be considered dissimilar needs and groups" (Sherrer, 1995, p. 26). It is not yet known whether a similar set of stimuli found in a typical college library also triggers anxiety responses in other types of libraries. Is the service model a determining factor of the level of library anxiety to be experienced by users in these different information-providing environments? Do users in these nonacademic libraries also undergo "feelings of being lost stemmed from four causes: (a) the size of the library, (b) a lack of knowledge about where things were located, (c) how to begin, and (d) what to do" (Mellon, 1986, p. 162)? Do users in these nonacademic information-providing environments behave differently because of the unique combination of the service model and the type of queries? To expand the fledging theory of library anxiety, more data need to be collected in different library environments and on different types of users, including school libraries, public libraries, special libraries, and academic libraries, as well as libraries in foreign countries. Ideally, future research efforts would be divided evenly among these different types of libraries because there are scant data in existence regarding the causes and components of library anxiety among the vast number of non-academic library users. Yet, given the relatively small number of researchers and limited resources available, a more focused effort will be the way to go for future library anxiety research. How do we decide which type of libraries to research next? Library count statistics and literature have already provided a direction for us.

During 1993–94, the United States had 91,587 public and private elementary and secondary schools with library media centers (National Center for Education Statistics, 2000, p. 473), 3,408 college and university libraries during 1996–97 (National Center for Education Statistics, 2000, p. 478), 16,512 public libraries including branches, and 11,017 special libraries (Bowker, 2001, p. xii), with a total of 122,524 libraries. Elementary and secondary school libraries are the largest group, accounting for approximately 75% of the country's total libraries. Public libraries are the next largest group, with approximately 13% of the total. These libraries provide essential information, services, and education for an enormous number of school population as well as adult users. According to U.S. government statistics, during the fall of 1997, there were more than 51 million students enrolled in various public and private elementary and secondary schools and more than 14 million students enrolled in various institutions of higher learning (National Center for Education Statistics, 2000, p. 11); also, approximately 3 million adult learners were enrolled in the basic and secondary education programs in 1998 (National Center for Education Statistics, 2000, p. 391). Future library anxiety research endeavors should focus on the users of the largest category of libraries, namely, school library media centers. However, school students not only comprise the users of school library media centers but also make up a large proportion of the public library user population. Terrie and Summers (1987) found that students are very active users of public libraries in Florida. Users under 18 years of age borrow 26% of all library materials, even though they constitute less than 15% of the total user population.

As early as the 1950s and 1960s, school students began to make demands on public library services, especially for reference and school-based needs that could not be met with available resources and services in school libraries (American Library Association, 1964). The survey by the U.S. Department of Education (National Center for Education Statistics, 1996) indicates that although many schools contain library media centers, there is a great variation in staffing and collection not only across states but also between elementary and secondary schools and between large and small schools. Much of the limited funding is being allocated to the installation of computer hardware and automated systems in school library medial centers. This situation, coupled with the fact that school library media centers are operated with different hours and under different service models, has driven many school students to public libraries for their school-related, cultural, recreational, and educational needs.

The public library has taken on new roles since the 1980s. Avner (1989) suggests that because of the many home-schooled children, public libraries need to provide materials for parents who teach these children. Adding textbooks and other curricular materials to the existing library collection is being reconsidered by some public libraries. Sager (1992) addresses the role of the public library in the improvement of public education. In addition to the existing preschool and literacy programs, parent and caretaker education programs, homework centers, tutoring programs, career information services, and workshops on computer literacy, extended services have addressed the needs of the recent educational trends, such as home schooling, alternative schools, and year-round schools. Shannon (1991) recognizes the overlap between the patrons served and the types of information and services provided by both school library media centers and public libraries.

Both public libraries and school library media centers provide materials and resources relating to school curricula and students' assignments. In fact, they "offer complementary and mutually reinforcing programs for children and young adults from infancy to eighteen years of age" (Mathews, Flum, & Whitney, 1990, p. 197) and play a unique role to complement students' curricular and literacy needs. When the school day ends, public libraries are available to continue to serve students' educational needs. Are the 51 million potential users of school library media centers and public libraries suffering from any kinds of known or unknown effects of library anxiety, which is found to be a prevalent phenomenon among college students? If so, what can the school library media specialist and public librarian do to help alleviate the anxiety responses of their young patrons? School and public libraries provide a fertile ground for future library anxiety researchers to explore. Because a paucity of library anxiety research has been undertaken in these settings, the initial research findings are likely to be descriptive and exploratory. Future researchers will have the opportunity to conduct a grounded theory study of library anxiety, similar to the one developed by Mellon (1986) for college students, in order to determine the extent to which library anxiety is prevalent in these different library environments.

## Exploring the Library Anxiety Process

On the academic library front, there is a need for further theory and research to investigate the process of library anxiety among college students in order to understand better the role of affective components on the nature of library anxiety and how they influence students' library and information-seeking processes. Library anxiety research has been focusing on the specific sources of anxiety-provoking stimuli in the library physical environment as well as on academic library users' psychological and personality characteristics. Several components or dimensions of library anxiety have been discovered. These components have contributed to the emerging theory of library anxiety. Future library anxiety studies, however, should not be limited to looking for anxiety-provoking stimuli in library physical settings such as library equipment, signage, furniture arrangement, and library homepage designs. Researchers also should explore the more elusive world of perceived library information–seeking contexts because the amount of library anxiety experienced and the mix of actual, potential, and perceived situations vary widely from user to user.

Library anxiety responses or reactions are quite different among users, depending on their past experiences, their psychological traits, the nature of the library tasks, and the context of the library and information problems. Every user enters the library-related situation with a unique set of personal characteristics that include assumptions, beliefs, concerns, and expectations from his or her prior knowledge and experience about the library. Library anxiety is often evoked by the perceived threatening stimuli, situations, or circumstances in the library or library use setting (Jiao & Onwuegbuzie, 1999b; Mellon, 1986, 1988; Onwuegbuzie & Jiao, in press). Situations in which there is ambiguity as to what to be expected, whether help will be offered, if they are in control of the situation, how well they can handle the task, and what kind of threat exists are believed to be particularly conducive to the development of anxiety (Onwuegbuzie & Jiao, in press). Although the physical library situation contains many anxiety-provoking stimuli, it is the personal interpretation or appraisal of the perceived library use situations that causes anxiety among many college students (Onwuegbuzie & Jiao, 1998c, 2000).

Mellon (1988) found that undergraduate "students become so anxious about having to gather information in a library for their research paper that they are unable to approach the problem logically or effectively" (p. 138). This suggests that library anxiety is an emotional process that has at least a cognitive and an affective component. Indeed, this result is supported by Onwuegbuzie and Jiao's (in press) Anxiety-Expectation Mediation (AEM) Model of Library Anxiety, which was described in chapter 3. The cognitive components such as worry, task-irrelevant thinking, appraisal, hope, judgment, and procrastination directly impact the performance of the library information–gathering task, whereas affective components appear to impact students' performance only under situations where students also experience high levels of cognitive anxiety.

Mellon (1986) has identified seven major sources of library anxiety among college students with two underlying themes. The four sources of the "lost" theme stem from "(1) the size of the library; (2) a lack of knowledge about where things were located; (3) how to begin, and (4) what to do" (Mellon, 1986, p. 162). The three sources of the "fear" theme concern the fact that "students' fear is due to a feeling that other students are competent at library use while they alone are incompetent, this lack of competence is somehow shameful and must be kept hidden, and asking questions reveals their inadequacies" (Mellon, 1988, p. 138). Based on Mellon's qualitative research findings, Bostick (1992) empirically discovered the following five dimensions of library anxiety, using the statistical method of factor analysis: (a) barriers with staff, (b) affective barriers, (c) comfort with the library, (d) knowledge of the library, and (e) mechanical barriers. These findings have greatly increased our understanding of the library anxiety phenomenon among college students. Yet, many questions remain unanswered. For example, what is the relationship between the cognitive components of the "lost" theme and the affective components of the "fear" theme? How do these themes impact the information seeking process of students?

Most library anxiety research has tended to view the cognitive components as central to the performance of students' library information gathering, while viewing the affective components such as feelings, values, beliefs, enthusiasms, motivations, and attitudes as less stable and carrying less predictive value. However, studies in emotions and motivation have demonstrated that emotions may be the triggering mechanism for self-regulating strategies that facilitate performance (Carver & Scheier, 2000; Ellsworth & Smith, 1988; Schutz & Davis, 2000). Mellon (1988) also notes that "the emotional attitudes that students bring to the learning situation strongly affect what and how much will be learned" (p. 139). In addition, Jiao and Onwuegbuzie's (1999b) study in self-perception indicates that "graduate students with the lowest levels of perceived scholastic competence, perceived intellectual ability, perceived creativity, and perceived social acceptance . . . [tend] to have the highest levels of library anxiety associated with affective barriers and comfort with the library" (p. 145). Thus, the role of affective components of library anxiety deserves to be studied further.

There is another possible component that may have the potential to contribute to our understanding of the process of library anxiety among college students. Analysis of the situation-specific factors and the contextual influences that often lead to library anxious thoughts and behaviors of college students has resulted in at least one other possible component of library anxiety—the presence of the library information–seeking task itself. The historical Yerkes-Dodson law (Yerkes & Dodson, 1908) attempted to explain that the relation between anxiety and performance seems to depend on the difficulty and complexity of the task. But this conceptualization of an anxiety situation seems too simple.

Kuhlthau's (1993) work on the research process of students has provided an in-depth analysis of how students respond to assigned research projects, but her analysis does not treat the type of assignment as a possible cognitive and affective factor in the student's information-seeking process. Recent studies of the imposed query by Gross (1995, 1998,

1999a, 1999b, 2000) have provided a new way of thinking about the possible impact of different types of library queries on the performance of students' library information–gathering task. According to Gross (1995), information seeking that is externally motivated and set in motion when a person gives a question to someone else to resolve is called an imposed query, while information seeking that is internally motivated in response to the context of an individual's life situation is called self-generated query. One example of the imposed query is the class assignment. The teacher is the imposer. The student is the agent who is asked to respond to a question or to work on a research assignment that the student did not construct but is responsible to undertake. The imposed query can affect the way in which it is perceived and handled later by the agent student, especially during the initial stage of the process. How the imposed query will be perceived and appraised by the agent student within the activity setting will influence the type and intensity of emotions that may emerge. And the way students choose to control the situation-specific emotions will affect their performance levels.

Research on students' appraisal process has tried to link the appraisals they make to the experience of particular emotions (Ellsworth & Smith, 1988; Frijda, 1993; Lazarus, 1991; Morris & Reilly, 1987; Roseman, 1991; Smith, 1991). Boekaerts (1993) reported that appraisals about self-efficacy, effort, and interest in learning tasks were related to different types of emotional experiences. Low self-efficacy was associated with more intense, unpleasant emotions and fewer pleasant emotions (Boekaerts, 1993). The student's cognitive appraisals of an assignment may result from his or her personal theories, experiences, and beliefs about the world and the goal of his or her education. The research conducted by Folkman and Lazarus (1985) on college examination suggests that the perceived importance of the exam is the key to the appraisal process. These researchers found that believing the examination represented high stakes testing, and anticipating that the examination would be difficult were significantly related to threat emotions (e.g., anxiety, anger, distress, or guilt), which, in turn, would have the potential to influence the choice of actions for the anticipated task.

Schutz, DiStefano, Benson, and Davis (1999) have identified four key appraisals that influence the type of emotions that emerge during a test-taking situation: perceived importance of the test, perceived goal congruence or incongruence, perceived locus of control, and perceived self-efficacy. Taken together, these studies in educational psychology, testing, and imposed information seeking provide us with some insights into the nature of the interaction among the affective, cognitive, and task dimensions in a typical educational setting. Library information gathering is one of the most commonly required tasks a college student has to undertake. There is a need for further research and theory development concerning the dimensions of the library research assignment. What kind of library-related tasks (imposed or self-generated) tend to evoke library anxiety among what type of users? How do they affect the information-seeking task? What is the appraisal process like once students receive the imposed library research assignment? How do they regulate their emotions in the process?

A related area that has not been extensively investigated is how students' beliefs, experiences, and attitudes are related to the appraisal process of an imposed library information-gathering task. It appears that students' appraisals of a task are closely related to the emotions that emerge before and during the actual library information gathering. If we are going to understand the emotional processes underlying the choices they make and the subsequent coping strategies adopted, we need a better understanding of what those personal beliefs, experiences, and attitudes are and how they have been acquired or formed. Do students with high levels of library anxiety have different beliefs, attitudes, and experiences about library use and goals than do students with low levels of library anxiety? If so, how are they different? Can those unaccommodating beliefs, attitudes, and experiences be changed or modified? What kind of library experiences foster positive attitudes toward the library? What experiences induce negative memories? How do students cope with unpleasant library anxiety responses when they first experience them? Why can some students handle library anxiety better than others? The situational library context is paramount in determining the behaviors of users at any moment. In the future, it will be very beneficial to approach the seemingly complex subject of library anxiety process from multiple dimensions and perspectives.

## Research on Library Anxiety Intervention Procedures

The challenge facing academic librarians over the years has been to arrive at effective intervention procedures based on evolving and insufficient research findings and limited understanding of the library anxiety phenomenon. This is a typical example of the theoretical research that is "not always congruent with the demands of professional practice, or the needs of its practitioners" (Dowler, 1996, p. viii). Although it has been recognized that library anxiety can interfere with the users' information-seeking process, there has been relatively little research concerned with reducing anxiety per se in real library and information settings. Most current intervention procedures are designed either to prevent or to reduce the disruptive effects of library anxiety on students' library use. A high level of anxiety is believed to be disruptive to the execution of cognitive processes required for performance of a given library task (see Information Literacy Process Model of Library Anxiety, chapter 2). Intervention procedures aimed at supplementing the affected cognitive processes, such as bibliographic instruction, tours, reference assistance, roving, and research consultation, have been shown to help reduce the debilitating effects of library anxiety to some extent. But the overall improvement of students' library use can only be assumed to have transpired either through a reduction of the effects of the library anxiety symptoms or through mediation and alteration of the task such that the demands have become more congruent with the abilities of library-anxious users.

Future research on intervention procedures designed to lower library anxiety of college students needs to address the question of whether these methods can reasonably be expected to reduce both cognitive and emotional symptoms. One approach to this question is to analyze the components of library anxiety and to set up specific intervention conditions that will modify these components. However, not all components of library anxiety may be manifested with equal intensity in every college student. At times, one or more components may not be noted at all. In these instances, intervention conditions need to align the components that overly present themselves. What would be the most facilitative condition or state of mind for working on an imposed library search task? How can educators and librarians help create an educational environment where the student would see a library research assignment as important and worth pursuing and also feel in control and confident enough to deal with any potential challenges from the task? Perhaps, McClelland's (1953) conception of achievement motivation and Atkinson's (1964) hypothesis can serve as theoretical bases for creating such learning environments.

McClelland (1953) believes that individuals acquire a need for achievement as they grow. Based on this conception, Atkinson (1964) hypothesizes that each individual has a need for achievement. Individuals with a high need for achievement tend to have a stronger expectation of success for most tasks. Individuals with a low need for achievement avoid such tasks because their fear of failure greatly outweighs their expectation of success. Therefore, they anticipate feelings of shame. Anxiety-ridden individuals tend to be more concerned about avoiding failure than achieving success. They would set goals that are too low in order to maximize successes. Educators and librarians can help create learning environments in which students experience success instead of failure because the need for achievement can be increased by making success a desirable goal and encouraging realistic goal setting.

A closely related area that needs further investigation is how maladaptive library anxiety responses can be transformed to more adaptive modes of effective coping strategies. For example, researchers can compare the coping strategies adopted by those students who tend to face challenging library assignments with ease and confidence and those who experience anxiety, distress, fear, shame, tension, helplessness, resignation, and worry when presented with the same task. Sarason (1980, p. 6) has noted that one of the adaptive responses to a stressful situation is "a task-oriented attitude that leads the individual to take specific steps toward successfully coping with the stress-arousing situation." Task-focusing strategies seem to be important. But the task-focusing strategies must be based on having as much information about the library task as possible. That information would help with developing the clarity about the nature of the imposed library task and subsequent coping strategies for dealing with any associated negative emotions.

It seems that we tend to emphasize the detrimental effects of library anxiety. Maybe we are too ready to accept the assumed damaging effects of library anxiety on the performance of students' library information–gathering task. The poor performance of library-anxious students or the avoidance behaviors may be related to the fact that there is a lack of clarity about the library research task necessary for library anxious students "to plan ways to achieve their goals" (Onwuegbuzie & Jiao, 1998c, p. 13). It can be assumed that if there were a clear course of action available for the potential library-anxious students, they would use it and apply it to their library information–seeking tasks. How can we facilitate the students' information-seeking process with a clearer course of action for them to follow? More research is needed to find the appropriate ways to help students modify their behaviors when experiencing library anxiety and to help them feel more comfortable and accomplish what is desired with greater competence because anxiety is believed to be adaptive. It is hoped that wider applicable library anxiety coping and adaptive strategies can be developed to guide the design of large-scale effective intervention procedures.

Experimental manipulations of instructional and mediating procedures in the library and information environment also will provide valuable first-hand information on the effects of these procedures. One example is the study conducted by Kracker (2002) on the effects of reducing college students' research anxiety through a 30-minute presentation of the research paper process. Kracker's (2002) study employed a research design using a control and an experimental group of students, an educational treatment, and pre-, post-, and interim testing. The future library anxiety research also can focus on the possible effects on the reduction of library anxiety from instructional procedures that provide both an awareness of how the student is cognitively self-generating anxiety and what the alternative coping strategies are. Both lines of research are designed to assess the effect of a designated aspect of instructional or mediating procedure on levels of library anxiety.

## Measurements of Library Anxiety

To deal effectively with the unpleasant effects of library anxiety and to enhance library use, librarians and other information professionals must be able to access the users' level of library anxiety with an instrument that consistently yields reliable and valid scores. By measuring changes in levels of library anxiety in the course of actual as well as potential library use, librarians will be able to determine the appropriate forms of intervention procedures for those library-anxious users. Schwab (1980) notes that without sound measurement, the theoretical progress of the field is in jeopardy. Statistical procedures and analysis are of little importance if the data are collected with measures that have not been shown to generate reliable and valid data (Nunnally & Bernstein, 1994).

Thus far, only two measures of library anxiety have been developed. The Library Anxiety Scale, or LAS (Bostick, 1992), the most utilized scale in this area, was discussed in chapter 1. The only other direct measure of library anxiety has been constructed by Mizrachi (2000) and Shoham and Mizrachi (2001). These researchers developed a Hebrew version of Bostick's (1992) LAS, which they called the Hebrew Library Anxiety Scale (H-LAS). Using exploratory factor analysis techniques, these researchers identified the following seven factors: Staff, Knowledge, Language, Physical Comfort, Library Computer Comfort, Library Policies/ Hours, and Resources (see chapter 2). However, this scale has been used in only one study. Moreover, four out of these seven dimensions yielded scores with unacceptably low reliability estimates (i.e., .60). Clearly, more work is needed on the H-LAS. Nevertheless, the researchers should be applauded for attempting to provide an alternative measure of library anxiety.

The fact that the LAS (Bostick, 1992) has been the only widely used instrument to measure library anxiety in academic libraries to date suggests that more scales are needed that measure various components of library anxiety, such as Mellon's (1986) "lost" and "fear" themes. Indeed, the LAS was based on the psychological construct of library use from the academic library user population in the early 1990s. It is believed that one of the most significant changes in the library and information field during the past decade has been the transition from the location-specific information environments to more open, virtual information settings. Although this empirically developed instrument still yields reliable and valid scores among college library users, as demonstrated in chapter 1, its construct domain needs to be expanded in order to measure the potential anxiety responses from students in virtual as well as physical library situations.

To strengthen the construct-related validity of this library anxiety measure, future research may begin with an expanded operational definition of the psychological construct of library use that reflects the challenging library and information environment of the 21st century. Current definition of the psychological construct of library use and the existing literature will serve as a basis for future endeavors in this area. Further, new evidence needs to be collected in different library use situations. Indeed, creating the scale of library anxiety for academic libraries was a lengthy, difficult, and extremely time-consuming process. Yet, the task for strengthening and expanding the existing LAS is equally challenging. Experiential insights and professional judgment are called on to generate new questions that sample the expanded construct domain of library anxiety in the new century.

The task of measuring the latent construct of library anxiety has been found to be very challenging for library anxiety researchers. It seems that the most appropriate time to measure library anxiety is just prior to the student's library information–seeking task. Yet, few studies have attempted to measure students' thoughts and feelings just prior to or during their library information–seeking processes. Most measurements obtained by researchers are either before or after students' library use. This is due to the methodological and ethical problems of assessing students while they are engaged in the actual information-gathering activity in a library setting. In an effort to overcome these methodological and ethical issues, library anxiety researchers have chosen to focus their research on what happens before or after library use.

Others have attempted to avoid the problem by asking participants to situate themselves in the library information–gathering situation. Tennyson and Boutwell's (1973) study indicates that measurement of trait or state anxiety prior to task performance provides a very poor estimate of task performance relative to measures of state anxiety during performance. Measuring library anxiety itself may be considered as a form of intervention that may have effects not only on the results but also on later behaviors. One area for future library anxiety researchers to study is whether or not library anxiety can be measured accurately enough just before or after library use. Or what will be the ideal time or conditions to assess a student's level of library anxiety? Is the level of self-reported anxiety consistent over time for each individual student despite the variations of his or her imposed library task?

Another challenging reality of measuring library anxiety is in the interpretation of results. The self-reported scores obtained from the LAS may not measure the true anxiety level of those defensive students who choose to repress their anxiety. According to Freudian theory, a person is driven toward tension reduction in order to reduce feelings of anxiety (Freud, 1936). Thus, a low composite score on the scale may indicate either the absence of anxiety or the denial or repression of intense anxiety. If the student's anxiety scores drop under the increasingly anxious situation, we may suspect the defense mechanism of repression is probably in operation. Therefore, the composite anxiety scores may mean different things for defensive students. These scores may not directly parallel the effects of library anxiety on behavior. To identify defensiveness in a single anxiety scale or questionnaire would be difficult but not entirely impossible.

Theories of psychological constructs state that scores yielded by a measure of the construct should correlate with scores from another instrument measuring the same construct (i.e., convergent validity). To really pin down the effects of library anxiety, researchers probably need to undertake comparative studies. Unfortunately, there are few other scales of comparable construct in existence to assess the convergent validity of the LAS scale. Onwuegbuzie and Jiao (2002b) correlated LAS scores with scores from measures of other academic-related anxiety (e.g., research anxiety, writing anxiety). Although their results helped provide evidence of divergent validity of the LAS (see chapter 1), correlating the LAS with other measures of library anxiety would enable the evaluation of convergent validity. Therefore, this can be another area for potential development. The study by Jerabek et al. (2001) regarding the construct-related validity of the LAS, as well as Onwuegbuzie and Jiao's (2002b) investigation, can serve as models for future comparable studies of this nature.

Given the multifaceted nature of the library anxiety phenomenon and the breadth of situations believed to be anxiety inducing, we may need to develop multiple instruments to measure library anxiety adequately. Perhaps, for example, there is a need in the future to have one instrument sampling a range of potentially anxiety producing situations; one tapping the intensity of anxiety typically elicited, another dealing with styles of reaction to anxiety such as avoidance behaviors, worry, tension, and mental disorganization; and still another measuring the physiological reactions of anxious students. Encouragingly, Onwuegbuzie et al. (2002) presently are developing the Information Literacy Process Anxiety Scale that will attempt to measure library anxiety at the input, processing, and output stages of the information literacy process.

Finally, researchers could investigate the facilitative nature of library anxiety. Currently, it has been assumed by researchers that library anxiety has a debilitative effect on library users. Yet, it is possible that a certain amount of library anxiety has a facilitative impact on library patrons. For example, library users who experience little or no library anxiety may become complacent about undertaking the library task to the extent that they procrastinate on that task, leaving it to the last possible moment, thereby compromising the quality of the output. In such a case, low levels of library anxiety may prevent the library user from being complacent about undertaking library tasks. If facilitative library anxiety does exist, at what point do the facilitative responses become debilitative? To answer this and other questions on this topic, a measure of library anxiety containing items that tap both facilitative and debilitative forms of library anxiety is needed.

## ISSUES AND CHALLENGES OF
## LIBRARY ANXIETY RESEARCH

Researchers who study library anxiety, like other social and behavioral scientists, encounter many practical, methodological, and ethical problems and challenges. New and future researchers need to be aware of these practical issues and challenges in their attempts to conduct library anxiety investigations. This section will discuss and illustrate a range of issues and challenges related to library anxiety research, covering the importance of the research, the pool of researchers, funding and support, ethical considerations, the expectation and interpretation of research results, and the dissemination and utilization of research findings.

### Library Anxiety Research and Researchers

Library science is a field-centered discipline from which research derives and contributes to both theory and practice. Library anxiety is rooted in the definable situational context of libraries. Library anxiety research can be characterized as both basic library science research and applied or developmental research. It falls into two interrelated domains. On one hand, library anxiety research seeks to understand the underlying processes involved in the interference of users' information use and to explain the psychological impact on users in the library-related environment. It deals mainly with the "why" aspect of the phenomenon. The findings from basic research can help illuminate library practice and offer guidance for changes in policy and procedures. On the other hand, library anxiety research develops and tests practical solutions to mitigating the negative impact of library anxiety responses. It focuses on the "how to" aspect. The findings from the applied research can help librarians make more immediate, informed, and operational decisions. Thus, library anxiety research is a potentially broad area relating to several other disciplines such as psychology, education, sociology, linguistics, anthropology, and computer and information sciences.

One possible reason for the passion and interest in library anxiety research is the fact that library anxiety is found to be a prevalent phenomenon within educational systems. Its undesirable effects on the large number of potential users are considered an impediment to the goal of general and higher education in the information society and to the democratic process of the country. Libraries make democracy work by providing free access to information so citizens can make the decisions necessary to govern themselves. With the advent of the Internet and other online services, libraries have evolved from being primarily collections of printed information to information facilities for accessing vast amounts of global electronic and digital information resources. Although libraries do not directly link to the economic prosperity of the country, they contain the wealth of knowledge capable of educating and bettering the lives of citizens (Gorman, 1999). Yet, library anxiety debilitates citizens of their free information-seeking capability.

Given the complexity of studying the library anxiety phenomenon and the significance of its potential effects on users, more people with research backgrounds and expertise need to be involved in this research endeavor. Fortunately, people with strong research backgrounds continue to work in library and information fields. A lot of research expertise in library and information science come from the transfer of skills and knowledge from other disciplines. People in library science have come from backgrounds in nearly all fields but particularly from the social sciences, where research methods have been extensively developed. They have brought with them a wide range of research skills from their own disciplines. They often modify and adapt the skills and methods to the special needs of library and information problems and phenomena. Their research has become social science research applied to the particular case of the library and information field.

So far, very few people are engaged in research on library anxiety. The current library anxiety researchers consist of a small number of motivated librarians, library administrators, and faculty in the fields of education, psychology, and library and information science. This group of researchers has been working diligently trying to understand the components and antecedents of library anxiety. A growing body of research literature on library anxiety has been built as a result. However, the research that has been conducted often is isolated and uncoordinated. What will motivate more researchers and practicing librarians to participate in the library anxiety research is a very complex and challenging issue involving many factors. Library anxiety research may have been undertaken to further the academic careers of researchers, or to challenge the results of previous researchers, or just for fun. While many librarians recognize the need for research, few actually conduct research. Some in the library and information field still think conducting research as simply an intellectual game that is harmless but consumes valuable time and resources. In fact, a great deal of library science research has been conducted out of interest. This should be regarded as quite natural for the development of any field of research. Besides the assumed motivations on the part of current researchers, it is a big challenge to get more practicing librarians involved in the library anxiety research. Librarians are hard-working individuals who have limited time to accomplish all the tasks demanding their attention. Yet, the academic librarian as scholar is not a new concept. Practicing librarians have much to offer as researchers. Experienced librarians can bring to the library anxiety research not only the wisdom of practice but also a wealth of knowledge about the institutional, political, social, and cultural contexts of libraries. Such knowledge can only be derived from the lived experiences of day-by-day practices. The negative attitudes directed toward library anxiety research by librarians who either don't question anything or never read any research papers can be ignored.

What is needed most in the future is a larger number of people who have the curiosity and attitudes about library anxiety research, the skills to collect evidence and to analyze it in a helpful way, and the ability to create theories and to test these theories to join the existing researchers in helping to bring library anxiety research to a new level. The challenge is how to raise the profile of library anxiety research among the library professionals and how to engage their attention and involvement so that they can see more clearly the relevance of library anxiety research to the current information literacy initiatives and to the future generation of information literate citizens.

## Funding and Support for Library Anxiety Research

There is no doubt that if library anxiety research were funded by large sums of money, the amount of research would increase greatly. To some extent, the amount of library anxiety research depends not only on the opportunities and interests of researchers, but also on adequate funding and support because it seeks answers to the complex question of why some users avoid using library and information services even when they are badly in need of information. In general, the appropriateness of external research funding is often dependent on the dimension of time within which researchers and practitioners seek answers to questions. There is no alternative to just guessing the answers to the complicated questions, such as how library anxiety interferes with the information-seeking process, if we are in a hurry to arrive at some solutions.

The interdisciplinary, long-term, fundamental research of the library anxiety phenomenon deserves funding from all possible sources. However, no known library anxiety research has been supported with grants or other outside funding thus far. There is a shortage of funds throughout the research and development world. While some disciplines can look to both private and public sectors for a considerable degree of financial and technical support, the same is not true for the field of library and information science. Limited funding exists only at various levels of library associations and organizations, academic institutions, philanthropic foundations, and the federal government. Federal funding for library research during 1960s and 1970s under the disguise of science information research has been almost completely eliminated (White, 1994).

Government funding for library research peaked in 1987, according to a recent study commissioned by the National Institute on Postsecondary

Education, Libraries, and Lifelong Learning of the U.S. Department of Education (Libraries for the Future, 1998). Researchers in this study found that a very small amount of the federal dollars allocated to educational research was actually applied toward library and information science projects during the period of 1983 to 1997. The investigation also noted that total funding for library research has been approximately 3.25 million dollars, translating to less than $275,000 per year since 1983, while nonfederal funding for library research since 1983 has been under $6 million, or approximately $430,000 per year. The combined funding for library research, federal and private, has averaged less than three-quarters of a million dollars per year since 1983 (Libraries for the Future, 1998).

One likely explanation for the lack of support of library science research in general lies not in the success or failure of library research itself but in the perceived value of libraries among policy makers, administrators, and educators. As noted by White (1994), "Not only do educators claim that librarians are a subset of their profession, but many librarians, particularly in universities and the school systems agree with that assessment" (p. 30). Educators tend to make the assumption that "there is really nothing for libraries to research. Educators often articulate the value system that libraries exist to respond to the specific requests of their educator clients" (30).

The creation and maintenance of digital resources and the pressure to deliver immediate services to users are other reasons why so few resources have been applied to fundamental research into the information needs of users and into the development of an understanding of the difficulties during information seeking and information use. A more fundamental reason, however, is that library research has been so diverse and diffuse and intellectually so weakly governed, that researchers never have come together to devise a national research agenda and to seek support for it. The unfocused nature of library research, the relatively low levels of federal funding in relation to other disciplinary areas, and the recent shifts in research support toward electronic library issues all suggest the need for a coordinated national agenda for library research. A national center for library research might help strengthen the library-based information infrastructure and delivery system nationally and to build a research program that helps to inform public and private investment in library development. Without such a program, library research likely would remain chaotic, haphazard, and nonstrategic (Libraries for the Future, 1998). However, a national library research agenda is practically meaningless if funding is not available.

Although the funding picture for both current and future library anxiety researchers is bleak, alternative solutions may be found in the form of organizational support and encouragement. To pursue more scholarly activities of their own, librarians would like more support by their employers and associations for education in research methodology (Dimitroff, 1996). Numerous studies have been conducted on the significant role of institutional support in fostering research among librarians (Lee, 1995). Encouragement and support may come in different forms. Examples of support include release time, funding options, and a progressive work environment (Gratch, 1989). Increased clerical staff support can help free librarians from their routine clerical tasks. A librarywide policy or strategic plan regarding the importance and aims of research and development also helps librarians set up priorities among the multiple tasks they have to perform.

Breivik (1998, p. 90) has observed that "it is never easy to quit doing good things to do better or more important things although some decisions are easier than others." Lee (1995) has reported that an in-house library research advisory committee provides an equitable support mechanism for encouraging research by librarians. The committee offers both administrative and peer support for counseling and advising in the formulation and development of research proposals. It also increases the awareness of and motivation about library research. Because there is a spectrum in the nature of library research, the committee helps foster the research skills among librarians so that researchers can operate in their appropriate spheres of research interests.

Arlen and Santizo (1990) have found that there is a distinct "attitudinal dichotomy" between those librarians with administrative support and those without. Librarians who have received formal support often display hopeful and optimistic attitudes, whereas those without have experienced frustration and anger. Hare (1989) has found that the most important factors in encouraging professional development are availability of funds and release time. Montanelli and Stenstrom (1986, p. 482) cite the major benefits of research for academic librarians as "job advancement, personal recognition, improved relationships with teaching faculty, increased responsiveness to change and innovation, and better library service through shared knowledge and experience." Havener and Stolt (1993) have confirmed in their study that institutional support does make a positive difference for librarians' professional development activities. More opportunities for research funding and support can lead to improved library and information services. The resultant research findings will put librarians and information professionals in a better position to provide a higher quality service than they can provide at the moment.

## Ethical Considerations of Library Anxiety Research

Although most library anxiety research involves library users, students, staff, and faculty as research participants, it is quite different from those biomedical experiments where clinical trials of new drugs and innovative treatment procedures are used on patients and other human participants. Library anxiety research falls at the benign end of the continuum in terms of the effects on potential research participants. While there are no reported library anxiety studies that have utilized risky or harmful research procedures on the participants, library anxiety researchers do encounter moral dilemmas in their studies at almost any stage of the research process. Thus, it is very important that library anxiety researchers are aware of the possible ethical implications of their research and ensure that their work is of a high ethical standard. Major ethical issues in library anxiety research can be divided into the following three interrelated areas: treatment of research participants, professional conduct, and observance of ethical principles.

Library anxiety researchers must face the challenge of trying to achieve a satisfactory compromise among three objectives of protecting the rights and welfare of the research participants, minimizing the research cost, and advancing the scientific understanding of library anxiety phenomenon. A typical ethical dilemma is how to advance the knowledge of library anxiety without infringing on the rights and welfare of those library users who participate in the research. Regardless of the methods used, library anxiety research is likely to yield private sensitive data concerning participants' psychological traits, learning styles, attitudes, and academic preparation. In addition to the private information about the participating users, the scientifically valid procedures to be employed by the researchers during library research, such as interviewing, survey, questionnaire, psychological testing, and various anxiety intervention strategies, may cause undesirable effects on participants. These effects may induce unpleasant feelings, stress, humiliation, or leave research participants "wondering about their adequacy" (Sarason, 1980, p. 28).

The most general solution to the recurrent problem of protecting the rights and welfare of research participants has been the practice of informed consent, which allows potential research participants to make their own decisions regarding involvement in a research project that might have negative effects on them, presumably in a voluntary and informed way (Gay & Airasian, 2000; Johnson & Christensen, 2000). Informed consent is meant to provide confidence that all potential participants will be able to make decisions that allow their best interests to be fully considered in those decisions (Gay & Airasian, 2000; Johnson & Christensen, 2000).

Allowing potential participants to make their own decisions reflects a respect for the right of self-determination. It also shifts part of the responsibility to the participant for any of the negative effects that they might experience. Although most potential library anxiety research participants are mature, responsible, competent, rational, and capable of making the correct decisions, given the available information about the research, there are certain types of potential participants who may not have the capacity to provide consent and to exercise their rights to self-determination. Those considered not competent to make their own decisions as research participants usually include young school children and elderly persons who are not necessarily mentally incompetent but may nonetheless be in a position where they are unable to consider the implications of involvement in library anxiety research to give free or comprehending consent. For these special participants, provisions have to be made to ensure that informed consent is obtained from parents or guardians or even a durable power of attorney.

There are four basic conditions under which the potential participant is assumed to be able to exercise his or her rights to self-determination. These conditions are (a) competence to make a decision, (b) a setting that is void of coercion or undue pressure to induce a library user to participate in the research, (c) available information about the overall purpose of a research, and (d) comprehension of that information. Presumably, potential participants who are able to exercise their rights and liberties would not agree to be involved in research procedures that would lead to severe pain or psychological trauma.

Yet, the implementation of a complete informed consent procedure may lead to two research dilemmas for library anxiety researchers. A complete informed consent procedure may not add significantly to the cost of conducting a research when the number of potential participants is manageably small. However, if a research project involves a large number of participants, say in the thousands, and each has to be contacted briefly for disclosing the purpose and possible effects, the time and resources required to complete the elaborate informed consent procedure may be a considerable financial burden to the researcher. An empirically based study on library anxiety, for instance, requires research that systematically examines the interrelationship among many variables, a process that can only be carried out when a large number of users are involved. This type of research demands a multitude of human participants for collecting adequate empirical data in order to develop confidence in the generated research findings. It is not unreasonable to expect that in some library anxiety research situations, the costs of obtaining informed consent may be greater than that of conducting the research itself.

Another undesirable but likely problem is when a complete informed consent procedure introduces bias among the participants in a research. For instance, in a controlled social psychological experiment, some fully informed participants may try to behave as "good participants" and to produce "socially desirable responses" that are consistent with the research hypothesis, without realizing that their very behaviors defeat the scientific objective of the research project and make them less representative of the population the research intends to study. It is common for a research participant at the end of a psychological experiment to try to find out how well he or she performed during the research process and whether he or she performed adequately. This tendency is known as the experimenter effect and was studied extensively by Rosenthal (1967, 1968) and Barber and Silver (1968). The experimenter effect occurs when the research allows the participants to fall victim to experimenter bias (Gay & Airasian, 2000; Johnson & Christensen, 2000; Onwuegbuzie, 2003a). Full disclosure of the purpose and procedures of a library anxiety research study can have substantial effects on the phenomenon under investigation and contaminate the results regardless of research methods to be used (e.g., experimental study, survey research, field observation). It can be argued that the objective of a library anxiety research study would be better achieved if the true purpose of the research was not fully disclosed until after the study had been completed.

Apparently, there is a challenging issue with regard to application of a complete informed consent procedure in library anxiety research. The heart of the issue lies in the dichotomous notion of labeling research as either "ethical" or "unethical" on the basis of whether or not a complete informed consent procedure is implemented. In many cases, a full informed consent procedure is expected, even when there is almost no possibility of negative effects for the participants and practically no threats to participants' rights and liberties. However, insistence on implementing an elaborate informed consent procedure to all library anxiety research involving library users, regardless of the possible impact on research costs and experimenter effects, may obscure its application to those research endeavors where it may be an important asset. It may also coerce a researcher into a situation where he or she sees no obvious getaway but giving up the research altogether.

A prudent but not blind application of informed consent might be more productive in library anxiety research because it would prevent the trivialization of ethics (Ingelfinger, 1975) and avoid complicating the relatively innocuous library anxiety research with procedures that seem to provide limited benefit. Library anxiety researchers also need to understand the limits on the extent to which the informed consent procedure provides. In most research, the informed consent by itself is inadequate as a source of confidence that all rights and welfare of participants are protected and given full consideration. Often the context in which potential participants make their decisions is more important than is the actual document of agreement, especially when participation of a library anxiety research will have no obvious personal advantages other than contributing to scientific understanding of the debilitating phenomenon. What prompts potential participants to agree to participate in a library research study, and the degree of willingness to participate in a library anxiety research probably depend on the nature of potential research effects on them, the informed consent procedure, and the research activities. No matter what potential research participants have agreed to do, and regardless of what they may have signed, library anxiety researchers are assumed to retain a major responsibility for the participants' well-being throughout the research process. This leads to the issue of ethical conduct of library anxiety researchers.

Research ethics are guidelines and principles that help uphold the values of researchers. Ethical principles are not simply prohibitions, but guidance for positive responsibilities (Diener & Crandall, 1978). Researchers have a responsibility to conduct research as competently as they can and to communicate their findings accurately. Library anxiety researchers need to have a working set of principles to guide their research activities when they face ethical decisions regarding the conduct, management, and supervision of research personnel in the case of a research team, publication, and storage of research data.

It is generally assumed that library anxiety researchers show their concern for the research participants in a number of ways, including treating them in a dignified manner, ensuring that any negative psychological effects are quickly detected and promptly reduced, avoiding demeaning or condescending descriptions of the participants and their actions, and taking extra precautions to keep personal data confidential. Privacy and confidentiality are very important concerns in library anxiety research. The research data gathered from background information about participants, self-reported measures, performance measures, interviews, and observed events are all sensitive and should not be stored with names or other unique identifiers attached. The library anxiety researcher must devise a system of removing names and other related identifiers from all data before even starting the research and the data should not be disclosed to others. Besides these important ethical considerations, there are many other regulatory mechanisms and policies at different levels to help guide library anxiety researchers who plan to involve library users in their studies.

At the federal level, the major ethical principles regarding all research involving humans as participants are set forth in the report of the National Commission for the Protection of Human Subjects of Biomedical and Behavioral Research, sometimes known as the "Belmont Report" (Department of Health, Education, and Welfare, 1979). And a major shared federal policy regarding human research subjects is known as the

Common Rule, which was adopted by 16 federal departments and agencies in 1991 and revised in 2001. The Common Rule, which is identical to the basic Department of Health and Human Services policy for the protection of research participants, contains a general set of regulatory provisions governing protections for human participants and specifies how research that involves human participants is to be conducted and reviewed, including specific rules for obtaining informed consent. The regulatory framework for protecting human participants in research is detailed in Title 45 of the Code of Federal Regulations, Part 46, subparts A and D (Office for Human Research Protections, 2001), to which all library anxiety researchers whose research involving library users regardless of funding and sponsorship must conform.

Although all library anxiety researchers whose research involving library users as research participants are bound by these federal laws, they may or may not have a local oversight body to help them conform to these federal ethical policies and requirements at or near the site of their research. For researchers who are affiliated with a public school system or a research institution such as a college, university, medical school, or a hospital, they must go through a local review process to be sure that the rights and welfare of the research participants will be properly protected in the research activities. The local oversight body is normally called the Institutional Review Board (IRB), which has the authority delegated by federal agencies and the institution to certify research proposals involving human participants. However, for researchers who are not affiliated with any of these institutions, the means to seek compliance with federal laws can be very difficult.

For a cooperative research project, in which at least one of the researchers belongs to a signatory research institution, the entire research team can submit their research proposal or protocol to the institution's IRB for review. If none of the researchers are affiliated with any research institutions or federal agencies, they have options of either requesting a review by the IRB in a nearby research institution or seeking an independent review board to have its proposal reviewed. The chair of the IRB in a research institution has under his or her jurisdiction the power to decide whether or not the IRB will review a research proposal for a nonaffiliated researcher. The most important thing for library anxiety researchers to keep in mind is that it is an ethical conduct to request an authorized IRB to review their research protocols involving users as participants, no matter where these IRBs are located or to which institution they belong.

In addition to the more legally binding federal regulations regarding using human participants in biomedical and behavioral research, many social science professional associations have developed their consensus-based ethical principles and codes of conduct for their members and others who choose to adopt them. The one discipline with a substantial number of national codes of ethics is psychology. Library anxiety researchers can consult with the American Psychological Association's Ethical Principles of Psychologists and Code of Conduct (American Psychological Association, 2002) when faced with ethical dilemmas in their research. They can also refer to the American Sociological Association Code of Ethics (American Sociological Association, 1997).

Conforming to regulations of the conduct of research with human participants in foreign countries can be even more complicated. Library anxiety researchers from the United States who are conducting research on library users in a foreign country are still bound by the federal regulations and the policies and procedures enforced by various local IRBs. In addition, they must also follow the regulations of the host country because the federal "policy does not affect any foreign laws or regulations which may otherwise be applicable and which provide additional protections to human subjects of research" (Code of Federal Regulations, 1991).

## Universally Applicable Theories or Context-Bound Realities

The notion that universally applicable theories can be found to solve various libraries' problems across the board still dominates the view of many practicing librarians and continues to shape the goal of some researchers. The expectations of these librarians and library administrators are deeply rooted in the deterministic viewpoint of library research. There is great thirst for the answer, yet, little patience for an answer to the frustrating and complex problems in the field, such as the phenomenon of library anxiety. This thirst for the right answer may lead to the rapid appropriation of solutions that may or may not have a relationship to the problems at hand.

Another view of library research is based on the belief that the complexity of the information-seeking process in the ever-changing library and information environment makes it very difficult, if not impossible, to find valid principles and rules of universal applications to librarianship. Technological advancement, demographic changes, digital revolution, library budget cuts, and other cultural, historical, and sociopolitical events all interfere with the context wherein the library research is conducted. Issues and problems facing libraries and librarianship such as library anxiety, information literacy, bibliographic instruction, information seeking and use, and digitization of library collection are all rooted in the cultural, social, and political contexts of the time. These multiple, dynamic library and information environments make the pursuit of universal rules, laws, and principles for library practices and services almost unachievable. For good and responsible reasons, library research in general and library anxiety research in particular, needs to involve more particularistic studies investigating limited areas of inquiry within which interactions between variables can be understood better. Both experimental and ethnographic studies of users and libraries have asserted an epistemology of incremental understanding, whereby knowledge is created not with the aim of arriving at a single explanatory model or solution, but of creating context-sensitive understanding of multiple library and information environments.

There can be many different realities of library settings, depending on one's values, culture, perceptions, and beliefs. As Kuhn (1962) noted, even science cannot be totally value free or completely objective. There have been many research paradigms that have differed in the assumptions made, in the questions asked, in the phenomenon observed, and in the ways the data were interpreted. Researchers working under different paradigms often believe some events are more important than others and they tend to think of the same events in quite different ways. According to Diener and Crandall (1978), "Value issues also arise in the social sciences because scientific theories and findings often represent powerful social forces in themselves" (p. 185). Library anxiety research has and will continue to represent a constructed effort of understanding the library environmental and service realities within the broader social and cultural contexts.

While pursuing more particularistic studies of library anxiety, the library research community must be aware of the hidden challenges in the future. The variety of context-bound and component-oriented library anxiety studies and their lack of unity may be an advantage at the present stage of our knowledge when it is desirable to provide the greatest possible number of explorations of the complex phenomenon of library anxiety. However, this makes it difficult to summarize these studies in a cohesive way. Narrowly focused studies of library anxiety in a variety of library environments may produce quite a few scholarly pieces of work whose value is less than the sum of its parts because the context sensitivity and multiple effects could become a barrier to generalizations. For example, researchers who study library anxiety, more than most other researchers, encounter the problems of systematic versus representative sampling. With potential interactions among library anxiety, academic anxiety, and other state and trait anxieties and also among the nature of different library tasks, intervention procedures, and library situations or circumstances, the problem of representative sampling of all these variables becomes virtually impossible. This suggests that the usefulness of a particular procedure to facilitate information seeking of highly anxious individuals in one situation may not be generalizable to other situations of similar tasks or tasks of greater difficulty. This lack of generality may frustrate or even annoy some practicing librarians and library administrators who still wish for universalistic answers. But the lack of replicability may point to the influence of variables that otherwise might be overlooked.

## Dissemination and Utilization of Library Anxiety Research

If library anxiety research is to have any impact on practice at all, findings in this area have to be widely disseminated. Dissemination of library anxiety research findings is a challenge for both current as well as potential library anxiety researchers. We all know that there is more to dissemination of research than just publishing the findings in professional journals. The traditional model of research communication follows the approach where researchers publish the findings in the appropriate journal and keep up with other researchers' findings by constantly monitoring the abstracting and indexing services within their special fields. This model works well for a target audience consisting of other researchers with a similar passion and interest in the subject matter. It perpetuates the share of research results within a small circle of researchers. However, when the potential audience comprises a huge group of educators, administrators, practicing librarians, social scientists, policymakers, and politicians in local government with wide-ranging research interests, abilities, and expectations, the traditional scientific communication model does not work well for disseminating the findings of library and information science research, nor does it help promote application of these research findings.

There is a gap between library anxiety research and the application of its findings in the every day library practice. Caplan, Morrison, and Stambaugh (1975) argued that researchers and practitioners existed in different communities separated by a gulf wide enough to defy conventional attempts to report publishing. The scholarly pursuit of understanding the nature of library anxiety phenomenon involves conducting the research, writing up the results, and advancing the leading edge of knowledge and the careers of the researchers. However, the real world of library practice is not concerned much about research output but with practical outcomes. The value of library anxiety research lies in the timely and appropriate applications. Librarians want research to be practical and directed toward real problem solving. But the real change is difficult to be achieved by simply communicating research findings through professional journals to those in a position to make the change such as library practitioners, administrators, and policy makers. The time-honored methods of sharing research findings such as seminars, conferences, and research reports are useful, but they have their own drawbacks. Conferences reach comparatively few of the total intended audience. Publications are expensive and time consuming to produce. Detailed research reports are often more than busy librarians need.

The utilization of research findings is a complicated psychological, organizational, and social issue. Practicing librarians are not all equally interested in the results of library research in general and library anxiety research in particular. Some people are more inclined than others to seek out, assimilate, apply research findings, and advocate their implementation. Libraries and library management teams also vary in their receptiveness to research findings. Research findings may be sought after when there is a pressing need. A library working group or an ad hoc committee charged to improve a specific aspect of library service and to come up with recommendations is likely to be most receptive to new research findings especially when the findings are noticed early enough in the group decision-making process. Meyer and Scott (1983) argued that some institutions are torn by conflicting needs for efficient coordination of task activities on the one hand and the demand for conformity with established institutional conventions on the other. Under such circumstances, a library may choose to guard its existing service practices against the immediate demands for change suggested by research findings and to protect the practices from close scrutiny and evaluation.

Another obstacle to effective dissemination of library research findings includes the absence of a librarywide or systemwide policy regarding research and utilization of research findings. This sometimes leads to library research being conducted in a vacuum and having little impact on the practice as a result. Nowotny (1990) studied the growing interlinkages between scientific-technological knowledge and their practical applications in a wider societal context and argued that the utilization context in which research findings are received is made and structured by social forces and organized interests. This utilization context determines how research findings are to be understood and used according to a constantly changing balance of conflicting forces.

There is an obvious need to explore some of the issues and challenges of dissemination, reception, and utilization of library anxiety research findings. Future studies need to take into account the psychological, organizational, and social complexities involved in the potential utilization context. A more research-oriented environment in libraries and information service institutions need to be promoted by administrators at various levels of management. In addition, efforts should be made on the part of researchers to try to bridge the gap between themselves as producers of research findings and the consumers of the library and information science community, even though sometimes researchers are not always the best people to publicize their results because they are too close to them and they have poor grasp of writing for a wider audience. Options include collaborative research projects where the researchers interact with practitioners; creation of networks of practitioners with an active interest in making change happen in the libraries; and encouraging research strategies that involve the practicing librarians as researchers (i.e., action research).

## SUMMARY AND CONCLUSIONS

Library anxiety research is part of the overall library and information science research aimed at advancement of the library profession, which is currently undergoing constant changes and adaptations due to the impact of emerging technologies, societal change, and globalization. The traditional library and information service models are no longer adequate for accommodating the wide range of user needs and demands in the information age. Increased access to vast amounts of information requires librarians to help users not only to locate sources of information but also to interpret and to use the information. The library and information environment has become increasingly complicated. Information services must be redefined in order to respond to the demands of the ever-changing environment. Instead of passively reacting to the pressure of changing environment, the library profession needs directions and guidance to move itself forward. An active and concerted research effort by members of the entire library profession is one of the viable solutions to its own problem of lacking directions. Widely participated library research will help find solutions to the profession's immediate as well as future problems.

This chapter has highlighted potential areas for future library anxiety research as well as the commonly encountered issues and challenges facing library anxiety researchers. Library anxiety research and other related studies, such as computer anxiety, writing anxiety, and research anxiety, will increasingly be used as a language to understand and to discuss library users' information seeking and educational problems. The role of library anxiety research for advocating, explaining, and justifying service policies and decisions, as well as for promoting professional discourse from both within and outside the field of librarianship will continue to unfold and become clearer. The future of libraries and librarianship depends on a substantial and ever-increasing body of knowledge based on substantive and sound research, which must be distinguished from reports merely on opinions, ideology, or personal experience and "must be more than localized, non-replicated action research that is not directly linked to decision making" (Hernon, 1994, p. 191). The emerging information technologies will have a tremendous impact on the quality of our lives. Practically every aspect of life will revolve around the creation, exchange, and consumption of information. To ensure equitable participation in society, all citizens regardless of their location and socioeconomic status, will require access to a broader set of telecommunications services, among them a basic package of library and public information services (Tyson, 1995).

There are hopeful signs in library anxiety research in particular, and library science research in general. The past decade has been a period of growing attention to differential effectiveness among libraries and librarians and more sophistication in the investigation of such matters. High-quality research focusing on theory building and understanding of the foundations of library services in the information age will play a key role in contributing to the transition of librarianship from a practice-based profession to a theory-rooted discipline. Library anxiety research can assist in resolving some of the significant psychological problems of library users as they live on the 21st century.

# Appendix A

# Library Anxiety Scale
### Sharon L. Bostick

You are being asked to respond to statements concerning your feelings about college or university libraries. Please mark the number which most closely matches your feelings about the statement. The numbers range from:

1 = Strongly Disagree    2 = Disagree    3 = Undecided    4 = Agree    5 = Strongly Agree

| | | | | | | |
|---|---|---|---|---|---|---|
| 1. | I'm embarrassed that I don't know how to use the library. | 1 | 2 | 3 | 4 | 5 |
| 2. | A lot of the university is confusing to me. | 1 | 2 | 3 | 4 | 5 |
| 3. | The librarians are unapproachable. | 1 | 2 | 3 | 4 | 5 |
| 4. | The reference librarians are unhelpful. | 1 | 2 | 3 | 4 | 5 |
| 5. | The librarians don't have time to help me because they're always on the telephone. | 1 | 2 | 3 | 4 | 5 |
| 6. | I can't get help in the library at the times I need it. | 1 | 2 | 3 | 4 | 5 |
| 7. | Library clerks don't have time to help me. | 1 | 2 | 3 | 4 | 5 |
| 8. | The reference librarians don't have time to help me because they're always busy doing something else. | 1 | 2 | 3 | 4 | 5 |
| 9. | I am unsure about how to begin my research. | 1 | 2 | 3 | 4 | 5 |
| 10. | I get confused trying to find my way around the library. | 1 | 2 | 3 | 4 | 5 |
| 11. | I don't know what to do next when the book I need is not on the shelf. | 1 | 2 | 3 | 4 | 5 |
| 12. | The reference librarians are not approachable. | 1 | 2 | 3 | 4 | 5 |
| 13. | I enjoy learning new things about the library. | 1 | 2 | 3 | 4 | 5 |

| | | | | | | |
|---|---|---|---|---|---|---|
| 14. | If I can't find a book on the shelf the library staff will help me. | 1 | 2 | 3 | 4 | 5 |
| 15. | There is often no one available in the library to help me. | 1 | 2 | 3 | 4 | 5 |
| 16. | I feel comfortable using the library. | 1 | 2 | 3 | 4 | 5 |
| 17. | I feel like I am bothering the reference librarian if I ask a question. | 1 | 2 | 3 | 4 | 5 |
| 18. | I feel safe in the library. | 1 | 2 | 3 | 4 | 5 |
| 19. | I feel comfortable in the library. | 1 | 2 | 3 | 4 | 5 |
| 20. | The reference librarians are unfriendly. | 1 | 2 | 3 | 4 | 5 |
| 21. | I can always ask a librarian if I don't know how to work a piece of equipment in the library. | 1 | 2 | 3 | 4 | 5 |
| 22. | The library is a comfortable place to study. | 1 | 2 | 3 | 4 | 5 |
| 23. | The library never has the materials I need. | 1 | 2 | 3 | 4 | 5 |
| 24. | I can never find things in the library. | 1 | 2 | 3 | 4 | 5 |
| 25. | There is too much crime in the library. | 1 | 2 | 3 | 4 | 5 |
| 26. | The people who work at the circulation desk are helpful. | 1 | 2 | 3 | 4 | 5 |
| 27. | The library staff doesn't care about students. | 1 | 2 | 3 | 4 | 5 |
| 28. | The library is an important part of my school. | 1 | 2 | 3 | 4 | 5 |
| 29. | I want to learn to do my own research. | 1 | 2 | 3 | 4 | 5 |
| 30. | The copy machines are usually out of order. | 1 | 2 | 3 | 4 | 5 |
| 31. | I don't understand the library's overdue fines. | 1 | 2 | 3 | 4 | 5 |
| 32. | Good instructions for using the library's computers are available. | 1 | 2 | 3 | 4 | 5 |
| 33. | Librarians don't have time to help me. | 1 | 2 | 3 | 4 | 5 |
| 34. | The library's rules are too restrictive. | 1 | 2 | 3 | 4 | 5 |
| 35. | I don't feel physically safe in the library. | 1 | 2 | 3 | 4 | 5 |
| 36. | The computer printers are often out of paper. | 1 | 2 | 3 | 4 | 5 |
| 37. | The directions for using the computers are not clear. | 1 | 2 | 3 | 4 | 5 |
| 38. | I don't know what resources are available in the library. | 1 | 2 | 3 | 4 | 5 |
| 39. | The library staff doesn't listen to students. | 1 | 2 | 3 | 4 | 5 |
| 40. | The change machines are usually out of order. | 1 | 2 | 3 | 4 | 5 |
| 41. | The library is a safe place. | 1 | 2 | 3 | 4 | 5 |
| 42. | The library won't let me check out as many items as I need. | 1 | 2 | 3 | 4 | 5 |
| 43. | I can't find enough space in the library to study. | 1 | 2 | 3 | 4 | 5 |

*Appendix B*

# Scoring Protocols for the Library Anxiety Scale

The Library Anxiety Scale contains 12 items that are written in the opposite direction (i.e., in the positive direction). Thus, these items need to be key-reversed before the scale is totaled. These items are: 13, 14, 16, 18, 19, 21, 22, 26, 28, 29, 32, and 41.

## METHOD 1 FOR KEY-REVERSING ITEMS

In order to key-reverse the responses to these items, you subtract the item response from 6. This can be undertaken using a statistical software package such as SPSS. For example, suppose Item 13 was called "ITEM13." Using SPSS, you would click on the "TRANSFORM" icon, then the "COMPUTE" icon.

In the "TARGET" space under the "COMPUTE" option, you could type in "NEWIT13" (or any other meaningful name that has less than 9 characters). Then, under the "NUMERIC EXPRESSION" space, you type in "6 – ITEM13." That is, you will use the equation "NEWIT13 = 6 – ITEM13." This equation will change a response of "1" to a "5," a "2" to a "4," a "3" to a "3," a "4" to a "2," and a "5" to a "1." Then you repeat this for the other 11 items above.

## METHOD 2 FOR KEY-REVERSING ITEMS

Alternatively, you could use the "TRANSFORM" icon, then the "RECODE" icon, followed by the "INTO SAME VARIABLES" icon.

Thus, item 13 could be changed by clicking on "Old and New Values" and then:

1. Under "OLD VALUE" TYPE "1"; and then under "NEW VALUE" type a "5"; then click on the "ADD" icon.
2. Under "OLD VALUE" TYPE "2"; then under "NEW VALUE" type a "4"; then click on the "ADD" icon.
3. Under "OLD VALUE" TYPE "3"; then under "NEW VALUE" type a "3"; then click on the "ADD" icon.
4. Under "OLD VALUE" TYPE "4"; then under "NEW VALUE" type a "2"; then click on the "ADD" icon.
5. Under "OLD VALUE" TYPE "5"; then under "NEW VALUE" type a "1"; then click on the "ADD" icon.

After performing Steps 1 to 5, in the box on the bottom right-hand side, you will see the five above changes displayed. Then you repeat these five steps for the remaining 11 key-reverse items.

## OBTAINING COMPOSITE
## (TOTAL SCALE) SCORES

When you have key-reversed all 12 items, you will be ready to obtain a total score for each participant. All you need to do is use the "COMPUTE" command under the "TRANSFORM" icon. Then, in the "TARGET" space, you could type in "TOTAL" (or any other meaningful name that has less than 9 characters). Then, under the "NUMERIC EXPRESSION" space, you type in "ITEM1 + ITEM2 + ITEM3 + . . . + ITEM43" (or whatever name you gave for the 43 anxiety items). This will add up each participant's set of responses to the 43 items—giving a score that ranges from 43 to 215, which will be created under the variable called "TOTAL."

You could then use the variable "TOTAL," as a dependent variable, to perform your statistical analyses (e.g., compare males and females using the "INDEPENDENT SAMPLES T-TEST" option under the "STATISTICS" option in SPSS).

## OBTAINING TOTAL (SUBSCALE) SCORES

Additionally, or alternatively, you could create the five LAS subscales. The items for each of the five subscales are as follows:

> **Barriers with Staff:** 3–8, 12, 14–15, 21–22, 27, 33–34, 39
> **Affective Barriers:** 1–2, 9–11, 16–17, 24, 37–38, 42–43
> **Comfort with the Library:** 18–20, 23, 25–26, 31–32
> **Knowledge of the Library:** 13, 28–29, 35, 41
> **Mechanical Barriers:** 30, 36, 40

You could then use the procedure in the *"Obtaining Composite (Total Scale) Scores"* section to obtain subscale scores for the Barriers with Staff, Affective Barriers, Comfort with the Library, Knowledge of the Library, and Mechanical Barriers" dimensions.

Statistical analyses could then be conducted using these five subscale scores either individually (i.e., using a series of univariate statistical analysis procedures such as an independent samples *t*-test and an analysis of variance) or simultaneously (i.e., using multivariate statistical analysis procedures such as multiple analysis of variance and canonical correlation). However, we suggest strongly that the comprehensive guidelines provided in chapters 4–6 be used before conducting any statistical analysis.

# References

Abelson, R. P. (1997). A retrospective on the significance test ban of 1999 (If there were no significance tests, they would be invented). In L. L. Harlow, S. A. Mulaik, & J. H. Steiger (Eds.), *What if there were no significance tests?* (pp. 117–141). Mahwah, NJ: Erlbaum.

Abusin, K. A. (1998). Library anxiety among IIUM first year students. Unpublished manuscript, International Islamic University, Malaysia.

Aiken, L. S., West, S. G., Sechrest, L., Reno, R. R., Roediger, H. L., Scarr, S., Kazdin, A. E., & Sherman, S. J. (1990). The training in statistics, methodology, and measurement in psychology. *American Psychologist, 45*, 721–734.

Allen, M. J., & Yen, W. M. (1979). *Introduction to measurement theory.* Monterey, CA: Brooks/Cole.

Allen, S. M. (1997). Preventing theft in academic libraries and special collections. *Library & Archival Security, 14*(1), 29–43.

Alpert, R., & Haber, R. (1960). Anxiety in academic achievement situations. *Journal of Abnormal and Social Psychology, 61*, 207–216.

American Educational Research Association, American Psychological Association, & National Council on Measurement in Education. (1999). *Standards for educational and psychological testing* (rev. ed.). Washington, DC: American Educational Research Association.

*The American heritage college dictionary* (3rd ed.). (1993). Boston: Houghton Mifflin.

American Library Association. (1964). *Student use of libraries: An inquiry into the needs of students, libraries and the educational process.* Chicago: author.

American Library Association. (1989). American Library Association Presidential Committee on Information Literacy. Final report (ERIC Document Reproduction Service No. ED 315 074).

*American Library Directory* (2001, 54th ed.). New York: R. R. Bowker.

American Psychological Association. (2001). *Publication manual of the American Psychological Association* (5th ed.). Washington, DC: author.

American Psychological Association. (2002). American Psychological Association ethical principles of psychologists and code of conduct. Retrieved April 10, 2003, from http://www.apa.org/ethics/code.html.

American Sociological Association. (1997). American Sociological Association code of ethics. Retrieved April 9, 2003, from http://www.asanet.org/members/ecoderev.html.

Amstutz, D., & Whitson, D. (1997). University faculty and information literacy: Who teaches the students? *Research Strategies, 15,* 18–15.

Andrews, J. (1991). An exploration of students' library use problems. *Library Review, 40,* 5–14.

Anonymous. (n.d.). Retrieved April 8, 2003, from http://www.wiu.edu/users/mma108/litreview.html.

Arkin, R. M., Kolditz, T. A., & Kolditz, K. K. (1983). Attributions of the test-anxious student: Self-assessments in the classroom. *Personality and Social Psychology Bulletin, 9,* 271–280.

Arkin, R. M., & Schumann, D. W. (1984). Effects of corrective testing: An extension. *Journal of Educational Psychology, 76,* 835–843.

Arlen, S., & Santizo, N. (1990). Administrative support for research: A survey of library faculty. *Library Administration and Management, 4,* 211–212.

Atkinson, J. W. (1964). *An introduction to motivation.* Princeton, NJ: Van Nostrand.

Avner, J. A. (1989). Home schoolers: A forgotten clientele? *School Library Journal, 35,* 29–33.

Bailey, P., Onwuegbuzie, A. J., & Daley, C. E. (1998). Anxiety about foreign language: Comparison of French, Spanish, and German classes. *Psychological Reports, 82,* 1007–1010.

Bailey, P., Onwuegbuzie, A. J., & Daley, C. E.. (2000a). Correlates of anxiety at three stages of the foreign language learning process. *Journal of Language and Social Psychology, 19*(4), 475–492.

Bailey, P., Onwuegbuzie, A. J., & Daley, C. E. (2000b). Using learning style to predict foreign language achievement at the college level. *System, 28,* 115–133.

Bailey, P., Onwuegbuzie, A. J., & Daley. C. E. (2000c). Study habits and anxiety about learning foreign languages. *Perceptual and Motor Skills, 90,* 1151–1156.

Bailey, P., Onwuegbuzie, A. J., & Daley, C. E. (in press). Foreign language anxiety and student attrition. *Academic Exchange Quarterly.*

Bandura, A. (1977). Self-efficacy: Toward a unifying theory of behavioral change. *Psychological Review, 84,* 191–215.

Bandura, A. (1982). Self-efficacy mechanisms in human agency. *American Psychologist, 37,* 122–147.

Bandura, A. (1986). *Social foundations of thought and action: A social cognitive theory.* Englewood Cliffs, NJ: Prentice Hall.

Bandura, A. (1997). *Self-efficacy: The exercise of control.* New York: Freeman.

Barber, T. X., & Silver, M. J. (1968). Fact, fiction, and the experimenter bias effect. *Psychological Bulletin, 70*(6, Pt. 2), 1–29.

Bazillion, R. J., & Braun, C. (1995). *Academic libraries as high-tech gateways: A guide to design and space decisions.* Chicago: American Library Association.

Beasley, T. M., & Leitner, D. W. (1994, February). The p-problem with stepwise multiple regression. Paper presented at the annual meeting of the Eastern Educational Research Association (ERIC Document Reproduction Service No. ED 367 669).

Becker, H. S. (1970). *Sociological work: Method and substance.* New Brunswick, NJ: Transaction Books.

Becker, H. S., Geer, B., Hughes, E. C., & Strauss, A. L. (1977). *Boys in white: Student culture in medical school.* New Brunswick, NJ: Transaction Books. (Original work published by University of Chicago Press, 1961.)

Ben Omran, A. I. (2001). Library anxiety and Internet anxiety among graduate students of a major research university. (Doctoral dissertation, University of Pittsburgh.) *Dissertation Abstracts International, 62,* 05A, 1620.

Benson, J. (1989). Structural components of statistical test anxiety in adults: An exploratory model. *Journal of Experimental Education, 57,* 247–261.

Benson, J., & Bandalos, D. (1989). Structural model of statistical test anxiety. In R. Schwarzer, H. M. van der Ploeg, & C. D. Spielberger (Eds.), *Advances in test anxiety research* (Vol. 6, pp. 137–149). Lisse, The Netherlands: Swets and Zeitlinger; Hillsdale, NJ: Lawrence Erlbaum.

Bentler, P. M. (1990). Comparative fit indexes in structural models. *Psychological Bulletin, 107,* 238–246.

Bentler, P. M., & Bonett, D. G. (1980). Significance tests and goodness of fit in the analysis of covariance structures. *Psychological Bulletin, 88,* 588–606.

Beswick, G., Rothblum, E. D., & Mann, L. (1988). Psychological antecedents to student procrastination. *Australian Psychologist, 23,* 207–217.

Biaggio, M. K., & Nielsen, E. C. (1976). Anxiety correlates of sex-role identity. *Journal of Clinical Psychology, 32,* 619–623.

Bickel, P. J., & Doksum, K. A. (1977). *Mathematical statistics.* San Francisco: Holden-Day.

Blair, R. C., & Higgins, J. J. (1980). A comparison of power of Wilcoxon's rank-sum statistic to that of Student's t statistic under various nonnormal distributions. *Journal of Educational Statistics, 5,* 309–335.

Blandy, S. G., & Libutti, P. O. (1995). As the cursor blinks: Electronic scholarship and undergraduates in the library. *Library Trends, 44*(2), 279–305.

Boekaerts, M. (1993). Being concerned with well-being and with learning. *Educational Psychologist, 28*(2), 149–167.

Bollen, K. A. (1986). Sample size and Bentler and Bonett's nonnormed fit index. *Psychometrika, 51*, 375–377.

Bollen, K. A. (1989). *Structural equations with latent variables.* New York: Wiley.

Bosman, E., & Rusinek, C. (1997). Creating the user-friendly library by evaluating patron perceptions of signage. *Reference Services Review, 25*(1), 71–82.

Bostick, S. L. (1992). The development and validation of the library anxiety scale. (Doctoral dissertation, Wayne State University.) *Dissertation Abstracts International, 53*–12, A4116.

Bostick, S. L., & Onwuegbuzie, A. J. (2002a). Age as a predictor of library anxiety among students in England and Ireland. Manuscript in preparation.

Bostick, S. L., & Onwuegbuzie, A. J. (2002b). Library anxiety in the United States, England, and Ireland: A cross-cultural comparison. Manuscript in preparation.

Bowling Green State University Libraries. *Reference services.* Retrieved April 7, 2003, from http://www.bgsu.edu/colleges/library/infosrv/ref/assist/IDR.html.

Bradley, J. V. (1968). *Distribution-free statistical tests.* Englewood Cliffs, NJ: Prentice-Hall.

Brandt, D. S. (2001). Information technology literacy: Task knowledge and mental models. *Library Trends, 50*(1), 73–86.

Breivik, P. S. (1998). *Student learning in the information age.* Phoenix: Oryx Press.

Brett, J. E., & Kernaleguen, A. (1975). Perceptual and personality variables related to opinion leadership in fashion. *Perceptual and Motor Skills, 40*, 775–779.

Bridge, P. K., & Sawilowsky, S. S. (1999). Increasing physician's awareness of the impact of statistical tests on research outcomes: Investigating the comparative power of the Wilcoxon Rank-Sum test and independent samples *t* test to violations from normality. *Journal of Clinical Epidemiology, 52*, 229–235.

Brinberg, D., & McGrath, J. E. (1987). *Validity and the research process.* Newbury Park, CA: Sage.

Browne, M. W., & Cudeck, R. (1993). Alternative ways of assessing model fit. In K. A. Bollen & J. S. Long (Eds.), *Testing structural equation models* (pp. 136–162). Newbury Park, CA: Sage.

Buckland, M. K. (1974). *Book availability and the library user.* New York: Pergamon.

Bungard, T. (1987). Reducing library anxiety and defining "teaching." *Research Strategies, 5*, 146–148.

Butterfield, E. (1964). Locus of control, test anxiety, reactions to frustration and achievement attitudes. *Journal of Personality, 32*, 355–370.

Bryk, A. S., & Raudenbush, S. W. (1992). *Hierarchical linear models. Applications and data analysis methods.* Newbury Park, CA: Sage.

Byrd, P. (1982). A descriptive study of mathematics anxiety: Its nature and antecedents. (Doctoral dissertation, Indiana University.) *Dissertation Abstracts International, 43*(08A), 2583.

Byrne, B. M. (1989). A primer of LISREL: *Basic applications and programming for confirmatory factor analytic models.* New York: Springer-Verlag.

Campbell, D. T. (1957). Factors relevant to the validity of experiments in social settings. *Psychological Bulletin, 54*, 297–312.

Campbell, D. T. (1963a). From description to experimentation: Interpreting trends as quasi-experiments. In C. W. Harris (Ed.), *Problems in measuring change* (pp. 212–242). Madison: University of Wisconsin Press.

Campbell, D. T. (1963b). Social attitudes and other acquired behavioral dispositions. In S. Koch (Ed.), *Psychology: A study of science: Investigations of man as socius* (Vol. 6). New York: Rand McNally.

Campbell, D. T., & Fiske, D. W. (1959). Convergent and discriminant validation by the ultitrait-multimethod matrix. *Psychological Bulletin, 56*, 81–105.

Campbell, D. T., & Stanley, J. C. (1963). *Experimental and quasi-experimental designs for research.* Chicago: Rand McNally.

Campbell, D. T., & Stanley, J. C. (1990). *Experimental and quasi-experimental designs for research.* Boston: Houghton Mifflin.

Caplan, N. S., Morrison, A., & Stambaugh, R. J. (1975). *The use of social science knowledge in policy decisions at the national level: A report to respondents.* Ann Arbor: Institute for Social Research, University of Michigan.

Caracelli, V. W., & Greene, J. C. (1993). Data analysis strategies for mixed-methods evaluation designs. *Educational Evaluation and Policy Analysis, 15*, 195–207.

Carver, S. C., & Scheier, M. F. (2000). On the structure of behavioral self-regulation. In M. Boekaerts, P. R. Pintrich, & M. Zeidner (Eds.), *Handbook of self-regulation* (pp. 41–84). San Diego: Academic Press.

Cattell, R. B. (1966). Anxiety and motivation: Theory and crucial experiments. In C. Spielberger (Ed.), *Anxiety and behavior* (pp. 23–62). New York: Academic Press.

Cattell, R. B., & Scheier, I. H. (1961). *The meaning and measurement of neuroticism and anxiety.* New York: Ronald Press.

Claxton, C. H., & Ralston, V. (1978). *Learning styles: Their impact on teaching and administration*. Washington, DC: Association for the Study of Higher Education.

Cleveland, A. M. (2001). Library anxiety in first-year students: Computer assisted instruction vs. bibliographic instruction. Unpublished Master's thesis, University of North Carolina, Chapel Hill.

Cliff, N. (1987). *Analyzing multivariate data*. San Diego: Harcourt Brace Jovanovich.

Cliff, N., & Krus, D. J. (1976). Interpretation of canonical analysis: Rotated vs. unrotated solutions. *Psychometrika, 41*, 35–42.

Code of Federal Regulations. (1991). Title 45, Part 46.101(g). Subpart A: Federal policy for the protection of human subjects.

Cohen, A., & Cohen, E. (1979). *Designing and space planning for libraries: A behavioral guide*. New York: R. R. Bowker Co.

Cohen, J. (1965). Some statistical issues in psychological research. In B. B. Wolman (Ed.), *Handbook of clinical psychology* (pp. 95–121). New York: McGraw-Hill.

Cohen, J. (1968). Multiple regression as a general data-analytic system. *Psychological Bulletin, 70*, 426–443.

Cohen, J. (1983). The cost of dichotomization. *Applied Psychological Measurement, 7*, 249–253.

Cohen, J. (1988). *Statistical power analysis for the behavioral sciences*. New York: Wiley.

Cohen, J. (1994). The earth is round ($p < .05$). *American Psychologist, 49*, 997–1003.

Collins, B. L., Mellon, C. A., & Young, S. B. (1987). The needs and feelings of beginning researchers. In C. A. Mellon (Ed.), *Bibliographic instruction: The second generation* (pp. 73–84). Littleton, CO: Libraries Unlimited.

Collins, K. M. T., & Veal, R. E. (in press). Off-campus adult learners' levels of library anxiety as a predictor of attitudes toward the Internet. *Library & Information Science Research*.

Connolly, P. (1998). "Dancing to the wrong tune": Ethnography generalization and research on racism in schools. In P. Connolly and B. Troyna (Eds.), *Researching racism in education: Politics, theory, and practice* (pp. 122–139). Buckingham, England: Open University Press.

Constas, M. A. (1992). Qualitative data analysis as a public event: The documentation of category development procedures. *American Educational Research Journal, 29*, 253–266.

Cornett, C. E. (1983). *What you should know about teaching and learning styles*. Bloomington, IN: Phi Delta Kappa Educational Foundation.

Courville, T., & Thompson, B. (2001). Use of structure coefficients in published multiple regression articles: $\chi$ is not enough. *Educational and Psychological Measurement, 61*, 229–248.

Covington, M. V. (1985). Test anxiety: Causes and effects over time. In H. M. van der Ploeg, R. Schwarzer, & C. D. Spielberger (Eds.), *Advances in test anxiety research* (Vol. 4, pp. 55–68). Lisse, The Netherlands: Swets & Zeitlinger.

Creswell, J. W. (1994). *Research design: Qualitative and quantitative approaches.* Thousand Oaks, CA: Sage.

Creswell, J. W. (1998). *Qualitative inquiry and research design: Choosing among five traditions.* Thousand Oaks, CA: Sage.

Creswell, J. W. (2002). *Educational research: Planning, conducting, and evaluating quantitative and qualitative research.* Upper Saddle River, NJ: Pearson Education.

Crocker, L., & Algina, J. (1986). *Introduction to classical and modern test theory.* Orlando, FL: Holt, Rinehart, & Winston.

Cruise, R. J., Cash, R. W., & Bolton, D. L. (1985, August). Development and validation of an instrument to measure statistical anxiety. Paper presented at the annual meeting of the Statistical Education Section. Proceedings of the American Statistical Association.

Cruise, R. J., & Wilkins, E. M. (1980). STARS: Statistical Anxiety Rating Scale. Unpublished manuscript, Andrews University, Berrien Springs, MI.

Daly, J. A., & Miller, M. D. (1975a). Apprehension of writing as a predictor of writing intensity. *Journal of Psychology, 89*, 175–177.

Daly, J. A., & Miller, M. D. (1975b). Further studies in writing apprehension: SAT scores, success expectations, willingness to take advanced courses, and sex differences. *Research in the Teaching of English, 9*, 250–256.

Daly, J. A., & Miller, M. D. (1975c). The empirical development of an instrument to measure writing apprehension. *Research in the Teaching of English, 9*, 242–249.

Daly, J. A., & Shamo, W. (1976). Writing apprehension and occupational choice. *Journal of Occupational Psychology, 49*, 55–56.

Daly, J. A., & Shamo, W. (1978). Academic decisions as a function of writing apprehension. *Research in the Teaching of English, 12*, 119–126.

Daly, J. A., & Wilson, D. (1983). Writing apprehension, self-esteem, and personality. *Research in the Teaching of English, 17*, 327–341.

Daniel, L. G. (1988). Statistical significance testing: A historical overview of misuse and misinterpretation with implications for the editorial policies of educational journals. *Research in the Schools, 5*(2), 23–32.

Daniel, L. G. (1989a, March). Commonality analysis with multivariate data sets.

Paper presented at the annual meeting of the American Educational Research Association, San Francisco (ERIC Document Reproduction Service No. ED 314 483).

Daniel, L. G. (1989b, November). Comparisons of exploratory and confirmatory factor analysis. Paper presented at the annual meeting of the Mid-South Educational Research Association, Little Rock, AR (ERIC Document Reproduction Service No. ED 314 447).

Daniel, L. G. (1997). Kerlinger's research myths: An overview with implications for educational researchers. *Journal of Experimental Education, 65*, 101–112.

Daniel, L. G. (1998a). Statistical significance testing: A historical overview of misuse and misinterpretation with implications for editorial policies of educational journals. *Research in the Schools, 5*, 23–32.

Daniel, L. G. (1998b). The statistical significance controversy is definitely not over: A rejoinder to responses by Thompson, Knapp, and Levin. *Research in the Schools, 5*, 63–65.

Daniel, L. G. (1998c, December). Use of statistical significance testing in current "general" educational journals: A review of articles with comments for improved practice. Paper presented at the annual meeting of the Association for the Advancement of Educational Research, Ponte Vedra, FL.

Daniel, L. G., & Onwuegbuzie, A. J. (2000, November). Toward an extended typology of research errors. Paper presented at the annual conference of the Mid-South Educational Research Association, Bowling Green, KY.

Daniel, L. G., & Onwuegbuzie, A. J. (2002, November). Reliability and qualitative data: Are psychometric concepts relevant within an interpretivist research paradigm? Paper presented at the annual meeting of the Mid-South Educational Research Association, Chattanooga, TN.

Darlington, R. B., Weinberg, S. L., & Walberg, H. J. (1973). Canonical variate analysis and related techniques. *Review of Educational Research, 42*, 131–143.

Davidson, B. M. (1988, November). The case against using stepwise regression methods. Paper presented at the annual meeting of the Mid-South Educational Research Association, Louisville, KY (ERIC Document Reproduction Service No. ED 303 507).

Dennis, S., & Broughton, K. (2000). FALCON: An interactive library instruction tutorial. *Reference Services Review, 28*(1), 31–38.

Denzin, N. K. (1978). *The research act: A theoretical introduction to sociological methods*. New York: Praeger.

Denzin, N. K. (1989). *The research act: A theoretical introduction to sociological methods* (3rd ed.). Englewood Cliffs, NJ: Prentice-Hall.

Denzin, N. K. (1994). Evaluating qualitative research in the poststructural moment: The lessons James Joyce teaches us. *Qualitative Studies in Education, 7,* 295–308.

Department of Health, Education, and Welfare. (1979). The Belmont report. Retrieved April 7, 2003, from http://ohrp.osophs.dhhs.gov/humansubjects/guidance/belmont.htm.

Diener, E., & Crandall, R. (1978). *Ethics in social and behavioral research.* Chicago: University of Chicago Press.

Dimitroff, A. (1996). Research knowledge and activities of special librarians: Results of a survey. *Special Libraries, 87*(1), 1–9.

Doris, J., & Sarason, S. B. (1955). Test anxiety and blame assignment in a failure situation. *Journal of Abnormal and Social Psychology, 50,* 335–338.

Dowler, L. (1996). Foreword. In C. LaGuardia, M. Blake, L. Farwell, C. Kent, & E. Tallent (Eds.), *Teaching the new library: A how-to-do-it manual for planning and designing instructional programs.* New York: Neal-Schuman Publishers, Inc.

Doyen, S. E. (1989). Effects of conceptual instruction on subject-searching performance in a computerized library catalog. *Dissertation Abstracts International, 50*(11), A3399 (UMI No. AAG9010201).

Duffy, E. (1962). *Activation and behavior.* New York: John Wiley & Sons.

Dunn, J. A. (1965). A stability of the factor structure of the Test Anxiety Scale for Children across age and sex groups. *Journal of Consulting Psychology, 29,* 187.

Dzurec, L. C., & Abraham, J. L. (1993). The nature of inquiry: Linking quantitative and qualitative research. *Advances in Nursing Science, 16,* 73–79.

Edelmann, R. J. (1992). *Anxiety: Theory, research and intervention in clinical and health psychology.* New York: Wiley Series in Clinical Psychology.

Edirisooriya, G. (1995, November). Stepwise regression is a problem, not a solution. Paper presented at the annual meeting of the Mid-South Educational Research Association, Biloxi, MS (ERIC Document Reproduction Service No. ED 393 890).

Eisenhart, M. A., & Howe, K. R. (1992). Validity in educational research. In M. D. LeCompte, W. L. Millroy, & J. Preissle (Eds.), *The handbook of qualitative research in education* (pp. 643–680).

Eisner, E. W. (1975). *The perspective eye: Toward the reformulation of educational evaluation.* Occasional papers of the Stanford Evaluation Consortium. Stanford, CA: Stanford University Press.

Eisner, E. W. (1991). *The enlightened eye: Qualitative inquiry and the enhancement of educational practice.* New York: Macmillan.

Elliott, A. J., & McGregor, H. A. (1999). Test anxiety and the hierarchical model of approach and avoidance achievement motivation. *Journal of Personality and Social Psychology, 76,* 628–644.

Ellis, A., & Knaus, W. J. (1977). *Overcoming procrastination.* New York: Institute for Rational Living.

Ellsworth, P. C., & Smith, C. A. (1988). From appraisal to emotion: Differences among unpleasant feelings. *Motivation and Emotion, 12*(3), 271–302.

Elmore, P. B., & Woehlke, P. L. (1988). Statistical methods employed in *American Educational Research Journal, Educational Researcher,* and *Review of Educational Research* from 1978 to 1987. *Educational Researcher, 17*(9), 19–20.

Elmore, P. B., & Woehlke, P. L. (1996, April). Research methods employed in *American Educational Research Journal, Educational Researcher,* and *Review of Educational Research* from 1978 to 1995. Paper presented at the Annual Meeting of the American Educational Research Association, New York.

Elmore, P. B., & Woehlke, P. L. (1998, April). Twenty years of research methods employed in *American Educational Research Journal, Educational Researcher,* and *Review of Educational Research.* Paper presented at the annual meeting of the American Educational Research Association, San Diego.

Ely, M., Anzul, M., Friedman, T., Garner, D., & Steinmetz, A. C. (1991). *Doing qualitative research: Circles within circles.* New York: Falmer.

Endler, N., & Edwards, J. (1982). Stress and personality. In L. Goldberger & S. Breznitz (Eds.), *Handbook of stress: Theoretical and clinical aspects* (pp. 36–48). New York: The Free Press.

Epstein, S. (1972). The nature of anxiety with emphasis on its relationship expectancy. In C. Spielberger (Ed.), *Anxiety: Current trends in theory and research.* New York: Academic Press.

Ercegovac, Z., & Yamasaki, E. (1998). *Information literacy: Search strategies, tools and resources* (ERIC Document Reproduction Service No. ED 421 178).

Erdfelder, E., Faul, F., & Buchner, A. (1996). GPOWER: A general power analysis program. *Behavior Research Methods, Instruments, & Computers, 28,* 1–11.

Erickson, F. (1986). Qualitative methods of research on teaching. In M. Wittrock (Ed.), *Handbook for research on teaching* (pp. 119–161). New York: Macmillan.

Erlandson, D. A., Harris, E. L., Skipper, B. L., & Allen, S. D. (1993). *Doing naturalistic inquiry: A guide to methods.* Newbury Park, CA: Sage.

Ermarth, M. (1978). *Wilhelm Dilthey: The critique of historical reason.* Chicago: University of Chicago Press.

Everson, H. T., Millsap, R. E., & Rodriguez, C. M. (1991). Isolating gender differences in test anxiety: A confirmatory factor analysis of the Test Anxiety Inventory. *Educational and Psychological Measurement, 51*, 243–251.

Ezekiel, M. (1930). *Methods of correlational analysis.* New York: Wiley.

Feather, N. T. (1967). Some personality correlates of external control. *Australian Journal of Psychology, 19*, 253–260.

Fein, L. G. (1963). Evidence of a curvilinear relationship between IPAT anxiety and achievement at nursing school. *Journal of Clinical Psychology, 19*, 374–376.

Feld, S., & Lewis, J. (1967). Further evidence of the stability of the factor structure of the Test Anxiety Scale for Children across age and sex groups. *Journal of Consulting Psychology, 31*, 434.

Felder, R. M., & Henriques, E. R. (1995). Learning and teaching styles in foreign and second language education. *Foreign Language Annals, 28*(1), 21–31.

Fennema, E., & Sherman, J. A. (1976). Fennema-Sherman mathematics attitudes scales: Instruments designed to measure attitudes toward the learning of mathematics by males and females. *Catalog of Selected Documents in Psychology, 6*, 1–32.

Ferrari, J. R. (1991). Compulsive procrastination: Some self-reported characteristics. *Psychological Reports, 68*, 455–458.

Fetterman, D. M. (1989). *Ethnography: Step by step.* Newbury Park, CA: Sage.

Fielding, N., & Fielding, J. (1986). *Linking data.* Beverly Hills, CA: Sage.

Fleming, D. (1988, April). The literature on teacher utilization of research: Implications for the school reform movement. Paper presented at the annual meeting of the American Educational Research Association, New Orleans.

Fliotsos, A. (1992). Anxiety layering: The effects of library and computer anxiety on CD-ROM use. *The Southeastern Librarian, 42*, 47–49.

Folkman, S., & Lazarus, R. S. (1985). If it changes it must be a process: Study of emotion and coping during three stages of a college examination. *Journal of Personality and Social Psychology, 48*, 150–170.

Fox, J. (1997). *Applied regression analysis, linear models, and related methods.* Thousand Oaks, CA: Sage.

Freud, S. (1936). *The problem of anxiety.* New York, The Psychoanalytic Quarterly Press and W.W. Norton & Company, Inc.

Frick, E. (1975). Information structure and bibliographic instruction for undergraduates. *Journal of Academic Librarianship, 1*(4), 12–14.

Frick, E. (1982). Teaching information structure: Turning dependent researchers into self-teachers. In C. Oberman & K. Strauch (Eds), *Theories of bibliographic education: Designs for teaching* (pp. 193–208). New York: R. R. Bowker Company.

Frijda, N. H. (1993). The place of appraisal in emotion. *Cognition and Emotion, 7*, 357–387.

Gall, M. D. (1969). The relationship between masculinity-femininity and manifest anxiety. *Journal of Clinical Psychology, 25*, 294–295.

Gay, L. R., & Airasian, P. W. (2000). *Educational research: Competencies for analysis and application* (6th ed.). Englewood Cliffs, NJ: Prentice Hall.

Gay, L. R., & Airasian, P. W. (2003). *Educational research: Competencies for analysis and application* (7th ed.). Upper Saddle River, NJ: Pearson Education

Gaudry, E., & Spielberger, C. D. (1971). *Anxiety and educational achievement.* New York: Wiley.

Geen, R. G. (1980). Test anxiety and cue utilization. In I. G. Sarason (Ed.), *Test anxiety: Theory research and applications* (pp. 43–62). Hillsdale, NJ: Lawrence Erlbaum.

Gibbons, J. D. (1993). *Nonparametric measures of association* (Sage University Paper series on Quantitative Applications in the Social Sciences, series no. 07B091). Newbury Park, CA: Sage.

Glaser, B. G., & Strauss, A. L. (1967). *The discovery of grounded theory: Strategies for qualitative research.* Chicago: Aldine.

Glass, G. V., Peckham, P. D., & Sanders, J. R. (1972). Consequences of failure to meet assumptions underlying the fixed effects analyses of variance and covariance. *Review of Educational Research, 42*, 237–288.

Glesne, C., & Peshkin, A. (1992). *Becoming qualitative researchers: An introduction.* White Plains, NY: Longman.

Goetz, J. P., & LeCompte, M. D. (1984). *Ethnography and the qualitative design in educational research.* New York: Academic Press.

Gold, D. (1968). Some correlation coefficients: Relationships among I-E scores and other responsibility variables. *Psychological Reports, 22*, 983–984.

Goldstein, H. (1987). *Multilevel models in educational and social research.* London: Griffin.

Goldstein, H. (1995). *Multilevel statistical models.* London: Edward Arnold.

Goodwin, L. D., & Goodwin, W. L. (1985). Statistical techniques in *AERJ* articles, 1979–1983: The preparation of graduate students to read educational research literature. *Educational Researcher, 14*(2), 5–11.

Gorman, G. E. (1999). The future for library science education. *Libri, 49*(1), 1–10.

Gorsuch, R. L. (1983). *Factor analysis* (2nd ed.). Hillsdale, NJ: Lawrence Erlbaum.

Gourgey, A. F. (1984). *The relationship of misconceptions about math and mathematical self-concept to mathematics anxiety and statistical performance* (ERIC Document Reproduction Service No. ED 254 417).

Gratch, B. (1989). Fostering research activity: Examples of institutional support. Statements or policies. *College & Research Libraries News, 50*(11), 979–980.

Gray, J., & Wilcox, B. (1995). *Good school, bad school: Evaluating performance and encouraging improvement*. Buckingham, England: Open University Press.

Green, G. S. (1876). Personal relations between librarians and readers. *American Library Journal, 1*, 74–81.

Green, K. E., & Kvidahl, R. F. (1990, April). Research methods courses and post bachelor's education: Effects on teachers' research use and opinions. Paper presented at the annual meeting of the American Educational Research Association, Boston.

Green, S. B. (1991). How many subjects does it take to do a regression analysis? *Multivariate Behavioral Research, 26*, 499–510.

Greenberg, J., Solomon, S., Pyszczynski, T., Rosenblatt, A., Burling, J., Lyon, D., Simon, L., & Pinel, E. (1992). Why do people need self-esteem? Converging evidence that self-esteem serves as anxiety buffering function. *Journal of Personality and Social Psychology, 63*, 913–922.

Greene, J. C., Caracelli, V. J., & Graham, W. F. (1989). Toward a conceptual framework for mixed-method evaluation designs. *Educational Evaluation and Policy Analysis, 11*, 255–274.

Greenwald, A. G., Pratkanis, A. R., Leippe, M. R., & Baumgardner, M. H. (1986). Under what conditions does theory obstruct research progress. *Psychological Review, 93*, 216–229.

Gressard, C. P., & Loyd, B. H. (1987). An investigation of the effects of mathematics anxiety and sex on computer attitudes. *School Science and Mathematics, 87*(2), 125–135.

Gross, M. (1995). The imposed query. *RQ, 35*, 236–243.

Gross, M. (1998). The imposed query: Implications for library service evaluation. *Reference and User Services Quarterly, 37*, 290–299.

Gross, M. (1999a). Imposed versus self-generated questions: Implications for reference practice. *Reference and User Services Quarterly, 39*, 53–61.

Gross, M. (1999b). Imposed queries in the school library media center: A descriptive study. *Library & Information Science Research, 21*, 501–521.

Gross, M. (2000). The imposed query and information services for children. *Journal of Youth Services in Libraries, 13*, 10–17.

Guba, E. G., & Lincoln, Y. S. (1989). *Fourth generation evaluation*. Newbury Park, CA: Sage.

Hair, J. F., Anderson, R. E., Tatham, R. L., & Black, W. C. (1995). *Multivariate data analysis* (4th ed.). Englewood Cliffs, NJ: Prentice Hall.

Hall, B. W., Ward, A. W., & Comer, C. B. (1988). Published educational research:

An empirical study of its quality. *Journal of Educational Research, 81*, 182–189.

Hall, S. M. (1972). Self-control and therapist control in the behavioral treatment of overweight women. *Behavior Research and Therapy, 10*, 59–68.

Halpern, E. S. (1983). Auditing naturalistic inquiries: The development and application of a model. Unpublished doctoral dissertation, Indiana University.

Hammersley, M., & Atkinson, P. (1995). *Ethnography: Principles in practice* (2nd ed.). New York: Routledge.

Hanson, N. R. (1958). *Patterns of discovery: An inquiry into the conceptual foundations of science*. Newbury Park, CA: Sage.

Hare, A. (1989). Professional development in the 1980s in college libraries in the Southeast. *The Southeastern Librarian, 39*, 18–19.

Harris, A. L., & Harris, J. M. (1987). Reducing mathematics anxiety with computer assisted instruction. *Mathematics and Computer Education, 21*, 16–24.

Harris, R. M. (1992). Bibliographic instruction: Views of academic, special and public librarians. *College & Research Libraries, 53*, 249–256.

Hatcher, L. (1994). *A step-by-step approach to using the SAS system for factor analysis and structural equation modeling*. Cary, NC: SAS Institute Inc.

Havener, W. M., & Stolt, W. A. (1993). The professional development activities of academic librarians: Does institutional support make a difference? *College & Research Libraries, 55*, 25–36.

Henson, R. K. (1998, November). ANCOVA with intact groups: Don't do it! Paper presented at the annual meeting of the Mid-South Educational Research Association, New Orleans (ERIC Document Reproduction Service No. 426 086).

Henson, R. K. (2000). Demystifying parametric analyses: Illustrating canonical correlation as the multivariate general linear model. *Multiple Linear Regression Viewpoints, 26*, 11–19.

Henson, R. K., Capraro, R. M., & Capraro, M. M. (2001, November). Reporting practices and use of exploratory factor analyses in educational research journals. Paper presented at the annual meeting of the Mid-South Educational Research Association, Little Rock, AR.

Henson, R. K., & Roberts, J. K. (in press). Exploratory factor analysis reporting practices in published research. In B. Thompson (Ed.), *Advances in social science methodology* (Vol. 6). Stamford, CT: JAI Press.

Hernon, P. (1994). Need for research: Regaining "the foundation of understanding." *Journal of Academic Librarianship, 20*(4), 119–120.

Hetzel, R. D. (1996). A primer on factor analysis with comments on patterns of practice and reporting. In B. Thompson (Ed.), *Advances in social science methodology* (Vol. 4, pp. 175–206). Greenwich, CT: JAI Press.

Hewitt, P. L., & Flett, G. L. (1991a). Perfectionism in self and social contexts: Conceptualization, assessment, and association with psychopathology. *Journal of Personality and Social Psychology, 60,* 456–470.

Hewitt, P. L., & Flett, G. L. (1991b). Dimensions of perfectionism in unipolar depression. *Journal of Abnormal Psychology, 100,* 98–101.

Hill, K. T. (1984). Debilitating motivation and testing: A major educational program, possible solutions, and policy applications. In R. E. Ames & C. Ames (Eds.), *Research on motivation in education* (Vol 1, pp. 245–274). New York: Academic Press.

Hill, K. T., & Sarason, S. B. (1966). A further longitudinal study of the relation of test anxiety and defensiveness to test and school performance over the elementary school years. *Child Development Monographs, 31,* 1–76.

Hodges, H. (1944). *Wilhelm Dilthey: An introduction.* London: Routledge & Kegan Paul.

Hodges, H. (1952). *The philosophy of Wilhelm Dilthey.* London: Routledge & Kegan Paul.

Hogarty, K. Y., & Kromrey, J. D. (2001, April). We've been reporting some effect sizes: Can you guess what they mean? Paper presented at the annual meeting of the American Educational Research Association, Seattle.

Hollander, M., & Wolfe, D. A. (1973). *Nonparametric statistical methods.* New York: John Wiley & Sons.

Hollandsworth, J. G., Jr., Glezski, R. C., Kirkland, K., Jones, G. E., & Van Norman, L. R. (1979). An analysis of the nature and effects of test anxiety: Cognitive behavioral and physiological components. *Cognitive Therapy and Research, 3,* 165–180.

Hope, C. B., Kajiwara, S., & Liu, M. (2001). The impact of the Internet: Increasing the reference librarian's role as teacher. In D. Su (Ed.), *Evolution in reference and information services: The Impact of the Internet* (pp. 13–36). Binghamton, NY: Haworth Information Press.

Horwitz, E. K., Horwitz, M. B., & Cope, J. (1986). Foreign language classroom anxiety. *Modern Language Journal, 70,* 125–132.

Howe, K. R. (1988). Against the quantitative-qualitative incompatability thesis or dogmas die hard. *Educational Researcher, 17,* 10–16.

Howe, K. R., & Eisenhart, M. (1990). Standards for qualitative (and quantitative) research: A prolegomenon. *Educational Researcher, 19*(4), 2–9.

Hu, L. T., & Bentler, P. M. (1999). Cutoff criteria for fit indexes in covariance structure analysis: Conventional criteria versus new alternatives. *Structural Equation Modeling, 6*(1), 1–55.

Huberty, C. J. (1989). Problems with stepwise methods—better alternatives. In

B. Thompson (Ed.), *Advances in social science methodology* (Vol. 1, pp. 43–70). Greenwich, CT: JAI Press.

Huberty, C. J. (1994). *Applied discriminant analysis.* New York: Wiley & Sons.

Huberty, C. J., & Barton, R. (1989). An introduction to discriminant analysis. *Measurement and Evaluation in Counseling and Development, 22,* 158–168.

Huberty, C. J., & Morris, J. D. (1989). Multivariate analysis versus multiple univariate analyses. *Psychological Bulletin, 105,* 302–308.

Huberty, C. J., & Wisenbaker, J. (1992). Discriminant analysis: Potential improvements in typical practice. In B. Thompson (Ed.), *Advances in social sciencemethodology* (Vol. 2, pp. 169–208). Greenwich, CT: JAI Press.

Hughes, H. (1958). *Consciousness and society.* New York: Knopf.

Humphries-Wadsworth, T. M. (1997, April). Features of published analyses of canonical results. Paper presented at the annual meeting of the American Educational Research Association, San Diego (ERIC Document Reproduction Service No. ED 418 125).

Hunsley, J. D. (1985). Test and mathematics anxiety: An examination of appraisal and attributional processes. (Doctoral dissertation, University of Waterloo [Canada].) *Dissertation Abstracts International, 46,* 12B, 4402.

Hunsley, J. D. (1987). Cognitive processes in mathematics anxiety and test anxiety: The role of appraisals, internal dialogue, and attributions. *Journal of Educational Psychology, 79,* 388–392.

Ingelfinger, F. J. (1975). The unethical in medical ethics. *Annals of Internal Medicine, 83,* 264–269.

Jacobson, F. F. (1991). Gender differences in attitudes toward using computers in libraries: An exploratory study. *Library & Information Science Research, 13,* 267–279.

Jenkins, S. J., Fuqua, D. R., & Froehle, T. C. (1984). A critical examination of the use of nonparametric statistics in the *Journal of Counseling Psychology. Perceptual and Motor Skills, 59,* 31–35.

Jennings, S. E., & Onwuegbuzie, A. J. (2001). Computer attitudes as a function of age, gender, math attitude, and developmental status. *Journal of Educational Computing Research, 25,* 367–384.

Jerabek, J. A., Meyer, L. S., & Kordinak, S. T. (2001). "Library anxiety" and "computer anxiety": Measures, validity, and research implications. *Library & Information Science Research, 23,* 277–289.

Jiao, Q. G., & Onwuegbuzie, A. J. (1997). Antecedents of library anxiety. *The Library Quarterly, 67,* 372–389.

Jiao, Q. G., & Onwuegbuzie, A. J. (1998). Perfectionism and library anxiety among graduate students. *Journal of Academic Librarianship, 24,* 365–371.

Jiao, Q. G., & Onwuegbuzie, A. J. (1999a). Is library anxiety important? *Library Review, 48,* 278–282.

Jiao, Q. G., & Onwuegbuzie, A. J. (1999b). Self-perception and library anxiety: An empirical study. *Library Review, 48*(3), 140–147.

Jiao, Q. G., & Onwuegbuzie, A. J. (1999c). Identifying library anxiety through students' learning modality preferences. *Library Quarterly, 69,* 202–216.

Jiao, Q. G., & Onwuegbuzie, A. J. (2001a). Library anxiety and characteristic strengths and weaknesses in graduate students' study habits. *Library Review, 50,* 73–80.

Jiao, Q. G., & Onwuegbuzie, A. J. (2001b). Library anxiety among international students. *Urban Library Journal, 11,* 16–27.

Jiao, Q. G., & Onwuegbuzie, A. J. (2002a). Dimensions of library anxiety and social interdependence: Implications for library services. *Library Review, 51*(2), 71–78.

Jiao, Q. G., & Onwuegbuzie, A. J. (2002b). The odds of visiting the library as a function of anxiety. Unpublished manuscript, Baruch College, The City University of New York.

Jiao, Q. G., & Onwuegbuzie, A. J. (2002c). Reliability generalization of the Library Anxiety Scale scores: Initial findings. Unpublished manuscript, Baruch College, The City University of New York.

Jiao, Q. G., & Onwuegbuzie, A. J. (2003a). Relationship between library anxiety and computer anxiety. Manuscript submitted for publication.

Jiao, Q. G., & Onwuegbuzie, A. J. (2003b). Library anxiety: A function of race? Manuscript submitted for publication.

Jiao, Q. G., & Onwuegbuzie, A. J. (2003c). Reading ability as a predictor of library anxiety. *Library Review, 52*(4), 159–169.

Jiao, Q. G., Onwuegbuzie, A. J., & Bostick, S. L. (2003). Racial differences in library anxiety among graduate students. Manuscript submitted for publication.

Jiao, Q. G., Onwuegbuzie, A. J., & Lichtenstein, A. (1996). Library anxiety: Characteristics of "at-risk" college students. *Library & Information Science Research, 18,* 151–163.

Jick, T. D. (1979). Mixing qualitative and quantitative methods: Triangulation in action. *Administrative Science Quarterly, 24,* 602–611.

Joe, V. C. (1971). Review of the internal-external construct as a personality variable. *Psychological Reports, 28,* 619–639.

Joesting, J., & Whitehead, G. I. (1977). Relationships of state and trait anxiety to grades in educational psychology. *Psychological Reports, 40,* 705–706.

Johnson, R. B. (1999). Examining the validity structure of qualitative research. *Education, 118,* 282–292.

Johnson, B., & Christensen, L. (2000). *Educational research: Quantitative and qualitative approaches.* Boston: Allyn & Bacon.

Johnson, B., & Turner, L. A. (2003). Data collection strategies in mixed methods research. In A. Tashakkori & C. Teddlie (Eds.), *Handbook of mixed methods in social and behavioral research* (pp. 297–319). Thousand Oaks, CA: Sage.

Joseph, M. E. (1991). The cure for library anxiety—it may not be what you think. *Catholic Library World, 63,* 111–114.

Kaiser, H. F. (1958). The varimax criterion for analytic rotation in factor analysis. *Psychometrika, 23,* 187–200.

Kazdin, A. E. (1999). The meanings and measurement of clinical significance. *Journal of Consulting and Clinical Psychology, 67,* 332–339.

Keefer, J. A. (1993). The hungry rats syndrome: Library anxiety, information literacy, and the academic reference process. *RQ, 32,* 333–339.

Kemper, E. A., Stringfield, S., & Teddlie, C. (2003). Mixed methods sampling strategies in social science research. In A. Tashakkori & C. Teddlie (Eds.), *Handbook of mixed methods in social and behavioral research* (pp. 273–296). Thousand Oaks, CA: Sage.

Kerlinger, F. N. (1960). The mythology of educational research: The methods approach. *School and Society, 85,* 35–37.

Kerlinger, F. N. (1986). *Foundations of behavioral research* (3rd ed.). New York: Holt, Rinehart & Winston.

Kerlinger, F. N. (1999). *Foundations of behavioral research* (4th ed.). Fort Worth, TX: Harcourt Brace College Publishers.

Kerlinger, F. N., & Pedhazur, E. (1973). *Multiple regression in behavioral research.* New York: Holt, Rinehart & Winston.

Keselman, H. J., Huberty, C. J., Lix, L. M., Olejnik, S., Cribbie, R. A., Donahue, B., Kowalchuk, R. K., Lowman, L. L., Petoskey, M. D., Keselman, J. C., & Levin, J. R. (1998). Statistical practices of educational researchers: An analysis of their ANOVA, MANOVA, and ANCOVA analyses. *Review of Educational Research, 68,* 350–386.

Kidder, L. H. (1981). Qualitative research and quasi-experimental frameworks. In M. B. Brewer & B. E. Collins (Eds.), *Scientific inquiry and the social sciences.* San Francisco: Jossey-Bass.

Kieffer, K. M. (1999). An introductory primer on the appropriate use of exploratory and confirmatory factor analysis. *Research in the Schools, 6*(2), 75–92.

Kirk, R. E. (1996). Practical significance. A concept whose time as come. *Education and Psychological Measurement, 56,* 746–759.

Knapp, T. R. (1978). Canonical correlation analysis: A general parametric significance testing system. *Psychological Bulletin, 85,* 410–416.

Koehler, B., & Swanson, K. (1988). ESL students and bibliographic instruction: Learning yet another language. *Research Strategies, 6*(4), 148–160.

Koenig, K. P., & Masters, J. (1965). Experimental treatment of habitual smoking. *Behavior Research and Therapy, 3,* 235–243.

Kracker, J. (2002). Research anxiety and students' perceptions of research: An experiment. Part I. Effect of teaching Kuhlthau's ISP model. *Journal of the American Society for Information Science and Technology, 53,* 282–294.

Kracker, J., & Wang, P. (2002). Research anxiety and students' perceptions of research: An experiment. Part II. Content analysis of their writings on two experiences. *Journal of the American Society for Information Science and Technology, 53,* 295–307.

Kramer, E. H. (1996). Why roving reference: A case study in a small academic library. *Reference Services Review, 24,* 67–80.

Kreft, I., & De Leeuw, J. (1998). *Introducing multilevel modeling.* Thousand Oaks, CA: Sage.

Krug, S. E., Scheier, I. H., & Cattell, C. B. (1976). *Handbook for the IPAT anxiety scale.* Champaign, IL: Institute for Personality and Ability Testing.

Kuhlthau, C. C. (1983). The library research process: Case studies and interventions with high school seniors in advanced placement English classes using Kelly's theory of constructs. Unpublished doctoral dissertation, The State University of New Jersey, Rutgers.

Kuhlthau, C. C. (1985). A process approach to library skills in instruction. *School Library Media Quarterly, 13,* 35–40.

Kuhlthau, C. C. (1987). An emerging theory of library instruction. *School Library Media Quarterly, 16,* 23–28.

Kuhlthau, C. C. (1988a). Developing a model of the library search process: Cognitive and affective aspects. *RQ, 28,* 232–242.

Kuhlthau, C. C. (1988b). Longitudinal case studies of the information search process of users in libraries. *Library & Information Science Research, 10,* 257–304.

Kuhlthau, C. C. (1989). The information search process of high-middle-low achieving high school seniors. *School Library Media Quarterly, 17,* 224–228.

Kuhlthau, C. C. (1991). Inside the search process: Information seeking from the user's perspective. *Journal of the American Society for Information Science, 42*(5), 361–371.

Kuhlthau, C. C. (1993). *Seeking meaning: A process approach to library and information services.* Norwood, NJ: Ablex Publishing.

Kuhlthau, C. C. (1994). Students and the information search process: Zones of intervention for librarians. *Advances in Librarianship, 18,* 57–72.

Kuhlthau, C. C., Turock, B. J., George, M. W., & Belvin, R. J. (1990). Validating a model of the search process: A comparison of academic, public and school library users. *Library & Information Science Research, 12*, 5–31.

Kuhn, T. S. (1962). *The structure of scientific revolutions*. Chicago: University of Chicago Press.

Kvale, S. (1995). The social construction of validity. *Qualitative Inquiry, 1*, 19–40.

LaGuardia, C., Blake, M., Farwell, L., Kent, K., Tallent, E. (1996). *Teaching the new library: A how-to-do-it manual for planning and designing instructional programs*. New York: Neal-Schuman Publishers, Inc.

Lambert, Z. V., & Durand, R. M. (1975). Some precautions in using canonical analysis. *Journal of Market Research, 12*, 468–475.

Lather, P. (1986). Issues of validity in openly ideological research: Between a rock and a soft place. *Interchange, 17*, 63–84.

Lather, P. (1993). Fertile obsession: Validity after poststructuralism. *Sociological Quarterly, 34*, 673–693.

Lawley, D. N., & Maxwell, A. E. (1971). *Factor analysis as a statistical method*. New York: Macmillan.

Lazarsfeld, P. F., & Barton, A. (1955). Some functions of qualitative data analysis in sociological research. *Sociologica, 1*, 324–361.

Lazarus, R. S. (1991). *Emotion and adaptation*. New York: Oxford University Press.

Leach, L. F., & Henson, R. K. (2003, February). The use and impact of adjusted $R^2$ effects in published regression research. Paper presented at the annual meeting of the Southwest Educational Research Association, San Antonio, TX.

Lechner, J. V. (1989). Bibliographic instruction evaluation: A study testing the correlation among five measures of the impact of a bibliographic instruction program on undergraduates' information searching behavior in libraries. *Dissertation Abstracts International, 50*(5), A 1124. (UMI No. AAG8914373)

Lee, T. P. (1995). The library research committee: It has the money and the time. *Journal of Academic Librarianship, 21*(2), 111–115.

Leech, N. L., & Onwuegbuzie, A. J. (2002, November). A call for greater use of nonparametric statistics. Paper presented at the annual meeting of the Mid-South Educational Research Association, Chattanooga, TN.

Leech, N. L., & Onwuegbuzie, A. J. (2003, April). A proposed fourth measure of significance: The role of economic significance in educational research. Paper presented at the annual meeting of the American Educational Research Association, Chicago.

Libraries for the Future. (1998). Library research: 1983–1997. A report to the

U.S. Department of Education, Office of Educational Research and Improvement, The National Institute on Postsecondary Education, Libraries, and Lifelong Learning and The National Library of Education. Retrieved November 1, 2002, from http://www.ed.gov/offices/OERI/PLLI/LibraryResearch/title.html.

Liebert, R. M., & Morris, L. W. (1967). Cognitive and emotional components of test anxiety: A distinction and some initial data. *Journal of Counseling Psychology, 20,* 975–978.

Lincoln, Y. S., & Guba, E. G. (1985). *Naturalistic inquiry.* Beverly Hills, CA: Sage.

Line, M. B. (1991). Research policy in librarianship and information science: Keynote address. In C. Harris (Ed.), Research policy in librarianship and information science. Papers presented to a conference of the library and information research group and the public libraries research group, Salford, 1990, organized with the support of the British Library Research and Development Department. British Library Research and Development Report 6010, Taylor Graham, London and Los Angeles.

Lipsett, L. P. (1958). A self-concept scale for children and its relationship to Children's Form of the Manifest Anxiety Scale. *Child Development, 29,* 463–472.

Liu, M., & Redfern, B. (1997). Information seeking behavior of multicultural students: A case study at San Jose State University. *College & Research Libraries, 58,* 348–354.

Llabre, M. M., & Suarez, E. (1985). Predicting math anxiety and course performance in college women and men. *Journal of Counseling Psychology, 32,* 283–287.

Lockridge, J. (1997, January). Stepwise regression should never be used by researchers. Paper presented at the annual meeting of the Southwest Educational Research Association, Austin, TX (ERIC Document Reproduction Service No. ED 407 425).

Loftin, L. B., & Madison, S. Q. (1991). The extreme dangers of covariance corrections. In B. Thompson (Ed.), *Advances in educational research: Substantive findings, methodological developments* (Vol. 1, pp. 133–147). Greenwich, CT: JAI Press.

Loomis, R. J., & Parsons, M. B. (1979). Orientation needs and the library setting. In D. Pollet & P. C. Haskell (Eds.), *Sign systems for libraries* (pp. 3–16). New York: R. R. Bowker Company.

Lopez, K. A. (1989, November). Testing interaction effects without discarding variance. Paper presented at the annual meeting of the Mid-South Educational Research association, Little Rock, AR (ERIC Document Reproduction Service No. ED 322 167).

Loyd, B. H., & Gressard, C. (1984). *The effects of sex, age, and computer experience on computer attitudes* (ERIC Document Reproduction Service No. ED 246 878).

MacIntyre, P. D., & Gardner, R. C. (1991a). Language anxiety: Its relation to other anxieties and to processing in native and second languages. *Language Learning, 41*, 85–117.

MacIntyre, P. D., & Gardner, R. C. (1991b). Investigating language class anxiety using the focused essay technique. *The Modern Language Journal, 75*, 296–304.

MacIntyre, P. D., & Gardner, R. C. (1991c). Methods and results in the study of anxiety and language learning: A review of the literature. *Language Learning, 41*, 85–117.

MacIntyre, P. D., & Gardner, R. C. (1994a). The subtle effects of language anxiety on cognitive processing in the second language. *Language Learning, 44*(2), 283–305.

MacIntyre, P. D., & Gardner, R. C. (1994b). The effects of induced anxiety on three stages of cognitive processing in computerized vocabulary learning. *Studies in Second Language Acquisition, 16*, 1–17.

Mandler, G. (1972). Helplessness: Theory and research in anxiety. In C. Spielberger (Ed.), *Anxiety: Current trends in theory and research*. New York: Academic Press.

Mardikian, J., & Kesselman, M. (1995). Beyond the desk: Enhanced reference staffing for the electronic library. *Reference Services Review, 23*, 21–28.

Massachusetts Board of Library Commissioners. (1997, August). Needs assessment. In *Library services and technology act Massachusetts long-range plan, 1998–2002*. Retrieved April 7, 2003, from http://www.mlin.lib.ma.us/mblc/ldev/lsta/lrp.shtml.

Mathews, V. H., Flum, J. G., & Whitney, K. A. (1990, Spring). Kids need libraries: School and public libraries preparing the youth of today for the world of tomorrow. *Journal of Youth Services in Libraries, 3*, 197–207.

Maxwell, J. A. (1992). Understanding and validity in qualitative research. *Harvard Educational Review, 62*, 279–299.

Maxwell, J. A. (1996). *Qualitative research design*. Newbury Park, CA: Sage.

Maxwell, S. E., & Delaney, H. D. (1990). *Designing experiments and analyzing data: A model comparison perspective*. Belmont, CA: Wadsworth.

May, R. (1950). *The meaning of anxiety*. New York: The Ronald Press Company.

McClelland, D. C. (1953). *The achievement motive*. New York: Appleton-Century-Crofts.

McGregor, J. (1999). Teaching the research process: Helping students become lifelong learners. *NASSP Bulletin, 83*, 27–34.

McKelvie, S. (1978). Graphic rating scales: How many categories? *British Journal of Psychology*, *69*, 185–202.

McKenzie, K. M. (2000). The impact of bibliographic instruction on the library anxiety of adult non-traditional college students. Unpublished Bachelor's thesis, Bethel College.

McMillan, J. H. (1999). Unit of analysis in field experiments: Some design considerations for educational researchers (ERIC Document Reproduction Service No. ED 428 135).

McNemar, Q. (1960). At random: Sense and nonsense. *American Psychologist*, *15*, 295–300.

McReynolds, P. (1976). Assimilation and anxiety. In M. Zuckerman & C. Spielberger (Eds.), *Emotions and anxiety: New concepts, methods and applications*. Hillsdale, NJ: Lawrence Erlbaum.

McSeeney, M., & Katz, B. M. (1978). Nonparametric statistics: Use and nonuse. *Perceptual and Motor Skills*, *4*(3), 1023–1032.

Mech, T. F., & Brooks, C. I. (1995). Library anxiety among college students: An exploratory study. Paper presented at the 7th National Conference of the Association of College and Research Libraries, Pittsburgh, March 30–April 2.

Mech, T. F., & Brooks, C. I. (1997). Anxiety and confidence in using a library by college freshmen and seniors. *Psychological Reports*, *81*, 929–930.

Mellon, C. A. (1982). Information problem-solving: A developmental approach to library instruction. In C. Oberman & K. Strauch (Eds.), *Theories of bibliographic education: Designs for teaching* (pp. 79–81). New York: R. R. Bowker Company.

Mellon, C. A. (1986). Library anxiety: A grounded theory and its development. *College & Research Libraries*, *47*, 160–165.

Mellon, C. A. (1988). Attitudes: The forgotten dimension in library instruction. *Library Journal*, *113*, 137–139.

Mellon, C. A. (1989). Library anxiety and the non-traditional student. Paper presented at the 16th national LOEX Library Instruction Conference, Bowling State Green State University, Bowling Green, OH, May 5–6, 1988.

Merriam, S. (1988). *Case study research in education: A qualitative approach*. San Francisco: Jossey-Bass.

Meyer, J. W., & Scott, W. R. (1983). *Organizational environments: Ritual and rationality*. Beverly Hills, CA: Sage.

Meyers, J., & Martin, R. (1974). Relationships of state and trait anxiety to concept-learning performance. *Journal of Educational Psychology*, *66*, 33–39.

Micceri, T. (1989). The unicorn, the normal curve, and other improbable creatures. *Psychological Bulletin*, *105*(1), 156–166.

Miles, M., & Huberman, A. M. (1994). *Qualitative data analysis: An expanded sourcebook* (2nd ed.). Thousand Oaks, CA: Sage.

Miles, M. B., & Huberman, A. M. (1984). Drawing valid meaning from qualitative data: Toward a shared craft. *Educational Researcher, 13*, 20–30.

Milgram, N. A. (1991). Procrastination. In R. Dulbecco (Ed.), *Encyclopedia of human biology* (Vol. 6, pp. 149–155). San Diego: Academic Press.

Miller, W. (1992). The future of bibliographic instruction and information literacy for the academic librarian. In B. Baker & M. E. Litzinger (Eds.), *The evolving educational mission of the library* (pp. 144–150). Chicago: Association of College and Research Libraries.

Minor, L. C., Onwuegbuzie, A. J., Witcher, A. E., & James, T. L. (2002). Preservice teachers' educational beliefs and their perceptions of characteristics of effective teachers. *Journal of Educational Research, 96*, 116–127.

Mitchell, J. V., Jr. (1959). Goal-setting behavior as a function of self-acceptance, over- and under-achievement, and related personality variables. *Journal of Educational Psychology, 50*, 93–104.

Mizrachi, D. (2000). Library anxiety and computer attitudes among Israeli B.Ed. students. Unpublished Master's thesis, Bar-Ilan University, Israel.

Montanelli, D. S., & Stenstrom, P. F. (1986). The benefits of research for academic librarians and the institutions they serve. *College & Research Libraries, 47*, 482–485.

Mood, T. (1982). Foreign students and the academic library. *RQ, 22*, 175–180.

Moore, J. D. (1996, January). Stepwise methods are as bad in discriminant analysis as they are anywhere else. Paper presented at the annual meeting of the Southwest Educational Research Association, New Orleans (ERIC Document Reproduction Service No. ED 395 041).

Morris, W. N., & Reilly, N. P. (1987). Toward the self-regulation of mood: Theory and research. *Motivation and Emotion, 11*, 215–249.

Morrison, R. L. (1992). The effects of learning modules on teaching library skills to doctoral students in education. *Dissertation Abstracts International, 53*(8) A2706. (UMI No. AAG9237321)

Morse, J. M. (1991). Approaches to qualitative-quantitative methodological triangulation. *Nursing Research, 40*, 120–123.

Mueller, J. H. (1979). Anxiety and encoding processes in memory. *Personality and Social Psychology Bulletin, 5*, 288–331.

Myers, R. H. (1986). *Classical and modern regression with applications*. Boston: Duxbury Press.

Nanna, M. J., & Sawilowsky, S. S. (1998). Analysis of Likert scale data in disability and medical rehabilitation evaluation. *Psychometric Methods, 3*, 55–67.

National Center for Education Statistics. (1996). *SASS by state: 1993–94 schools and staffing survey: Selected state results*. Washington, DC: National Center for Education Statistics.

National Center for Education Statistics. (2000). *Digest of education statistics 2000*. Washington, DC: U.S. Department of Education, Office of Educational Research and Improvement, National Center for Education Statistics.

Nelson, L. R., & Zaichkowsky, L. D. (1979). A case for using multiple regression instead of ANOVA in educational research. *Journal of Experimental Education, 47*, 324–330.

Newman, I., & Benz, C. R. (1998). *Qualitative-quantitative research methodology: Exploring the interactive continuum*. Carbondale: Southern Illinois University Press.

Nottleman, E. D., & Hill, K. T. (1977). Test anxiety and off-task behavior in evaluative situations. *Child Development, 48*, 225–231.

Nowotny, H. (1990). *In search of usable knowledge*. Boulder. CO: Westview Press.

Nunnally, J. C., & Bernstein, I. H. (1994). *Psychometric theory* (3rd ed.). New York: McGraw-Hill.

Office for Human Research Protections (OHRP). (2001). 45 CFR 46—Protection of Human Subjects. Retrieved April 6, 2003, from http://ohrp.osophs.dhhs.gov/humansubjects/guidance/45cfr46.htm.

Oling, L., & Mach, M. (2002). Tour trends in academic ARL libraries. *College & Research Libraries, 63*(1), 13–23.

Onwuegbuzie, A. J. (1996). Development of the Research Anxiety Rating Scale. Unpublished manuscript, University of Central Arkansas (Conway).

Onwuegbuzie, A. J. (1997a). Writing a research proposal: The role of library anxiety, statistics anxiety, and composition anxiety. *Library & Information Science Research, 19*, 5–33.

Onwuegbuzie, A. J. (1997b). The teacher as researcher: The relationship between enrollment time and achievement in a research methodology course. *Reflection and Research, 3*(1) [On-line]. Available:http://www.gonzaga.edu/rr/v3n1/tony.html

Onwuegbuzie, A. J. (1997c). Development of the Research Anxiety Rating Scale. Unpublished manuscript, University of Central Arkansas (Conway).

Onwuegbuzie, A. J. (1997d). The teacher as researcher: The relationship between research anxiety and learning style in a research methodology course. *College Student Journal, 31*, 496–506.

Onwuegbuzie, A. J. (1997e). The role of technology in the library anxiety of Arkansas college students. *Instructional Media Quarterly, 30*, 6–8.

Onwuegbuzie, A. J. (1998a). The relationship between writing anxiety and learning styles among graduate students. *Journal of College Student Development, 39*, 589–598.

Onwuegbuzie, A. J. (1998b). Teachers' attitudes towards educational research courses: Implications for the teacher-as-researcher movement. *GATEways to Teacher Education, 11*, 39–51.

Onwuegbuzie, A. J. (1999a). Writing apprehension among graduate students: Its relationship to self-perceptions. *Psychological Reports, 84*, 1034–1039.

Onwuegbuzie, A. J. (1999b). Statistics anxiety among African-American graduate students: An affective filter? *Journal of Black Psychology, 25*, 189–209.

Onwuegbuzie, A. J. (1999c). Underachievement of African-American graduate students in research methodology classes: Possible implications for the supply of school administrators. *The Journal of Negro Education, 67*, 67–78.

Onwuegbuzie, A. J. (2000a). Statistics anxiety and the role of self-perceptions. *Journal of Educational Research, 93*, 323–335.

Onwuegbuzie, A. J. (2000b, November). Validity and qualitative research: An oxymoron? Paper presented at the annual meeting of the Association for the Advancement of Educational Research (AAER), Ponte Vedra, FL.

Onwuegbuzie, A. J. (2000c, November). Expanding the framework of internal and external validity in quantitative research. Paper presented at the annual meeting of the Association for the Advancement of Educational Research (AAER), Ponte Vedra, FL.

Onwuegbuzie, A. J. (2001, November). A new proposed binomial test of result direction. Paper presented at the annual meeting of the Mid-South Educational Research Association, Little Rock, AR.

Onwuegbuzie, A. J. (2002a). Common analytical and interpretational errors in educational research: An analysis of the 1998 volume of the British Journal of Educational Psychology. *Educational Research Quarterly, 26*(1), 11–22.

Onwuegbuzie, A. J. (2002b). Three-stage model of statistics anxiety. Manuscript in preparation.

Onwuegbuzie, A. J. (2002c). Positivists, post-positivists, post-structuralists, and post-modernists: Why can't we all get along? Towards a framework for unifying research paradigms. *Education, 122*, 518–530.

Onwuegbuzie, A. J. (2003a). Expanding the framework of internal and external validity in quantitative research. *Research in the Schools, 10*(1), 71–90.

Onwuegbuzie, A. J. (2003b). A three-dimensional typology of mixed methods research designs. Manuscript submitted for publication.

Onwuegbuzie, A. J. (2004). Academic procrastination and statistics anxiety. *Assessment & Evaluation in Higher Education, 29*, 3–18.

Onwuegbuzie, A. J. (in press-a). Prevalence of statistics anxiety among graduate students. *Journal of Research in Education.*

Onwuegbuzie, A. J. (in press-b). Modeling statistics achievement among graduate students. *Educational and Psychological Measurement.*

Onwuegbuzie, A. J. (in press-c). Effect sizes in qualitative research: A prolegomenon. *Quality & Quantity: International Journal of Methodology.*

Onwuegbuzie, A. J., Bailey, P., & Daley, C. E. (1999a). Factors associated with foreign language anxiety. *Applied Psycholinguistics, 20,* 217–239.

Onwuegbuzie, A. J., Bailey, P., & Daley, C. E. (1999b). Relationship between anxiety and achievement at three stages of learning a foreign language. *Perceptual and Motor Skills, 88,* 1085–1093.

Onwuegbuzie, A. J., Bailey, P., & Daley, C. E. (1999c). The validation of three scales measuring anxiety at different stages of the foreign language learning process: The input anxiety scale, the processing anxiety scale, and the output anxiety scale. *Language Learning, 50*(1), 87–117.

Onwuegbuzie, A. J., Bailey, P., & Daley, C. E. (2000). Cognitive, affective, personality, and demographic predictors of foreign language achievement. *Journal of Educational Research, 94,* 3–15.

Onwuegbuzie, A. J., Bailey, P., & Daley, C. E. (2001). Self-enhancement versus self-derogation biases in learning a foreign language. *Educational Research Quarterly, 25*(1), 3–11.

Onwuegbuzie, A. J., Bailey, P., & Daley, C. E. (2002). The role of foreign language anxiety and students' expectations in foreign language learning. *Research in the Schools, 9,* 33–50.

Onwuegbuzie, A. J., & Collins, K. M. T. (2001). Writing apprehension and academic procrastination among graduate students. *Perceptual and Motor Skills, 92,* 560–562.

Onwuegbuzie, A. J., & Daley, C. E. (1996). The relative contributions of examination-taking coping strategies and study coping strategies on test anxiety: A concurrent analysis. *Cognitive Therapy & Research, 20,* 287–303.

Onwuegbuzie, A. J., & Daley, C. E. (1999a, May). The effects of academic-related anxiety among college students. Paper presented at the Universidad Nacional de Río Cuarto, Río Cuarto, Argentina.

Onwuegbuzie, A. J., & Daley, C. E. (1999b). Perfectionism and statistics anxiety. *Personality and Individual Differences, 26,* 1089–1102.

Onwuegbuzie, A. J., & Daniel, L. G. (2002a). Uses and misuses of the correlation coefficient. *Research in the Schools, 9,* 73–90.

Onwuegbuzie, A. J., & Daniel, L. G. (2002b). A framework for reporting and interpreting internal consistency reliability estimates. *Measurement and Evaluation in Counseling and Development, 35,* 89–103.

Onwuegbuzie, A. J., & Daniel, L. G. (2003, February 12). Typology of analytical and interpretational errors in quantitative and qualitative educational research. *Current Issues in Education* [On-line], 6(2). Available: http://cie.ed.asu.edu/volume6/number2/

Onwuegbuzie, A. J., & Daniel, L. G. (in press). Reliability generalization: The importance of considering sample specificity, confidence intervals, and subgroup differences. *Research in the Schools.*

Onwuegbuzie, A. J., Daniel, L. G., & Roberts, J. K. (in press). A proposed new "what if" reliability analysis for assessing the statistical significance of bivariate relationships. *Measurement and Evaluation in Counseling and Development.*

Onwuegbuzie, A. J., DaRos, D., & Ryan, J. (1997). The components of statistics anxiety: A phenomenological study. *Focus on Learning Problems in Mathematics, 19,* 11–35.

Onwuegbuzie, A. J., & Jiao, Q. G. (1997a). Prevalence and reasons for university library usage. *Library Review, 46,* 411–420.

Onwuegbuzie, A. J., & Jiao, Q. G. (1997b). Academic library usage: A comparison of native and non-native English-speaking students. *The Australian Library Journal, 46,* 258–269.

Onwuegbuzie, A. J., & Jiao, Q. G. (1998a). The relationship between library anxiety and learning styles among graduate students: Implications for library instructors. *Library & Information Science Research, 20,* 235–249.

Onwuegbuzie, A. J., & Jiao, Q. G. (1998b). Understanding library-anxious graduate students. *Library Review, 47,* 217–224.

Onwuegbuzie, A. J., & Jiao, Q. G. (1998c). I hope that I am not anxious about using the library: The relationship between hope and library anxiety among graduate students. *Florida Journal of Educational Research, 38*(1), 13–26.

Onwuegbuzie, A. J., & Jiao, Q. G. (2000). I'll go to the library tomorrow: The role of procrastination in library anxiety. *College & Research Libraries, 61*(1), 45–54.

Onwuegbuzie, A. J., & Jiao, Q. G. (2002a). Library anxiety as a function of library use. Manuscript submitted for publication.

Onwuegbuzie, A. J., & Jiao, Q. G. (2002b). Criterion-related validity of Library Anxiety Scale scores. Unpublished manuscript, University of South Florida, Tampa.

Onwuegbuzie, A. J., & Jiao, Q. G. (2002c). Library anxiety and the educational use of the Internet. Manuscript submitted for publication.

Onwuegbuzie, A. J., & Jiao, Q. G. (2002d). The Dispositional-Situational-Environmental model of library anxiety. Manuscript in preparation.

Onwuegbuzie, A. J., & Jiao, Q. G. (2002e). Confirmatory factor analysis of the Library Anxiety Scale. Manuscript in preparation.

Onwuegbuzie, A. J., & Jiao, Q. G. (in press). Information search performance and research achievement: An empirical test of the anxiety-expectation model of library anxiety. *Journal of the American Society for Information Science and Technology (JASIST)*.

Onwuegbuzie, A. J., Jiao, Q. G., & Bostick, S. L. (2002). Development of the Information Literacy Process Anxiety Scale. Manuscript in preparation.

Onwuegbuzie, A. J., & Johnson, R. B. (2004). Mixed research. In B. Johnson & L. Christensen, *Educational research: Quantitative, qualitative, and mixed approaches*. Needham Heights, MA: Allyn & Bacon.

Onwuegbuzie, A. J., & Leech, N. L. (2003a). A framework for conducting qualitative power analyses. Manuscript submitted for publication.

Onwuegbuzie, A. J., & Leech, N. L. (2003b, February). Taking the "Q" out of research: Teaching research methodology courses without the divide between them. Paper presented at the annual meeting of the Southwestern Educational Research Association, San Antonio, TX.

Onwuegbuzie, A. J., & Leech, N. L. (in press). Post-hoc power: A concept whose time has come. *Understanding Statistics*.

Onwuegbuzie, A. J., & Levin, J. R. (2003a). A proposed three-step method for assessing the statistical and practical significance of multiple hypothesis tests. Manuscript submitted for publication.

Onwuegbuzie, A. J., & Levin, J. R. (2003b). Without supporting statistical evidence, where would reported measures of substantive importance lead? To no good effect. *Journal of Modern Applied Statistical Methods, 2*, 133–151.

Onwuegbuzie, A. J., Slate, J., Paterson, F., Watson, M., & Schwartz, R. (2000). Factors associated with underachievement in educational research courses. *Research in the Schools, 7*, 53–65.

Onwuegbuzie, A. J., & Teddlie, C. (2003). A framework for analyzing data in mixed methods research. In A. Tashakkori & C. Teddlie (Eds.), *Handbook of mixed methods in social and behavioral research* (pp. 351–383). Thousand Oaks, CA: Sage.

Onwuegbuzie, A. J., & Wilson, V. A. (2003). Statistics anxiety: Nature, etiology, antecedents, effects, and treatments: A comprehensive review of the literature. *Teaching in Higher Education, 8*, 195–209.

Osgood, C. E., Suci, G. J., & Tannenbaum, P. H. (1957). *The measurement of meaning*. Urbana: University of Illinois Press.

Outhwaite, W. (1975). *Understanding social life: The method called Verstehen*. London: Allen & Unwin.

Outhwaite, W. (1983). *Concept formation in social science*. London: Routledge & Kegan Paul.

Patton, M. Q. (1990). *Qualitative evaluation and research methods* (2nd ed.). Newbury Park, CA: Sage.

Pearce, R. (1981). The overseas student and library use—A special case for treatment. In Peter Fox (Ed.), *Proceedings of the Second International Conference on Library User Education, Oxford University, July 7–10, 1981*, Loughborough, England.

Pedhazur, E. J. (1982). *Multiple regression in behavioral research: Explanation and prediction* (2nd ed.). New York: Holt, Rinehart & Winston.

Peet, M. W. (1999, November). The importance of variance in statistical analysis: Don't throw the baby out of the bathwater. Paper presented at the annual meeting of the Mid-South Educational Research Association, Point Clear, AL (ERIC Document Reproduction Service No. ED 436 571).

Perry, Jr., W. G. (1970). *Forms of intellectual and ethical development in the college years: A scheme*. New York, Holt, Rinehart & Winston.

Phillips, B. N. (1971). *Anxiety and school related interventions*. Albany: The University of the State of New York.

Phillips, B. N., Martin, R. P., & Meyers, J. (1972). Interventions in relation to anxiety in school. In C. Spielberger (Ed.), *Anxiety: Current trends in theory and research* (p. 2). New York: Academic Press.

Phillips, D. C. (1987). Validity in qualitative research: Why the worry about warrant will not wane. *Education and Urban Society, 20*, 9–24.

Plotnick, E. (2000). Definitions/perspectives. *Teacher Librarian, 28*, 27–29.

Polkinghorne, D. (1983). *Methods for the human sciences*. Albany: University of New York Press.

Pollet, D., & Haskell, P. C. (1979). *Sign systems for libraries*. New York: R.R. Bowker Company.

Popper, K. R. (1959). *The logic of scientific discovery*. New York: Basic Books.

Procicuk, T. J., & Breen, L. J. (1973). Internal-external control, test anxiety, and academic achievement: Additional data. *Psychological Reports, 33*, 563–566.

Prosser, B. (1990, January). Beware the dangers of discarding variance. Paper presented at the annual meeting of the Southwest Educational Research Association, Austin, TX (ERIC Document Reproduction Service No. ED 314 496).

Pyszczynski, T., & Solomon, S. (1986). The causes and consequences of a need for self-esteem: A terror management theory. In R. F. Baumeister (Ed.), *Public self and private self* (pp. 189–207). New York: Spring-Verlag.

Rackliffe, G. (1988, April). Obstacles to teacher use of the knowledge base for school reform. Paper presented at the annual meeting of the American Educational Research Association, New Orleans.

Ramirez, J. L. (1994). Reference rover: The hesitant patron's best friend. *College & Research Libraries News, 6,* 354–357.

Ravid, R., & Leon, M. R. (1995, April). Students' perceptions of the research component in Master's level teacher education programs. Paper presented at the annual meeting of the American Educational Research Association, San Francisco (ERIC Document Reproduction Service No. ED393 840).

Ray, W. J., & Katahn, M. (1968). Relation of anxiety to locus of control. *Psychological Reports, 23,* 1196.

Razani, J. (1972). Ejaculatory incompetence treated by deconditioning anxiety. *Journal of Behavior Therapy and Experimental Psychology, 3,* 65–67.

Reichardt, C. S., & Rallis, S. F. (1994). Qualitative and quantitative inquiries are not incompatible: A call for a new partnership. In C. S. Reichardt & S. F. Rallis (Eds.), *The qualitative-quantitative debate: New perspectives* (pp. 85–92). San Francisco: Jossey-Bass.

Reynolds, L., & Barrett, S. (1979). *Signs and guiding for libraries.* London: Clive.

Richards, T. J., & Richards, L. (1994). Using computers in qualitative research. In N. K. Denzin & Y. S. Lincoln (Eds.), *Handbook of qualitative research* (pp. 445–462). Thousand Oaks, CA: Sage.

Richardson, F. C., & Suinn, R. M. (1972). The Mathematics Anxiety Rating Scale: Psychometric data. *Journal of Counseling Psychology, 19,* 551–554.

Roberts, A., & Blandy, S. (1989). *Library instruction for librarians.* Englewood, CO: Libraries Limited.

Roberts, D. M., & Bilderback, E. W. (1980). Reliability and validity of a statistics attitude survey. *Educational and Psychological Measurement, 40,* 235–238.

Rochester Institute of Technology Libraries. (2003). *RIT Libraries.* Retrieved April 7, 2003, from http://wally.rit.edu/depts/ref/instruction/studentrequest.html.

Rogers, E. M. (1995). *Diffusion of innovations* (4th ed.). New York: The Free Press.

Roman, L., & Apple, M. (1990). Is naturalism a move away from positivism? Materialist and feminist approaches to subjectivity in ethnographic research. In E. Eisner & A. Peshkin (Eds.), *Qualitative inquiry in education: The continuing debate* (pp. 38–73). New York: Teachers College Press.

Rose, M. (1984). *Writer's block: The cognitive dimension.* Carbondale: Southern Illinois University Press.

Roseman, I. J. (1991). Appraisal determinants of discrete emotions. *Cognition and Emotion, 5,* 161–200.

Rosenberg, M. (1962). The association between self-esteem and anxiety. *Journal of Psychiatric Research, 1,* 135–151.

Rosenthal, R. (1967). Covert communication in the psychological experiment. *Psychological Bulletin, 67*(5), 356–367.

Rosenthal, R. (1968). Experimenter expectancy and the reassuring nature of the null hypothesis decision procedure. *Psychological Bulletin, 70*(6, Pt. 2), 30–47.

Rossman, G. B., & Wilson, B. L. (1985). Numbers and words: Combining quantitative and qualitative methods in a single large-scale evaluation study. *Evaluation Review, 9,* 627–643.

Rothblum, E. D., Solomon, L. J., & Murakami, J. (1986). Affective, cognitive, and behavioral differences between high and low procrastinators. *Journal of Counseling Psychology, 33,* 387–394.

Rothstein, S. (1994). Reference services. In W. A. Wiegand & D. G. Davis (Eds.), *Encyclopedia of Library History* (pp. 541–546). New York: Garland Publishing, Inc.

Rounds, J. B., & Hendel, D. D. (1980). Measurement and dimensionality of mathematics anxiety. *Journal of Counseling Psychology, 27,* 138–149.

Sager, D. (1992). Professional views: The best intentions; the role of the public library in the improvement of public education. *Public Libraries, 31,* 11–17.

Sager, H. (1995). Implications for bibliographic instruction. In G. M. Pitkin (Ed.), *The impact of emerging technologies on reference service and bibliographic instruction.* Westport, CT: Greenwood Press.

Sandelowski, M. (1986). The problem of rigor in qualitative research. *Advances in Nursing Science, 8*(3), 27–37.

Sappington, T. E. (1987). Emotional experiences of returning students in nontraditional degree programs. (Doctoral dissertation, The Fielding Institute). *Dissertation Abstracts International, 48,* 10A, 2514.

Sarason, I. G. (1963). Test anxiety and intellectual performance. *Journal of Abnormal and Social Psychology, 66,* 73–75.

Sarason, I. G. (1980). *Test anxiety: Theory, research, and application.* Hillsdale, NJ: Lawrence Erlbaum.

Sarason, S. B., Davidson, K., Lighthall, F., & Waite, R. (1958). Rorschach behavior and performance of high and low anxious children. *Child Development, 29,* 277–285.

Sarkodie-Mensah, K. (1998). Using humor for effective library instruction sessions. *Catholic Library World, 68*(4), 25–29.

SAS Institute Inc. (1999). *SAS/STAT User's Guide* (Version 6.12) [Computer software]. Cary, NC: SAS Institute.

SAS Institute Inc. (2002). *SAS/STAT User's Guide* (Version 8.2) [Computer software]. Cary, NC: SAS Institute Inc.

Schacht, S., & Stewart, B. J. (1990). What's funny about statistics? A technique for reducing student anxiety. *Teaching Sociology, 18,* 52–56.

Schmidt, F. L., & Hunter, J. E. (1997). Eight common but false objections to the discontinuation of significance testing in the analysis of research data. In L. L. Harlow, S. A. Mulaik, & J. H. Steiger (Eds.), *What if there were no significance tests?* (pp. 37–64). Mahwah, NJ: Lawrence Erlbaum.

Schumacker, R. E., & Lomax, R. G. (1996). *A beginner's guide to structural equation modeling.* Mahwah, NJ: Lawrence Erlbaum.

Schutz, P. A., & Davis, H. A. (2000). Emotions and self-regulation during test taking. *Educational Psychologist, 35,* 243–256.

Schutz, P. A., DiStefano, C., Benson, J., & Davis, H. A. (1999, April). The emotional regulation during test-taking scale. Paper presented at the annual meeting of the American Educational Research Association, Montreal, Quebec, Canada.

Schwab, D. P. (1980). Construct validity in organization behavior. In B. M. Staw & L. L. Cummings (Eds.), *Research in organizational behavior* (Vol. 2) (pp. 3–43). Greenwich, CT: JAI Press.

Schwartz, R., Slate, J., & Onwuegbuzie, A. J. (1999). Empowering teachers: Acting upon action research. *GATEways to Teacher Education, 11*(2), 44–59.

Schwarzer, R., & Jerusalem, M. (1992). Advances in anxiety theory: A cognitive process approach. In K. A. Hagtvet & T. B. Johnsen (Eds.), *Advances in test anxiety research* (Vol. 7, pp. 2–31). Lisse, The Netherlands: Swets & Zeitlinger.

Scriven, M. (1974). Maximizing the power of causal investigations: The modus operandi method. In W. J. Popham (Ed.), *Evaluation in education—current applications* (pp. 68–84). Berkeley, CA: Sage.

Sechrest, L., & Sidani, S. (1995). Quantitative and qualitative methods: Is there an alternative? *Evaluation and Program Planning, 18,* 77–87.

Semb, G., Glick, D. M., & Spencer, R. E. (1979). Student withdrawals and delayed work patterns in self-paced psychology courses. *Teaching of Psychology, 6,* 23–25.

Sen, A. K., & Srivastava, M. S. (1990). *Regression analysis: Theory, methods and applications.* New York: Springer-Verlag.

Shannon, D. M. (1991). Cooperation between school and public libraries: A study of one North Carolina county. *North Carolina Libraries, 49,* 67–70.

Shapiro, S. S., & Wilk, M. B. (1965). An analysis of variance test, for normality and complete samples. *Biometrika, 52,* 592–611.

Shapiro, S. S., Wilk, M. B., & Chen, H. J. (1968). A comparative study of various tests for normality. *Journal of the American Statistical Association, 63,* 1343–1372.

Shaver, J. P., & Norton, R. S. (1980a). Populations, samples, randomness, and replication in two social studies journals. *Theory and Research in Social Education, 8*(2), 1–20.

Shaver, J. P., & Norton, R. S. (1980b). Randomness and replication in ten years of the *American Educational Research Journal. Educational Researcher, 9*(1), 9–15.

Sherrer, J. (1995). Implications of new and emerging technologies on reference service. In G. M. Pitkin (Ed.), *The impact of emerging technologies on reference service and bibliographic instruction* (pp. 25–47). Westport, CT: Greenwood Press.

Shoham, S., & Mizrachi, D. (2001). Library anxiety among undergraduates: A study of Israeli B.Ed. students. *Journal of Academic Librarianship, 27,* 305–311.

Shuman, B. (1997). The devious, the distraught and the deranged: Designing and applying personal safety into library protection. *Library & Archival Security, 14*(1), 53–73.

Sieber, J. E., O'Neil, Jr., H. F., & Tobias, S. (1977). *Anxiety, learning, and instruction.* Hillsdale, NJ: Lawrence Erlbaum.

Sieber, S. D. (1973). The integration of fieldwork and survey methods. *American Journal of Sociology, 73,* 1335–1359.

Siegel, S. (1956). *Nonparametric statistics for the behavioral sciences.* New York: McGraw-Hill.

Smalley, T. N., & Plum, S. H. (1982). Teaching library researching in the humanities and the sciences: A contextual approach. In C. Oberman & K. Strauch (Eds.), *Theories of bibliographic education: Designs for teaching* (pp. 135–170). New York: R. R. Bowker Company.

Smith, C. A. (1991). The self, appraisal and coping. In C. R. Snyder & D. R. Forsyth (Eds.), *Handbook of social and clinical psychology: The health perspective* (pp. 116–137). Elmsford, NY: Pergamon Press.

Smith, D. (1980). *Systems thinking in library and information management.* New York: K. G. Saur.

Smith, J. K. (1983). Quantitative versus qualitative research: An attempt to clarify the issue. *Educational Researcher, 12,* 6–13.

Smith, J. K., & Heshusius, L. (1986). Closing down the conversation: The end of the quantitative-qualitative debate among educational inquirers. *Educational Researcher, 15,* 4–13.

Smith, M. L., & Glass, G. V. (1987). *Research and evaluation in education and the social sciences.* Englewood Cliffs, NJ: Prentice Hall.

Snyder, P., & Lawson, S. (1993). Evaluating results using corrected and uncorrected effect size estimates. *Journal of Experimental Education, 61,* 334–349.

Solomon, L. J., & Rothblum, E. D. (1984). Academic procrastination: Frequency and cognitive-behavioral correlates. *Journal of Counseling Psychology, 31,* 503–509.

Sommer, R. (1969). *Personal space: The behavioral basis of design.* Englewood Cliffs, NJ: Prentice-Hall.

Spielberger, C. D. (1966). *Anxiety and behavior.* New York: Academic Press.

Spielberger, C. D. (1972). Current trends in theory and research on anxiety. In C. D. Spielberger (Ed.), *Anxiety: Current trends in theory and research* (pp. 3–23). New York: Academic Press.

Spielberger, C. D., Gorsuch, R. L., & Luchene, R. E. (1968). *The State-Trait Anxiety Inventory.* Palo Alto, CA: Consulting Psychologists Press.

SPSS Inc. (2001). *SPSS 11.0 for Windows.* [Computer software]. Chicago, IL: SPSS Inc.

Stake, R. (1976). *Evaluating educational programs: The need and the response.* Washington, DC: OECD Publications Center.

Stake, R. (1995). *The art of case study research.* Thousand Oaks, CA: Sage.

Steiger, J. H. (1990). Structural model evaluation and modification: An interval estimation approach. *Multivariate Behavioral Research, 25,* 173–180.

Strauss, A., & Corbin, J. (1990). *Basics of qualitative research: Grounded theory procedures and techniques.* Newbury Park, CA: Sage.

SUNY-Brockport Drake Memorial Library. (2003). *Individual research consultations.* Retrieved April 7, 2003, from http://www.brockport.edu/~library5/consult.htm.

Swope, M. J., & Katzer, J. (1972). Why don't they ask questions? The silent majority. *RQ, 12*(2), 161–166.

Tabachnick, B. G., & Fidell, L. S. (1996). *Using multivariate statistics* (3rd ed.). New York: HarperCollins College Publishers.

Tashakkori, A., & Teddlie, C. (1998). *Mixed methodology: Combining qualitative and quantitative approaches.* Applied Social Research Methods Series (Vol. 46). Thousand Oaks, CA: Sage.

Tennyson, R. D., & Boutwell, R. C. (1973). Pretask versus within-task anxiety measures in predicting performance on a concept acquisition task. *Journal of Educational Psychology, 65,* 88–92.

Tenopir, C. (1999). Electronic reference and reference librarians: A look through the 1990s. *Reference Services Review, 27*(3), 276–279.

Terrie, E. W., & Summers, F. W. (1987). *Libraries improve Florida's education: A report on the role of public libraries in the education of Florida's children and illiterate adults.* Tallahassee: Florida Department of State, Division of Library and Information Services.

Thompson, B. (1980, April). Canonical correlation: Recent extensions for modeling educational processes. Paper presented at the annual meeting of the American Educational Research Association, Boston.

Thompson, B. (1984). *Canonical correlation analysis: Uses and interpretations.* Newbury Park, CA: Sage Publications (ERIC Document Reproduction Service No. ED 199 269).

Thompson, B. (1986). ANOVA versus regression analysis of ATI designs: An empirical investigation. *Educational and Psychological Measurement, 46,* 917–928.

Thompson, B. (1988a). Discard variance: A cardinal sin in research. *Measurement and Evaluation in Counseling and Development, 21,* 3–4.

Thompson, B. (1988b, April). Canonical correlation analysis: An explanation with comments on correct practice. Paper presented at the annual meeting of the American Educational Research Association, New Orleans (ERIC Document Reproduction Service No. ED 295 957).

Thompson, B. (1991). Methods, plainly speaking: A primer on the logic and use of canonical correlation analysis. *Measurement and Evaluation in Counseling and Development, 24,* 80–93.

Thompson, B. (1992a, April). Interpreting regression results: Beta weights and structure coefficients are both important. Paper presented at the annual meeting of the American Educational Research Association, San Francisco (ERIC Document Reproduction Service No. ED 344 897).

Thompson, B. (1992b, April). Misuse of ANCOVA and related "statistical control" procedures. *Reading Psychology: An International Quarterly, 13,* iii–xvii.

Thompson, B. (1994a). Common methodological mistakes in dissertations, revisited. Paper presented at the annual meeting of the American Educational Research Association, New Orleans (ERIC Document Reproduction Service No. ED 368 771).

Thompson, B. (1994b). The pivotal role of replication in psychological research: Empirically evaluating the replicability of sample results. *Journal of Personality, 62,* 157–176.

Thompson, B. (1995). Stepwise regression and stepwise discriminant analysis need not apply here: A guidelines editorial. *Educational and Psychological Measurement, 55,* 525–534.

Thompson, B. (1997). The importance of structure coefficients in structural equation modeling confirmatory factor analysis. *Educational and Psychological Measurement, 57,* 5–19.

Thompson, B. (1998a, April). Five methodological errors in educational research: The pantheon of statistical significance and other faux pas. Paper presented at the annual meeting of the American Educational Research Association, San Diego.

Thompson, B. (1998b). Statistical testing and effect size reporting: Portrait of a possible future. *Research in the Schools, 5,* 33–38.

Thompson, B. (1999, April). Common methodology mistakes in educational research, revisited, along with a primer on both effect sizes and the bootstrap. Invited address presented at the annual meeting of the American Educational Research Association, Montreal [On-line]. Available: http://www.coe.tamu.edu/~bthompson/acraad99.htm.

Thompson, B. (2000). Ten commandments of structural equation modeling. In L. Grimm & P. Yarnold (Eds.), *Reading and understanding more multivariate statistics* (pp. 261–284). Washington, DC: American Psychological Association.

Thompson, B. (2002). What future quantitative social science research could look like: Confidence intervals for effect sizes. *Educational Researcher, 31*(3), 25–32.

Thompson, B., & Borrello, G. (1985). The importance of structure coefficients in regression research. *Educational and Psychological Measurement, 45,* 203–209.

Thompson, B., & Daniel, L. G. (1996). Factor analytic evidence for the construct validity of scores: A historical overview and some guidelines. *Educational and Psychological Measurement, 56,* 197–208.

Thompson, B., Smith, Q. W., Miller, L. M., & Thomson, W. A. (1991, January). Stepwise methods lead to bad interpretations: Better alternatives. Paper presented at the annual meeting of the Southwest Educational Research Association, San Antonio, TX (ERIC Document Reproduction Service No. ED 327 573).

Thompson, B., & Vacha-Haase, T. (2000). Psychometrics is datametrics: The test is not reliable. *Educational and Psychological Measurement, 60,* 174–195.

Tidwell, S. L. (1994). Reducing library anxiety with a creative video and in-class discussion at Brigham Young University. *Research Strategies, 12,* 187–190.

Tobias, S. (1977). A model for research on the effect of anxiety on instruction. In J. Sieber, H. F. O'Neil, Jr., & S. Tobias (Eds.), *Anxiety, learning and instruction* (pp. 223–240). Hillsdale, NJ: Lawrence Erlbaum.

Tobias, S. (1980). Math anxiety: What you can do about it. *Today's Education, 69*(3), 26–29.

Tobias, S. (1985). Test anxiety: Interference, defective skills and cognitive capacity. *Educational Psychologist, 3,* 135–142.

Tobias, S. (1986) Anxiety and cognitive processing of instruction. In R. Schwarzer (Ed.), *Self-related cognitions in anxiety and motivation* (pp. 35–54). Hillsdale, NJ: Lawrence Erlbaum.

Tuckett, H. W., & Stoffle, C. J. (1984). Learning theory and the self-reliant library user. *RQ, 24,* 58–66.

Tyson, J. C. (1995). The impact of emerging technologies on library clientele. In G. M. Pitkin (Ed), *The impact of emerging technologies on reference service and bibliographic instruction* (pp. 63–73). Westport, CT: Greenwood Press.

University of North Carolina at Wilmington Randall Library. (2003). *STAR: Student thesis assistance @ Randall.* Retrieved April 7, 2003, from http://library.uncwil.edu/star.html.

Vacha-Haase, T. (1998). Reliability generalization: Exploring variance in measurement error affecting score reliability across studies. *Educational and Psychological Measurement, 58,* 6–20.

Vacha-Haase, T., Kogan, L. R., & Thompson, B. (2000). Sample compositions and variabilities in published studies versus those in test manuals: Validity of score reliability inductions. *Educational and Psychological Measurement, 60,* 509–522.

Vacha-Haase, T., Ness, C., Nilsson, J., & Reetz, D. (1999). Practices regarding reporting of reliability coefficients. A review of three journals. *The Journal of Experimental Education, 67,* 335–341.

Van Allen, P. (1984). A good library sign system: Is it possible? *Reference Services Review, 12,* 102–106.

Vidmar, D. J. (1998). Affective change: Integrating pre-sessions in the students' classroom prior to library instruction. *Reference Services Review, 26,* 75–95.

Vincent, C. P. (1984). Bibliographic instruction and the reference desk: A symbiotic relationship. *Reference Librarian, 10,* 39–47.

Vockell, E. L., & Asher, W. (1974). Perceptions of document quality and use by educational decision makers and researchers. *American Educational Research Journal, 11,* 249–258.

Wahl, M., & Besag, F. (1986, April). Gender, attributions, and math performance. Paper presented at the Annual Meeting of the American Educational Research Association: 67th, San Francisco (ERIC Document Reproduction Service No. ED 276 620).

Waid, L. R., Kanoy, R. C., Blick, K. A., & Walker, W. E. (1978). Relationship of state-trait anxiety and type of practice to reading comprehension. *Journal of Psychology, 98,* 27–36.

Ward, A. W., Hall, B. W., & Schramm, C. E. (1975). Evaluation of published educational research: A national survey. *American Educational Research Journal, 12,* 109–128.

Ward, C., & Salter, C. A. (1974). The effects of trait and state anxiety on verbal learning. *Psychology*, *11*, 56–62.

Watson, D. (1967). Relationship between locus of control and anxiety. *Journal of Personality and Social Psychology*, *6*, 91–92.

Wayman, S. G. (1984). The international student in the academic library. *Journal of Academic Librarianship*, *9*, 336–341.

Webb, E. J., Campbell, D. T., Schwartz, R. D., & Sechrest, L. (1966). *Unobtrusive measures*. Chicago: Rand McNally.

Weiner, B. (1966). The role of success and failure in the learning of easy and complex tasks. *Journal of Personality and Social Psychology*, *3*, 339–344.

Weiner, B., & Schneider, K. (1971). Drive versus cognitive theory: A reply to Boor and Harmon. *Journal of Personality and Social Psychology*, *18*, 258–262.

Welge, P. (1990, January). Three reasons why stepwise regression methods should not be used by researchers. Paper presented at the annual meeting of the Southwest Educational Research Association, Austin, TX (ERIC Document Reproduction Service No. ED 316 583).

Westbrook, L., & DeDecker, S. (1993). Supporting user needs and skills to minimize library anxiety: Considerations for academic libraries. *The Reference Librarian*, *40*, 43–51.

Wherry, R. J., Sr. (1931). A new formula for predicting the shrinkage of the coefficient of multiple correlation. *Annals of Mathematical Statistics*, *2*, 440–457.

White, H. S. (1994). Library research and government funding: A less than ardent romance. *Publishing Research Quarterly*, *10*(4), 30–38.

Wigfield, A., & Meece, J. L. (1988). Math anxiety in elementary and secondary school students. *Journal of Educational Psychology*, *80*, 210–216.

Wilkinson, L., & Task Force on Statistical Inference. (1999). Statistical methods in psychology journals: Guidelines and explanations. *American Psychologist*, *54*, 594–604 (Reprint available through the APA Home Page: http://www.apa.org/journals/amp/amp548594.html).

Williams, D. D. (1986). Naturalistic evaluation: Potential conflicts between evaluation standards and criteria for conducting naturalistic inquiry. *Educational Evaluation and Policy Analysis*, *8*, 87–99.

Willson, V. L. (1980). Research techniques in *AERJ* articles: 1969 to 1978. *Educational Researcher*, *9*(6), 5–10.

Wine, J. (1980). Cognitive-attentional theory of test anxiety. In I. G. Sarason (Ed.), *Test anxiety: Theory, research and applications* (pp. 349–385). Hillsdale, NJ: Lawrence Erlbaum.

Witcher, A. E., Onwuegbuzie, A. J., & Minor, L. C. (2001). Characteristics of effective teachers: Perceptions of preservice teachers. *Research in the Schools*, *8*, 45–57.

Witta, E. L., & Daniel, L. G. (1998, April). The reliability and validity of test scores: Are editorial policy changes reflected in journal articles? Paper presented at the annual meeting of the American Educational Research Association, San Diego (ERIC Document Reproduction Service No. ED 422 366).

Wolcott, H. F. (1990). On seeking—and rejecting—validity in qualitative research. In E. W. Eisner & A. Peshkin (Eds.), *Qualitative inquiry in education: The continuing debate* (pp. 121–152). New York: Columbia University, Teachers College Press.

Wolpe, J. (1973). *The practice of behavior therapy*. Elmsford, New York: Pergamon Press.

Yerkes, R. M., & Dodson, J. D. (1908). The relation of strength of stimulus to rapidity of habit-formation. *Journal of Comparative Neurology and Psychology*, *18*, 459–482.

Yin, P., & Fan, X. (2001). Estimating $R^2$ shrinkage in multiple regression: A comparison of analytical methods. *The Journal of Experimental Education*, *69*, 203–224.

Young, D. J. (1991). Creating a low anxiety classroom environment: What does language anxiety research suggest? *The Modern Language Journal*, *75*, 426–439.

Young, T. E., Jr. (1999). Keeping the Ahhh! alive. *Library Talk*, *12*(2), 8–11.

Zahner, J. (1993). Thoughts, feelings and actions: Integrating domains in library instruction. Paper presented at the annual meeting of Association for Educational Communications and Technology, New Orleans, January 13–17, 1993. Proceedings of Selected Research and Development Presentations (ERIC Document Reproduction Service No. ED 362 215).

Zeidner, M. (1991). Statistics and mathematics anxiety in social science students—some interesting parallels. *British Journal of Educational Psychology*, *61*, 319–328.

Zuckerman, M. (1972). State and trait anxiety. In S. B. Sells & R. C. Demaree (Eds.), *Needed research on stress and anxiety* (IBR report No. 72–10). Fort Worth: Texas Christian University, Institute of Behavioral Research.

Zuckerman, M. (1976). General and situation specific traits and states: New approaches to assessment of anxiety and other constructs. In M. Zuckerman & C. D. Spielberger (Eds.), *Emotions and anxiety* (pp. 133–174). Hillsdale, NJ: Lawrence Erlbaum.

# Subject Index

Please note that italic page numbers refer to illustrations.

# Author Index

# About the Authors

**Anthony J. Onwuegbuzie** is an associate professor in the Department of Educational Measurement and Research at the University of South Florida in Tampa, Florida. He earned his Ph.D. in educational research and two of his three Master's degrees (M.S. in statistics and M.Ed. in testing and measurement) at the University of South Carolina. Also, he earned a postgraduate diploma in statistics at the University College, London. His research topics primarily involve disadvantaged and underserved populations such as minorities, learning disabled students, and juvenile delinquents. In the last four years, he has secured more than 130 publications in reputable nationally refereed journals. To date, he has made or has been invited to make more than 250 presentations and keynote addresses at the international, national, regional, and university levels, presenting in North America (including Canada), Europe, and Africa.

**Qun G. Jiao** is an associate professor and reference librarian at Newman Library, Baruch College, The City University of New York. His major research interest is in the psychological aspects of library use among college students, especially in library anxiety and its effects on students' learning. He has published numerous scholarly articles in national and international journals of library and information science. He is also the author of three reference books, among the most recent titles: *Internet Resources and Services for International Finance and Investment* (Oryx Press, 2001) and *Internet Guide to Personal Finance and Investment* (Oryx Press, 2002). Professor Jiao holds a Master of Library and Information Science degree from the University of South Carolina, an M.A.

degree from Columbia University in New York, and an M.Ed. degree from Miami University in Ohio.

**Sharon L. Bostick** has had a long career in libraries, working in the user services field. She began as a reference librarian at a public library, then moved to academic libraries. She served as the director of the Oakland University Reference Hotline, an award-winning, grant-funded program providing reference services to public libraries in two Michigan counties, was head of reference at Wichita (KS) State University, assistant director at the University of Toledo Library, and director of libraries at the University of Massachusetts, Boston. She is currently president of S. L. Bostick and Associates, which provides consulting services to libraries. Her research includes developing the Library Anxiety Scale and continued study of library anxiety in the United States and internationally. She also writes on the role of library consortia. She holds a B.A. from Oakland University, an AMLS from the University of Michigan, and a Ph.D. from Wayne State University.